Funny Pictures

The publisher gratefully acknowledges the generous support
of the Ahmanson Foundation Humanities Endowment Fund of
the University of California Press Foundation.

Funny Pictures

Animation and Comedy
in Studio-Era Hollywood

Edited by

Daniel Goldmark and Charlie Keil

UNIVERSITY OF CALIFORNIA PRESS

Berkeley   Los Angeles   London

University of California Press, one of the most distinguished university presses in the United States, enriches lives around the world by advancing scholarship in the humanities, social sciences, and natural sciences. Its activities are supported by the UC Press Foundation and by philanthropic contributions from individuals and institutions. For more information, visit www.ucpress.edu.

University of California Press
Berkeley and Los Angeles, California

University of California Press, Ltd.
London, England

Library of Congress Cataloging-in-Publication Data

Funny pictures : animation and comedy in studio-era Hollywood / edited by Daniel Goldmark and Charlie Keil.
    p. cm.
  Includes bibliographical references and index.
  ISBN 978-0-520-26723-7 (cloth : acid-free paper)
  ISBN 978-0-520-26724-4 (pbk. : acid-free paper)
    1. Animated films—United States—History and criticism.   2. Wit and humor in motion pictures.   I. Goldmark, Daniel.   II. Keil, Charlie.
  NC1766.U5F86   2011
  791.43′340973—dc22   2011005494

Manufactured in the United States of America

19 18 17 16 15 14 13 12 11
10 9 8 7 6 5 4 3 2 1

In keeping with a commitment to support environmentally responsible and sustainable printing practices, UC Press has printed this book on Cascades Enviro 100, a 100 percent postconsumer waste, recycled, de-inked fiber. FSC recycled certified and processed chlorine free. It is acid free, Ecologo certified, and manufactured by BioGas energy.

CONTENTS

FIGURES

Introduction

What Makes These Pictures So Funny?

Charlie Keil and Daniel Goldmark

In Preston Sturges's *Sullivan's Travels* (1941) John Sullivan, a movie director traversing the United States in an attempt to define the soul of America, finds himself wrongly imprisoned and part of a chain gang. Invited with the other prisoners to attend a screening at an African American church in a southern bayou, Sully discovers what really speaks to the human condition when he notes the spontaneous and heartfelt peals of laughter generated by the film chosen to amuse black parishioner and white jailbird alike. The film in question? A Disney cartoon.[1]

In asserting that Hollywood entertainment finds its purest expression in the cartoon hijinks of Pluto and Mickey, *Sullivan's Travels* confirms what has become a strongly held assumption; namely, studio-era animation, in particular shorts, has been long associated with comedy. At least as far back as E. G. Lutz's book, *Animated Cartoons: How They are Made, Their Origin and Development* (1920), a volume that greatly inspired the young Walt Disney, comedy has loomed large in the success of cartoons, evidenced by an entire chapter, "On Humorous Effects and on Plots," dedicated to the topic. Lutz even begins the chapter with the seemingly obvious statement: "The purpose of the animated cartoon being to amuse, the experienced animator makes it his aim to get, as the saying goes in the trade, a laugh in every foot of film."[2] But if equating the short cartoon with Hollywood humor now strikes us as axiomatic, much as it did Lutz in the early days of the studio era, we should resist accepting the logic of the association at face value, if only to explore how the animator's pen came to be enlisted consistently as a primary tool for entertaining the masses through cartoon merriment.

Of course, studio-era animation need not be funny, nor was it so at all times.

But insofar as the studio system assigned prescribed roles to the types of films produced under its control, and inasmuch as that system's primary goal was to entertain—as the example of *Sullivan's Travels* is at pains to demonstrate—cartoons chiefly carried out the task of making audiences laugh. Studio executives believed that cartoons were ideally suited to this mission; audiences reinforced that belief by responding to the studio-era cartoon with appreciative laughter; and animators complied by rolling out dozens upon dozens of mirth machines for the nearly five decades that the studio system held sway in the United States. So entrenched was this equation of cartoons and humor that the assumptions underlying it have gone largely unexamined. Why were cartoons assigned this role? Why did cartoon makers, studio executives, and audiences all subscribe to the idea that animation would be most effective if enlisted to engender laughter? If we try to determine how this connection was made and sustained so effectively, do we find its roots in the nature and lineage of animation, the structure and logic of the studio system, or some combination?

Surprisingly, these questions have gone unanswered for the most part. In analyzing the long-standing association of comedy and cartoons forged during the years of the studio system, this volume ultimately points to an unavoidable by-product of that association: our ideas about (American) animation have been shaped by the commercial success and social impact of the Hollywood cartoon. Whether by design or by fiat, the role of the animated short became prescribed to the point where few other competing functions could be entertained or imagined. This predominance of "funny pictures," both within the production system and the public consciousness, demands a thoroughgoing exploration of the process by which the broader-based term *animation* became synonymous with the label *cartoon.* The aim of *Funny Pictures,* then, is not to drain the humor out of studio-era animation by explaining it away but rather to elaborate on the ramifications of comedy finding itself so fully ingrained within the form of the Hollywood cartoon for so long.

Acknowledgment of the complex nature of the relationship between humor and animation guides the organization of this anthology, prompting balanced consideration of both the historical dimensions and theoretical implications of their union. Adhering to an arrangement that accounts for both the development of animation's role during the fifty-year sweep of the studio era and the relevance of numerous conceptual frames—of representation, narratology, and authorship—to our understanding of animation's social impact and formal functions, *Funny Pictures* also maintains a clear eye on the influence of the studio system during this period. Any simple assertions that we might be tempted to put forth concerning animation, comedy, the studio era, or any combination of the three, find themselves complicated by the range of arguments and insights advanced by the chapters to follow. Even so, a roadmap seems in order, an overview that sorts out the conflicting messages—of conformity and anarchy, of repetition and deviation, of racism and iconoclasm, of control and resistance—that emerge from any collection as diverse as this one on a topic so rife with its own internal contradictions. So, while the cartoons under examination may simply seem to be playing for laughs, we must forestall for the moment the reactions of the patrons in that swamp-bound church. For *Sullivan's Travels,* screening *Playful Pluto* to a roomful of appreciative spectators affirms the studio system's main goal as purveying lighthearted entertainment; for *Funny Pictures,* the task is to arrest the projector long enough to interrogate how and why humor and animation became so productively intertwined.

COMEDY + ANIMATION = ?

Is Hollywood animation a subset of the broader field of comedy, or is the cartoon a particular (and distractingly popular) strand of animation practice? Can we assume that the general principles of comedy address themselves as fittingly to animated filmmaking of the studio era as to its live-action counterparts? Certainly the gag, the pratfall, and the punch line—all staples of filmed comedy—are prevalent in the Hollywood cartoon. Paul Wells's examination of the links between silent comedy and animation in this volume goes so far as to say that the latter "as a form enabled the greatest possible development and expression of the 'gag' as the new art of the impossible." But if we move beyond checklists of comic ingredients, would we find the same comic spirit informing cartoons? As Scott Curtis demonstrates in his chapter, when applying the Bergsonian notion of the mechanical to the output of Tex Avery, a figure who looms large in the history of Hollywood animation in general, animated work of the studio era not only conforms to canonical precepts of comic creation; it epitomizes the automatism and inversion inherent in the comic process.

Automatism is a central concept here, for not only is much of comedy predicated on recognizing the mechanical dimension of human behavior, but animation itself depends on the automatic repetition of near-identical images. Cartoons derive, literally and historically, from single comic images, which served as both the base material of an animated sequence and the antecedents for cinematic animated forms. While the comic-cartoon lineage has been chronicled at length elsewhere,[3] less time has been spent exploring the theoretical and practical implications of the relationship, particularly as it relates to cartoons' perceived affinity for comedy. Writing some thirty years ago, Kristin Thompson, in "Implications of the Cel Animation Technique," offered some of the earliest modern critical theories concerning assumptions about cel animation. The relegation of cartoons to the comic dustbin, in her view, comes in part from animated cartoons' strong relationship with comic strips: "Cartoon production was broadly stylized, usually in imitation of comic strips; it used caricature, stretchiness and flatness in general defiance of the laws of nature. These are all familiar aspects of animation. Hence, only certain types of narratives were considered appropriate to the animated medium: all cartoons were supposed to be comic. Possibly this view originated partly from the fact that virtually all the animators of the silent period came into business from being newspaper comic strip artists (Disney, coming from commercial art, was the first major exception)."[4]

While some of Thompson's assertions have given way in the light of more recent scholarship (Max Fleischer was a commercial artist as well as a cartoonist, as Mark Langer's essay here discusses at length), some of the larger points she makes in the above excerpt have not been pursued by film or animation historians. However, it is the remainder of the paragraph that complicates the discussion: "Also, comedy has traditionally been a mode which motivates extreme departures from canons of verisimilitude (as when Groucho advises the audience to go out to the lobby during a musical interlude in *Horse Feathers*). Since comedy so easily permitted the stylization thought 'natural' to the animated film, an ideological view of cartoons as comic developed."[5]

The idea that cartoons suffered from marginalization (in terms of their mode of production, their placement within the exhibitor's bill of fare as a prelude to features, signifying their subordinate status, and their relationship to more conventional forms of filmed entertainment) aligns itself to the differences comedy encourages (straining verisimilitude, facilitating excess, encouraging exaggeration). Several essays in this collection take up particular aspects of the broader question of how humor shapes the operations of cartoons, analyzing how the production of gags affects the construction of cartoon narrative, how humor spurs animation's tendency toward self-referentiality, and how being funny allows Hollywood's cartoons to push the boundaries of Code-enforced decorum, often resulting in laughs that are provocative for their testing of societal and formal norms.

What emerges from such investigations is the idea that cartoons used economically enforced limitations (that is, profoundly restricted budgets compared to live-action features or shorts) and aesthetic proclivities in conjunction to boldly go where few other products from Hollywood (save the most enterprising of comic live-action films) ventured. This led cartoons into often uncharted terrain, where unbounded physical transformations rubbed up against decidedly unconvincing backdrops, where merciless lampooning slid into racist caricature and masculinist fantasies. Cartoons push boundaries, often literally, as when the formal parameters of the screen find themselves stretched by the activities of their animated denizens. But they also challenge our social pieties, making us deliberately uncomfortable by celebrating unbridled violence and engaging in crude stereotyping. Yet with this discomfort comes pleasure, be it the shock of seeing our worst impulses rendered in stylized form, the delight in embracing the exaggeration that can only come from a world entirely untethered to a photographic reality, or the recognition bred by repeated familiar styles of drawing.

Hollywood animation typically tied this pleasure to humorous ends, often using the extremities of the form as a baseline for comic inventiveness. Perhaps the very obviousness of linking the cartoon and comedy explains why analyses of film comedy have neglected studio-era animation, though one senses this lacuna may owe more to the manner in which animation as a whole is cordoned off in most discussions of film, its isolation from the mainstream of film study mirroring the marginalization of animation as a production practice. But this isolation has prevented those studying film comedy (and no less those examining animation) from determining what is common to both forms. As many of the essays in this collection demonstrate time and again, the interchange between animated humor and live-action comedy is fluid and ongoing: not so much because personnel moved from the one domain to the other but because gags, the stock and trade of film comedy, found themselves repeated and revised as they hopscotched from live-action comic film to cartoon and back again. Influence was reciprocal: seminal live-action comedians from the silent era proved inspirational for certain tenets of animated humor at the same time that animation fed the comic imagination of later film performers. Whether it be Paul Wells arguing for the importance of Chaplin's rhythmic movement to the physicality of the cartoon, or J.B. Kaufman tracing the lineage of the firehouse stock comedy situation from Chaplin through Lloyd and Langdon on to Mickey Mouse, the contributors to *Funny Pictures* view Hollywood comedy as a phenomenon that meaningfully incorporates animated work rather than standing to one side of it. Perhaps the most powerful example comes from Frank Tashlin, a veritable nexus for all the forms under consideration here, as his work bridges not only animation and live-action filmmaking but also print cartoons (with his strip *Van Boring*). Ethan de Siefe's essay explores in detail just how acutely Tashlin's identity as a comedic artist forged a continuity between his animated work and the later live-action films he directed.

The cultural and aesthetic bonds linking comedy and animation come into clear focus in Henry Jenkins's suggestive extension of J. Hoberman's concept of vulgar modernism to describe a matrix of popular comic creativity that links Avery, Olsen and Johnson, and Spike Jones. Jenkins is at pains to suggest that the traditional boundaries separating comic illustration, vaudeville theater, and the cartoon needn't—and shouldn't—keep us from noting the similarities among artists working across a spectrum of media. That observation can be extended to erode the wall that has been erected between live-action comedy and the cartoon. Attending too closely to what is unique in animation has encouraged scholars to overlook what keeps it in close dialogue with the mainstream of filmed comedy.

One of the chief aims of *Funny Pictures* is to illuminate what ties together the effect of humor and the practice of animating, reinforcing a productive dialectic that the separation of comedy from animation has too often suppressed.

OUT OF THE INKWELL, INTO THE STUDIO SYSTEM

Whether cartoons could have been anything other than humorous shorts once Hollywood reached a state of industrial maturity can only be a matter of conjecture, for the fact of the studio era remains that animation found itself assigned the role of court jester. Comedy and animation are not synonymous, by any means, but clearly the former found an ideal expression in the latter. The industry's decision to relegate animation to the peripheral sphere of nonfeature production probably helped foster a perception that the goal of the cartoon was to amuse. Once the film industry moved away from a model of single-reel production in the mid-1910s, one sees comedy commonly associated with the short, as the feature format was generally reserved for more "weighty" material. As early as 1914, industry doxa deemed comedy unsuitable for the extended running time of the feature, exemplified by Stephen Bush's pronouncement in *Moving Picture World*: "Nor do we believe that multiple reel comedy will ever successfully rival the short snappy comedy of a thousand feet. On the screen as in the newspaper and on the stage brevity is the soul of wit."[6] As Rob King documents in his study of Charlie Bowers, by the 1920s this tendency to equate the short format with humor prompted the Short Feature Advertising Association to devise a campaign promoting "National Laugh Month."

In part, the labor-intensive nature of animation dictated that it be restricted to the short format, facilitating the fusion of animation and comedy. But even as the extensive work required to produce a few moments of animation on the screen rendered it an inefficient (and overly expensive) means of producing features during the studio era, the thoroughgoing manipulation of the image track during the drawing process invested cartoons with a special quality of humor. Unlike live-action comedies, where humor could well emerge from the interactions between actors or derive from seemingly spontaneous occurrences before the camera, everything about animation was necessarily premeditated. One can claim with some justification, then, as does Ethan de Seife, that animated comedy was a comedy of extreme preparation, the timing of gags tied to the duration of the moment as it unfolded via the number of cels required. The unique profilmic dimension of animated filmmaking renders it the apogee of studio-era principles of manufacture: nothing is left to chance; everything can be calibrated. Even if the contours of classical editing and camerawork were emulated, they were incorporated into a governing aesthetic of totalizing control via the animation desk. For these reasons animation fits well within the studio system's logic of reducing risk through employment of the most reliable procedures available. Susan Ohmer shows how Disney extended this principle by employing audience research tools, noting that "producing laughter on schedule and for profit, that was the challenge."

Film studies' examination of the principles and practices of the studio system has confirmed the truism that predictability of manufacture and variation of product were the two foundational supports for the system's proper operation. Yet this insight into the studio system is largely based on the centerpiece of Hollywood's output, the A feature. How did the ancillary products from the system fit into its broader goals, and to what degree did they represent possible alternatives precisely because of their marginal status?

On the one hand, animated shorts share many qualities with the B-studio serials and weekly newsreels that accompanied them as part of the bill of fare preceding the main feature. The output of the animation mills at Warner Bros. and MGM, at Disney and Fleischer, was tied to an idea that audiences wanted the same thing week after week, only slightly different. Perhaps that is why animation has often been described as a genre—because various formulae and conventions proved so determinative of the contours that animation assumed. But at the same time, animation differed radically from fictional features, with their stars and narratives tied to ninety minutes and longer; from serials, with their cliffhanger endings leading audiences to the next installment; and from newsreels, which were tied to events of the day. And of course the distinctiveness of animation's appearance—regardless of the genre (western, musical, melodrama, etc.) that the story might be appropriating—seals once and for all its identity as cinematic "other."

If animation was (and is) not a genre, in its Hollywood incarnation it still very much adhered to the generic traits of comedy, borrowing situations and gags passed down from that mode's development in earlier entertainment forms. Fostered as they were by traditions of comedy developed in the funny pages of newspapers, the vaudeville theaters and burlesque halls of turn-of-the-century America, and the slapstick antics of the silent comedians, the cartoon shorts of the studio era developed and extended certain tendencies of American humor by virtue of combining them with the principles of exaggeration and parody that animation could cultivate. What resulted was a hybrid form, one that borrowed brazenly from recognized comic conventions but expanded on them in the artificial, hothouse world of the animated drawn image.

If the comic performative traditions of vaudeville informed the content of animation's mise-en-scène, the artisanship of the comic strip artist defined the cartoon's mode of production. From the outset cinematic animation struggled with how to reconcile the painstaking craft of image-making with the rote repetitive manufacture of the multiple cels required to render such images in movement. With some prominent early film animators emerging from the ranks of celebrated still-image comic artists, the lineage manifests itself in obvious ways, particularly the vogue for "lightning sketch" films, an early form of filmic animation. Perhaps the most celebrated example is Winsor McCay, whose early animated films self-consciously explore the possibilities of cinematic space and animation's capacity for instantaneous metamorphosis (as in Little Nemo), as well as the animator's relationship to his fictive creations (Gertie the Dinosaur). As Nicholas Sammond points out in his contribution to this volume, the insistent trope of the animator's hand in many early animated films foregrounds the act of creating these moving pictures, stressing their handmade quality and, by extension, what Philip Brophy identifies as an outright refutation of the screened body's "fleshiness," pointing to its inherent lack of corporeality. As mentioned, animators, seemingly emboldened by the capacity of their chosen medium, often took situations to comic extremes impossible to realize in live-action film, and the fact that cartoon characters are drawn necessarily complicated standard notions of performance and "physical humor."

But the trope of the animating hand also points to the labor involved in the drawing of the images at the core of any animated work, a labor laid bare when the animator is personified within his own comic creation. Such overt acknowledgment of the work underlying studio manufacture runs counter to the general aura of mystification that pervades the studio system. It also implicitly tweaks the overarching principle of process over practitioner that defines the classical era. And the idea of an animation auteur seems to fly in the face of not only the faceless animation mills dependent on cadres of assembly-line workers but also the studio's determination that story and product remain paramount, not the creative individual. Small wonder, then, that those animators whom we might be tempted to nominate as authorial figures were responsible for works that resoundingly reinforced the drudgery of the animation process and the near-existential conundrums defining the depicted realm of most Hollywood cartoons.

The twinned forces of mechanical reproduction and formal repetition offset the spirit of comic invention infusing the most spirited cartoons of the studio era. While Rob King highlights how technology could carry with it the promise of "magical productivity," Scott Curtis counters that it also threatened relentless tedium. As a symbolic figure, the studio animator, crafting individual images that would then be endlessly replicated, fused the traditional qualities of the workshop with the modern logic of the factory. This reflects the dual nature of animation itself, which epitomized Benjamin's age of mechanical reproducibility at the same time that it inspired the surrealists. And if the animator could indulge his penchant for what J. B. Kaufman calls the "plausibly impossible," he was also responsible for churning out dozens of derivative cartoon stories that the animation factories produced for decades on end, relying on canonical comic situations in the process. These plot structures formed the basis of much of the cartoons' humor at the same time that they satisfied the compositional principles underlying classical narrative construction. As Richard Neupert demonstrates through a formal analysis of selected works from the 1930s, "most American cartoons are built around carefully unified narratives motivated by clearly defined, goal-oriented characters and chronologically arranged actions that lead toward a strong thematic resolution and discursive closure." Other contributors to this volume are more circumspect, citing the influence of both vaudeville and the comic strip on what Mark Langer calls the "heterogeneous and polyphonic" quality of studio-era animation.

If the latter position views the Hollywood cartoon as engaging in what was often a productively uneasy relationship with the overarching principles of classicism, few would dispute that, as products of the studio system, animated shorts were bounded and influenced by that system. Whether independent producers (like Disney or the Fleischers), whose work would be handled by a distributor within a national network, or units within an integrated major (such as the animators at Warner Bros. and MGM), all those making cartoons knew that their product was destined for distribution within a stable and highly controlled system. The oligopolistic nature of the film industry during the studio era delivered a large audience through established distribution channels, but it also dictated that a uniformity of product be maintained, diminishing the chance of radical formal experimentation or contestatory ideological statements. By obeying the dictates of entertainment, the makers of cartoons during this era ensured that their work fell within the studio-sanctioned limits of decorum; at the same time, comedy provided a degree of license that many animators pushed to the extreme.

If discussing the studio era as a homogeneous period allows us to forge meaningful connections among works from diverse producers, downplaying the surface noise created by technological innovations (color, sound) and events more pertinent for world history than studio manufacture (World War II), it can also blind us to the distinct changes occurring within this fifty-year period. Many of the contributors align themselves with more period-specific observations tied to distinct eras within the broader swatch of the studio era. If J. B. Kaufman's interest is ultimately the Disney cartoon of the mid-1930s, Susan Ohmer focuses her attention much more on the post–World War II activities of the same studio. Both Donald Crafton and Richard Neupert concentrate on Depression-era Hollywood animation, the former attending to its cultural significance, the latter to its formal qualities. Scott Curtis looks at Tex Avery's efforts at MGM during the 1940s and 1950s; Ethan de Seife tends to concentrate on the same period in Frank Tashlin's career. Henry Jenkins understands the current of vulgar modernism as accelerating in the postwar period, while the tendencies analyzed by Paul Wells and Rob King (in the work of Chaplin and Charley Bowers, respectively) occur primarily in the silent era. Their collective efforts point to the varied nature of animation during the studio years, at the same time that they reveal how different practitioners negotiated their relationships with their industrial overseers.

MAKING MODERN AMERICA LAUGH

The majority of the entries in this volume concede that many of the qualities that Hollywood cartoons trade on—the elasticity of the depicted space, the porousness of the cinematic frame, the exaggerated lines, and the fantastical universe within which so many of the inhabitants of the animated world reside—lend themselves to humor. But, as Henry Jenkins says, "Comedy is always a messy business." If nostalgic recollection has tended to transform these cartoons into innocent vessels of unalloyed mirth, the contributors to *Funny Pictures* offer a corrective: they remind us that studio-era animation traded in racist imagery, sexist stereotyping, and mockery of societal mores. Cartoons, even when eliciting laughter, could also prompt tears, and at times the humor could curdle, transforming a comic sensibility into something far darker. Donald Crafton, for one, though acknowledging the escapist potential of animated entertainment, also points to its capacity to instill a sense of alienation, convey a cloaked critique, or even offer the hope of transcendence, all of these functions embodied in the shared audience reaction of communal laughter.

Still, figuring out how to make a moving drawing elicit laughter remained a key motivation for cartoons of this era. While the gags depicted in these films may well share a heritage with comic traditions established elsewhere, be it vaudeville, music-hall knockabout, or comic strips, the fusion of drawn imagery and the kineticism of movement lent to filmic animation an added dimension of fanciful expression. Doubtless this spurred some commentators to align Hollywood animation with the anarchic spirit of more obviously modernist art movements, while others saw its humorous vitality as indicative of the most salutary aspects of the modern era. More than a few of the contributors to this volume tie cartoons to the uncertainties promoted by modernity, be it Paul Wells in his reading of animation's tendency toward rapid metamorphosis or Philip Brophy's analysis of the endless Coyote-Roadrunner saga as the ne plus ultra of absurdism. In Wells's words, "the human condition, in the view of the absurdists, could only be understood through a perverse, ironic, and sometimes bleak model of humor. Arguably, this sense of 'absurdism' becomes the condition of the animated film per se."

Standing in opposition to such a reading of animation is the salutary effect of *Playful Pluto* on those diegetic viewers depicted in *Sullivan's Travels,* who might otherwise succumb to despair. According to Donald Crafton, Preston Sturges selects the Disney short in part to demonstrate how cartoons offer the power of redemption by provoking laughter. Ultimately, these funny pictures distill, in line and movement, the essentials of comedy and the rhythms of modern life. In the essays that follow, the contributors explore the ways in which the laughter-making potential of animation connects to broader aesthetic impulses, industrially developed conventions, and ingrained legacies of ideology. Collectively, this volume's contributions offer a penetrating analysis of the pleasures offered by a staple of American entertainment during the studio system's heyday while also pointing forward to a vital tradition within American entertainment still evident today in works ranging from *The Simpsons* to the output of Pixar. That the book ends with a look to the future is thus not accidental. Both Daniel Goldmark's and Linda Simensky's essays share a common purpose: the desire to illuminate how the path staked out by methods and techniques developed during the studio era, whether in narrative construction or sound design, has snaked its way into contemporary animation. With the connection made to more recent work, this book not only shows the indebtedness of modern animators to their studio forebears but also makes a strong case as to the continuing pertinence of a moment in animation history when movies were so often defined by funny pictures.

NOTES

The editors want to thank Alex Bonus, Lauren Davine, Tony Pi, and Jeremy Butler for their assistance with this collection, along with the ever-persevering Mary Francis, Eric Schmidt, Suzanne Knott, the redoubtable Joe Abbott, and everyone at UC Press.

1. The film in question is *Playful Pluto* (1934). In his essay in this volume Donald Crafton elaborates on this cartoon's significance to *Sullivan's Travels*.

2. Lutz, *Animated Cartoons*, 223.

3. See, e.g., Crafton, *Before Mickey*.

4. Thompson, "Implications of the Cel Animation Technique," 110.

5. Ibid.

6. Bush, "The Single Reel—II," 36.

PART ONE

The (Filmic) Roots of Early Animation

cious, she nevertheless also hints at a way of viewing Chaplin that has been, perhaps surprisingly, relatively unexplored. In many senses the lingua franca of the animated cartoon was the anthropomorphized animal figure, and it is surely possible, particularly given that this figure's early phases of development parallel Chaplin's career, that in discovering "the cat or the penguin, the monkey or the poodle" in Chaplin, and even more pertinently, vice versa, the relationship between Chaplin and the animated film might reward exploration. Indeed, I will go as far as to say that Chaplin is one of animation cinema's unsung and undervalued figures and, more provocatively, one of its greatest implicit auteurs.

Chaplin's work and identity were also extremely significant to the animation community, which embraced his performance skills and outlook as intrinsically related to the development of the newly emergent language of animated film and its own particular claims to becoming a modernist art. Chaplin combined particular qualities in his performance persona and in his ideological stance that proved engaging to other artists, who drew on his work both in a spirit of respectful imitation and as the stimulus and catalyst for more experimental approaches. An immediate barometer of this may be found in what has become a bible of sorts for animators: Frank Thomas's and Ollie Johnston's *Disney Animation: The Illusion of Life,* which references the ways that renowned figures like Fred Moore imitated Chaplin's movement. Thomas and Johnston themselves imagined how Chaplin would play a scene, saw Chaplin's engagement with "personality" as the key point of access to what was intrinsically funny about a situation, and examined the score as a major facilitator of "mood."[2] In the first instance this might immediately suggest that it was in the American context that animators borrowed freely from his films, and used his gags in unacknowledged "homage," and that it was in Europe that his work was used in a more progressive fashion. This is partly true but ignores the ways in which Chaplin himself straddled the European and American contexts, like Mickey Mouse, mediating his symbolic identity. Chaplin's "Little Tramp" or "little fellow" was a highly resonant figure in many cultures both in relation to the metaphoric import of his styling and in the ways that his comedy reflected the plight of the underdog in luckless contexts and oppressive regimes of everyday existence. At one level Chaplin's comedy is a model of defiance in the face of adversity; at another it is a triumph of tragic-comic defeatism, leavened only by the sheer power of Chaplin's personality. Chaplin's personality is, of course, key here, in the sense that Chaplin can never be read purely "in character," his own self-reflexive presence as an artist constantly inflecting the self-conscious nature of his performance. It is this presence at the heart of Chaplin's work that allies him with the same kind of self-figuration that Donald Crafton has suggested permeates animated film,[3] both in its clear examples of the appearance of the animator himself (in work like the Fleischer brothers' Out of the Inkwell series) and in the obvious artifice and illusionism of creating animated material in general. In this analysis, then, I will explore how the self-reflexive dynamics of Chaplin's persona influence the whole developing vocabulary of the animated film, casting much "mainstream" American animation as more experimental than previously acknowledged, and how notions of European "absurdism" find purchase in a number of American idioms.

Chaplin's work is characterized by a tension between scripted intentions and extensive improvisation, by the refining of physical gags and routines until the actor is satisfied that he has achieved both the funniest option and the greatest resonance with his assumed audience. Richard Schickel has suggested that "his was essentially, a kinetic genius. . . . It was in motion—the ability to convey emotion in seemingly heedless, thoughtless, purely instinctive action—that his unique gift resided."[4] This sense of the cultivation of meaning through the dynamics of motion itself is, of course, profoundly related to the dynamics of the cartoon and begins to suggest how Chaplin *as animator* might be defined and understood. Chaplin recognized that he could create scenarios in which his own status as a comic artist, versed in the arts of pantomimic performance and theatrical staging, could readily combine with narrative contexts rich with sociocultural significance, prompting engagements with issues of class, status, empowerment and suffering. Like the animator, Chaplin essentially created an art that remained invisible until interrogated for its construction and execution. A high degree of planning was required to achieve spontaneity. Schickel argues, though, that Chaplin "was a consumer of big ideas, not a creator of them,"[5] a suggestion that undermines how Chaplin's gift for "visualization" helps to facilitate the "openness" of the text in a spirit of foregrounding ideas and issues. Though Chaplin's own ideological stance may have been incoherent—it was essentially that of a well-meaning, left-leaning liberal—his radicalism lay in his ability to create a protoanimated space in which the *dialectic* principles of an issue might be addressed, without the fixity and certainty of didacticism—a context that was to some extent disrupted with the advent of sound and the intervention of "the word."[6]

Chaplin's comic scenarios became dramatizations of constantly shifting social circumstances and everyday anxiety, which were essentially overcome by his own romanticized vision of one man's ability, through accident and design, literally and metaphorically, to achieve a modicum of success, which redeemed a situation on his own terms and conditions. By reworking material culture through the practices of one individual's ability to secure change, played out through substituting comic bravura for the exigencies of daily experience, Chaplin remade the social environment, recasting it in his own light and changing its political implications. In evacuating the social and material environment of its inevitable sense of oppressive routine, and in undermining and reversing the operations of power and authority, Chaplin creates a quasi-cartoonal space in which the reinterrogation of the material world becomes a challenging reinterpretation of social conditions and attitudes. As Elia Faure wrote in 1923, "He imagines the drama. He gives it its laws. He stages it. He plays the parts of all his associates, as well as his own, and re-unites them all in the final drama after having explored it and examined it in all of its aspects."[7]

What I am essentially suggesting here is that Chaplin helped to create a particular vocabulary of expression in the live-action context, which has profound echoes of, and was profoundly influential in, developing the specific conditions of animated film. When Lejeune says, "Chaplin shuffles along down the middle of his film, touching here a hat, there a flower, here a cigarette, there a coat-sleeve, and each thing he touches becomes suddenly and passionately alive, playing its part for a moment in the comic succession,"[8] she is surely describing the work of the animator, and it is clear that this model of work chimed not merely with the "new realism" of European modernist art but also with the specific advances in the progressive delineation of the animated film in the United States and Europe. Fernand Léger, who began his *Le ballet mécanique* (1924) with an animated puppet of Chaplin, exhibited by Friedrich Kiesler for the first time at the International Exhibition of New Theatre Techniques in Vienna in 1924, was intent on engaging with his view that "all current cinema is romantic, literary, historical expressionist etc. Let us forget all this and consider, if you please: A pipe—a chair—a hand—an eye—a typewriter—a hat—a foot, etc, etc, just as they are—in isolation—their value enhanced by every known means . . . in the new realism the human being, the personality, is very interesting only in these fragments and that these fragments should not be considered of any more importance than any of the other objects listed."[9] Léger's list, like Lejeune's, acknowledges the primacy of the physical and material object as the focus of the new modern subjectivity and, crucially, the ways in which this constitutes new representational forms outside established conventions. This "plasticity" of the image itself was recognized as the core signifier at the heart of experimental film, particularly in Europe, where it was seen as a chief aspect in the construction of nonnarrative, nonlinear, nonobjective cinema, but it remains less acknowledged as the primary basis not merely of Chaplin's expressive vocabulary but of the language of animation. It is no accident that Sergei Eisenstein noted the very same "plasmaticness" at the heart of the animated form, particularly in Disney's Silly Symphonies,[10] an attribute that, in the same way as Chaplin's "purely cineplastic"[11] imagery, constituted a liberating language of expression, easy to read as a model of political metaphor. Within the American context it is very important to recognize, however, that the plasticity of the image was used primarily for experimental *narrative* and *performative* effects, not purely as the abstract expression of form, which was to dominate the development of animated film in Europe. In essence, abstraction in the American context took the form of "the gag," the primary combination of motion and meaning, comic event and concept, content and continuity. Animation as a form enabled the greatest possible development and expression of "the gag" as the new art of the impossible. Chaplin remained its source and inspiration. But what then of finding the cat or penguin, monkey or poodle? Crucially, in America, Chaplin becomes "the animal" before the abstract.

The animation historian William Moritz, himself skeptical of Léger's claims to creating *Le ballet mécanique*,[12] was equally unpersuaded by the ways in which he believed that Chaplin and his ilk were co-opted into cartoon narratives:

> Endless chase and mayhem cartoons (Bugs Bunny, Tom and Jerry, etc) . . . attempt to revive the exhausted vocabularies of the silent film comedians, from Méliès and Linder to Laurel and Hardy and The Three Stooges, by substituting animals for humans. Now, the convention of animal fables is ancient and honorable, and whether it be classical Greece's Aesop, medieval Europe's Reynard the Fox or Heian Japan's Choju Scrolls, the use of animal personae allows the storyteller to say something that could not be said by talking about humans due to political, religious or social taboos. But watching a drawn coyote crash through walls, fall down stairs, be crushed by falling objects or burned to a crisp by the explosives he holds is certainly not as amazing or funny as seeing Buster Keaton or Charlie Chaplin or Harold Lloyd or the Keystone Kops do those same stunts live right before our "camera never lies" eyes.[13]

I have explored elsewhere how animation has represented animals,[14] but in this context I wish to take up Moritz's suggestion that "the gag" does not function as well in the cartoon form as it does in the live-action performances of the silent cinema clowns. "The gag" in the animated form is, of course, different, but it is Chaplin who once more points the way to how it is different. As Mark Winokur notes, "What distinguishes Chaplinesque comedy is a certain transformative ability: whether the ability to transform objects into other objects, himself into an object, pathos into comedy (and vice versa) or the tramp into a gentleman." Winokur goes on to add that "although Chaplin is only one of many silent comics to use transformation, he is the only one whose life thematically connects physical transformation and the fairy-tale transformation of immigrant into American."[15] This idea of "transformation" is again fundamental to animated forms, but it differs significantly in that while Chaplin can work with the material or conceptual conditions of change, he is still at the corporeal center of the transition. He can only ultimately achieve *metaphorical* change because while he can affect the function and meaning of figures, objects, and environments, he cannot change the properties of these things in themselves. Animation, of course, in many of its forms, can literally change properties, having the capacity, through metamorphosis, to translate some figures, objects, and environments from one state to another. Animation can erase and efface a former image and create another image, showing another state, creating not merely new physical relationships but achieving translations that create unusual, alternative, or seemingly impossible relationships. Animation can achieve material change and operate as an almost inherently *metaphorical*, if not *metaphysical*, form. Chaplin is in essence the progenitor of the conditions by which animation as a form demonstrates this vocabulary. Chaplin defines a terrain in live action that is extended and developed by "the cartoon" and other animated forms, one essentially validating the other as a "modernist" practice.

While Chaplin's personal "translation" from his status as a British performer to an American movie star usefully articulates mythic narratives of "rags to riches" transformation in the United States, within this context it signals a very particular physical and aesthetic transition, which informs some of the tensions at the heart of Chaplin's status as animator. Winston Churchill was a friend and confidante of Chaplin's during the 1930s. Churchill was persuaded by Chaplin's intrinsically "English" persona, which he believed had its roots in the work of Charles Dickens. Churchill was nevertheless of the view that Chaplin possessed less of the defeated and defeatist aspects of the British tramp and more of the romantic adventure and defiance of the American hobo.[16] Though inevitably, critics have made much of how Chaplin's styling as the Tramp reflects a particular tension between the material status of the down and out—the baggy trousers—and the desire to ascend to polite society—the buttoned waistcoat, bow tie, and cane, I wish to suggest that the costume is an apt metaphor for the tension between the restraints of British cultural life and the performative vitality of American show business and, furthermore, an important recognition of the imperatives of control and dynamic, purposive movement in animation. While Chaplin's costume in Britain represented the tensions of the "lower middle class," and in Europe became an iconic metaphor for leftist dialectic thought in French and Russian political contexts, in America it becomes the signifier of the latent graphic mark in Hollywood cartoons. While Fred Miller Robinson stresses that "for Americans, Charlie's decline into vagrancy is the opportunity for him to aspire to something beyond social contingency—one of the regnant American ideals,"[17] it is also a material metaphor by which psychological, emotional, and physical contingency is also liberated and readily informs the currency of the animated film. Chaplin's styling enables him, therefore, to be read as Brecht viewed him—as a "document," as an objective interrogator of social mores—but also, and fundamental to the claims for Chaplin as animator, as a barometer of subjective motion, emotion, and praxis. So what of Chaplin's presence in early American cartoons?

Charlie cartoons were made as early as 1916 by the Movca Film Service, but it was the series made in 1918, directed by Pat Sullivan, animated by Otto Messmer, and released by Nestor/Universal, that had significant popular impact and was a direct forerunner of the Felix the Cat cartoons, also made by Sullivan and Messmer. As Messmer recalls, "Chaplin sent at least thirty or forty photographs of himself in different poses. He was delighted, of course; this helped the propagation of his pictures, you see, and he encouraged us; we copied every little movement that he did; later on that rubbed off and we used a lot of that kind of action in Felix; Chaplin had a great influence on us."[18] In some senses this propagation of movement from stills echoes the references animators later made to Muybridge's photo sequences of human and animal motion. Disney was probably the first to consult Muybridge's sequences in the quest to develop and ultimately perfect the language of "full animation" in the classic style, but Messmer's address of the Chaplin images was more in a spirit of capturing both the clownlike business and balletic lyricism of Charlie's performance idioms. In this, completely by coincidence, Messmer was engaging with a modernist imperative to capture the choreographic line and the sense of symbolic abstraction in Chaplin *as an image* and to exploit and expand on its implied vocabulary of movement. Charlie's black-and-white iconic styling translated readily into cartoon representation, but his strategic motion as a performer equally underpinned the choreography of animated movement and its implied narrative and meaning in cartoon form. This stress upon the line and a new spatial condition was important because it constituted a high degree of modernity within the American context. In Europe Léger had used a puppet Chaplin to anticipate and evidence the plasticity of the image in the fragmentary culture of the new realists, but as early as 1922, the artist Vavara Stepanova drew a picture of "Charlie Chaplin Turning Somersaults," one of ten illustrations produced for the publication *Kino-Fot,* a journal largely predicated on Constructivist perspectives and a desire to explore the social dynamics of technology. Admired by Lev Kuleshov and the artist Alexander Rodchenko for his economy of movement and resonance of ideas, Chaplin was viewed as a progressive figure but, significantly, because his choreography seemed to have the precision and specificity of "a machine." Stepanova's work reflected this as it "simplified his physique, transforming it into a series of bold geometric forms and distilling the poses and movements into vital combinations of rectangular planes. The sparse quality of visual language parallels Chaplin's economy of gesture."[19] Furthermore, at the same time that Léger and Dudley Murphy produced *Le ballet mécanique,* Wassily Kandinsky had created highly reduced analytical line drawings of the dancer Gret Palucca, from photographs by Charlotte Rudolph, including "Three Curves Meeting at a Single Point" (1925) and "Two Large Parallel Lines Supported by a Simple Curve" (1925), focusing on the precision of motion in what he called "dance curves." These drawings, however, were merely static suggestions of dominant choreographic arcs. These kinds of works operated as "reductive" models of Chaplin's animation in the service of a functionalist understanding of motion aesthetics. It was only in the United States that the *abstract* poses, "dance curves," and choreographic dynamics of Chaplin's performance were used as a "constructive model," extending the potential and possibility of the cartoon and its motion graphic comic events as the very semblance of American modernity.

Such a view is sometimes compromised by the dismissal of animation and many of its comic strip sources as merely the work of popular culture, media with little relationship to the prerogatives of traditional art forms. The relationship to Chaplin legitimized the motives of the work, however, and literally illustrated the new mobilities of both the animated film and American culture. Many of the early silent shorts provided gag templates for animated cartoons—the person approaching a manhole, an amateur handyman on a roof with some tools, the disassembling vehicle in a chase, the exaggerated violent exchange—but Chaplin's choreographic skills and eye for the compression of time, space, and the environment into specific images often rendered them as quasi-graphic idioms lending themselves to the maximum of suggestion in the minimum of imagery. Examples include the placing of bread in an oven with a long pole or the balancing of a tray loaded with bread and cakes on his head in *Dough and Dynamite* (1914); the playing against physical types in *The Bounders* (1914), with Fatty Arbuckle, or *Tilly's Punctured Romance* (1914), with Marie Dressler; "the park, policeman and a pretty girl" model, the touchstone of much Chaplinesque pathos in the dream-based *His Prehistoric Past* (1914); the sustained engagement with conspiratorial props in *His New Job* (1915); the dance idioms and use of an animal in *The Champion* (1915); and, most significant, the use of distance and isolation in physical "blocking" to enhance the idea of a longing and desire for the "unattainable girl" in *The Bank* (1915) and *The Tramp* (1915). When Chaplin wakes up to find himself kissing a mop, rather than the oneiric Edna he had embraced in his dream adventure in *The Bank,* he sets the template for the tragic-comic as image, performance, and narrative, which in the mature features became his trademark.

All the choreographic idioms Chaplin was to employ throughout his career were explored in these films and consolidated in the slightly later works like *The Rink* (1916), *Easy Street* (1916), and *The Immigrant* (1916). It is this collective imagery that enters the vocabulary of the early cartoon, but crucially, it is explored not merely as the dynamics of motion but through Chaplin's essential "animality," which translates readily into the animated animals that characterized the radical language of expression available in cartoons and sets American modernity in the field apart from its European counterparts. As T. S. Eliot asserted, "The egregious merit of Chaplin is that he has escaped in his own way from the realism of the cinema and invented a *rhythm*. Of course the unexplored opportunities of the cinema for eluding realism must be very great."[20] With this he touches on Chaplin's essential quality as animator—to suggest the very rhythm that bridges the gap between the material limitations of the real, both in relation to the physical environment and the live-action lens, and the open conditions of the cartoon. This is not, then, merely a formalist principle but a recognition of an intuitive, inarticulable, physical expression that I am naming here as an intrinsic "animality." Apocryphal, or not, Chaplin was said to envy the perfect timing of gags in animated cartoons, as they were not subject to the limits of the physical body, but here again, Chaplin set a template that the cartoon was to advance and perfect.[21] As a child, the master animator Chuck Jones observed Chaplin working on his sets off Sunset Boulevard and was inevitably influenced by Chaplin's determination to get things absolutely perfect in relation to the "timing" of the gag, sometimes likening the numerous takes Chaplin would do to secure this perfection with the numerous drawings that he threw away in a spirit of executing an exact sequence of graphic choreography.[22] This is intrinsically bound up with Eliot's observation of Chaplin's "rhythm," which was not merely an improvised "flow" but an instinctive engagement with an established set of rules and outcomes. The deliberate limitations that Chaplin imposed on himself were essentially the conditions by which the gag might be achieved, and these became the touchstone for Jones when he imposed a set of rules on his Roadrunner cartoons.[23]

By limiting the discipline, and by establishing a core motivation for the joke—usually predicated on "survival," most notably in relation to hunger or imminent danger, and normally too, in the desperate avoidance of humiliation in some way—it was possible to create a structure for a comic event that crucially revealed its "emotional" content as well as its humor. Jones recalls, "My dad first saw Chaplin do those funny little hoppy runs, where he bounces up and down a few times as he rounds a corner, and I loved that and used it a lot. It wasn't really required, but it had the kind of exaggeration you could use in a cartoon. Chaplin used to do that all the time—exaggerated a move to show surprise, excitement, even understanding, using his body to let you know that something was funny but it had a point too."[24] Partly, Chaplin's rhythm drew attention to the very "momentum" of the modern world and constantly revealed his own status as an individual "out of kilter" with the changing environment around him. It is this fundamental trope that underpins many characters in the American animated cartoons in their formative years up to the mid-1930s and, at one and the same time, points up that the inherent change embedded in modernity ironically left humankind without a complete sense of security or purpose—a condition ultimately, and literally, played out in the metamorphoses of the cartoon. At the very same time in which the modern world seemed to be subject to an extraordinary sense of progress, supposedly in the service of humankind, it seems clear that humankind became increasingly alienated from it, finding ways to cope with "difference" through more radical languages of expression—ironically, in this case, the populist idioms of comic forms like vaudevillian performance, comic strips, and cartoons. This irony anticipates and informs later conceptions of the "absurd" advanced in the European works of André Gide, Albert Camus, Samuel Beckett, and Eugene Ionesco, who effectively distilled a view of modern life in their art and philosophy predicated on the incongruity that people occupied a godless, seemingly meaningless, world yet still constantly struggled to secure meaning, revelation, and contentment in their existence. The human condition, in the view of the absurdists, could only be understood through a perverse, ironic, and sometimes bleak model of humor. Arguably, this sense of "absurdism" becomes the condition of the animated film per se and is informed by the way Chaplin charges the cartoon with a core "animality," which in turn becomes the preserve of an essential humanity, in the midst of an increasingly inhumane and dehumanized world.

Chaplin himself is featured in Pat Powers's and Otto Messmer's *Felix in Hollywood* (1923), where he confronts Felix's attempts to imitate his appearance and gait with the accusation, "Stealing my stuff, eh?," a free acknowledgment of the cartoon's debt to his work. His narratives are parodied again in *Felix the Cat in the Cold Rush* (1925), and many Felix cartoons borrow freely from the speed and simplicity of Chaplin's Keystone era and the choreographic strategies noted above. As a crude simplification, I wish to suggest that Chaplin's influence on Mickey Mouse correlates with the self-conscious relationship-based comedies of the Essanay and Mutual periods, where in some senses Chaplin starts to signify his own recognition of the "comic" as a significant language of modernity. Esther Leslie has mapped Walter Benjamin's response to Chaplin, in this spirit, for example, noting how Benjamin suggests that Chaplin reconciles the performance of a marionette-like, noninvolvement with objects and environments, with an empathetic insight about humanity that understood how people were amused and emotionally affected, resulting in the "revolutionary" expression of "laughter."[25] There is much in this reading, though, that seeks to abstract Chaplin into the avant-garde through an elision of his performance with the mechanistic machinations played out by Léger and suggested in the work of Stepanova and Kandinsky earlier, but this idea of the parody automata is ultimately belied in the work, where it is Chaplin's "animality," not his abstracted or political stance, that permeates the narratives. This might equally be read as a more "vulgar" or "direct" set of imperatives, but this is to undermine again the key expressions of thought and emotion through choreographic motion and composition *in itself*. It was this that Chaplin—the animator—brought to the American cartoon.

Norman Klein has argued persuasively that there is a correlation between Chaplin's career and the significant changes that came about in the animated cartoon by the mid-1930s. Klein suggests that Chaplin necessarily had to finesse his work with increasing sentimentality to move away from the anarchic pantomime that spoke to blue-collar rather than middle-class sensibilities, and this was echoed in animated film.[26] Klein cites *The Kid* (1921) as the key transitional film in this respect but notes that "the early Chaplin of the teens is another species compared to the mature Chaplin. The same profound split holds true for full animation. It is a species in itself compared to cartoons made earlier. It emerges from different sources and to different ends. Disney's personality animation is as big a jump as Chaplin's *The Kid*."[27] While this is in some senses true in the self-evident changes in the narrative, technical, and aesthetic developments within the cartoon, it is equally true that the unselfconscious animality of the more primitive cartoon became the conceptual animality before Silly Symphonies debuted. The Silly Symphonies themselves were effectively American animation's version of "the experimental film," privileging new idioms and models of expression—often drawing from melodrama and more mature genres—but still echoing Chaplin's visualization and choreography. In some senses this conceptual animality might be understood as a core step in the move toward full personality animation.

It is worthwhile addressing one of Chaplin's most influential features in this respect. *Modern Times* (1936) is perhaps best remembered for Chaplin's antics as he becomes literally caught in the cogs and mechanisms of modern machine culture or is subjected to force feeding, gags that clearly operate in a quasi-cartoonal way, privileging impossible physical and material situations as the subject and object of the gag. An even more revealing metaphoric action, though, is when Chaplin roller-skates with Paulette Goddard on the edge of an abyss. Chaplin plays out the dramatic irony of the audience's knowledge of their predicament and its potential consequences, prompting suspense and concern, but Chaplin's knack was in the precision of his choices about what "visually" imbued the narrative with motion and metaphysical weight, at one and the same time pointing up "the absurd" as the material condition of experience and the philosophical character of "modern times." This was directly echoed by Disney in, for example, *Building a Building* (1933)[28]; the horror pastiche *The Mad Doctor* (1933); the improvisational bravura of keeping a plane in the air in *The Mail Pilot* (1933); *Mickey's Mechanical Man* (1933), a "modern" update of *The Champion;* the recognition of the significance of *King Kong* (1933) in the clash of the old and new worlds in *The Pet Store* (1933); the direct emulation of Chaplin's physical business in *Playful Pluto* (1934); Mickey's Charlie-like abandonment of material responsibility when distracted by his desire "for the girl" in *Mickey's Steam Roller* (1934); the tension between the "barnyard" and "classicism" in *The Band Concert* (1934); the sheer surrealism of *Mickey's Garden* (1934), which reconfigures space and scale to challenging effect; the oppressive moral incitement of *Pluto's Judgement Day* (1934); the aesthetic and cultural reversals of *Thru the Mirror* (1935); and, most important, in direct homage to Chaplin routines, the profound engagement with modernity in *Modern Inventions* and *Clock Cleaners* (both 1937).

As Faure has suggested, "Chaplin is a conceptualist. It is his profound sense of reality which he imposes on all appearances and movements, upon nature itself, and upon the soul of men and objects. He organises the universe into a cineplastic poem and flings forward into the future, in the manner of a god, this organisation which is capable of directing certain sensibilities and intelligences, and by means of these, of acting more and more upon the mind of mankind."[29] Once more, it is not hard to see the omnipotent characteristics of the animator here, in the construction of a highly particular "reality," the development of movement as metaphor, and the embedded sense of an immediacy in the image-making that has a direct effect on the viewer, emotionally, intellectually, and physically. It was this that Disney readily embraced in his experimental cartoons of the late 1920s and the 1930s, like Chaplin, slowly moving from the dynamics of pure "animality" to the conceptual leanings of pure "personality." This direct-ness, though, has an increasing clarity of purpose in the gag, which operates in and of itself and is merely part of an accumulation of comic perspectives that demonstrate that Chaplin, the animator, can still be aligned with the most com-mon creations and agency of the cartoon in this period. There is a technical as well as conceptual reason for this. Cartoon animators necessarily resist executing "animation for its own sake" because of the labor-intensive nature of the work. Simply, each choreographic or comic principle has to be motivated, and it must be executed with a precision that delivers the gag but does not involve extensive choreographic excess. This means much greater planning in the devising and visualization stage of the work.

Stark Young, writing in 1928 of Chaplin's seminal short *The Circus,* engages with something of this by commenting on the essence of Chaplin's visualization:

> They are too perfect images, too aptly expressive and too final to be mere symbols. By a perfect image I mean a motive, an action, a personage or event that parallels a thing in nature, a hill, a tree, the wind blowing; it can be taken simply in itself, it carries for the simplest person, and it carries with it its elemental idea, which it is inseparable from. But at the same time it is capable of the whole idea; it can exist with or without amplification or comment; it can hold as much meaning as you put into it."[30]

Chaplin's capture of the "elemental idea" represents his greatest influence on the cartoon, which readily evidences how intrinsic outcomes are bound up with the inherently authorial process. Where Chaplin and cartoon diverge, it is largely in the contextualization and aestheticization of "the gag" or "the elemental idea"— Chaplin seeking out a lyrical, one might say literary, underpinning to the wit of his invention; the cartoon epitomizing the radicalism of "the line" and its freedoms. When "Chaplin" influences the cartoon, he is the embodiment of its innate choreographies; when he ceases to "animate" and affect, he surrenders his cultural corporeality to the social surreality of the animated langue. But even in this "limitation" Chaplin is still instrumental in prompting an important dynamic in the cartoon. Žižek has suggested, "Neither death nor crime exist in the polymorphous world of the burlesque where everybody gives and receives blows at will, where cream cakes fly and where, in the midst of the general laughter, buildings fall down. In this world of pure gesticularity, which is also the world of cartoons (a substitute for lost slapstick), the protagonists are generally immortal . . . violence is universal and without consequences, [and] there is no guilt."[31] Žižek's easy elision of the burlesque, slapstick, and the cartoon, while noting the fantasy-collapse of the modern in the face of its anarchy, anxiety, and supposedly guilt-free expression of violence, fails to take into account the resonance of the "animality," "personality," and capture of the "elemental idea" as the emotive and affective resonances that insist on the address of mortality. Chaplin's comic melodramas and Disney's later Silly Symphonies and early features are often chastised for their apparently sentimental, sometimes mawkish, tendencies, but this is to misread the function of sentiment and to insufficiently take into account its status as an interrogation of changing emotional states that resist transience. Furthermore, it does not recognize the ways in which Chaplin and the American cartoon, in its evolution from the mid-1910s to the mid-1930s, function as a commentary on the ways in which "modernity" is understood through the repositioning of modernist creative idioms and conceptual outlooks in populist forms. The very specificity in the creation of the image in both the conception of "Chaplin as animator" and the traditional animator, as that figure emerged in this early period, was effectively a mediation between the recollection of the old world and the construction of the new. As Stark Young has remarked:

> I think of how much went into the creation of a single movement, a single perfect invention or motive or image, even a pause; exactly as so many centuries went into the development of an organ like the eye, or as so many forces, seasons, wind, rain, and so much of the chemistry of dust, went to the half-lights in the depths of the flower. I wonder if art is always like this, if it is something out of the memory, a voice of something past, the immortal come to us out of death; I wonder if art is like the return of a soul to its old life, of a ghost to its memory.[32]

Chaplin, and the animators of the 1920s and 1930s, saw the intrinsic "absurdity" of a world that sought progress and advance while sacrificing the intrinsic humanity it was supposedly serving. An "old life" was being lost, a "memory" made, but Chaplin, his "animation," and the American animators, from Messmer to those who ultimately became "the Nine Old Men" at Disney, insisted on reanimating the soul of the new world and being the ghosts in the machine—the "gag," the epitome of the animal, the personal and the elemental, the art of modernity.

NOTES

1. Lejeune, *Cinema,* 27.
2. See Thomas and Johnston, *Disney Animation,* esp. 21, 79, 120, 223, 285, 293, 415, 417.
3. Crafton, *Before Mickey,* 11.
4. Schickel, "Introduction: The Tramp Transformed," 9.
5. Ibid., 25.
6. See Žižek, *Enjoy Your Symptom!* 1–9.
7. Faure, "The Art of Charlie Chaplin," 79.
8. Lejeune, *Cinema,* 29.
9. Léger, "A New Realism—the Object," 279.
10. Leyda, *Eisenstein on Disney,* 21.
11. Faure, "The Art of Charlie Chaplin," 74.
12. See Moritz, "Americans in Paris."
13. Moritz, "Some Observations on Non-Objective and Non-Linear Animation," 21.
14. See Wells, *The Animated Bestiary.*
15. Winokur, *American Laughter,* 75, 76.
16. See Churchill, "Everybody's Language."
17. Robinson, *The Man in the Bowler Hat,* 123.
18. Quoted in John Canemaker's documentary *Otto Messmer and Felix the Cat* (Phoenix Films and Video, 1977), film.
19. Wilk, *Modernism,* 137.
20. Quoted in Seldes, "I Am Here Today," 108.
21. See Canemaker, *Tex Avery,* 102.
22. Chuck Jones, interview with the author, Aug. 1992.
23. Jones, *Chuck Amuck,* 225.
24. Chuck Jones, interview with the author, Aug. 1992.
25. See Leslie, *Hollywood Flatlands,* 194–96.
26. See Klein, *Seven Minutes,* 102–3.
27. Ibid., 104.
28. See, e.g., Wells, "Building a Building."
29. Faure, "The Art of Charlie Chaplin," 78.
30. Young, "*The Circus,*" 185.
31. Žižek, *Enjoy Your Symptom!* 1.
32. Young, "*The Circus,*" 186–87.

2

Polyphony and Heterogeneity in Early Fleischer Films

Comic Strips, Vaudeville,
and the New York Style

Mark Langer

Most examinations of the early films of Max and Dave Fleischer portray them as failed narratives, despite their considerable virtues in other areas. Leonard Maltin has characterized the Fleischer cartoons as examples of "raw, peasant humor . . . that relied more on technical ingenuity and comical invention than artistic expertise. There was no storyboard, just a general idea of what the picture was about."[1] Bob Baker's criticism was based on his feeling that the Fleischer "films give the impression sometimes of having been made up as they went along, from cel to cel. The plots frequently take off in odd directions or just peter out altogether."[2] Animation history generally posits Disney's narrative organization as the standard by which all animated films are compared. Good animation narrative is linear, unified, and coherent. Bad animation narrative (or at least, inferior animation narrative) is anything that doesn't conform to this. The Fleischer films, on the whole, do not conform to this.

Scholarly examinations of Disney's work often attribute Disney's tendencies toward mimesis, small-town or rural values, and linear, moralistic narratives to his boyhood in small towns and rural settings like Marceline and Kansas City or to the influence of American theatrical tradition.[3] Animation historians tend toward evolutionary or teleological approaches in their examinations of narrative; the episodic, gag-oriented structures typical of early Fleischer films and those made by Fleischer contemporaries are seen as early stages leading up to the development of more coherent structures in the Disney product. This follows a tradition seen in work on early cinema in the immediate post-Brighton period, where pre-1907 discontinuous narrative structures were seen as a developmental stage to more integrated, linear forms of expression.[4] Just as later examinations have contested this view of early cinema, this study will offer a differing analysis of the alterity presented by early Fleischer films. The Fleischers' work was produced in a geographical area different from Disney's and stemmed from other traditions in media, such as comic strips and vaudeville. Rather than viewing their films as failed or primitive projects in terms of narrative organization, I argue that the polyphonic and heterogeneous forms of expression seen in early Fleischer films grew out of the expressive practices, cultural milieu, and urban setting from which the studio and its artists originated. Later animated films relying on the discontinuous style inherent in polyphonic and heterogeneous structures (with their voices of multiple creative perspectives and disconnected arrangement of visual styles, narrative forms, etc.) that privilege separate visual gags over linearity are not naive holdovers from the primal era of animation; instead, they represent both the deliberate continuation of media traditions and the effusion of a specific ethnocultural context.[5] Both the traditions and context were related, in large part, to the Fleischers' background in early twentieth-century New York City, which differed dramatically from traditions in the Midwest that resulted in Disney's "West Coast" style of animation.

New York City's status as the birthplace of American animation is indisputable. Through the 1910s and 1920s the city and surrounding area was home to dozens of animation companies—Associated Animators, Bray Studios, the Bud Fisher Films Corporation, Celebrated Players, Earl Hurd Productions, Fables Pictures, Carpenter Goldman Studio, Harry Palmer, International Film Service, the Jefferson Film Corporation, Macdono Cartoons, Out of the Inkwell Films, the Pat Sullivan Studio, and the Tony Sarg Studio—all of which were practitioners of a similar style of animation.[6] The Fleischers' Out of the Inkwell Films and its later incarnation, Fleischer Studios, became the most successful and longest-lived of animation businesses that used what has become known as the "New York style" of animation. New York–style animation preceded and later existed in opposition to a more realistic "West Coast style," which developed during the late 1920s through the 1930s at studios like Walt Disney Productions, Harman-Ising, and Ub Iwerks' Celebrity Productions. The earlier New York style had a number of characteristic features that stemmed partly from the location of the industry and partly from the nature of the early careers of its first participants. Most early New York studios were founded by practitioners of newspaper and magazine cartooning and illustration, such as Winsor McCay (*Little Nemo in Slumberland, Dreams of the Rarebit Fiend*), Raoul Barré (*Les contes du Père Rhault*), John Bray (*Little Johnny and the Teddy Bears*), Bud Fisher (*Mutt and Jeff*), or Pat Sullivan (*Sambo and His Funny "Noises"*). In addition, several founders, like McCay or J. Stuart Blackton, were veterans of vaudevillian "chalk talk" and "lightning sketch" performances.[7]

NEW YORK AND WEST COAST STYLES

The artificiality of the characters and their drawn nature were emphasized through design, movement, and narrative in New York–style animation. One thinks of the animated series that derived directly from newspaper cartoons, such as the Fleischers' Popeye the Sailor, Van Beuren's Little King, Fontaine Fox's Toonerville Folks, or Charles Mintz's Krazy Kat. Original characters developed by these studios conformed to a stylized, "cartoony" format. Betty Boop, Cubby Bear, and Scrappy were simple, flat, "inkblot" designs. These were both easy to animate and visually arresting. More important within the terms of this study, such characters were graphic descendants of earlier animated characters like the Fleischers' Ko-Ko the Clown or Sullivan and Messmer's Felix the Cat, which themselves were designs similar to those used in newspaper cartoons.[8]

Ethnic and working-class characters were common in these films, in contrast to the middle-class small-town or rural characters of the Disney, Iwerks, and Harman-Ising products. Felix and Ko-Ko were marginal *luftmenschen*. Disney's Mickey Mouse may have begun as a deckhand in *Steamboat Willie* (1928), but the Fleischers' working-class Popeye remained one. In most screen appearances Mickey Mouse appeared as an exemplar of an upwardly mobile middle class employed in a minor managerial or professional capacity.[9] Iwerks's Flip the Frog or Willie Whopper may have had fantastic adventures (entirely imaginary in Willie's case) but were usually seen in the context of lower-middle-class small-town America.

West Coast animation reflects a Protestant sense of morality more typical of the rural or small-town backgrounds of many of its leading figures, with Disney being the chief exemplar. While New York–style films often reveled in risqué behavior, West Coast–style films were invested with normative ideological meanings endorsing middle-class values. Moral homilies were common in these pictures, such as Snow White's counsel to "whistle while you work" in *Snow White and the Seven Dwarfs* (1938) or the hard-working pig's adage, "I'll be safe and you'll be sorry, when the wolf comes to your door," in *The Three Little Pigs* (1933).

New York animated films were far less likely to demonstrate moral homilies than those of West Coast studios. In an unfavorable comparison with the Disney product, William Kozlenko deploringly opined of Popeye:

> Here is a man who, after swallowing the contents of a can of spinach . . . goes completely berserk and with a series of powerful punches destroys buildings, knocks down trees, and annihilates men normally stronger than himself. His philosophy of action is the doctrine that with physical strength man can overcome every obstacle; and his justification for this display of unbridled power usually takes the form of saving his girl from the unsavory clutches of the gargantuan villain. We are speedily convinced by all this that if a man cannot get satisfaction by persuasion, he can certainly get it by a knockout blow.[10]

In contrast to the products of West Coast studios, animated films made in New York reflected the multiethnic and more worldly view of New York in the era just before and during Prohibition. Eschewing the fable convention of using animal or child characters common to studios like Disney, Iwerks, and Harman-Ising, New York animation tended to present adult characters with adult concerns, including (un)employment, sex, and death. Many New York films expressed and even endorsed forms of forbidden behavior. Vices exhibited in early Out of the Inkwell films include gluttony (in *Reunion* [1922]), sloth (in *Bedtime* [1923] or *Ko-Ko's Klock* [1928]), vengeance (in *Ko-Ko in the Fade-Away* [1926] or *Ko-Ko's Hot Ink* [1929]), homosexuality (in *Ko-Ko the Convict* [1926]), and lust (in *Ko-Ko's Magic* [1928] or *No Eyes Today* [1929]). Similar sins are found in other products of New York–based studios: cheating in Van Beuren's *Opening Night* (1933), infidelity in Sullivan's *Felix the Cat in Flim Flam Films* (1927), and drunkenness in *Felix the Cat in Whys and Otherwhys* (1927).

In films made by New York companies human figures abound, with protagonists such as Colonel Heeza Liar, Bobby Bumps, or Dinky Doodle at the Bray Studio; Tom and Jerry,[11] the Little King, Amos 'n' Andy, the Great Katrinka, and the Terrible-Tempered Mr. Bang at Van Beuren; Ko-Ko, Popeye, Olive Oyl, Bluto, Wimpy, Betty Boop, and Grampy at Out of the Inkwell Studios or its successor the Fleischer Studios; Farmer Al Falfa at Fables Studio; or Terrytoons and Oopie and Scrappy at Mintz. West Coast style incorporated a nativist, rural orientation with barnyard settings. Animal characters like Mickey Mouse, Bugs Bunny, Flip the Frog, and Barney Bear were common. Human figures did inhabit West Coast films, but they were used relatively infrequently. While both New York and West Coast studios intermingled animal and human characters, West Coast studios were far more likely to use them as stars. The Disney studio was particularly rigorous in its definition of separate worlds for animals and humans. The two rarely interacted on the same level as would Ko-Ko and Fitz, Betty Boop and Bimbo, or Farmer Al Falfa and Kiko. Barnyard environments appeared far less frequently in New York than in West Coast films. For eastern studios, gritty urban streets were the abode even of such animal characters as Cubby Bear.

Perspective, in New York–style films, retained the flatness of a drawing or foregrounded its existence through exaggerated effects. For example, Max Fleischer's Rotograph and his later Stereoptical Process both combined flat animated characters with three-dimensional backgrounds. The Rotograph, in use at the Fleischers' company as early as 1925, combined animated images with a live-action background by means of a rear-projection system on the animation camera rostrum. The Stereoptical Process combined animated characters with three-dimensional model backgrounds and, occasionally, foregrounds. While Disney's later multiplane camera smoothly integrated flat drawings with the idea of three-dimensional space by blurring distinctions among different planes of action, through the contrast of two- and three-dimensional images, the Fleischer processes foregrounded the very existence of a three-dimensional process.[12]

Often, in New York films, there was an acknowledgment of the cartoon as an artificial device or a manufactured object. For example, Little Nemo, Ko-Ko the Clown, Dinky Doodle, and occasionally Bobby Bumps appeared as characters originating on a drawn sheet of paper, interacting with a world outside the drawing. At the Fleischer Studios this convention lasted at least as long as the film *Goonland* (1938). In *Goonland* Popeye and Pappy are locked in a losing battle with the Goons. So violent is the struggle that the film "breaks." The Goons tumble out of the bottom of the frame. The hands of (presumably) an animator enter the screen, place Popeye and Pappy securely back in the frame, and repair the film with a safety pin. Popeye mutters, "That was a lucky break," and the picture continues.[13]

Rather than utilizing lifelike personality animation, New York studios, until about 1934, tended to use a style called "rubber animation" or "rubber hose animation" in which both animate and inanimate objects moved with a bouncy flexibility as if they were made of rubber. Objects took on the function or characteristics of other things, emphasizing mutability and metamorphosis. Morbid imagery and themes of death, violence, and mutilation were common in New York series. Examples include Felix the Cat cartoons like *Sure-Locked Homes* (1928), where, in a parody of contemporary horror thrillers, Felix is menaced by giant spiders, gorillas, and bats, or such Fleischer efforts as *No Eyes Today* and *Ko-Ko's Harem Scarum* (1929), where the clown is blinded or beheaded.[14]

If the visual style was literally "loose," narrative structure was metaphorically so. Few, if any, of the New York studios had formal story departments before 1932. Often, a vague outline would be improvised, but bits of business would be left to head, or even individual, animators. Consequently, narratives were often loose aggregations of illogical gags, often set in a recognizably "New York" environment. Many previous examinations of these narratives tried to explain their genesis in terms of the loose organization of studio authority.[15] While these examinations have value, it might also be useful to look at the organization of studio authority not as the cause of narrative form in New York–style animation but as the result of the media traditions from which New York style originated. I want to propose another reason for the Fleischer practice of assigning a great deal of autonomy to individual animators and of making most of their films a loose collection of "bits" with a decidedly urban flavor. In particular, the polyphonic and heterogeneous style of the Fleischer films may be explained partly by Max and Dave Fleischer's boyhoods in Jewish neighborhoods of New York and by the early experience of the Fleischer brothers in comic strip art, vaudeville theater, and related entertainment forms.

THE ROAD FROM BROWNSVILLE

Although both Max and Dave Fleischer were born elsewhere, their formative years were spent mostly in the Brownsville neighborhood in Brooklyn. In the late nineteenth century, land speculators purchased and developed farmland surrounding Brown's Village in Brooklyn. Originally these land speculators touted the area as an escape from the urban congestion of Manhattan's Lower East Side. After the destruction of blocks of tenements in the Lower East Side during the construction of the entrance ramps to the Williamsburg Bridge and the Manhattan Bridge in 1903 and 1909, many of the displaced residents moved to Brownsville. This exodus was followed by garment manufacturers and light industry. By 1914 the neighborhood's Jewish population was estimated at 102,000. Brownsville had the highest concentration of Jews in New York City, which itself was the most Jewish city in the United States. On one of the streets where the Fleischer family rented accommodations, Stone Avenue, there were ten synagogues, most of them in storefronts or basements.[16]

Alfred Kazin, who grew up within a few blocks of the various Fleischer flats, later recalled the longings of his youth in the neighborhood: "Whenever I went off on my favorite walk to Highland Park in the 'American' district in the north, on the border of Queens, and climbed the hill to the old reservoir from which I could look straight across to the skyscrapers of Manhattan, I saw New York as a foreign city. . . . They were New York, the Gentiles, America: we were Brownsville—*Brunzvil,* as the old folks said—the dust of the earth to all Jews with money, and notoriously a place that measured all success by our skill in getting away from it."[17]

Social conditions were deplorable, resulting in the attendant presence of crime. The office of the United Jewish Aid Societies stated that "some of the most unfortunate dependent classes" were to be found in the neighborhood. Indeed, among the sons of Brownsville were the Mafia banker Meyer Lansky and Murder Inc.'s Jacob "Gurrah" Shapiro. The Fleischers led lives of considerable privation in tenements on Stone Avenue, Powell Avenue, and Sackman Street, where each floor had one sink in a common hallway and toilet facilities consisted of a multiple-seat outhouse in the backyard. Decades later, minor financial windfalls still played large in the memories of family members. In an interview with Joe Adamson, Dave Fleischer shares a sixty-five-year-old recollection of his good fortune in finding a dime on the way to school. "I rushed home, and I gave it to my mother. She bought a tomato herring. I remember that. And we all ate out of that tomato herring can."[18]

Despite their poverty, the Fleischer family were believers in an age of progress. Family members were fascinated with modern technology and tinkered endlessly with inventions. William Fleischer, the family patriarch, created a number of devices for use in the tailoring trade, and the oldest brother, Charles, took out a series of patents on amusement park machines, including the popular claw-digger vending machine. Joe Fleischer was an early practitioner of wireless telegraphy. Both Max and Lou received technical education in engineering, mechanics, and art.[19]

Sometime early in the year 1900, Max Fleischer walked into the offices of the *Brooklyn Daily Eagle* looking for a job and was offered a position at two dollars a week to help deliver newspapers. Soon, he was employed as a copyboy and began to work in the art department as a photo retoucher. At the threshold of the twentieth century the *Brooklyn Daily Eagle* was one of the major daily newspapers in the United States. From its magnificent new headquarters at Washington and Johnson Streets the *Eagle* published thirty-five thousand daily and forty-five thousand Sunday papers. The editor-in-chief of the *Eagle* was the charismatic St. Clair McKelway, who ran the paper with a sense of personal mission until his death in 1915. Raymond A. Schroth said of the paper under the conservative editorship of McKelway that the "*Eagle* . . . became a symbol of its own age and of its community; but seen against the backdrop of its own time, the clear image of prosperity, stability and upper-class respectability projected to turn-of-the century Brooklynites now seems narrow and unreal. In contrast to a larger metropolitan culture torn by philosophical, class, ethnic and religious factions, the *Eagle's* Brooklyn remained stable, homogeneous, business-oriented and Protestant."[20]

COMIC STRIPS

In this milieu Max Fleischer began his working life. Employment at the *Eagle* represented the first step on the voyage from the proletarian, ethnic world of Brownsville to the established society of corporate, Protestant America. By 1901 Max began to get his drawings published in the *Brooklyn Daily Eagle,* and before the following year began, he was publishing regular strips. While some of his early drawings were signed "M. Fleischer," most were signed with a more ethnically misleading, or at best ambiguous, "Mack."[21] His first strip, *Little Algy,* was in many ways typical of the "kid strips" that were popular at the beginning of the century through the success of James Swinnerton's *Jimmy,* R. F. Outcault's *Yellow Kid* and *Buster Brown,* Rudolph Dirks's *Katzenjammer Kids,* and Winsor McCay's *Little Sammy Sneeze* and *Little Nemo.* These strips, according to Bill Blackbeard and Martin Williams, stemmed from a preexisting literary tradition that had featured earlier characters like Mark Twain's Huckleberry Finn, George W. Peck's Bad Boy, and Edward W. Townsend's Chimmie Fadden.[22] In their comic strip adaptations these traditional archetypes shifted from rural and small-town settings to more urban and multicultural environments. For

FIGURE 2.1. Max Fleischer, "Algy's St. Valentine's Scheme," undated clipping from the *Brooklyn Daily Eagle* (c. Feb. 1901) in *Scrapbook*, Fleischer family private collection.

example, the Hogan's Alley setting of Outcault's *Yellow Kid* was a slum populated with immigrant Irish and other ethnic groups.

Max Fleischer's *Little Algy* was set in surroundings not unlike Brownsville. It was an environment in which conflicts (sometimes violent) between young Jews and non-Jewish youth gangs were common.[23] The strip's protagonist, Algy, is a young boy with what appears to be a Yiddish accent. Algy is perpetually in innocently amorous pursuit of May McGinnis in an assimilationist narrative anticipating such later Hollywood productions as *The Jazz Singer* (1927) or *Abie's Irish Rose* (1929). In one strip Algy cuts a heart-shaped hole in a fence (a "val" as he pronounces it) and prints around it the message "My dear May, Wen Yew pass this, axcept me for your Valentine, Algy." Algy goes to the other side of the fence and sticks his head through the hole. Swipsey, Algy's rival for May's affections, ropes Algy and, together with members of his gang, proceeds to beat the hapless boy. May, unaware of the beating going on behind the fence, dismisses Algy as a chump since he is evidently shedding tears for love (Fig. 2.1).[24] Algy's childhood world is one in which the hero is the outsider in an environment dominated by a gentile gang. The protagonist's plans for acceptance or attempts to improve his lot are constantly frustrated by the hostility of his surroundings. The strip exhibits conflicting voices that polyphonically represent not only the tragic point of view of the disadvantaged immigrant but also the point of view of a dominant culture that finds the frustration of minority attempts at acceptance and assimilation to be a comical subject. It simultaneously voices the perspectives of the new immigrant and of groups more established in America.

Max's other early strip, *E. K. Sposher, the Camera Fiend*, was also consistent with a preexisting genre of comic publications featuring a character that Blackbeard and Williams characterize as "the well-meaning, even saintly, fool" found in such strips as C. M. Payne's *S'Matter Pop?*, Fred Opper's classic "hobo strip" *Happy Hooligan*, or Charles Schultz's *Foxy Grandpa*.[25] Reflecting the Fleischer family's love of technology, *E. K. Sposher, the Camera Fiend* detailed the adventures of an ardent middle-class shutterbug whose grasp of photographic technology falls far short of his ambition. In one instance Sposher tries to take a self-portrait by shooting into a mirror but becomes confused by the upside-down image that appears on the frosted glass of his bellows camera. Attempting to correct the situation, Sposher upends the apparatus and stands on his head. Inevitably, both camera and photographer fall over, smashing the mirror (Fig. 2.2).

Elements of Max's early strips can be seen in the later Out of the Inkwell films. Like the character that would later become Ko-Ko the Clown, Algy is smaller than his contemporaries and lives in a hostile environment. Both the clown and Algy are inscribed in terms of otherness in relation to established society. Like the strips, the films have polyphonic and heterogeneous points of view, invoking sympathy for the trials of the clown being tormented by his maker, and

FIGURE 2.2. *E. K. Sposher, the Camera Fiend* was Max Fleischer's second strip. This episode, "E. K. Sposher, the Camera Fiend: Fails Again to Take a Picture," appeared in the *Brooklyn Daily Eagle*, c. 1902, in *Scrapbook*, Fleischer family private collection.

for the exasperation of the artist confronted with the mischievous antics of his creation. E. K. Sposher and Ko-Ko the Clown are "fool" characters. The Out of the Inkwell films mirror concerns found in *E. K. Sposher, the Camera Fiend* in their comic preoccupation with the process and apparatus of a modern, mechanically reproducible medium. Consequently, the mimetic conventions of straight photographic live-action images and the realism implicit in the lifelike movement afforded through the use of the rotoscope are undermined through the foregrounding of the mechanical process of filmmaking.[26] The Fleischer films, like the strips that preceded them, created a space combining these multiple perspectives and viewpoints.

VAUDEVILLE

Several entertainment media competed for a mass audience in the early twentieth century.[27] While Max's career began in comic strips, Dave was interested in the theatrical business. In 1913 he was hired at the Palace Theater in New York, one of the leading venues for vaudeville. The workday began at eight o'clock in the morning, when Dave would be assigned to polish the brass trim and clean the theater. At two in the afternoon he put on an usher's uniform and worked through matinees and evening performances until eleven at night. Dave Fleischer later credited the repeated viewing of vaudeville routines by people like Weber and Fields, Timburg and Rooney, Gus Edwards, and Joe Jackson for teaching him the fundamentals of comic performance. "I watched the laughs and I watched the reactions. And as many times as they rehearsed, I would watch every bit of it, all the way through. Watch for the timing and everything."[28]

The team of Weber and Fields was perhaps the most successful comedy act of its time. Like the Fleischers, Joe Weber and Lew Fields came from proletarian Jewish immigrant backgrounds. During the 1870s the two vaudevillians did a variety of dialect acts that mocked the habits of new immigrants such as the Irish, Germans, and Jews. By the 1880s the two had perfected the act for which they would become famous. The comedians appeared as bearded Jewish immigrants. Fields, the tall thin one, played the character of Meyer—a sharpster somewhat more *au fait* with the conventions of American society than was his companion. Meyer would physically abuse the diminutive Mike, the character played by Weber. Mike was the *naif*—the more recent newcomer to America. Meyer would instruct Mike in the intricacies of American society and simultaneously con his companion as the two talked in comical Jewish accents. The act always concluded with Mike being forced off the stage by his partner as the little fellow protested "Don't poosh me Meyer!" By the time that Dave Fleischer saw the two at the Palace, Weber and Fields were able to command as much as $4,000 a week for their performances.

Weber and Fields were one of the most successful examples of what was known as the "two-act," a form of comic performance that depended on the interaction of two characters (although other minor characters could, on occasion, be incorporated into the act). The two-act, as Albert F. McLean has pointed out, depended more on situation and action than did other forms of comedy, such as the monologue. Traditionally, the dialogue in the two-act relied on insult, repartee, and ridicule. Weber and Fields, according to McLean, represented the experience of the new immigrant in America: "The Mutt and Jeff relationship symbolizes the contradictory needs of these new mass men. If on the one hand they desire a dialogue and companionship, on the other they find themselves, by virtue of their urban predicament, in a state of unrelieved competition. In the material order of an industrial society, the very closeness that brings friendship brings also exploitation, antagonism and ultimately violence."[29]

The vaudeville traditions in which Weber and Fields participated were relevant to the immigrant experience of the Fleischers and a major influence on their later work. The Out of the Inkwell cartoons take the classical form of the "two-act." As with Weber and Fields, the conflict between Max Fleischer and the clown is one between a large character with a little more life experience and the smaller one who is tormented by his partner. McLean's comments about the two-act apply perfectly to the relationship between the protagonist and antagonist in the silent Fleischer films. Live-action Max is depicted as more integrated into society than the smaller cartoon clown. As joint performers in films and coworkers in an animation studio, Max and Ko-Ko are presented in a partnership of dialogue and companionship. But the working and personal relationship in the films also results in exploitation, antagonism, and violence.

There is something else that Dave Fleischer may have picked up from such acts as Weber and Fields: the convention of repetition. Although Weber and Fields experimented with many different kinds of acts early in their career, once they set on their Mike and Meyer characters, the repetition of certain stock situations became central to their popularity. Perhaps their most famous routine, and the one that Dave Fleischer specifically cited in his AFI interview with Joe Adamson, was the "pool hall sketch." Audiences would return time after time to see this performed over a period of decades. Such acts were common. For example, the comedy team of Smith and Dale were famous for their "Dr. Krankheit" sketch, which they performed together for more than sixty years. Joe Jackson, who performed a comic tramp bicycle act for a similar period of time, was succeeded by his son Joe Jackson Jr., who performed the same routine. Obviously, these acts were not repeated for decades just in front of fresh audiences. The very fact that these acts would be enjoyed by spectators who would view them over and over was part of their charm. This is not unlike the pleasure that more modern audiences might get from Abbott and Costello's "Who's on

First" routine (repeated on stage, radio, and television) or from multiple listenings to old Firesign Theatre albums.

To humorously surprise repeat spectators, vaudevillians would often pepper their familiar routines with variations and ad-libs. This pattern of repetition with variation became fundamental to the Fleischer narrative. The Out of the Inkwell cartoons and other early Fleischer silents often made direct reference to well-known vaudeville routines, with visits to dentists, doctors, and chiropractors that mirror Smith and Dale's act in films like *The Cure* (1924), *Another Bottle Doctor* (1927), *Ko-Ko's Germ Jam* (1928), and *Ko-Ko's Kink* (1928) or the Joe Jackson reference in the use of a bicycle act of *Invisible Ink* (1921). Notable, too, is the number of films that have vaudeville or showbiz settings, such as *The Circus* (1920), *The Dancing Doll* (1922), *The Show* (1922), *The Contest* (1923), *Vacation* (1924), *Vaudeville* (1924), *Ko-Ko at the Circus* (1926), *It's the Cats* (1926), *Ko-Ko Makes 'Em Laugh* (1927), and the entire live-action Carrie of the Chorus series (1926). These locations were repeated throughout the sound era in the showbiz settings of many Betty Boop and Screen Song cartoons, as well as the frequent vaudeville, carnival, or nightclub themes used in many Popeye shorts, including *Popeye the Sailor* (1933), *The Hyp-Nut-Tist* (1935), *King of the Mardi Gras* (1935), *Organ Grinder's Swing* (1937), or *Puttin' on the Act* (1940). Stage performances also play a part in later features in instances like the banquet scene in *Gulliver's Travels* (1938) or the nightclub sequence in *Mr. Bug Goes to Town* (1941).

More important, Fleischer narrative patterns depended on the repetition principle through the ritualized use of stock plots. The Out of the Inkwell cartoons always depended on the repeated convention of Ko-Ko's being drawn and returning to the inkwell. The short-lived Carrie of the Chorus series of 1926–27 featured repeated situations involving a small traveling burlesque company in conflict with stodgy pillars of society. In the sound era the Popeye cartoons depended on a recurrent narrative of Popeye and Bluto in comic rivalry for Olive's affections, leading to a battle that is settled following the ingestion of spinach. Similarly the Fleischers' Superman series was based on a stock transformation of Clark Kent into the Man of Steel.

There is another aspect of the films that comes from related vaudeville, musical revue, or carnival traditions. With the additional income earned by Max and Dave Fleischer, in 1914 the Fleischer family was able to move from Brownsville to a more upscale neighborhood in Coney Island. Dave later recalled to Joe Adamson that on his days off work, he would hang around watching the entertainment in dance halls and saloons. After viewing clowns in Steeplechase Park, Dave decided that he too would like to be a clown. Dave's father, William, provided some black cloth from his tailor shop, and Dave fabricated a black clown suit with three oversized white "pom-pom"-style buttons, white trim on the neck frill, and a pointed hat decorated with three large white buttons. In costume he set out for

FIGURE 2.3. Sheet music from 1922 implicitly acknowledges the Fleischers' debt to Bessie McCoy, the "Yama
Yama Girl." Courtesy David A. Jasen.

Steeplechase Park and was hired as a clown. Dave worked with two or three other
clowns by the park entrance to entertain people waiting to get in. As part of his
job he was given an electrically charged whip. The floor on which he worked was
equipped with holes through which air was forced. When women would walk
over the hole, the air would blow their dresses up, resulting in their embarrassment and the general entertainment of the crowd. When victims were reluctant
to step over the hole, Dave was to touch them with the whip and move them over
to the compressed air blast.[30]

Dave Fleischer's recollections of this costume make no mention of any influence other than that of the clowns at Steeplechase Park, but his earlier employment and interest in vaudeville suggest another influence—Bessie McCoy. The
daughter of vaudeville dancers Billy McCoy and Minnie McEvoy, Bessie McCoy
grew up in the entertainment business. By 1905 she was a headliner. McCoy's

appearance in *A Yankee Circus on Mars* opened the six-thousand-seat Hippo-drome Theatre in New York in 1905. On January 27, 1908, Bessie McCoy appeared in the musical comedy *Three Twins* at the Herald Square Theatre in New York, where she performed a number called the "Yama-Yama Man." *Three Twins* was an immense hit, running for 288 performances, and McCoy would henceforth be known as the "Yama Yama Girl." According to Marjorie Farnsworth, "thousands came to see Bessie sing and dance as the Yama Yama Girl and then came to see her again. . . . Her knack of dancing her songs became so effective that she often did them in pantomime with the audience filling in the words." McCoy's perfor-mance of the "Yama-Yama Man," according to Joe Laurie Jr., became one of the most imitated routines in vaudeville.[31] McCoy went on to tour vaudeville theaters with her act—Bessie McCoy and her Yama Yama Girls.

The clown outfit worn by Dave Fleischer seems to owe much to McCoy's. Both were made of loose black material and had three large white pom-poms in the front and a white-trimmed neck frill. Both outfits included white gloves, white foot coverings, and a hat decorated with the same white pom-pom as the suit. Although Dave Fleischer did not use the floppy white bow worn by Bessie McCoy, the similarities between the two outfits, and the undoubted familiarity that Dave Fleischer would have had with McCoy's vaudeville success, suggest that the "Yama Yama Girl" was a strong influence (see Fig. 2.3).[32]

INTERRELATIONSHIP OF MEDIA
FORMS AND SYSTEMS

The emergence of film in general, and animation in particular, must be seen in the context of the advent and development of other media. The late nineteenth century and the early twentieth saw an upheaval in American popular culture. Older, regional forms of popular entertainments began to be displaced by more technologically based mass media, such as comic strips, sound recordings, and film. Vaudeville grew out of earlier music halls and museums as a mass medium in this period. The form of vaudeville entertainments was that of a variety show, with its hodgepodge of acts varying from singers, dancers, and comedians to animal acts, acrobats, contortionists, and magicians. Behind this was a rigidly centralized business structure, where organizations like the Keith Albee circuit disseminated a standardized cultural product nationally.

There were similarities between the newspaper industry where Max Fleischer began his career and the vaudeville industry that influenced Dave Fleischer. Comic strips may have appeared as a hodgepodge on the funny pages, but behind them stood businesses like the King Features or McClure's syndicates, which were as centralized as any vaudeville booking office. But both systems dissemi-nated similar cultural forms. Robert W. Snyder has pointed out that "vaudeville theatre's polyphony was partly caused by the contrast between the old and new popular culture. . . . They paid close attention to local audiences but knit them into a modern mass constituency. They featured blackface minstrels straight out of Jacksonian America and modern Jewish comedians from the Lower East Side."[33] Comics also appeared in a polyphonic format. As in vaudeville, traditional and modern American culture coexisted on the printed page, where strips featuring the middle-class Anglo Buster Brown rubbed shoulders with the working-class immigrant strip *The Katzenjammer Kids.* Small-town strips like *And Her Name Was Maude, Happy Hooligan,* and *Toonerville Trolley* could appear in conjunction with the urban settings of *Bringing Up Father, Abie the Agent,* or *Polly and Her Pals.* Fantasies like *Krazy Kat* coexisted with the ordinary family life of *Gasoline Alley.* Both forms were organized heterogeneously. On the stage musical numbers would be interspersed with magicians, dog acts, jugglers, and other acts. While individual comic strips, like individual vaudeville numbers, might exhibit narrative coherence, their brevity and random arrangement on the funny pages were a departure from the more continuous experience of reading a book or viewing a "well-made" play.

Early cinema exhibition owed a greater debt to vaudeville for the structure of the film program than it did to the conventions of middle-class theater. In their earliest release, around World War I, in combination with other live-action and animated films in "screen magazines" such as the Paramount-Bray or Goldwyn-Bray Pictographs, the Fleischer films appeared in a format similar to that of comic strips or vaudeville routines. Even during the classical Hollywood period, from the 1920s through the 1950s, audiences watched animated film shorts combined in a program of entertainment that included live-action shorts, newsreels, previews, and a feature film.[34] The polyphonic and heterogeneous format of a newspaper page of comic strips or the mixed vaudeville bill were similar to the way in which silent Fleischer films were exhibited in theaters. This format was also internalized into the very structure of their movies. On the rare occasion that a linear, continuous narrative was a concern in silent Fleischer films, it was a minor consideration. In *Ko-Ko Makes 'Em Laugh,* Max draws a background and then pours Ko-Ko out of the inkwell. The clown pulls out his canine companion, Fitz. Max draws a large stone-faced Indian in a village of tepees with a sign offering a reward to anyone who can make the native laugh. Ko-Ko and Fitz parade comically, Ko-Ko juggles his nose and Fitz, and finally the clown transforms himself into a monkey as Fitz tickles the Indian, all to no avail. Fitz snaps the Indian's suspenders, causing the native's head to fall onto Fitz's head. Fitz climbs onto the Indian's shoulders. Ko-Ko plays his nose like a flute and thinks that he has made the Indian laugh, but it just turns out to be Fitz. In frustration Ko-Ko kicks the Indian off of the screen. The clown and Fitz rearrange the lines of the Indian village background drawing into a proscenium arch and begin to entertain the extrafilmic audience. Fitz dances with a canine chorus line and does tricks by throwing rocks and shooting arrows at Ko-Ko. The clown does a weight-lifting act. A mouse joins Ko-Ko in performance and then turns into Fitz. The clown and dog take a bow and the curtain comes down.[35]

The almost incoherently episodic and nonlinear nature of the narrative in *Ko-Ko Makes 'Em Laugh,* with its mixture of live action and animation, representations of different ethnicities (and species), and varying modes of performance contained both within and without the spaces of the animation drawing and the screen, can be seen as an extension of the heterogeneous structures of vaudeville performance and the newspaper comic strip. Similarly, the shifting from the point of view of a live-action protagonist to that of animated characters (both human and animal) presents the action polyphonically. The heterogeneity and polyphony of vaudeville were experienced by audiences sequentially on each program bill, although the order of bills could theoretically change from show to show. Comic strips, however, could be experienced by readers both synchronically and sequentially in that strips could be viewed whole on one page or viewed in any order chosen by the reader. Although cinema is experienced sequentially, with images and scenes proceeding in a predetermined order, the Fleischer films were organized both sequentially, with narratives proceeding through a series of loosely related "bits," and synchronically, with action within the cartoon space proceeding at the same time as action occurring within the live-action space of the film. This is often done either by showing animated actions on a sheet of drawing paper within a larger image that also depicts action in the live-action world or by parallel editing of actions done by live-action and animated characters.

From his position on a sheet of paper in *Bubbles* (1922), the clown sees a little live-action girl amusing herself with a bubble pipe and soapy solution. The clown wants to blow bubbles too. Max decides that he will compete with his creation in a bubble-blowing contest. As Max blows bubbles that take various bizarre forms, the clown tries to cope with different bubble mutations that alter his body shape. Max and the clown decide to see who can blow the biggest bubble. Max wins and hits the clown on the nose as a penalty. The clown escapes from the studio sketch in a bubble and takes refuge in the radiator of a car parked on the street outside. Unable to get the clown out, Max bends over the radiator cap and berates his creation. The car's owner returns to find Max apparently chastising the automobile. The clown squirts the car owner with radiator fluid. As Max tries to explain things to the car owner, the clown floats back to the bubble solution in the studio, causing it to foam over. Although the images in *Bubbles* are ordered sequentially, as is inherent in any film, in its depiction of actions taking place simultaneously on drawing paper and in live action, and in its use of parallel editing, the film suggests the synchronic quality seen in the traditional presentation of comic strips on a page of a newspaper.

While narrative organization of Fleischer films appears to stem in part from a comic strip and vaudeville tradition, a similar influence can be seen in the mode of production of these films. As I stated earlier, studio organization may not have been simply a contributor to the narrative organization of silent Fleischer films—it may have been the result of the same media traditions from which the New York style originated. Max and Dave Fleischer did not exercise the kind of tight production control practiced by Walt Disney. Max hired personnel, ran the company, and appeared in many of the Out of the Inkwell shorts. Dave was the rotoscoped basis for the clown, made occasional appearances in the films, and was nominally the director of the shorts. Both Max and Dave devised gags and exercised some informal supervisory control over the animation.[36] Individual animators were assigned their own sequences with an uncertain idea of what might precede or follow them. Animators were free to express their own voices through improvising new bits of business and gags. While wandering around to check production progress, Dave would suggest improvements or new gags to the animators. Story sketches and storyboards were not used in a formal way until the middle or late 1930s. Well into the sound era, story development was haphazard. The animator Shamus Culhane, who began at the studio in 1929, later recalled, "Our story conferences might last as much as a whole hour."[37]

The semiautonomous status enjoyed by Fleischer animators was typical in New York studios. Although certainly less than that experienced by the creators of individual comic strips or performers of vaudeville routines, the degree of autonomy was similar in kind. A typical case would be that of Al Eugster, who worked for both the Pat Sullivan Studio and Fleischer Studios during the 1920s. Eugster originally wanted to be a newspaper cartoonist, and he admired the sports cartoons of Robert Ripley, the editorial cartoons of Winsor McCay, and the strips of Percy Crosby, Cliff Sterritt, and Milt Gross. He entered the animation industry in 1925, when he was employed by the Pat Sullivan Studio. In April 1929 he was hired by the Fleischers, who were then working out of the Carpenter Goldman Studio in Long Island City, and Eugster followed the studio when it moved back to Broadway in New York. The animator later recalled that "it was off the cuff.... Dave would come around while we were animating on a scene and would add gags. The animator would contribute and Dave would contribute.... And that's how it worked. Well, you'd get ideas while you're animating."[38] Dick Huemer, who joined Out of the Inkwell Films in 1923, recalled that "I would yell across the room, 'Hey Dave . . . suppose we do this.' And then we'd sit down and talk it over and laugh our heads off at our great gags, and then it would be my job to animate what we had threshed out."[39] West Coast studios produced animated films in a rigidly hierarchical system that used the story department as a choke point to maintain production control. The more informal system used at the Fleischers' studio was determined by a management philosophy that encouraged polyphonic forms of expression in the finished works.

The polyphonic, mixed genre texts of vaudeville and comic strips were consumed by a mass, but heterogeneous, audience. In effect, the mass distribution of comic strips and tours of the "circuit" by vaudeville acts created a public space where citizens of different backgrounds and from different regions could interact. As Robert Snyder said of vaudeville performers, "Together they participated in a series of cultural transformations. They helped fashion new ethnic identities formed more from American popular culture than from Old World ways; they gave big-city popular culture much of its buoyant, egalitarian style; and they challenged and subverted the genteel Victorianism of middle-class, native-born Americans."[40] The nonhierarchical space of the Out of the Inkwell studio and later Fleischer Studios was imbued with similar qualities. As Eugster recalled, "The spirit was wild." While the Disney studio was physically compartmentalized into separate rooms for separate job categories, the early Fleischer studio, like its New York competitors, lumped all workers together in one large space.[41] Most Fleischer employees were either teenagers or twentysomethings during the Jazz Age. Studio artists and technicians had names like Huemer, Natwick, Zamora, Sharpsteen, Vernick, Gillett, Crandall, Rufle, Cannatta, and Schettler, names that suggest a broad cultural diversity. The films show it. With their multiethnic references and their religious pluralism, they effected a mass medium transformation of a New York culture, through polyphonic and heterogeneous forms, into the mass consciousness of the entire country.[42]

NOTES

The author wishes to acknowledge the contributions to the research for this chapter with a list of names as heterogeneous as those of Out of the Inkwell Studios employees. These include the Swann Foundation for Caricature and Cartoon, Livio Jacob and Piera Patat of the Cineteca Friuli, Jere Guldin of the UCLA Film and Television Archive, Paolo Cherchi-Usai and Ed Stratman of George Eastman House, Ron Magliozzi and Charles Silver of the Film Study Center at the Museum of Modern Art, Richard Fleischer, Ray Pointer, William Lorenzo, Harold Casselton, Mark Kausler, Rick Scheckman, Michael Dobbs, Jerry Beck, Harvey Deneroff, J. B. Kaufman, Greg Ford, Ronnie Scheib, Edward Borsboom of the Netherlands Filmmuseum, Vladimir Opela of the Narodni Filmovy Archiv, Susan Dalton, Zoran Sinobad, and Brian Taves of the Library of Congress, Greg Eaman of the Visual and Sound Archive at the National Archives of Canada, Maurice Zouary, David A. Jasen, Cole Johnson, and Rebecca Rice of the Southwest Film/Video Archives. An earlier version of this chapter appeared in *Persistence of Vision*, the journal of the Film Faculty of the City University of New York. It has been revised for this book.

1. Maltin, *Of Mice and Magic*, 80, 84.

2. Baker, "Max and Dave Fleischer," 27.

3. See Merritt, "The Little Girl/Little Mother Transformation"; Crafton, "The Last Night in the Nursery"; Schickel, *The Disney Version*, 35–41; and Finch, *The Art of Walt Disney*, 165, 167, 170–72.

4. This evolutionary and teleological view is most clearly articulated by John Fell, who asserted that "viewing the earliest surviving movies in rough chronological order, year-by-year at least, is to witness film exposition pull itself out of the mudbanks and evolve into a semblance of narrative shape. Its progress is erratic, with false starts and paths untaken, but seems to evidence a kind of inexorable logic; run-on time and space bow to predesigned complications with increasing regularity" (Fell, "Motive, Mischief, and Melodrama," 272).

5. Gunning, "Enigmas, Understanding, and Further Questions."

6. Other New York animation companies include the Queens Plaza Studio, Charles Bowers Studio, the Barré-Bowers Studio, and the John McCrory Studio. Various companies devoted primarily to live-action films also produced and distributed animation or incorporated animation in their films. Among such companies in New York or nearby New Jersey were Gaumont, Essanay, Pathé, Universal, Eclair, R. C. Pictures, and Short Film Syndicate.

7. See Martin, *In Search of Raoul Barré*, 10; Maltin, *Of Mice and Magic*, 3–5, 14–15; Canemaker, *Felix*, 27–39; and Crafton, *Before Mickey*, 140. Sullivan and Fisher did not actually animate their studios' films but owned the companies. Most of Sullivan's animation was supervised by Otto Messmer, while animation at Fisher's Mutt and Jeff Company (later Jefferson Films) was supervised or animated by artists like Charles Bowers and Raoul Barré.

8. The Mintz Studio is included in the list of companies practicing New York–style animation even though it moved to Los Angeles in 1930 after changing its distributor from Paramount to Columbia. The studio was almost entirely staffed by New Yorkers such as Manny Gould, Ben Harrison, Dick Huemer, and Sid Marcus, and the style of its productions did not appreciably change following the move.

9. Although Mickey began as a rural laborer in films like *Plane Crazy* (1928), by the early 1930s the character had changed. Mickey conducted an orchestra in *The Band Concert* (1935) and *Mickey's Grand Opera* (1936). He worked as a scientist in *The Worm Turns* (1936) and supervised the team of Goofy and Pluto in films like *Mickey's Service Station* (1935) and *Clock Cleaners* (1937). In contrast to this, Ko-Ko and Betty Boop were carnival or vaudeville entertainers, Bimbo had no visible means of support, and Popeye was a working-class sailor. Felix the Cat seems to owe much to the early version of Charlie Chaplin's "Little Tramp" character (who was copied by Sullivan and Messmer in a pre-Felix series of "Charlie Chaplin Cartoons"). Like the early Chaplin, Felix is a loner in a hostile or at best indifferent world, who combines resourcefulness and a touch of viciousness in order to survive.

10. Kozlenko, "The Animated Film and Walt Disney."

11. Van Beuren's comedy duo of Tom and Jerry should not be confused with the similarly named, but completely unrelated, cat-and-mouse team devised by Harman-Ising veterans Hanna and Barbera for release through MGM.

12. For more on these processes see Langer, "The Disney-Fleischer Dilemma."

13. This tradition survived at Famous Studios and the Paramount animation studio, both of which were successor companies to Fleischer Studios, most notably with such films as *Cartoons Ain't Human* (1943) or former Fleischer employee Shamus Culhane's *My Daddy the Astronaut* (1967), which has a deliberately primitive, childlike style. Isolated instances of this convention can be found at Warner Bros. in such films as Friz Freleng's *You Ought to Be in Pictures* (1940), Tex Avery's *Porky's Preview* (1940), or Chuck Jones's *Duck Amuck* (1953). These West Coast examples differ from their New York counterparts in that the boundary between animation and live action is blurred. The New York films make a distinction in kind between a human animator and his cartoon creations. Animated and live-action characters maintain the same status in West Coast films. For example, in *You Ought to Be in Pictures* Porky and Daffy are contract players who have essentially the same relationship to a live-action world as Oliver Hardy or Errol Flynn. In *Porky's Preview* and *Duck Amuck* both the animators and the animated figures are cartoon characters. Similar tendencies

can be seen in other West Coast productions, such as *Designs on Jerry* (1955) at MGM, or Woody Woodpecker's appearances with "My boss, Walter Lantz," beginning in 1957 on television's *The Woody Woodpecker Show*.

14. Personality animation means that a character's personality is expressed in terms of its movement. This psychologically oriented style of animation was commonly used at the Disney studio.

15. Langer, "Max and Dave Fleischer," 49–50; see also Langer, "Institutional Power and the Fleischer Studios"; and Wassenaar, "Strong to the Finish *[sic]*," 28.

16. Miller, Miller, and Karp, "The Fourth Largest City in America—A Sociological History of Brooklyn," 25; Sorin, *The Nurturing Neighborhood*, 9–10; Landesman, "A Neighborhood Survey of Brownsville"; Landesman, *Brownsville*, 50–56, 96; Moore, *At Home in America*, 20–23; Howe, *World of Our Fathers*, 135.

17. Kazin, *A Walker in the City*, 11–12.

18. Adamson, "'Where Can I Get a Good Corned Beef Sandwich?'" 6; see also Landesman, "A Neighborhood Survey," 4; and Fleischer, interview by Ray Pointer, 2.

19. Carbaga, *The Fleischer Story in the Golden Age of Animation*, 1–2; Lou Fleischer, interview, 14–15; Max Fleischer, résumé (Fleischer family collection); Vera Coleman to William Welling; Roberta, "Tintypes."

20. Schroth, *"The Eagle" and Brooklyn*, 92, 95, 97, 104–5; see also Howard, *Max Fleischer Autobiography*, 1; Langer, interview with Richard Fleischer, 4; Villard, "St. Clair McKelway," 37; Miller, Miller, and Karp, "The Fourth Largest City in America," 25; Syrett, *The City of Brooklyn, 1865–1898*, 233–45.

21. While to a European reader "Mack" may seem to have Scottish connotations, in American street slang the word has more generic overtones and is used interchangeably with such names as "Buddy," "Bub," or "Pal."

22. Blackbeard and Williams, *The Smithsonian Collection of Newspaper Comics*, 19.

23. For accounts of this see Fleischer, interview by Ray Pointer; and Adamson, "'Where Can I Get a Good Corned Beef Sandwich?'"

24. Algy was not Max Fleischer's only Jewish comic character. Another strip featured a Jewish caricature in the actor Hamfat Zanzill, likely a takeoff on the name of the Jewish author and playwright Israel Zangwill. See Max Fleischer, "Actor Hamfat Zanzill's Revenge; or How the Play Was Brought to an Untimely End," undated clipping from the *Brooklyn Daily Eagle* (c. 1901) in *Scrapbook* (Fleischer family collection).

25. Blackbeard and Williams, *The Smithsonian Collection of Newspaper Comics*, 20.

26. The rotoscope was a device invented by Max Fleischer with the possible participation of Jack Leventhal, Dave Fleischer, and Joe Fleischer. The rotoscope allowed the rear projection of live-action film frame-by-frame onto a translucent surface set into a drawing board. An animator could simply trace each live-action image onto a piece of paper, advance the film by another frame and repeat the process. By these means, the live-action images became a guide to detailed and lifelike animation. See Max Fleischer, "Method of Producing Motion Picture Cartoons," U.S. Patent no. 1,232,674 (Oct. 9, 1915); see also Langer, "The Fleischer Rotoscope Patent."

27. Allen, "Vaudeville and Film, 1895–1915," 177.

28. Quoted in Adamson, "'Where Can I Get a Good Corned Beef Sandwich?'" 14.

29. McLean, *American Vaudeville as Ritual*, 131.

30. Adamson, "'Where Can I Get a Good Corned Beef Sandwich?'" 8–14; Lou Fleischer, interview, 6; Lenburg, *The Encyclopedia of Animated Cartoon Series*, 19; McLean, *American Vaudeville as Ritual*, 55–56, 130–31; Marian Spitzer, *The Palace*, 3, 47.

31. Anthony Slide gives another date (June 3, 1908) for the opening of *Three Twins*. *Three Twins* featured performances by Bessie McCoy, Clifton Crawford, Joseph Allen, Willard Curtiss, Stella

Tracey, and Joseph Kaufman. The book was by Charles Dickson, from a story by R. Pancheco. The music was composed by Karl Hoschna, with lyrics by Otto Harbach. Along with "Yama-Yama Man" the show also produced the hit "Cuddle Up a Little Closer." See Slide, *The Encyclopedia of Vaudeville*, 339–40; Kinkle, *The Complete Encyclopedia of Popular Music and Jazz, 1900–1950*, 1:35; Farnsworth, *The Ziegfeld Follies*, 60–61; Gilbert, *American Vaudeville*, 162–64; Blum, *A Pictorial History of the American Theatre, 1860–1970*, 106; and Laurie, *Vaudeville*, 101.

32. McCoy did play the Palace as a headliner in March 1918, a mere three months before the release of the first film featuring the clown, *Experiment No. 1*, on June 10, 1918.

33. Snyder, *The Voice of the City*, xv.

34. Robert C. Allen's "Vaudeville and Film, 1895–1915" remains the classic study of the relationship between vaudeville and film. See also Jeanne Thomas Allen, "Copyright and Early Theater, Vaudeville, and Film Competition"; McLaughlin, *Broadway and Hollywood*, 4–5; and Smoodin, *Animating Culture*, 2.

35. I chose *Ko-Ko Makes 'Em Laugh* as a random sample, by closing my eyes and poking my index finger at a filmography of silent Fleischer films. Almost any silent Out of the Inkwell film would illustrate the point about heterogeneous narrative structure as well as this one.

36. Max's contribution to the animation gradually lessened after he left the Bray Studio to found Out of the Inkwell Films in partnership with Dave in 1921. It is probably safe to say that by 1923 Max was no longer animating and that his attention was more directed toward the development of the Fleischer-owned distribution company Red Seal Pictures. However, despite claims to the contrary by Dave Fleischer and others, Max never completely withdrew from active participation in story and character development. See Langer, "Institutional Power and the Fleischer Studios," 10, 20.

37. Culhane, interview by Greg Ford; Adamson, "Working for the Fleischers"; Maltin, *Of Mice and Magic*, 84; Allen, "Vaudeville and Film, 1895–1915," 179.

38. Eugster, interview by Mark Langer, 1; and Eugster, interview by Greg Ford, 10.

39. Quoted in Adamson, "Working for the Fleischers," 23.

40. Snyder, *The Voice of the City*, 43.

41. Eugster, interview by Greg Ford, 4; Adamson, "Working for the Fleischers," 23.

42. Multiethnic references occur in such films as *League of Nations* (1924), which portrays Ko-Kos from dozens of countries converging in the Fleischers' New York office. Religious pluralism can be seen in such examples as the kosher pig in *The Clown's Little Brother* (1920) or the Jewish and Muslim references in *Ko-Ko's Harem Scarum*.

3

The Heir Apparent

J. B. Kaufman

In the summer of 1933 the Walt Disney studio released a new Mickey Mouse cartoon short: *Mickey's Gala Premier [sic]*. In this cartoon all Hollywood, in the form of movie-star caricatures, turns out for the opening of Mickey Mouse's latest picture. The film-within-the-film (a western bearing a loose resemblance to the 1930 Mickey short *The Cactus Kid,* but augmented with a host of new gags) rolls 'em in the aisles: stars ranging from Douglas Fairbanks to Boris Karloff, from the Barrymore family to Mae West, are reduced to helpless convulsions of laughter by Mickey's antics. Among the star caricatures on hand, laughing and eagerly cheering Mickey on, are a number of legendary comedians—performers familiar to the audience from decades of vaudeville and two-reel comedies.

But in 1933 both vaudeville and the two-reel comedy were on their last legs. Their place in popular culture had, in large part, been usurped by Mickey Mouse. Never mind that the humor of *Mickey's Gala Premier* is founded on the incongruous spectacle of Hollywood royalty fawning over a mouse; never mind that this show of adulation turns out to be a dream at the end of the reel. The fact is that Mickey *was* an international celebrity by the summer of 1933. As Chaplin, Harold Lloyd, Will Rogers, and numerous other comedians swarm onto the stage in *Mickey's Gala Premier* to acclaim the Mouse, they're acknowledging a very real fact of American cultural history: Mickey is the heir apparent. For one moment in history a vital tradition of American comedy, traced through a legion of human performers, seems to have come to rest on the shoulders of a cartoon mouse.

In part this was a matter of simple economics: animated cartoons, even Disney's relatively costly product, were thriving in the early 1930s, while the steadily less profitable two-reel comedy was gradually being phased out. But if Mickey stepped naturally into the place of his human counterparts, it was also because Walt Disney and his staff were steeped in the popular culture of their time and had absorbed the gags, themes, and techniques of the great comedians. *Mickey's Gala Premier* offers its own evidence; the movie-star caricatures, designed by Joe Grant, are clearly the work of artists with a thorough awareness of Hollywood comedy tradition. In the opening scenes, as fans throng around the theater (Grauman's Chinese) to get a glimpse of Mickey, crowd control is exercised by a line of Keystone Cops—not simply faceless figures in Cop uniforms but specific caricatures: Ben Turpin, Ford Sterling, Mack Swain, Harry Langdon, and Chester Conklin, not all of whom had actually *been* Keystone Cops but all of whom had worked for Mack Sennett. This showbiz savvy, this thorough grounding in the craft and tradition of the great human comics, permeates the atmosphere of the classic Mickeys of 1928 to 1934.

Another important factor came into play during these years: Walt Disney was redefining the art of animation along unaccustomed new lines. During the 1920s, as he was learning and polishing his craft, Disney's films had belonged very much to the world of contemporary silent American animation. This was a world built on the principles of graphic design, a flat world of constantly chang-ing shapes and optical illusions, a world that made its appeal directly to the eye without detouring very far into the realms of logic or everyday reality. Here a cigar-smoking character could blow a smoke ring, then snatch it out of the air and use it as a spare tire; here Felix the Cat's tail could detach itself and form a question mark above his head; here Ko-Ko the Clown (in Fleischer's Out of the Inkwell series) could distort his body and his surroundings in a nonstop series of visual puns. For most of the 1920s Disney was content to follow the acknowledged animation leaders in this two-dimensional graphic world.

All that changed suddenly in 1928–29 with the success of Mickey Mouse and *Steamboat Willie*. No longer a follower, Disney moved seemingly overnight to the head of the pack. The growing and insatiable demand for Disney cartoons now made Walt the unquestioned leader of the animation industry, a position he would maintain for the rest of his life, and much of his new preeminence stemmed from his use of sound. *Steamboat Willie* created a sensation in theaters, not because it was the first sound cartoon (it wasn't)[1] but because it used sound with wit, charm, and ingenuity. In subsequent Disney films a new cartoon world took shape onscreen, one in which characters convincingly spoke, sang, and indulged in clever musical gags.

With this development came a subtle but distinct shift in the balance between fantasy and reality in Disney's films. His cartoon images, grounded in sounds that evoked the real, physical world, moved unmistakably, not toward *realism* but toward a more convincing form of fantasy. The effect was one that Disney himself later termed "the plausible impossible."[2] No, his films seem to tell us, the things you're seeing on the screen could never really happen—but if they *could* happen, this is *how* they would happen. The Disney sound cartoons, and ultimately all Hollywood cartoons, began to abandon abstract visual gags in favor of gags that evoked this more convincing, "plausibly impossible," world. As a result, as Mickey Mouse began to come into his own in the early 1930s, his adventures suggested little of Felix the Cat or Ko-Ko the Clown. Instead, thanks to his worldwide popularity and his newly transformed surroundings, he found himself in the company of the great flesh-and-blood comedians: the legendary stage comedians and—more immediately, and more visibly from today's perspective—the great comics of the silent screen.

At its most basic level this development comes down to the simple appropriation of standard gags. During the first few decades of the twentieth century, a long-standing repertoire of gags and situations had become part of the basic equipment that united the brotherhood of stage and screen comedians. Mickey, in effect, declared himself a member of that brotherhood by adopting some of those familiar conventions. Thus, in *The Mad Dog* (1932) Mickey tosses banana peels in the path of a pursuer; in *The Grocery Boy* (1932) he reaches for the wrong doorknob, opens the door, and instead of exiting the house is brained by a falling ironing board; in *Traffic Troubles* (1931) he struggles with a recalcitrant automobile. In *The Opry House* (1929), *Mickey's Revue* (1932), and other films he's shown actually performing on the variety stage. One time-honored vaudeville gag was the itinerant musician who stoops to pick up the coins that have been thrown to him, only to find that one of those objects is not a coin but a gob of spit. Chaplin immortalized this mildly disgusting gag on film in *The Vagabond* (1916); Mickey does the same in *The Klondike Kid* (1932).

Beyond the gag, comedy's basic unit of construction, we can make some broad generalizations about settings, themes, and motifs. In the early twentieth century it wasn't unusual to see comedians depicted as outsiders—tramps, outcasts, unfortunates living on the fringes of society. More often than not, police and other authority figures were automatically assumed to be their enemies. Despite the family-friendly image he would later adopt, Mickey too sometimes fell into this category in the early 1930s, running afoul of the law in a few films like *Traffic Troubles* and *Fishin' Around* (1931).[3] Occasionally some of the earlier comedians, like Buster Keaton in *Convict 13* (1920) and Laurel and Hardy in *The Hoosegow* (1929), had even been seen behind prison bars—and, yes, Mickey himself wound up in the slammer in *The Chain Gang* (1930). (And like some of his predecessors, he was seen unwittingly taking part in a jailbreak.)

Although this social-outsider image was common, it wasn't uncommon for a vaudeville or silent-film comic to align himself with the "average guy" in the audience by focusing his comedy on the character's job. Gags in the workplace became a standard format for sight-gag comedy. Mickey heartily embraced this convention in his early films, appearing as a hot dog vendor in *The Karnival Kid* (1929), a taxi driver in *Traffic Troubles,* a delivery boy in *The Delivery Boy* (1931), a laborer in *Building a Building* (1933) and *Mickey's Steamroller* (1934). *The Pet Store* (1933) opens with Mickey walking down a sidewalk and spotting a "Boy Wanted" sign outside the pet store. Without hesitation he seizes the sign and strolls inside to apply for the job.

But for the great comedians, this basic vocabulary of slapstick conventions was only a starting point. What sets the legendary performers apart is their ability to go beyond these gags and situations, to use them as a foundation on which to construct a unique, individual performance. More than a few comedians have built films or comedy routines around the paperhanger's trade; the opportunity to create slapstick mayhem with paper, ladders, and huge, messy globs of paste has been too much to resist. But it takes a Chaplin to transform such a routine into a film like *Work* (1915). In Chaplin's hands the messy slapstick is punctuated with subtle interludes, flashes of wit and brilliant pantomime, and as a result becomes much funnier—and distinctly his own.

Similarly, as Walt Disney's filmmaking style matured, he increasingly showed himself less interested in his story material than in what he could *do* with the material. As the 1930s proceeded, his films adapted standard gags, molding them toward the ends that most interested him. In the 1920 Larry Semon two-reeler *The Grocery Clerk,* a housecat jumps from a height and lands squarely on two sheets of flypaper—both front paws on one sheet, both hind paws on the other. With all four feet firmly glued to the sticky surfaces, the cat is temporarily immobilized. Even the most casual Disney fan, on seeing this scene, will be instantly reminded of the classic "Flypaper Sequence" in the Mickey Mouse short *Playful Pluto* (1934), with Pluto struggling to free himself from a sheet of flypaper. Why is one of these scenes all but forgotten, while the other is revered as a classic?

Answer: the flypaper in *The Grocery Clerk* is little more than a throwaway gag. In a film dominated by slapstick fights with molasses, fights with flour, fights with soot, and assorted chases, falls, and explosions, the flypaper incident functions as a relatively quiet interlude. And, in fact, having got the cat onto the flypaper, Semon is hard-pressed for a way to build on the gag. He simply produces a pair of scissors and trims away the excess flypaper, leaving the cat with a tiny pad stuck to each foot. The cat exits the scene, picking its way gingerly with high steps, as if wearing adhesive snowshoes.

By contrast, the flypaper in *Playful Pluto* is deliberately planted as a vehicle for what by 1934 had become Walt Disney's top priority in his films: *personality animation,* the delineation of personality by the movement and facial expressions of the character. Pluto, sniffing along the kitchen floor, plows nose-first into a sheet of flypaper and stops in his tracks, staring in amazement at the sticky object plastered to his nose. By planting both front feet on the paper, he can pull his snout loose—but now his feet are stuck to the paper, and he can't free one foot without regluing the other. As he tries to reason a way out of his predicament, he becomes increasingly tangled in the flypaper, his frustration growing all the while. His struggles consume well over a minute of screen time (a very long time in a one-reel cartoon), all brilliantly animated by one of Disney's top character animators, Norm Ferguson. The "Flypaper Sequence" became, not only a quick laugh but a milestone in the development of personality animation.[4]

To illustrate this in greater detail, it may be helpful to observe the various ways that an assortment of comedians, and Mickey Mouse, deal with the same basic material. Let's take a stock comedy situation, follow it as it passes through the hands of some of the great sight-gag comedians, and then see what Mickey does with it. The comedian as *fireman* is a venerable comedy tradition. The idea of a slapstick comedian dispatched to combat a burning building is a natural; it offers a calamitous situation against which the comic's ineptitude can stand out in sharp relief, not to mention a variety of great slapstick props: ladders, axes, fire hoses, and sometimes even the fire engine itself. In the hands of any number of lesser comedians the situation has been enough to carry a film by itself. But, true to form, the best comics have all found distinctive ways to put their own stamp on it.

For Charlie Chaplin in *The Fireman* (1916) the firehouse is simply a setting in which to unleash his natural playfulness. *The Fireman* was the second of Chaplin's twelve films for Mutual and, like the other films in that series, is filled to overflowing with the great comedian's fresh, spontaneous improvisation. With the firehouse as a playground, Charlie is all over the place: impishly sparring with hulking, ferocious fire chief Eric Campbell, flirting with visiting Edna Purviance, engaging in rough-and-tumble gags with his fellow firemen, and even indulging in some unaccustomed camera tricks. Here the firehouse pole is only a prop: Charlie slides down the pole and darts back up again with equal ease and balletic grace, then impudently taunts Campbell as the latter struggles up the pole in pursuit. When he finally gets around to fighting fires (two at once) in the second reel, Charlie gets some fun out of other props at his disposal—grappling with the mighty blast of the fire hose and demolishing most of his fire engine as he races madly from one conflagration to the other—but reserves most of his energy for a heroic rescue. Seeing Edna trapped on the second floor of her burning house, he climbs up the side of the building to her rescue without benefit of a ladder and, with Edna (an obvious mannequin) clinging to his neck, climbs back down the same way.

Two years after the release of Chaplin's film, Harold Lloyd took his turn as a fireman in one of his early "Glass Character" comedies.[5] In *Fireman, Save My Child* (1918) Lloyd becomes a fireman by default simply by crashing a firemen's ball; when a fire alarm interrupts the party, he's pressed into service. Although this is one of Lloyd's early, formative pictures (unlike *The Fireman,* which gives us Chaplin in the full flower of his comedic brilliance), Lloyd obligingly illustrates my point by recycling some of the same basic gag material Chaplin had used. Like Chaplin he maintains a running rivalry with his fire chief; like Chaplin he's surrounded by silly, Keystone-like firemen who are forever falling off the fire truck and getting in each other's way; and like Chaplin he must rescue his girl from a burning building at the picture's climax.

The point, of course, is that Lloyd's screen personality is so utterly different from Chaplin's that the same gag material emerges in an entirely different light. In fact, considering that Lloyd's "Glass Character" had been introduced less than a year earlier, it's striking to see how fully developed the character is in *Fireman, Save My Child.* Although he's supposed to be impoverished, Lloyd's character (introduced in a title as "'Iron Hat' Sammy") is essentially the same brash, arrogant young man-about-town that he plays in later features like *Why Worry?* and the first part of *For Heaven's Sake.* Accordingly, the film's firefighting gags are made subordinate to, and are funnier because of, Lloyd's cocky, abrasive personality. His fire chief is no hulking bully like Chaplin's but is played by wizened little Snub Pollard, whom Lloyd defeats with careless ease. At the sound of the alarm the rest of the firemen pile into the fire engine with frantic urgency but are forced to wait while Lloyd calmly dusts his shoes with a handkerchief, then imperiously occupies the driver's seat himself. Once at the fire, he assumes responsibility for rescuing the girl (Bebe Daniels), eventually accomplishing that goal on the third try. Like Chaplin's film, this one features a volatile fire hose, but it never poses a problem for Lloyd's character (although he falls over it a few times on his way into the burning house). Instead, following the rescue, he and Bebe stand on the hose gazing into each other's eyes, then step off—and it's the *other* firemen who are drenched by the mighty blast of water from the hose.

One element from Chaplin's film is missing here: gags built around the fire engine. That's probably because of the Roach studio's modest circumstances in 1918; the "fire engine" in *Fireman, Save My Child* appears to be simply an old truck with a boiler mounted none too convincingly in the back—hardly up to the rigors of extended slapstick gags. Six years later, now successful and with considerably greater resources, Lloyd inserted a bona fide fire engine into one of his features. *Girl Shy* (1924) climaxes with a legendary chase sequence in which Lloyd commandeers an assortment of vehicles in his race to save Jobyna Ralston from marriage to a bigamist. One of those vehicles is a fire engine, conveniently speeding in the same direction that Lloyd needs to go. He hops on the back of the truck and finds himself clinging, not to a solid handhold, but to the fire hose—which is rapidly unreeling. As he continues to grab frantically at the hose, hand over hand, the hose continues to unreel and trails along the street, far behind the racing engine.

Buster Keaton and Roscoe Arbuckle, in *The Garage* (1919), adapt their duties as firemen to their own offbeat and highly athletic brand of slapstick. *The Garage* is one of Arbuckle's starring two-reelers for Paramount, in which Keaton served a highly productive apprenticeship before embarking on his own starring series for Metro. There has been much speculation as to whether Arbuckle or Keaton deserves more credit for the distinctive gags in these films, but regardless of who is responsible for the gags in *The Garage,* they could never be mistaken for Chaplin or Lloyd material.[6] The film actually devotes most of its footage to the garage of the title. Only after Keaton and Arbuckle have exhausted the gag possibilities in their roles as automotive mechanics do they turn to another rich fund of gags: their function as a two-man police *and* fire department in their rural community. Among other things, this development allows the placement of a firemen's pole in the garage, leading to various falls and slapstick confrontations as the characters, like Chaplin, slide down and shinny up the pole.

Now the fire alarm rings, launching a series of dry, offbeat gags. Arbuckle and Keaton leap out of bed as an elaborate system of pulleys and ropes, activated by the alarm, whips off their nightshirts and reveals them fully dressed and ready for the emergency. Pulling their hose wagon by hand, they charge out of the fire station and go racing over hill and dale before discovering a serious oversight: they've brought their police helmets rather than their firefighters' hats. Dropping everything, they race back to the garage to switch to appropriate headgear. The location of the fire, naturally, turns out to be their own garage/fire station. Controlling the fire hose is no problem this time; thanks to a gushing leak in midhose, the nozzle produces only a thin trickle of water—until Arbuckle locates the fissure and arranges his ample bulk on top of it, stopping the leak and restoring water pressure at the far end of the hose. Once again the leading lady (Alice Lake) is trapped in an upper room, but there will be no gallant rescues by our heroes; instead, they spread a net and encourage her to jump. (And instead of landing safely in the net, Alice bounces high into the air and lands on some nearby electric wires. She's nearly stranded there when the noon whistle blows, and most of her would-be rescuers abandon her for lunch.)

That Harry Langdon would take his own turn as a fireman was inevitable, simply because, of all the silent comedians, Langdon's helpless, babylike, eternally hesitant character was the *least* equipped for the heroics of a firefighter's job. Langdon's short feature *His First Flame* (produced by Mack Sennett in 1925 but released in 1927),[7] like the other comedians' films, relegates its firefighting business to the end of the picture. For most of its length it focuses on Harry's relationships with his gold-digging fiancée (Natalie Kingston), her younger sister who really loves him (Ruth Hiatt), and his uncle (Vernon Dent), a self-proclaimed "woman-hater." The uncle is a fireman, and when he answers a fire alarm, Harry tags along—only to discover that the woman trapped in the burning building is

Natalie, his fiancée. Spurred into action, Harry tries to rescue her and fails, while his uncle saves her and wins her kisses. The despondent Harry succumbs to tears until the sister, Ruth, stages another fire: a tiny, easily contained blaze from which Harry can rescue *her* single-handedly.

Once again, and perhaps to a greater extent than any other film we've discussed, *His First Flame* (written by Arthur Ripley and Frank Capra) keeps its firefighting gags strictly secondary to the star comedian's personality. In effect, the conflagrations in this film exist only as settings to accentuate Harry's weak, bumbling, inept character. During the first one, while Vernon Dent is busy rescuing Natalie, Harry blunders around elsewhere in the building. He emerges from a window, not only with his own pants on fire but carrying a dressmaker's dummy that he thinks is a woman. (Characteristically, even after he begins to realize that she's an inanimate object, he continues to carry on a one-sided conversation with her.) The second fire, such as it is, displays Harry's ineptitude in even sharper relief. Arriving on the scene in his fire engine, Harry races around the house several times, knocking shrubbery left and right. No out-of-control fire hose in this scene; instead, Harry sprinkles the house with dainty handfuls of water. Then, entering the house—which is filled with smoke, not from the tiny flame Ruth has provided but billowing from the smokestack of Harry's own fire engine—he tries to light his way by striking a match. In the end, although Ruth has made his job as easy as possible, she's effectively forced to rescue *herself* and then pretend Harry has been responsible.

* * *

Disney himself tackled the fireman theme as early as 1926 in one of his silent Alice Comedies, *Alice the Fire Fighter*. By this time the familiar comedy firefighting situations had become standardized as conventions, and several of them dutifully reappear in *Alice the Fire Fighter*. But this film, like the other Alice Comedies, belongs very much to the world of silent American animation of the 1920s, the world of flat graphic shapes and optical illusions. As a result, traditional firefighting gags in *Alice the Fire Fighter* are recast in impossibly cartoony terms. As Disney's characters scurry out of their burning apartment building, one of them brings along a piano. He sits down and begins to play, producing a series of musical notes that appear in the air in graduated steps—and other occupants of the building step from their windows onto this "staircase" and calmly walk down to safety. Still others ride the spray from the fire hose as if it were an escape chute. Julius, the cat, climbing a ladder to rescue characters in some of the upper windows, finds that the ladder is positioned just a little too far away from the building.[8] He can't quite reach the trapped victims, so the other firemen helpfully push the *building* closer to the *ladder*.

At the cartoon's climax, Julius, true to tradition, must rescue a (previously unnoticed) lady trapped in an upper window. By now the building is burning furiously, barring his entry through the ground floor. How to reach her? Julius makes use of another "impossible" gag: running to the fire engine and climbing to the top of the smokestack, he rides a puff of smoke as it ascends past the upper reaches of the building. Passing the lady cat's window, he grabs her by the tail and plucks her out of harm's way. Now Alice reverses a lever on the fire engine so that it runs backward and the puffs of smoke reverse direction, floating back down *into* the smokestack. Julius and his lady simply ride the smoke back down into the fire box. Emerging safely, Julius gallantly revives the lady and removes the smoke from her lungs, by flattening her with a rolling pin.

Now we turn to Mickey Mouse, who dons the fireman's helmet in *The Fire Fighters* (1930). A mere four years separate this film from *Alice the Fire Fighter,* but considerable changes had taken place in those four years. As we've seen, Mickey had assumed his place in a world very different from that of Alice and Julius, a world closer to that of the great live-action comedians. *The Fire Fighters* illustrates the difference. To be sure, comedians other than Chaplin and company had essayed firefighting gags—and, as we've seen, Julius and other cartoon characters had done and would do the same. But in *The Fire Fighters* Mickey seems aware of his place in cultural history and steps boldly into the shoes of his most illustrious predecessors, tackling with zest the ritual motifs and situations of their films: gags in the firehouse, the race to the burning building, the struggle with the fire hose, and of course the obligatory climactic rescue of the heroine.

Viewed in this context, *The Fire Fighters* seems almost like an anthology of great firefighting gags—with a twist. The frantic character who runs to ring the fire alarm in the opening scenes calls to mind Leo White's panic-stricken call for help in Chaplin's *The Fireman.* Horace Horsecollar, as one of the firemen, hears the alarm and leaps out of bed into his harness and collar, which are suspended from a pulley contraption something like the Arbuckle-Keaton device in *The Garage.* The firehouse pole figures in this film too, except that this time the "pole" is the long, skinny neck of another crew member, an ostrich, who thrusts it up through the opening in the floor so the other firemen can slide down. Mickey's fire engine, falling apart piece by piece en route to the fire, seems another reminder of the Chaplin film; and as it does so, one little character tries to hang onto the rapidly unreeling fire hose, just as Lloyd had done in *Girl Shy.*

But *The Fire Fighters* is not merely a rehash of old ideas. By 1930 Walt Disney has begun to develop strong ideas of his own about the direction his films are taking, and if he enjoys a kinship with the earlier comedians, he's not content simply to mimic their gags. Mickey Mouse, barely two years old at the time of *The Fire Fighters,* is not an anonymous cipher channeling stock comedy material—a label that might more reasonably be applied to Julius the Cat—but has already developed strong individual character traits and bends that material to his own purposes. Paradoxically, he joins the company of Chaplin, Keaton, and the other giants by distancing himself from them, establishing his own distinctive identity.

For one thing, Mickey in 1930 is a proactive character, plucky, resourceful, and usually in command of any situation. Although Pegleg Pete is available to play a ferocious, hulking bully, the equivalent of Eric Campbell in the Chaplin films, he's nowhere to be seen in *The Fire Fighters*. Instead of enduring a constant stream of abuse from the chief, as Chaplin had done, or handily outwitting the chief along Lloyd's lines, here Mickey himself is the fire chief. Arriving at the scene of the fire, he faces a series of comedy obstacles but overcomes them through what has already become his characteristic blend of luck and ingenuity.

In 1930, of course, the Disney studio's use of *sound* is still one of its distinctive trademarks. Like other contemporary Disney shorts, *The Fire Fighters* finds room for a peppy musical number: in this case Mickey and his crew, en route to the fire, sing, whistle, and dance two choruses of "A Hot Time in the Old Town." In Mickey's sound-film breakthrough, *Steamboat Willie*, he had pulled a cat's tail and transformed the yowling feline into a musical instrument; here he does the same thing, and the cat becomes a wailing siren. Once at the fire, Disney works a variation on earlier fire-hose gags: here the problem is not the hose but the hydrant, which produces only a thin trickle of water (Fig. 3.1a). Mickey responds with another ingenious transformation, "milking" the hydrant as if it were a cow, then carrying the bucket back and forth between hydrant and flames. (He never manages to deliver more than a few drops of water, and ultimately the problem is solved by Horace, who drinks a nearby pond dry and then disgorges the water on the burning building!)

As we've seen, by 1930 comedy tradition dictates that Mickey must cap his firefighting adventure by rescuing Minnie from an upper window of the burning building. He meets the challenge with originality, relying neither on the earlier comedians' gags nor on *Alice the Fire Fighter*'s abstract graphics. His rescue also combines equal parts of heroism and comedy: he approaches Minnie's window riding in a large pair of overalls, suspended from a clothesline that runs between the burning structure and a neighboring building. Plucking Minnie from harm's way just in time, Mickey deposits her in the other leg of the overalls, then reverses direction and makes for the safety of the opposite side. Flames attack the clothesline, the oversized garment falls, and the two mice start to plummet earthward—until the overalls fill with air and balloon into a parachute, and Mickey and Minnie float safely to the ground. Mickey's entry in the comedy-firefighting genre is officially complete.

*　*　*

But Mickey assumes the mantle of the great comedians only to lay it down again almost immediately. In the restless, constantly evolving creative environment

a   b

FIGURE 3.1. Firefighter Mickey at work in (a) *The Fire Fighters* (1930) and (b) *Mickey's Fire Brigade* (1935).

that was the Disney studio in the 1930s, nothing stood still for very long. If Mickey embraced the American comedy tradition during his early years, he had actively abandoned it by the mid-1930s. In its place, as he matured, he began to appear in new and different kinds of stories, stories that had little to do with slap-stick or sight-gag comedy. By decade's end this career change would lead Mickey into some of his best films: *Thru the Mirror, Brave Little Tailor,* and *The Sorcerer's Apprentice.* These were roles that belonged to the ages, fitting assignments for the mouse who had become the greatest of all cartoon characters—but they hardly suggested the comedy tradition of Chaplin, Keaton, or Lloyd. Increasingly, comedy content in the Disney films was shunted to a new breed of characters: Donald Duck, Pluto, and an anthropomorphized dog who began life as Dippy Dawg but ultimately evolved into Goofy. Nor did *these* characters suggest the world of the vaudeville stage or the silent two-reel comedy; instead, their personalities and their gags were increasingly tailored to the new, colorful, richly detailed cartoon environment that was becoming ever more clearly defined in the Disney films. In effect, Mickey had pioneered this new "plausibly impossible" world; Donald and the other cartoon stars were born into it. And already it was a world very different from the one in which *The Fire Fighters* had taken place.

As if to illustrate all these changes, Mickey returned to the firefighting service in 1935, this time in Technicolor. In *Mickey's Fire Brigade* (Fig. 3.1b) Mickey is once again the fire chief, introduced in the driver's seat as the fire engine races toward a burning rooming house. This time, however, he leads a crew of two; this is one of the first in a new group of cartoons built around Mickey, Donald, and Goofy. *Mickey's Fire Brigade* demonstrates the pattern: on arriving at the scene the three-man brigade splits up, and the film alternates among characters, following each of them through solo comedy scenes, before bringing them all together again for a wrap-up sequence at the end. Mickey may be the nominal leader of this group, but for the film's purposes he's just one of the guys, sharing equal time with his two nominal supporting players.

And although there's plenty of slapstick action going on at this fire scene, it's a far cry from the firefighting gags in earlier comedy films. Instead, it features gags uniquely suited to the Disney cartoon world: a fireplace is wrenched loose from a wall with the fire still burning inside; flames cast into a fishbowl fill the water with smoke, so that the goldfish comes to the water's surface and blows smoke rings into the air (a gag that will be reprised five years later in *Pinocchio*). Mickey does struggle with an out-of-control fire hose, but this time the scene is strikingly unlike earlier hose gags. Here the water pressure lifts both Mickey and the hose into the air, and the sequence becomes a showcase for the kind of technical device that was starting to appear in Disney films, an aerial effect in which the camera seems to follow Mickey as he careens madly through space. By 1935, in fact, the Disney cartoon world is so self-contained that this short can indulge in self-reflexive gags: in one scene the flames (tiny humanized flames with legs) are trapped on sheets of flypaper, no doubt left over from *Playful Pluto;* in another they scamper onto a piano keyboard and play a quick chorus of "Who's Afraid of the Big Bad Wolf?," the hit song from *Three Little Pigs.*

Nothing could illustrate the gap between this film and its ancestors more clearly than the climactic rescue scene. *Mickey's Fire Brigade* does have a climactic rescue scene, but it's a bizarre departure from earlier such scenes, a parody of a parody. This time the rescuee is not a fair damsel but a cow: Clarabelle Cow, soaking in a bathtub on an upper floor, noisily engaged in her vocal exercises and unaware of the fire. At the intrusion of Mickey and company she screams and violently fends off their rescue attempt, swinging her long-handled brush at anyone within reach. The bathtub is bodily ejected from a window with Clarabelle still inside, the three would-be heroes tumble from the same window, and the film ends with the tub on the ground outdoors, Clarabelle clobbering each of the firemen as, one by one, they surface at the opposite end of the tub. This scene may have its roots in the Chaplin or Lloyd rescues of earlier years, but those roots have been so transformed as to be scarcely recognizable.

By 1935, then, Mickey Mouse—who might have been considered the heir apparent of the American comedy tradition only a few years before—had left that tradition behind or, at any rate, had retained only such elements of it as could be fundamentally transformed and carried off in an entirely new direction. After Mickey, what?

In 1935, of course, American comedy was hardly a dead language. Laurel and Hardy, W. C. Fields, and the Marx Brothers all appeared in major-studio releases during that year, and Chaplin's *Modern Times* was still a year away. But the breeding grounds that had produced these and so many other comedians, vaudeville and the two-reel short, were seriously endangered. Vaudeville, in fact, was already dead by most accounts. The two-reel comedy short would, technically, continue to survive for years at some studios, notably Columbia and RKO, but by the mid-1930s the form had become so unprofitable that most comedians were deserting it (Laurel and Hardy made their last two-reeler in 1935).[9] What happened next is open to interpretation, but it's a matter of consensus that American comedy was entering its declining years—passed down to lesser journeyman performers like Abbott and Costello, siphoned off in alternate directions such as the screwball comedy, or simply abandoned. Of course these are highly subjective judgments, subject to change with the passage of time. When James Agee wrote his classic essay "Comedy's Greatest Era" in 1949, he used a comparison between Buster Keaton (in 1924) and Bob Hope (in 1948) as a measuring stick to demonstrate how far American comedy films had slipped in the interim. From today's perspective, when comedy films have plunged to unprecedented new depths, Hope himself appears to be part of the "greatest" era.

In any case it's clear that a tradition that was still reasonably healthy in the mid-1930s had become a distant memory within a couple of decades. And what of the animated cartoon? When Mickey Mouse laid down the comedy torch, which other character picked it up? The answer, again, is arguable, but this writer would argue that no other character ever did—at least, not in the same way. Perhaps a case could be made for the cynical, street-smart comedy of the classic Warner Bros. cartoon shorts of the 1940s. But the dialogue-heavy nature of the Warner cartoons seems to suggest vaudeville's other stepchild, radio, far more than the brilliant and purely visual tradition of silent film comedy—less Buster Keaton, more Bob Hope.

As for the Disney studio, perhaps we can best illustrate the studio's changing atmosphere by returning once again to the fireman theme. In 1940 yet another firefighting Disney cartoon appeared: *Fire Chief,* starring Donald Duck in the title role, this time with a crew made up of his three nephews. *Fire Chief* is a handsomely produced cartoon on its own terms, and in addition it's notable for returning to the ruthless comedy logic of the Arbuckle-Keaton *The Garage:* the burning building turns out to be none other than Donald's own fire station. This time, in fact, the logic is even more ruthless: here it's Donald himself who has started the fire. But any resemblance to the classic American comedy tradition ends there; despite this coincidental similarity, Donald never remotely suggests Keaton or any of the other legendary comedians. Gags in *Fire Chief* are mostly built around the ongoing conflict between Donald and the nephews and couched in the visual language of Disney's plausibly impossible cartoon world. When Donald indulges in a fire-hose gag, for example, it has little to do with earlier hose gags. This time the hose, accidentally tied in a knot, continues to fill with water behind Donald's back, expanding to monstrous proportions until it resembles a three-story water balloon—then bursts in a mighty cataclysm of water, an image that could be seen only in the world of cartoons. Other traditional firefighting gags are made secondary to the dynamic between Donald and his nephews, or omitted altogether, and there is no climactic rescue scene. If the comedy roots of *Mickey's Fire Brigade* are difficult to discern, they've disappeared completely by the time of *Fire Chief.*

None of this is intended as a criticism of *Fire Chief* or of the vintage-1940 Disney studio in general. On the contrary, Walt Disney had simply appropriated the element of comedy, combined it with other cultural influences and his own original ideas, and seamlessly absorbed them into a brilliant artistic statement all his own. In a sense he reached the apex of his art in 1940 with the release of both *Pinocchio* and *Fantasia*—two monumental works that remain today the pinnacle of animation art. But it's worth noting that a kinship with a rich and vital comedy tradition was one facet of Disney's triumph and that that kinship can be seen most clearly in the early 1930s. Those images from the closing scenes of *Mickey's Gala Premier,* with Mickey surrounded by the giants of stage and screen comedy, are more than just Mickey's fantasy; they're the expression of a bonding of like talents, a bonding preserved on film to this day.

NOTES

The author would like to thank film comedy specialists Ben Urish and Annette D'Agostino Lloyd for their help in the preparation of this essay.

1. Other animation producers, notably the Fleischer studio, had experimented with sound cartoons as early as four years before *Steamboat Willie.*

2. "The Plausible Impossible," an episode of the *Disneyland* television series that explained this aspect of the art of animation, was broadcast Oct. 31, 1956.

3. On the other hand, he was himself an officer of the law in *The Dognapper* (1934)—and, again, this was not without precedent; see Chaplin's *Easy Street* (1917).

4. Ben Urish points out that the two scenes differ partly because Semon, not the cat, is the focus of the gag in *The Grocery Clerk.* If we look past the superficially similar images of animals stuck to flypaper, a better parallel to the "Flypaper Sequence" might be W. C. Fields's struggles with sticky wrapping paper in *The Golf Specialist* (1930) and *You're Telling Me* (1934)—which, indeed, help to make up two extended and memorable comedy set-pieces.

5. After starring in short comedies for three years as a character called "Lonesome Luke," Lloyd had recently introduced a new character, distinguished physically by the fact that he wore glasses. The "Glass Character" would bring Lloyd his greatest fame and is the image by which he is best remembered today.

6. In accounts of this "apprentice" period in Keaton's career it has been traditional to assume that the best, most inventive gags in the Arbuckle-Keaton films were supplied by Keaton, not Arbuckle (see, e.g., Kerr, *The Silent Clowns,* chap. 13). More recently, however (as in the notes and commentaries supplied with the 2005 Arbuckle DVD collection), Arbuckle partisans have argued that the "borrowing" could just as easily have gone the other way.

7. See Schelly, *Harry Langdon,* 88–89. Essentially, Mack Sennett produced the five-reel *His First Flame* in 1925 while Langdon was still in his employ but withheld it from release until Langdon had appeared in several successful features for First National.

8. For those unfamiliar with the Alice Comedies, Julius was a cartoon cat who functioned as a sidekick to the live-action Alice, the little girl who was the nominal heroine of the series. In fact, by 1926 Alice had been steadily reduced to a supporting role in "her" films, while Julius had become the real protagonist.

9. It's true that most of these comedians, including Laurel and Hardy, were simply appearing in feature-length films instead, a move that made economic sense and actually did produce some classic films. But the two-reel short had provided an ideal environment for sight-gag comedy, an environment that the feature—with its constant pressure to dilute the comedy with dramatic plot elements, musical numbers, and romantic subplots—could rarely duplicate.

PART TWO

Systems and Effects

Making Cartoons Funny

4

Infectious Laughter

Cartoons' Cure for the Depression

Donald Crafton

There are 1,583,687.62 laughs in this collection of treasures from the Looney Tunes vaults. Your count may vary and, of course, contents will settle during shipping.
—PACKAGE DESCRIPTION, *LOONEY TUNES GOLDEN COLLECTION*, VOL. 4

It is axiomatic that cartoons from the studio period were made to make us laugh. Big belly laughs. Speaking as someone who attended the local "show" almost weekly for most of the 1950s, after the big producers had been forced to divest themselves of their theaters, but before economic pressures, changes in audience-ship, and competing entertainments put the industry in its downward spiral, I can attest to the producers' and exhibitors' success in the jocularity department. We kids laughed like crazy at cartoons. But so did grownups. Movie audiences seem to have been much more exuberant then; if it was funny, we laughed. We cried when appropriate too. I recall my parents sniffling along with the kids when it dawned on us that Wendy unfairly could not fly with Peter Pan back to Neverland just because she was growing up. Was this the origin of our 1960s rage against injustice? Did the models of parenting so strongly presented (and so Victorian) affect our behavior as parents? I believe that, as my generation did, the young and old moviegoers of earlier days laughed en masse at cartoons. I have no way of proving it except to note that theatrical performance historically has involved responsive audiences, and there is no reason to think that classic cartoons were an exception.

I want to examine here how the films of the 1930s used the performative signature of infectious laughter to convey meaning. It is obvious when watching them that there was more to the films than just some sort of tickle. The filmmakers had multiple audiences in mind from the beginning. Hollywood cartoons before the age of television addressed adults as well as children. Since the films participated in the articulation of the visual culture of their day, meaning was densely and sometimes ambivalently packed. Assumptions about class, race, and gender were silently at work too.

BENIGN LAUGHTER: FORGETTING THE DEPRESSION

There are so many books on the nature and function of laughter, it makes you want to cry.[1] I won't try to reinvent a couple of hundred wheels here but, rather, introduce the subject by pointing out that interest in the connection between laughter and audience behaviors has established credentials. "Laughter must answer to certain requirements of life in common," Bergson wrote in 1904. "It must have a *social* signification." Bergson also recorded something obvious to anyone attending spectacles, sports, or lectures: "Our laughter is always the laughter of a group. . . . How often has it been said that the fuller the theatre, the more uncontrollable the laughter of the audience!"[2] In Freud's book on humor he devoted a chapter to "The Joke and the Varieties of the Comic" and claimed that it takes at least three people for a joke to work. For Freud humor was always about power, often favored the weaker side over the powerful, and was capable of use as a weapon to make someone "contemptible and rob him of any claim on dignity or authority."[3] So laughter seems to have a built-in proclivity toward group expressivity. How appropriate for Hollywood.

On the question of the social efficacy of their products, the movie moguls (and Disney was exhibit number one in animation) often retreated behind the "mere entertainment" apology, saying that they were in a business foremost and that they wanted to please most people while offending few, thus denying responsibility for whatever social message their films might contain.[4] Richard Maltby has commented on the entrenched politically and socially conservative stance in the production companies of Hollywood. "The entertainment ethic," he wrote, "proscribed an area of human activity, going to the movies, as being detached from political significance. Movies were, according to the accepted wisdom of their manufacturers, mere 'harmless entertainment,' at most influencing only fashion and shirts."[5] It should be added, though, that producers were willing to take credit for progressive social content when it suited their purpose—as Jack Warner did for the Warner Bros. social problem and crime films.

Many people object when writers, teachers, or cocktail party raconteurs "read too much" into films, but there also are serious scholars who defend the notion of benign entertainment. Peter Berger distinguishes between a dark Dionysian strain of humor and benign forms that "offer no threat to the social order or to the paramount reality of ordinary life. They provide a vacation from the latter's worries, a harmless diversion from which one can return refreshed to the business of living."[6] He further describes benign humor: "Unlike wit, it does not make excessive intellectual demands. Unlike irony and satire, it is not designed to attack. Unlike the extravagant creations of folly, it does not present a counterworld. Rather, it is harmless, even innocent. It is intended to evoke pleasure, relaxation, and good will. It enhances rather than disrupts the flow of everyday life." By contrast, humor that has passed down from "Dionysian ecstasies" always has the element of exposing weakness and attacking it. "One might perhaps argue that this darker side is always there, under the surface of the most innocuous jokes, but it is almost completely hidden, present if at all as a mere *soupçon*."[7] It is this smidgeon that ushers in the possibility of the instrumentality of laughter in art.

INSTRUMENTAL LAUGHTER

Although benign laughter may exist, say in the giggles of very young children, common sense suggests that it is very rare. Even kids laughing on the playground may have meanness, jealousy, or other "Dionysian" intents or inadvertent unhappy effects. Since Berger's term has a Manichean connotation, it may not be the best way to describe the complexity of humor. Even the most seemingly escapist productions can have other functions or meaning imputed by users, and those may be constructive, destructive, or neutral. For instance, there are many glosses on Disney's *The Three Little Pigs* (1933) that conclude something to the effect of "it helped get the nation through the Depression." I am calling this *instrumental laughter* because it is used as a means for bringing awareness to a subject, changing minds, or getting something done. We don't expect to find much of the latter because there is little overt political content in Hollywood cartoons.[8] But on close inspection, many cartoons contain social viewpoints in the work—a hidden agenda, if you will.

Instrumental laughter appears to have been a widespread rhetorical strategy put forward by Hollywood producers, even when most of the time they claimed to shun provocative content. This is apparent in the many references to the New Deal, to FDR, and even homages on soundtracks: "Happy Days Are Here Again" (by Jack Yellen and Milton Ager)[9] had been a film and radio favorite that Roosevelt adopted as his 1932 campaign song.[10] The reflexive plots of the Warner Bros. backstage musicals of the early 1930s, among other things, purported to show that show business can end hard times. A seldom-seen 1934 film that explicitly embraced the power of movies and popular entertainment as a cure was *Stand Up and Cheer!*[11] The president of the United States summons Broadway showman and lothario Lawrence Cromwell (Warner Baxter) to his office:

Mr. Cromwell, our country is gravely passing through a serious crisis. Many of our people's affairs are in the red, and, figuratively, their nerves are in the red. But thanks to ingrained sturdiness, their faith is not in the red. Any people, blessed with a sense of humor, can achieve such a victory. We are endeavoring to pilot the ship past the most treacherous of all rocks—fear. The government now proposes to dissolve that rock in a gale of laughter. To that end, it has created a new cabinet office, that of Secretary of Amusement, whose duty it shall be to amuse and entertain the people, to make them forget their troubles.[12]

A sympathetic parody of FDR, the film picks up on the president's inaugural address, delivered on March 3, 1933, in which he indicted both "fear itself" and "the rulers of exchange of mankind's goods" as causes of the Depression.[13] In *Stand Up and Cheer!* the song "I'm Laughin'" (by Lew Brown and Jay Gorney) asserts the need for actively infectious laughter: "I'm laughing. And I got nothin' to laugh about, so if I can laugh, sing, dance and shout, brother, so can you." This refrain is sung by an astonishing cross-section of down-and-out or marginalized Americans: an Irish mother with kids, some rural hayseeds, a Jewish seamstress in a sweatshop, cops, construction workers, chorines, sanitation workers, blacksmiths, a train engineer, and (!) Aunt Jemima. Cromwell does succeed in evading the shoals, and he brings the Depression to an official end with a victory parade. The crowds sing the theme song (by Harry Akst and Lew Brown), "Stand up and cheer! Banish all fear, let's take ahold . . . The Depression's over, we're out of the red. . . . Sing hallelujah, sing it loud, because the big bad wolf is gone." As Henry Jenkins observes, "The film's narrative offers an elaborate apologia for Hollywood's own role as a central national institution during a national crisis, arguing for the social importance of entertainment and the need to 'stand up and cheer' in the face of adversity."[14] We also see in this film an effort to represent in art the consensus that has brought the country together in its shared hardship.

This rhetoric touting the prophylactic power of humor also has been memorialized in a key scene in *Sullivan's Travels,*[15] the 1942 film by Preston Sturges set in the "present" but with a story that seems to take place in the mid-1930s. In the course of a plot that veers from initial broad comedy to averted tragedy, the protagonist's views on the nature of film art change when he realizes how movie laughter can create a community.

The hero is John L. Sullivan (Joel McCrea), a Hollywood director who is inspired to make the ultimate social realist genre movie of the early 1930s (adapted from a book with the Steinbeckian title *O Brother, Where Art Thou?*). One of his studio heads, LeBrand,[16] suggests that the book would make a nice musical, to which Sullivan responds, "How can you talk about a musical at a time like this, with the world committing suicide, with the corpses piled up in the street, with grim death gargling at you from every corner, with people slaughtered like sheep?" The boss replies, "Maybe they'd like to forget that." Sturges parodies

Hollywood producers' stance that musicals and other lighthearted fare succeed because they appeal to mindless plebeians intent on forgetting their troubles.

The hero's nickname, Sully, is perhaps an homage by the erudite Sturges to James Sully, author of an influential turn-of-the-century book on the psychology of laughter. James Sully concluded that satire is a socially tolerable form of derision and ridicule. Through a series of darkening mishaps, Sullivan ends up serving time on a southern work farm. The epiphanic plot point occurs when Sullivan, now on a chain gang, has been taken to a nearby African American church, where the preacher puts up a sheet and shows a Mickey Mouse cartoon from the 1930s. The congregation convulses with laughter when Pluto steps on some sticky flypaper. Immersed in Pluto's tormented battle, the differences between the men and women, blacks and whites, prisoners and guards dissolve in the shared hilarity of the cartoon. Seeing and hearing the races and classes brought together by unifying laughter convinces Sullivan to abandon his "social" pretensions as a director and embrace the restorative potential of his trademark genre, uproarious sex comedies. That this scene is an epiphany is made clear by the preacher's prophetic remarks shortly before the prisoners arrive: "For we is all equal in the sight of God, and He said, 'and the chains shall be struck from them, and the lame shall leap, and the blind shall see and glory in the coming of the Lord.'" And so it was that Sullivan's social and artistic blindness is indeed lifted by his redeemer, Pluto the Pup.[17]

Sturges's film makes a strong case for the cartoon as a vehicle for redemption, that is, a way to save oneself from a seemingly irreversible decline and add value to one's life. The animated sequence from *Sullivan's Travels* turns animation into a social and ethical practice. We wonder to what extent this attitude was typical among movie viewers of the times.

Scant empirical data are available about audience attitudes or opinions about 1930s cartoons. Until something better comes along, the best way to get an idea about whether animation humor was innocuous or instrumental is to look at some specimen films. While in principle one could select any year in cartoons for content analysis, I look at the year 1934 for two reasons. That was when the effects of the Great Depression were being felt hardest by most people (the Gross National Product turned around that year in the United States but not necessarily in other countries).[18] And *Playful Pluto* turned out to have an exceptional reception history.

SPENDING LIKE A SAILOR: SOME CARTOON CURES

Of course, in 1934 no one knew that—in the big economic picture—the nation's worst times were bottoming out and it was the beginning of a painfully slow recovery from the Crash of '29 that would last until 1940. To those ordinary people who had patronized the movies as long as they could afford to, times must have seemed dismal indeed. Against this background Hollywood film humor thrived. And it was the animated apotheosis of Mickey Mouse, the Silly Symphonies, and the rival series of a half-dozen cartoon studios competing with Walt Disney. The aggregate crazy laughter produced by all the bizarre plot twists, mindless gags, goofy characters, peppy music, and unbridled optimism during this era in the movies must have seemed manic as well as poignant, considering the unemployment, race riots, strikes, starvation, and general misery outside the theater doors. It is intuitive that the exuberant content and the presumed infectious laughter that comedies elicited from moviegoers was purely escapist, a desirable distraction to facilitate social forgetfulness, and that that was sufficient. But a film like *Playful Pluto* and some other cartoons of the 1930s show the counterintuitive instrumental possibilities of animation. My aim will be to unmask merriment's innocent veil.

Playful Pluto (Disney, 1934) is a domestic comedy showing brief vignettes of by-play between Mickey Mouse and his pet, Pluto. The pup is in a playful mood, while head-of-household Mickey is intent on raking leaves. Mickey throws a stick to distract the dog, but Pluto's retrieval ends up spilling Mickey's leaf basket. Mickey forgives the dog, though, and offers to shake hands/paw. Mickey tricks Pluto by playing the schoolyard gag "Shake-Spear" on him, that is, by snatching his hand away and pointing his thumb over his shoulder. The playful battle escalates until Pluto tears the garden hose and faucet off the house. Mickey and Pluto go to the cellar to fix the broken pipe, with Pluto acting as the plumber's helper. A mishap hilariously sends the flashlight into Pluto's innards, and he runs around yowling crazily, the light giving us an X-ray of his skeleton with every hiccup, until he crashes through the kitchen's screen door. All the flies in the neighborhood invade the kitchen, so Mickey retaliates with sheets of flypaper. Pluto, in one of the most celebrated sequences of character animation in the Disney canon, becomes hopelessly entangled in a sheet of "Tanglefoot." The animator, Norm Ferguson, portrays the dog's fleeting emotions as the paper migrates from limb to ear to, inevitably, the rump. Between panting efforts to free himself, Pluto pauses to "think," and we see each hopeful scheme and each defeat register in slow-motion cognition on the dog's benighted face. Finally, when his rolling disaster spreads to the window shade, Mickey comes to rescue him—only to become stuck on the flypaper himself. Now Pluto removes it from his master and offers to shake. When Mickey extends his hand, Pluto gives *him* the Shake-Spear. Mickey realizes that turnabout is fair play, and they laugh together.

Playful Pluto is a parable that teaches the virtues of civility and cooperation in the spirit of other Disney fables, such as *The Grasshopper and the Ants* or *The Flying Mouse*.[19] The audience's sympathies lie with Pluto and not with Mickey, since Mickey teases him and negligently causes him pain and suffering. (The cocky Max Hare gets his similar comeuppance after giving the Shake-Spear to sympathetic Toby the Tortoise in *The Tortoise and the Hare* [Disney, 1935]).[20] The infectious laughter that the flashlight and the flypaper scenes evoke is sympathetic. Viewers probably do not laugh because they cruelly like to see animals suffer but because Pluto is anthropomorphized and because they feel superior to mean Mickey. While the film is not overtly about the Depression, the upbeat message is consistent with Roosevelt's calls for courteous citizenship.

When My Ship Comes In (Fleischer, 1934) was released later the same year. The moments of infectious laughter are early in the film when a horse that Betty Boop has bet on wins the sweepstakes. She celebrates by liberating her pets. In a nice gag it appears that she is cruelly chucking the fish out the window. A cut to the outside of her house reveals, though, that a brook babbles by where we expected a sidewalk. Betty breaks into the title song (by Jack Scholl and Sammy Timberg), which tells how she will use her newfound wealth:

> I'll just start buying, buying until my money is spent,
> Trying, trying to make everybody content.
> We won't need relief or unemployment; we'll have work and everything.
> I'll be spending like a sailor 'cause my ship came in.

Then a fantasy sequence shows Betty addressing some Depression-specific issues. Police officers treat two hoboes in a park to a fine multicourse meal. The Betty Boop milk company uses silenced horses hooves and balloon-assisted quiet delivery. Continuing the food motif, some kids play on an ice-cream mountain. All these vignettes are accompanied by the background tune of "We're in the Money" (by Harry Warren and Al Dubin) from Gold Diggers of 1933 (Warner Bros., 1933). When the scene shifts to Betty Boop's animal farm, the music switches to the anthemic, "Happy Days Are Here Again." The barnyard folk should be very happy, with the squirrels getting free nuts from vending machines, the pigs enjoying a mud pool with a diving board, and so on. In Betty's victory parade we see her handing out cash to cheering throngs and witness the immediate results. Next to the Old Maids' Home, a Bachelor Hall is built, to the delight of the cheering women. Workingmen and women file into department stores with money and file out carrying goods and sporting evening clothes. A decrepit factory comes to life, fills with workers, and then dissolves into tableaux of money changing hands across a map of North America (Fig. 4.1). As in the Sturges film, the personae are of mixed race and gender. As Betty reprises her upbeat theme song, a village grows into a great metropolis before our eyes, complete with its own Chrysler Building.

Betty Boop's fantasies are humorous because they are so wildly improbable. It may be that we laugh not only at her solutions but also at their incongruity. Charles Darwin, in his own take on laughter, opined that "something incongru-

FIGURE 4.1. *When My Ship Comes In* (Fleischer, 1934).

ous or unaccountable, exciting surprise and some sense of superiority in the laugher, who must be in a happy frame of mind, seems to be the commonest cause [of laughter]. The circumstances must not be of a momentous nature: no poor man would laugh or smile on suddenly hearing that a large fortune had been bequeathed to him."[21] Besides the incongruity of the gags—the Bergsonian mechanical dog scratcher might be the best—we also may be laughing at, and feeling superior to, Betty, whose solution is witty and original but unworkable, making her look magnanimous but kind of stupid.

Betty's solution for the Depression was based on a widespread explanation for the trouble, that it was lack of spending by consumers that had damaged the retail sectors, decreased demand for goods, and led to shuttered factories. In hindsight the problem more likely was that because of unemployment, rising interest rates, and inflation, especially on agricultural goods, consumers did not have disposable cash to relieve manufacturers' excess inventories, even if they had wanted to, which, because of low confidence in the economy, they did not.[22] Among those industries laying off workers and slashing wages: motion pictures. In 1933 the New Deal provided for consumer spending through the agency of the NRA (the National Recovery Administration).

John Maynard Keynes did not have Betty Boop's Boop Oop a Doop, but Betty apparently shared the British economist's theory of redistributing wealth as a cure for depressions. The plan she advocates in her song acted out her Keynesian solution, giving workers jobs so they might spend money, which would create jobs, which would put money into the system and would start a cycle of improvement.[23] This essentially was the monetary philosophy behind Roosevelt's New

FIGURE 4.2. *Honeymoon Hotel* (Schlesinger, 1934).

Deal.[24] Betty's plan is funny because, on its face, it embraces the Keynesian/NRA fix while taking it to absurd extremes.

Two Warner Bros. cartoons from 1934 that juxtapose humor and Depression themes are *Honeymoon Hotel* (Schlesinger, 1934) and *Those Beautiful Dames* (Schlesinger, 1934). The former film is based on the bawdy "Honeymoon Hotel" number in *Footlight Parade* (Warner Bros., 1933). The cartoon uses the song by Harry Warren and Al Dubin with altered lyrics for about the first half. In the seeming utopia of Bugville, the village is an analogue to the world outside: "Goodbye to Depression, business here is fine." The protagonists are a Ladybug and a Tumblebug on their honeymoon. They reprise some of the erotic jokes in the Busby Berkeley production number. Eventually, the bugs' lovemaking becomes so "hot" that it sets the hotel on fire. Although rubble crashes down around their room, they just hang out the Do Not Disturb sign and carry on (Fig. 4.2). In this film, laughter comes from the erotic antics of the anthropomorphized insects and the consummation-delaying mishaps that they encounter. It also derives from the comic tradition of imagining a parallel universe that mirrors our own. The bugtopia now has problems, just like small towns in the nonanimated world.

Those Beautiful Dames revived a recurring favorite plot device, the starving child who dreams of bounteous food, toys, and playtime.[25] The Depression is not explicitly acknowledged, but the iconography of deprivation, the loss of family, and the effects of hard times on kids make the connection unmistakable. A ragged girl treks through the snow and pauses to look in the window of a toy store. She presses on as the storm rages. Inside her cabin, where apparently she lives alone, there is no fire in the stove. A mouse is starving. As she sleeps, the toys

FIGURE 4.3. *Those Beautiful Dames* (Schlesinger, 1934).

come to redecorate her room and perform the title song (by Herbert W. Spencer) for her. Then the curtains part to reveal a sumptuous banquet. She joins the toys to feast on cake and ice cream (Fig. 4.3).

No question, the benign reading of all four of these films is positive and uplifting. They promote values of forgiveness, compassion, charity, and goodwill—the kind of feel-good experience celebrated by the fictional Sullivan. There are plenty of gags that are "pointless." There also are alternative readings that reveal criticisms of institutions, of the status quo, and are thinly disguised attacks. Giuliana Muscio has concluded that "the relationship between the New Deal and Hollywood appears to be ambivalent."[26] This is reflected in the animated output, too, where the cartoonists used humor, traditionally a safe haven for the critique of authority, to counter Hollywood's optimism. Though one has to look for it, the instrumental aspect of these films is much more than laughter for its own sake.

"LAUGHTER IS THE THING PEOPLE WANT— NOT SOCIAL STUDIES"

Preston Sturges, who wrote as well as directed *Sullivan's Travels,* said that he borrowed the conceit of infectious laughter from philosophy: "Art, Tolstoy said, is a medium for the transmission of emotions."[27] In a rare moment, a Hollywood filmmaker is giving us a clue to the intellectual basis of a film. Furthermore, Sturges was correct in his application of Tolstoy.

The laughing scene, indeed, is a good illustration of the aesthetic theory that

Leo Tolstoy developed in *What Is Art?* According to Gary R. Jahn, "Feeling (in Russian, *chuvstvo*) is the central term of Tolstoy's aesthetic theory."[28] Tolstoy seized on the metaphor of infection, as in infectious laughter or crying, in his 1897 book to illustrate how works of art communicate the artist's emotion to the audience. (His guiding metaphor was probably inspired by the rapid acquisition of knowledge about the origins of contagious diseases toward the end of the nineteenth century, especially the first laboratory isolation of viruses by the Russian scientist Dmitri Iosifovich Ivanovski in 1892.) Tolstoy defined art according to these premises: artistic activities arise from natural expressions of feeling; they join men *[sic]* in humanity; and they are communicated as though by aesthetic infection.[29] Crucially for him, Tolstoy also insisted on a fourth, ethical, dimension to this communication process, which in itself was morally neutral. Good art conveyed positive spiritual (i.e., his rather idiosyncratic Christian) values, but "decadent" art either did not "infect" its consumers (for instance, Wagner's music) or instilled immoral thoughts in them (impressionist painting and the various fin de siècle art movements). Reductive though it may be, Tolstoy's "infection aesthetics" became the tagline for the novelist's theory of art.

By pressing Disney's cartoon into service as the turning point in his drama, Sturges represents animation as an exemplary infectious art. The scene succeeds twice, once as a "cure" for Sullivan's and the country's metonymical depression and again as an allegory of the instrumentality of art and the artist (that is, the filmmaker) to bring about social change. The medium—animation—is part of the message because it redeems individual isolation and existential despair through the unifying power of laughter.

Tolstoy's argument is of more than passing interest, for, just as it was utilitarian for Sturges's plot and his conception of the instrumental nature of laughter, it provides a model for inferring how audiences may have understood animation in the 1930s. Tolstoy was in vogue. His centenary had been celebrated in 1928. *What Is Art?* had been reissued in English in 1932, and his theory was more widely circulated then than it is now. There were five Hollywood adaptations of his novels in the early 1930s.[30] While Tolstoy was "in the air," it is neither expected nor necessary for ordinary moviegoers to have heard of his aesthetics, or even to have heard of him, to make our claim that Sturges's nod to his philosophy provides a historically grounded framework with which to describe the status of animation with its audiences in the mid-1930s.

Returning to Tolstoy's premises, animation can readily be seen as creating the illusion of an authentic vernacular expression, carefully cultivated by the producers, of course. Most important, cartoons use their tendency to generate infectious laughter to produce art that does not exist in the formal properties of the work, in the artist, or in anything innate in the audience but in the interaction between the audience and the work. He did not use the words, but Tolstoy's theory shares elements of modern-day performance theory and viral aesthetic theories. The former emphasizes the role of the interactivity of performer and audience, while the latter focuses on how reception communities constantly negotiate the uses of a work.[31] Sturges undoubtedly was attracted to this performative concept of art. Tolstoy wrote that the profoundest works of art communicate by building feverish and contagious excitement:

> The simplest example: a man laughs, and another man feels merry; he weeps, and the man who hears this weeping feels sad; a man is excited, annoyed, and another looking at him gets into the same state. With his movements, the sounds of his voice, a man displays cheerfulness, determination, or, on the contrary, dejection, calm—and this mood is communicated to others. A man suffers, expressing his suffering in moans and convulsions—and this suffering is communicated to others; a man displays his feeling of admiration, awe, fear, respect for certain objects, persons, phenomena—and other people become infected, experience the same feelings of admiration, awe, fear, respect for the same objects, persons or phenomena.
>
> On this capacity of people to be infected by the feelings of other people, the activity of art is based.[32]

It is the Tolstoyan feverish excitement of animation that the laughing scene in *Sullivan's Travels* documents. Whether Tolstoy could possibly have imagined cartoons is beside the point (and rather silly), but it did happen that that branch of film production and its reception seem to have matched pretty well his conception of how art communicates.

INFECTIOUS ANIMATION

Now the issue becomes, did the cartoons that we're studying do what Sturges claimed they were doing, that is, using emotions to communicate with viewers?

That *Playful Pluto* was made with the intention of disinclining bad behavior or reinforcing good seems obvious. Following the narrative form of fables, the film's redeeming message comes as an implicit "moral" at the end, which in this case is a version of the Golden Rule. Its laughter is instrumental in the sense that it's inspirational and sets an example. But even this film is not purely benign. While it does not reference the Depression directly, we infer it as a structuring absence in the film's setting and décor, a Barthesian "reality effect."[33] Mickey's home seems to be located on the edge of a small village, somewhere between town and country but far, far from the Dust Bowl. According to Maltby, "Rural simplicity . . . emerged again in the Depression as the cultural, if not the economic, bastion of American virtues. The populist mythos of the agrarian community or the small town pervaded the idealized solutions to the Depression."[34] Mickey

FIGURE 4.4. *Playful Pluto* (Disney, 1934).

seems comfortable enough, but the Mouse residence is becoming dilapidated, with cracked plaster, patched window shades, and broken panes (Fig. 4.4).

The kitchen stove is an old wood-burning model. Mickey's reliance on old-fashioned "Tanglefoot," rather than more effective and up-to-date insecticides, also stamps the time of the story as pre-1930s.[35] Furthermore, Pluto's plight seems designed to elicit empathy from Depression audiences. The dog, like the laborers, had done nothing to deserve entrapment. His victimization by uncontrollable overarching forces is a figure for 1934 America. Nostalgia for a pre-Depression Edenic state is implicit, as is an ethical position. While the plot might teach, "Don't allow yourself to be like Pluto," the film also suggests that his condition is predestined and inescapable. Sturges's choice of this film for its affinity with the incarcerated audience of *Sullivan's Travels* was inspired.[36] Moreover, the cartoon probably resonated with, that is, infected, larger audiences during its first run in the depth of the Depression by suggesting a more complex, and darker, understanding of the human condition in hard times.

Betty Boop, in her *When My Ship Comes In* parody of a New Dealer, presents an equivocal message when she generates infectious laughter. There is the affirmative reading: Workers and (implicitly) unions will be part of the recovery plan if they cooperate with management according to NRA terms. Then, there is the undermining reading: The proposed plan is an unworkable pipedream.

Although the film is a folly, its humor spotlights several fundamental flaws inherent in the quick-fix solutions of the NRA. Where is the seed money coming from? Rather than borrowing by the government to fund its projects (a Keynesian policy that earned the president the nickname Franklin Deficit Roosevelt),[37] Betty's wonderful windfall does not increase the national debt and does not have to be paid back. So her welfare scheme is exposed as a gambling long shot. The film shows clearly that Betty herself has not been doing her part. Rather than buying durable goods with her disposable cash to boost the economy, she's been using her money to gamble. This is consistent with critiques of Keynesian strategies that pointed out that workers tend to use cash to pay back loans, overdue rent, and personal expenses rather than spend it on big-ticket manufactured goods. The film also lampoons Roosevelt's appeal to the rich to help the poor through charitable giving. It didn't happen. And Betty's plan ignores one of the acknowledged causes of the Depression, the collapse of the agricultural economy. The urbanistà Fleischer brothers give none of Betty's largesse to distressed farmers, only to city folk. The film was produced when confidence in the New Deal was waning. "Six months after the NRA's inception," that is, by the fall of 1933, according to Meg Jacobs, "the euphoria that had surrounded it in its early days was gone. Employment and purchasing power had increased, but not enough."[38] Also, employers had countered the rapid growth of organized trade unions with their own company unions, and the summer of 1934 saw many bitter strikes. Workers were beginning to call the NRA the National Run Around.[39] It is quite appropriate to see in this seemingly cheerful cartoon anxiety about the current government's optimistic alternative.[40]

When My Ship Comes In uses the Swiftian technique of hyperbole by taking elements of the NRA and exaggerating them to ridiculous, and therefore laughable, extremes. Another technique, inversion, reverses the roles of humans and animals and real and imagined worlds. There perhaps is a hint, too, that the animators were slyly criticizing the policies of Fleischer Studios, since the working conditions were poor and the management's biases against unions were legion. The animation camera operators had formed a union in 1934; the animators began organizing in 1935, an action that would lead to a strike in 1937.[41]

Compared to, say, the Busby Berkeley "Shanghai Lil" sequence of *Footlight Parade*, which unambiguously lauds the intervention of the NRA, or to the Oswald the Rabbit cartoon *Confidence* (Lantz/Universal, 1933) that treats us to the spectacle of FDR in a song-and-dance number, *When My Ship Comes In* is not an endorsement of the government's or of the Fleischer Studios' ability to cure the Depression. The infectious laughter that Betty generates signals the gap between policy and reality that the rousing patriotism elided in *Footlight Parade* and *Confidence*. Audiences leaving the theater after the Warner musical might have kept Sousa's rousing "Stars and Stripes Forever" in their heads as it's played by a troop of marching soldiers who display a portrait of FDR, before re-forming into an NRA Blue Eagle, complete with firing rifles. How could one not experience

fleeting optimism? The same music accompanies the images of money changing hands at the finale of *When My Ship Comes In.* But here the effect is a joke,
since the proposition that money spent on nut-vending machines and the like
could resuscitate a moribund economy is patently absurd. If viewers recalled the
strains of Betty's ditty about "buying, buying" and the laughter it generated, they
also may have been haunted by the underlying policy weakness that the humor
ironically forces to the surface. Possibly more troubling, there is an implicit accusation that the Depression was caused to begin with by the abstemiousness of
laborers as consumers. So blame is being shifted from the government, business
management, and natural causes onto workers, many of whom constituted some
part of the cartoon's original audience. These viewers might have felt accusatory
cynicism in the laughter instead of inspiration.

In *Honeymoon Hotel* and *Those Beautiful Dames* the laughter is again double-
edged. Although it is benign if we see it as showing how to make it through
adversity by laughing and copulating, or by dreaming of dancing toys and feasts,
respectively, the films suggest that these activities actually are denials rather than
instrumental actions. Unlike the resulting creation of new jobs in the entertainment sector that films like *Stand Up and Cheer!* and *Footlight Parade* portray,
these two cartoons depict a crash (literally and symbolically referring to the
market crash of 1929) in the former film and imply starvation in the latter.

In *Honeymoon Hotel* the bugs' honeymoon begins as an idyll, but the film
slides steadily downward from utopia. Obstacles seem to pop up everywhere,
from snooping bell staff to a voyeuristic moon that leers through the window
at the lovers. While the final image of the bugs bedding happily as their world
crumbles around them is funny, it is not an altogether salutary message. Indeed,
the film seems to be saying: have your fun, have a good laugh, but don't get so
absorbed in your emotions that you lose touch with what's going on outside.

In *Those Beautiful Dames* there is a discrepancy between the superficial content of the film and the alternative reading, for, unlike many cartoons with the
"dream" narrative structure, the girl does not awaken at the end. The lack of
symmetry and narrative closure in the plot is itself unsettling, but some viewers
might also associate the story with Hans Christian Andersen's "The Little Match
Girl," which ends with the girl's death (she is frozen in the snow after enjoying
beautiful visions of a warm stove, an abundant feast, and a loving grandmother).[42]
The Warner Bros. cartoon ends with a laughing scene, but the gaiety subsides if
the viewer contemplates the grim implications of the story's incomplete ending
extrapolated to its logical conclusion. This film and *Honeymoon Hotel* seem to
condemn, not encourage, escapism.

So while all these cartoons deliver on their expectations of producing an
optimistic, even constructive, message about how individuals should feel and act
during the Depression, all four are susceptible to negative or dystopian interpre-

tations. These counterreadings seem to confirm that Tolstoyan infectiousness is at work; the films' ambivalent performances allow them to communicate preferred and alternative readings, while laughing all the way. This aspect, if it were understood by the films' original consumers (and I believe that it was at some level), helps us understand the original pertinence of cartoons for Depression audiences.

LAUGHTER BETRAYED

The instrumental nature of laughter, however, may not be necessarily a good thing. A school of thought typified by Siegfried Kracauer saw the dark side of infectious laughter. He was not at all swayed by Sturges's use of hilarity as a means for redemption, arguing that the laughter in *Sullivan's Travels* was not progressive but downright dangerous. He gave his essay, written on the occasion of the 1950 revival of the film, the caustic title "Laughter Betrayed." Kracauer reacted against the view that infectious laughter was desirable and harmless. Unthinking laughter could become a tool for hidden persuasion and social control. Singling out the Disney cartoon sequence, he observed that the antics of Pluto and Mickey presented "a paradise where wrongs right themselves automatically." Indeed, the degree to which the audience in the film instantly succumbs to the cartoon's allure is ominous. Their infectious laughing paints them contrarily as a mob. Kracauer goes on to make a distinction between farce and satire. Farce produces an easy but pointless laugh, whereas satire has an ideological effect. Sturges's "farce in the disguise of satire" is risky because it leaves the audience vulnerable to psychological manipulation.[43]

When Kracauer divides laughter into positive and negative strains, farce and satire, he puts into play a strategy we've seen other commentators do with different terminologies. If we extend his thinking to the four films we've studied, it might be accurate to see them as satires disguised as farces. That is, superficially the films seem to promote infectious laughter for its own "pointless" sake; but there is also satirical or ideological content just below the surface.

Kracauer's concern that audiences risked being duped by cartoons is consistent with his intellectual formation in Weimar Germany. In one of his most famous early film essays he observed that the movie palaces of Berlin were designed to lull their bourgeois patrons by distracting them from their social condition and by creating an amoeba-like entity, "the masses," the collective identity that the business elite nurtured in order to exploit. Kracauer wrote in 1926, concerning the intelligentsia, "They are being absorbed by the masses and this gives rise to the homogeneous cosmopolitan audience in which everyone has the same responses, from the bank director to the sales clerk, from the diva to the stenographer."[44] Kracauer's image of the masses absorbing an individual's identity is like a virulent strain of Tolstoy's infection model. The cinema institution's infectious laughter is instrumental, but it is directed by the culture industry.

There was controversy about laughter and animation among the intellectuals of the Frankfurt School, with which Kracauer had affinities. Indeed, the most widely read essay from the period, Walter Benjamin's "The Work of Art in the Age of Its Technological Reproducibility" (1935–36) also used Disney cartoons to probe the joys and dangers of communal laughter. Benjamin's first version of the essay specifically included a section on "Micky-Maus."[45] In his early thinking Benjamin, much as the fictional Sullivan did, looked to explosive film laughter as cathartic. He saw Mickey Mouse as a figure of a collective dream (or nightmare) caused by twentieth-century technology, which had taken control of the state. One visionary section presages the redemption by cinema that we witness in Sturges's film: "Our taverns and city streets, our offices and furnished rooms, our train stations and factories appeared to have us locked up beyond hope. Then came film and exploded this prison-world with the dynamite of one-tenth seconds, so that now, in the midst of its far-flung ruins and debris, we calmly embark on adventurous travels."[46] Perhaps in a reference (unconscious?) to the infection theory, Benjamin claimed that exposure to such films was a "psychic inoculation" against the military and industrial spread of technology. Moreover, films were a safety valve, sating the audience's desire for more assertive reactions. "The collective laughter signifies a premature and therapeutic eruption of such mass psychoses." Cartoons and slapstick disarm the destructive effects of technology "through technologically mediated laughter."

Benjamin's friend and critical antagonist, Theodor Adorno, however, dismissed this as romantic wishful thinking. "The laughter of the cinema audience is . . . anything but good and revolutionary; instead, it is full of the worst bourgeois sadism." This is also the essence of Kracauer's criticism of *Sullivan's Travels*. Much later in life, Adorno had an unsettling experience that revealed the redemptive power of humor. Oh, to be a fly on this wall, when Theodor Adorno encountered Charlie Chaplin and Harold Russell, the double-amputee from William Wyler's *The Best Years of Our Lives* (MGM, 1946). Adorno recalled:

> Together with many others we were invited to a villa in Malibu, on the coast outside of Los Angeles. While Chaplin stood next to me, one of the guests was taking his leave early. Unlike Chaplin, I extended my hand to him a bit absent-mindedly, and, almost instantly, started violently back. The man was one of the lead actors from *The Best Years of Our Lives*, a film famous shortly after the war; he lost a hand during the war, and in its place bore practicable claws made of iron. When I shook his right hand and felt it return the pressure, I was extremely startled, but sensed immediately that I could not reveal my shock to the injured man at any price. In a split second I transformed my frightened expression into an obliging grimace that must have been far ghastlier.

Chaplin stepped in to "save" Adorno from his embarrassment by reperforming the faux pas: "The actor had hardly moved away when Chaplin was already playing the scene back. All the laughter he brings about is so near to cruelty; solely in such proximity to cruelty does it find its legitimation and its element of the salvational."[47] Although Adorno was the butt of Chaplin's seemingly cruel and derogatory imitation, it triggered for him the same sort of epiphanic transformation that John Sullivan had undergone. Adorno generalized from it the essence of Chaplin's humor, which was funny because it was sadistic.

The social theories that the Frankfurt School writers formulated differed in most ways from Tolstoy's—the mass culture of the twentieth-century theorists did not exist in Tolstoy's day; the Germans were not promoting religion. But there were some similarities to infection theory. The art object is itself void of ethical content, and it is a product of popular expression (with varying levels of authenticity). In the presence of art a kind of osmosis takes place between the artist and the receiver, and neither party is in full control of the process. Therefore it is highly contested. The meaning is partly rational but mostly emotional, and therefore the effects may be subconscious. Whereas Tolstoy thought that the results of infection tended to be curative, the Frankfurt School tended to see the effects as mixed but mostly negative.

Both Sturges (following Tolstoy) and Kracauer (following Benjamin and Adorno) raise crucial issues for understanding the Hollywood cartoon of the 1930s. Did the form exist as escapism, stimulating belly laughs to distract audiences from their plight as social victims? Or did the films' "stimulation of involuntary and collective laughter . . . affect their viewers in a manner at once physiological and cognitive" (Hansen)? To express the dynamic another way, did the effects of early sound animation dupe audiences into perceiving the farce of everyday life as normalcy, or were the effects making them aware through parody and satire of their alienation, stuck in the flypaper of the culture industry?

GETTING HAPPY

Tolstoy's fourth premise explicitly identified shared religion as the channel by which the art infection was transmitted from sender to receiver: "art must be, and indeed has always been, understandable to everyone, because each man's relation to God is always the same. And therefore temples, and the images and singing in them, have always been understandable to everyone."[48] Significantly, even in the secular texts of the twentieth century the discourse of religion slips into discussions of laughter. Kracauer saw in *Playful Pluto* a duplicitous "paradise." Adorno found redemptive humor "salvational." Sullivan's transformation took place in a house of worship, as though Sturges saw the kinship between humor and the spark of conversion.

There is another salient genealogy showing the spiritual side of animated redemption by laughter. From 1931 to 1933 the Merrie Melodies theme song was "Get Happy." The music, composed by the young Harold Arlen in 1930, was his first big success and would have been instantly recognized by hip moviegoers. It plays under the title cards in every release. The words are not used, but they are relevant because they derive from African American religious traditions:

> Pack up your troubles and just get happy
> Ya better chase all your cares away
> Sing hallelujah, c'mon get happy
> Get ready for the judgment day.

Repeatedly, the nexus between African American performance and American popular culture has been affirmed. This is especially true of early animation.[49] In the case of "Get Happy," Ted Koehler, the lyricist, produced cabaret shows and was a future "legend of jazz" songsmith (e.g., "Stormy Weather").[50] Though filtered through layers of race appropriation and Cotton Club-ized, the song still captures the euphoria of the original meaning of "getting happy." Ethnomusicologists have traced this ecstatic experience of transcendence to African rituals that hybridized with American Christian worship. James Standifer observes, "Religious expression and black musical behavior almost from the start were one and the same thing. Both manifested themselves in the experience of singing . . . and a behavior resulting from this singing called 'getting happy.' This behavior of being 'hit by the spirit' consisted of behaviors including shouting, dancing, arm-waving, screaming or hollering, swaying back and forth, moaning, singing, fainting, and the like. It is highly individualistic behavior but extremely infectious to other participants."[51]

Peter Berger also has noticed the similarities between paroxysms of laughter and religious experience: "at least certain manifestations of the comic suggest that this other reality has redeeming qualities that are not temporary at all, but rather that point to that other world that has always been the object of the religious attitude. In ordinary parlance one speaks of 'redeeming laughter.' Any joke can provoke such laughter, and it can be redeeming in the sense of making life easier to bear, at least briefly."[52]

It is not coincidental, then, that John Sullivan's enlightenment takes place in a church where the congregants "get happy." In the church-cum-movie house the cartoon gets its viewers very happy indeed, transporting them by laughter, as well as by prayer, to paradise. Sturges thus links animation to true religion, much as the producers of the Merrie Melodies invited their viewers to think of the films as ecstatic interludes in the "service" that was the movie program. The infectious laughter induced by cartoons that has been dismissed as laughter for laughter's sake, or mere escapism, can alternatively be seen as offering to moviegoers a quasi-religious redemption.

CONCLUSION

We don't know much about what 1930s audiences thought of these cartoons. But producing infectious laughter was the cartoonists' stock in trade ("Gagging it," in Disney's words). The cartoons of the 1930s probably benefited from audiences' and exhibitors' expectations that the short films would be a funny distraction—especially if the short shared the program with "serious" films, and there were many in 1934. Additionally, since the cartoons brought with them the possibility of multiple readings, if the four cartoons that I have examined are typical of the era, and I think they are, it is reasonable to think that this multivalence was part of the generic expectation. In other words audiences probably anticipated that their cartoon entertainment would be charged with irony, contemporary observation, object lessons, and the filmmakers' points of view. This humor is not without social history, nor is it benign. Rather, the works are deeply imbued with what Maltby called "the invisible politics of style."[53] Cartoons tuck their meaning behind catchy tunes, hilarious slapstick, funny 'toon characters and wacky worlds of entertainment, but, using Kracauer's terms, they are satires, not farces. Vittorio Hösle observes, "In times of ideological uncertainty comedy may share the task of questioning, together with the philosophers, the basic conventions of the age."[54]

The notion that infectious laughter could be instrumental and ethical while delighting audiences can explain the strong moral component in Disney's mid-1930s product. The Fleischer and Schlesinger studios, conversely, did not appear to be seeking universal moral insight but rather were experiencing with their viewers the current trauma in the country, inducing awareness and, perhaps, guilt. In short, the Disney approach that combined comedy and meliorism prescribed ways for people to model their behavior; the other studios pointed out the ironic contrast between the way society was and the way it might be.

Audience members brought different expectations and competencies to movie theaters. Individuals may have come for distraction, but that would not preclude them from being discerning consumers, too. There is no one interpretation for all, but as we have seen, at least three aspects of "infection" were at work. At the level of the plot, that is, what is presented literally in the film, we find parody, farce, moral assertions, and implied recommendations for behavior. On the story level, that is, the more encompassing understanding of a film's implications, we find satire and inferences about deeper meanings, such as conclusions about Depression-fatigue in *Playful Pluto,* the inadequacy of government programs in Betty Boop, and malaise in the Warner cartoons.[55] Both these kinds of "infections" seem noncontroversial to me. It is the third aspect, which I will call the ideological level, that is the most troublesome. That is where the possibility of unconscious influence or subliminal communication takes place. This has not been proven definitely to exist under laboratory conditions, much less in the raucous worlds of aesthetics and critical theory. How can we know if people's minds were unknowingly changed or their actions influenced by watching escapist comedies, batty musicals, or violent gangster films?

Although I cannot answer this third question, I think that a viral theory can at least state that it was not the cartoons autonomously that were affecting viewers, either consciously or unconsciously, but rather something happening between the viewer and the screen. It is here that seeing infection as a type of collective performance reconciles the opposites that we have encountered in this study: benign/Dionysian; escapist/instrumental; farce/satire. The way that cartoon entertainment worked in the 1930s does seem to resemble a Tolstoyan infection in the sense that the films are constructed according to a certain convention, the seven-minute Hollywood cartoon, but they are incomplete performances, in which the audience invests meaning. The filmmakers may invite this investment, or not; viewers will do as they please. Practically, it is difficult to know what is going on in the mass mind. In the historical context, would rural farmers have been delighted by Betty Boop's cure for the Depression? Because of the widespread policy of segregated theaters in the 1930s, blacks and whites likely watched *Playful Pluto* under racially defined conditions. How did this affect, say, each group's perception of the Mickey-Pluto relationship? Going back to one of my personal musings, did watching *Peter Pan* (multiple times) subconsciously affect my attitudes or behavior when I became a spouse or parent? Possibly, but I don't think so. Anyway, if it were subliminal, it is unprovable.

But a common end result—infectious laughter—does not mean common motives or shared understanding; each viewer may be responding to interpretations vastly different from his or her neighboring viewer, while both laugh out loud. Using Sturges's example, it was only Sullivan, not the whole congregation, who had the sudden realization about the social efficacy of film genres. But this happened at the instant that his identity became one with the laughing audience, showing the tension between the individual and the audience. While Kracauer may be right to suspect that this behavior was instrumental, it need not signify monolithic conformity, but it does need at least a minimal consensus among the audience members to work.

In our everyday experience at the movies today, our laughter seems more restrained, individual, fragmented, and without the consensus implied in cartoons of the 1930s. The person in the front row may be susceptible to subtle moral suggestions. You may be thinking that Pluto's flypaper trap reminds you of your alienated existence. I just always laugh at stupid pet tricks.

NOTES

1. For a concise survey of humor theories and their practical application see the introduction to Goldstein, *Laughter Out of Place*, 1–17. Theories of comedy specifically in relation to media are woven throughout Jenkins, *What Made Pistachio Nuts?*

2. Bergson, *Laughter*, 6–8.

3. Freud, "The Joke and the Varieties of the Comic," 183.

4. Disney claimed to have been surprised that *The Three Little Pigs* was seen as a Depression-themed film: "It was just another story to us and we were in there gagging it just like any other picture" (quoted in Schickel, *The Disney Version*, 156).

5. Maltby, *Harmless Entertainment*, 55.

6. Berger, *Redeeming Laughter*, 114.

7. Ibid., 99.

8. One notable exception is the pacifist *Peace on Earth*, directed by Hugh Harman, produced by Harman and Fred Quimby, released by MGM on Dec. 9, 1939. Animation is certainly capable of delivering propaganda, as well as didactic content, but the major Hollywood producers avoided such films as part of the "entertainment ethic" and owing to monitoring by the Hays Office and exhibitor trade organizations.

9. All music and lyric citations are from the ASCAP ACE database, www.ascap.com/ace/.

10. Rubin, "Movies and the New Deal in Entertainment," 94. "Happy Days Are Here Again" may be heard in *Chasing Rainbows* (Paramount, 1930), *Rain or Shine* (Columbia, 1930), and *Thanks a Million* (Twentieth Century–Fox, 1935).

11. *Stand Up and Cheer!*, directed by Hamilton MacFadden, produced by Winfield Sheehan, released by Fox Film Corp. on May 4, 1934.

12. The author would like to express his gratitude to the Fox Movie Channel and his beloved Tivo. *Stand Up and Cheer!* is the film with the "back-flipping senators" routine, a line from which inspired the title of Jenkins's *What Made Pistachio Nuts?*

13. Franklin D. Roosevelt, First Inaugural Address, www.eric.ed.gov/.

14. Jenkins, *What Made Pistachio Nuts?* 1.

15. *Sullivan's Travels*, written and directed by Preston Sturges, produced by B. G. DaSilva, released by Paramount on Jan. 28, 1942.

16. *LeBrand* is a pun on the name of Paramount's William LeBaron, who executive produced Sturges's *Christmas in July* (1940), *The Great McGinty* (1940), and *The Lady Eve* (1941).

17. The interpretation of *Sullivan's Travels* is by no means unambiguous, laced as the film is with Sturges's own antagonism toward Hollywood's ambivalent politics, his sardonic humor, and his guilty conscience for participating in the system he was ridiculing. For a discussion of the film that is quite different from mine see Moran and Rogin, "What's the Matter with Capra?"

18. Edsforth, *The New Deal*, 150.

19. *The Grasshopper and the Ants*, directed by Wilfred Jackson, produced by Walt Disney, released by United Artists on Feb. 10, 1934; *The Flying Mouse*, directed by David Hand, produced by Walt Disney, released by United Artists on July 14, 1934.

20. *The Tortoise and the Hare*, directed by Wilfred Jackson, produced by Walt Disney, released by United Artists on Jan. 5, 1935.

21. Darwin, *The Expression of the Emotions in Man and Animals* (1872), quoted in Hösle, *Woody Allen*, 10.

22. See Edsforth, *The New Deal*.

23. See Keynes, *The Means to Prosperity*.

24. Keezer, "The Consumer under National Recovery Administration," 89.

25. Images of fantastic nutritional abundance abound in Depression-era cartoons. An earlier example is *The Shanty Where Santa Claus Lives,* directed by Hugh Harman and Rudolf Ising, released by Warner Bros. on Jan. 7, 1933. It is Santa who takes the orphan boy to his workshop for food and play. In the live-action film *Hollywood Party* (MGM, 1934), Disney provided a food-themed animated cartoon as an insert called *The Hot Chocolate Soldiers,* animated by Ben Sharpsteen. An example from the same week of release as *Those Beautiful Dames* is *Holiday Land,* directed by Arthur Davis, produced by Charles Mintz, released by Columbia Pictures on Nov. 9, 1934. Here Scrappy dreams of visiting the various holidays to get food, culminating with a Thanksgiving feast. That these films starring hungry children were released for the 1934 Thanksgiving holiday is especially poignant. A ragged girl saved by food also is featured in *The Cookie Carnival,* directed by Ben Sharpsteen, produced by Walt Disney, released by United Artists on May 25, 1935. I know of only one film with the Depression as its explicit subject, *Confidence,* directed by William Nolan, produced by Walter Lantz, released by Universal on July 31, 1933.

26. Muscio, *Hollywood's New Deal,* 102.

27. The title of this segment is from the Dec. 5, 1941, review of *Sullivan's Travels* in the *Hollywood Reporter.* Sturges's reference to Tolstoy is quoted in Curtis, *Between Flops,* 157.

28. Jahn, "The Aesthetic Theory of Leo Tolstoy's *What Is Art?*" 61. I disagree with Jahn when he writes, "If Tolstoy had written in English he might have employed the term 'expression' and 'impression,' thus establishing a verbal connection similar to that of the Russian" (65). It seems perfectly clear that Tolstoy meant to evoke the involuntary spread and absorption of emotions, which could be benign or malignant, as a viral metaphor.

29. Mounce, *Tolstoy on Aesthetics,* 27.

30. *Redemption* (MGM, 1930, based on *The Living Corpse*); *Resurrection* (Universal, 1931, also made in Spanish as *Resurrección*); *We Live Again* (Goldwyn/United Artists, 1934, based on *Resurrection*); *Anna Karenina* (MGM, 1935).

31. For a roundup of performance theory see Schechner, *Performance Studies.* John T. Caldwell has characterized the viral nature of contemporary film marketing: "Each multimedia platform (the Web site and the DVD with extras) serves as a 'host body' for the studio/network's mutating content, and various forms of industrial reflexivity (behind-the-scenes, making-ofs, bonus tracks, and interactively negotiated production knowledge) serve as the fuel that drives the endless mutation of this content across proprietary host bodies within the conglomerated world. As a form of constant textual renegotiation, onscreen critical analysis (whether from scholars, publicists, show-biz reports, or industrial marketing departments) facilitates the process of repurposing and mutation" (Caldwell, "Welcome to the Viral Future of Cinema [Television]," 94–95).

Note that Tolstoy does not attribute negative qualities to his concept of infection, which he sees as neutral. This is distinct from Philip Brophy's use of the term *infection* to describe the musical establishment's view of folk/popular music as a disease (Brophy, "The Animation of Sound," 97).

32. Tolstoy, *What Is Art?,* 38. This view of an aestheticized space between the artist and the audience resonates later in the writings of Eisenstein, Kuleshov, Stanislavski, and Godard.

33. See Barthes, "The Reality Effect." Barthes argues that it is the extraneous, nonnarrative details of description that make a written scene "real" for the reader.

34. Maltby, *Harmless Entertainment,* 155.

35. The prominent display of the Tanglefoot label is significant. This company had become synonymous with its principal product, Tanglefoot brand flypaper. Although commonly used from the 1880s onward, the use of Tanglefoot to trap insects began to decline in the 1920s, reflecting urbanization, the replacement of horses (and their attendant fly-breeding manure) with motorcars, and higher sanitation standards in the food industry. More convenient products, including spray insecticides such as Flit, had challenged Tanglefoot's business by the mid-1930s (see www.tanglefoot.com/history.htm).

36. Like many great inspirations this one was serendipitous. Originally Sturges had wanted a Chaplin short for the scene, but Charles Chaplin declined to give permission (Diane Jacobs, *Christmas in July: The Life and Art of Preston Sturges,* cited in Moran and Rogin). Paul Wells has noticed a similarity between the use of animated sequences in *Sullivan's Travels* and *The Blackboard Jungle* (MGM, 1955): "Both . . . foreground the animated film as the vehicle by which significant moments of revelation and understanding take place. Both films thus invest the animated film with a specific ability to communicate complex, and sometimes contradictory, ideas within the framework of an apparently accessible, yet taken for granted, form" (Wells, *Understanding Animation,* 6.)

37. Belington, "The New Deal Was a Joke," 17.

38. Jacobs, *Pocketbook Politics,* 128. See also Edsforth, *The New Deal,* 185.

39. Jacobs, *Pocketbook Politics,* 128.

40. The underlying tone of pessimism in this film is even more apparent in *Betty Boop for President* (Fleischer, 1932), when she cynically echoes Hoover's promise of prosperity in fantastic campaign promises. In one scene she becomes a caricature of the president's face.

41. Sito, *Drawing the Line,* 83–84; see also Deneroff, *Popeye the Union Man.*

42. A cinema precedent might have been Jean Renoir's celebrated short film *La petite marchande d'allumettes* (1928). An animated version that preserved the story's original ending was made in 1937: *The Little Match Girl,* directed by Arthur Davis and Sid Marcus, released by Columbia Pictures on Nov. 5, 1937. The starving mouse in the Warner Bros. film is an avatar of the girl's death after the film has ended.

43. Kracauer, "Preston Sturges or Laughter Betrayed," 47.

44. Kracauer, "Cult of Distraction," 93.

45. See Hansen, "Of Mice and Ducks," 54. I follow Hansen's literal translation of the essay's title and the mouse's German name.

46. Benjamin, quoted in Hansen, "Of Mice and Ducks," 30. In the following paragraphs I paraphrase Hansen's argument (pp. 30–33) regarding Benjamin and Adorno.

47. Adorno, "Chaplin in Malibu," 60–61.

48. Tolstoy, *What Is Art?,* 82.

49. See Cohen, *Forbidden Animation;* and Goldmark, *Tunes for 'Toons,* esp. chap. 3, "Jungle Jive: Animation, Jazz Music, and Swing Culture" (77–106).

50. Ferriano, "Did He Write That?" 10.

51. Standifer, "Musical Behaviors of Black People in American Society," 52.

52. Berger, *Redeeming Laughter,* 205.

53. Maltby, *Harmless Entertainment,* 182.

54. Hösle, *Woody Allen,* 84–85.

55. I am adapting the well-known story/plot distinction presented in Bordwell and Thompson, *Film Art,* 71.

5

"We're Happy When We're Sad"

Comedy, Gags, and 1930s Cartoon Narration

Richard Neupert

As this timely volume demonstrates, animated cinema has been undertheorized, particularly in the realm of humor and narrative. Some theorists and critics have concentrated their interest in the American commercial animated cartoon around the binary opposition between loose gag structures and more linear, developed narratives. One of the most extreme positions was taken by Brian Henderson, who dared ask, "Is there such a thing as a cartoon narrative?" He reduces cartoon series such as Tom and Jerry or the Roadrunner to repetitious chains of similar situations and patterns with arbitrary endings patched on. According to Henderson's scenario, the chain of events just stops until the next episode reopens another variation on the same basic plotline, often a chase.[1] However, while classical Hollywood cartoon narratives may abound in visual and audio gags, with a great deal of repetition within formulaic cartoon plots, such as the constant disappointment and humiliation of characters like Elmer Fudd or Wile E. Coyote, the average cartoon follows the norms of classical comedy storytelling. Most American cartoons are built around carefully unified narratives motivated by clearly defined, goal-oriented characters and chronologically arranged actions that lead toward a strong thematic resolution and discursive closure.

Historically, classical Hollywood animated shorts were institutionalized as a marginal product that, along with newsreels, preceded the main feature. In terms of their original distribution and exhibition, cartoons may thus all be considered cinematic attractions in the most fundamental sense of the term. Cartoons functioned as enticing spectacles or presentation acts and, much like live prologues, served as a brief distraction in the tradition of vaudeville routines. They were seemingly free, bonus attractions preceding the featured event. The term *attraction,* of course, is significant in itself. Tom Gunning's exemplary historical concept, the cinema of attractions, has been reworked and exploited by such a wide range of scholars that attractions and their implied radical effects sometimes seem to be everywhere, their functions occasionally far removed from Gunning's original definition.[2] Perhaps because of a strong, lingering tendency in film studies to impose crisp structural oppositions, the term *attraction* is often applied to any cinematic moment thought to call attention to textual processes, thereby derailing a naive narrativity. According to Donald Crafton, for instance, slapstick gags are disruptive and lend incoherence to plots. Their purpose is "to misdirect the viewer's attention, to obfuscate the linearity of cause-effect relations."[3] Other critics delight in isolating interrupting moments as well, which reveal the artifice and impossibility of a unified, naturalized product. For instance, Sylvain du Pasquier states, "The gag, like a parasite, corrupts the plot, and a corollary is that the multiple meanings hidden in normal or realistic discourse are exposed, unmasked, laid bare."[4] As many critics have noted, visual and audio gags may undermine classical narrative conventions, since they are a site of fascination and affect for the audience, but they are often balanced and motivated within coherent plots.[5] We should not evaluate all visual gags in animation as the pure opponent of narrative coherence or ideological unity.

Gags and story development are not as simply opposed as are a cartoon's rabbit and hunter but typically function together to create an efficient narrative. Nonetheless, beyond the specific use of Gunning's term, limited to a particular historical period and early silent cinema mode of production, the distinction between scenes or events that can be labeled "attractions" and the opposing "narrative" elements and structure is hardly a useful concept for evaluating visual gags or humor within comic cartoons. As we will see, some commercial animation retains exhibitionistic traits similar to the early cinema of attractions. However, comic narrative structures dominate most American animated cartoons, while each segment typically advances that central narrative line, ideally in increasingly entertaining, fast-paced farcical scenes. Moreover, by definition comedies end successfully for the protagonists, and the happy ending is a vital component for classical American cartoons, so each clever sequence helps the action, reinforcing the moral qualities and structures of sympathy within the specific film.[6]

There are certainly some commercial cartoons that defy these norms, as we will see, but most comic cartoons do not automatically revert to an earlier era of a cinema of attractions, nor do they escape or overturn classical Hollywood storytelling conventions; they merely condense them, often to the point of parody. For instance, the character with a set goal ("I'm going to shoot a rabbit") may lose every time, as in Elmer Fudd's inept forays against Bugs Bunny. The spectator's pleasure arises in large part from anticipating the clever ways in which Bugs will avoid capture, as the narrative blurs the roles of hunter and prey. Repeated visual gags create rather than challenge narrative unity and purpose. When Bugs repeatedly tricks some unfortunate pursuer into stepping off a cliff in cartoons such as *All This and Rabbit Stew* or *Heckling Hare* (both by Tex Avery, 1941), his strategy is the logical accumulation of escalating methods of proving his own superiority over the hunter. Rather than gags that somehow suspend the narrative, just as the characters are suspended in midair before finally realizing they will fall, these spectacular, if predictable, tactics are the very substance of the narrative situation: after being unable finally to dissuade hunters to give up and leave him alone, Bugs tries ever more drastic measures to remove them from his space.

Analysis of several 1930s cartoons can prove that such visual gags, the building blocks of Hollywood cartoons, function efficiently as micronarrative action codes that reinforce the larger central narrative thrust of these funny little films. In a classical, goal-oriented cartoon built around a central, recurring protagonist, such as *Adventures of Popeye* (1935), for instance, Popeye presents scenes from climactic fights in several of his previous cartoons to inspire a live-action, crying boy to eat spinach and beat up the neighborhood bully. Each of the scenes reveals Popeye overcoming tough situations to clobber assorted foes to save the day and rescue Olive Oyl. Every sequence is constructed around visual gags, many fitting Noël Carroll's "mimed metaphor" category.[7] During a bullfight, for example, Popeye is caught in a wrestling "scissors hold," and the bull transforms temporarily into a pair of scissors. Later, Popeye punches the jungle cats so hard they change into fur coats. Not only does Popeye succeed in each of his fights, but the live-action boy, taking his cue from Popeye's lessons, hits the bully so hard that the tough kid flies through a window. *Adventures of Popeye,* like many classical Hollywood narratives, ends with a double closure device thanks to the violent physical gags involving first Popeye, then his young pupil.

These sorts of character-centered cartoons, whether they feature Popeye, Betty Boop, or Bugs Bunny, provide clear-cut examples of condensed classical Hollywood cinema, with protagonists moving rather predictably toward a secure termination point, resolving yet again their narrative situation, much like a live-action romance or adventure film. A wide spectrum of narrative options exists within classical studio animation, however, with some commercial cartoons indeed avoiding some basic requirements of storytelling altogether. To evaluate the creative relations between humor and narration in animation, I want to concentrate on several cartoons from the mid-1930s, when Hollywood had standardized much about the length and content of the animated portion of the movie theater's daily program. Importantly, the three cartoons analyzed here all lack any spoken dialogue, which keeps them closer to visual slapstick gag traditions than cartoons that depend on clever wordplay. These three films also have no named characters, which distinguishes them further from more formulaic series built around recurring main characters such as Popeye, Mickey, or Bugs. Two of the three cartoons actually feature clusters of nearly identical characters or teams, further reducing the sense of a central "starring" role of a featured, familiar cartoon character with definable, individual traits. Thus, these three sample cartoons would seem to lie closer to the spectacle-attraction end of the spectrum, which is a perfect place to investigate the relations between story and gag.

One key test case for understanding comic animation is *The Sunshine Makers* (Ted Eshbaugh and Burt Gillett, 1935), a rather campy two-color cartoon from Van Beuren Studios, initially released by RKO and then sponsored by Borden Dairies. Less canonical than Disney or Warner cartoons of the 1930s, *The Sunshine Makers* later became a regular on 1950s television, after the sale of RKO's film library. I will analyze this cartoon, about two warring factions of gnomes, alongside the context of two Disney Silly Symphony cartoons of the same era: *Music Land* (1935) and *Funny Little Bunnies* (1934). On first glance *Sunshine Makers* may seem a weak example of classical Hollywood storytelling. Leonard Maltin, for instance, writes that "this curious cartoon tells a paper-thin story."[8] But *The Sunshine Makers* has much to teach us about the humorous narrative structure of short cartoons, especially about the relations between the visual comedy of specific scenes and the overall unity and progression of the story. Unlike cartoons centered on a single protagonist, such as Mickey Mouse trying to stage a band concert in nearly impossible circumstances, or Popeye rescuing Olive from Bluto's advances, *The Sunshine Makers* has no individualized or named characters. Instead, it is built around two communities of "good" vs. "bad" gnomes. This is a cartoon about two different factions and their opposing lifestyles, but unlike the similarly warring kingdoms in the Silly Symphony *Music Land,* there is no single figure representing each group who can help bridge a gap between their feuding ideologies. *The Sunshine Makers* is about two groups locked in combat and the eventual victory of the happy clan over the gloomy clan. Dueling philosophies rather than personal desires drive the narrative.

The film begins just before dawn as several little elflike men, built short like children but sporting adult-styled beards, wake up, leave their tiny homes, and sing "Hail His Majesty the Sun." All these happy gnomes are identical in every way. They quickly go to work in little round buildings on the hilltop where a large magnifying glass gathers the sun's rays, distilling the sunshine down to a white liquid poured into milk bottles. Thus, the conceit is quickly established that milk is a sort of natural product comically collected and bottled by these pleasant little people. (No cows are in evidence, even though Molly Moo-cow is a starring character in other films in this Van Beuren Rainbow Parade series.) The bottles are loaded into little carts pulled by grasshoppers, as more gnomes drive off to deliver the morning milk, singing, "Sunshine, Sunshine . . . it's just the thing to

FIGURE 5.1. *The Sunshine Makers* (Van Beuren, 1935).

keep you feeling fine" (Fig. 5.1). However, in a dark woods bordering this idyllic, apparently all-male community, a gloomy little elf from a neighboring, rival village fires an arrow at a happy milkman, who throws a bottle back at the villain, spilling some pure white light onto his coat. Terrified, the gloomy gnome runs toward his village, which is populated by identical, blue-clad fellows with sharper noses than the happy gnomes, and no beards. Instead of working together cheerfully these gnomes stomp about in unison singing, "We're happy when we're sad." Their village is dark blue, with a sinister black, swampy pond. The stricken gnome with the glowing white spot on his coat races home, but all his neighbors hide from him. This scene, with the gnome burying his bright jacket and clanging the village alarm, calling the others to arms, arrives precisely at the halfway point of this seven-and-a-half minute film.

The second half of the film involves the sad blue gnomes marching against the happy villagers. They spray dark swamp gas as their weapon to counter the purifying milk and its nearly radioactive bright white effects. The happy gnomes joyously mount a well-organized counterattack, using hollow trees as cannons to launch milk, and dragonflies as bombers to drop milk down their chimneys when the gloomy elves run home to hide. *The Sunshine Makers* suddenly becomes a curious mix of a war film and an elaborate snowball fight. The milk bombs' effects prove dramatic, reviving trees in the dark forest and turning a crow into a colorful bird. When one gloomy gnome is hit with milk, he even leaps out of his trench to begin singing "la-la-la" until his comrade sprays him with swamp gas to return him to his usual misery. Seconds later they are both hit with milk and begin to sing and dance, waving flowers in their hands. Immediately, the happy gnomes overwhelm the sad village and drag the grumpy blue elves to their pond, which has been transformed into a colorful, healing fountain of milk. There the sad gnomes, who still protest, "I don't want to be happy," are bathed in the fountain or have milk forcefully poured down their throats until they all cheer up, while their stomachs begin to glow like x-ray light bulbs. They sing, "I want to be happy, I want to be glad." Holding hands, the conquered gnomes dance and sing, "And now the world looks bright and fair, because there's sunshine everywhere," providing tight resolution and narrative closure to conclude the cartoon.

In its short screen time *The Sunshine Makers* establishes a unified diegetic time and space, introduces a stable narrative situation that is disrupted by an opposing force, and then provides a climactic battle, plus a tiny epilogue to prove peace and happiness have now descended on the land. Yet this is a narrative with no spoken dialogue. Visual cues, music, and song provide all the information. Moreover, the characters remain indistinguishable. The two gnomes who initiate the war, the fellow with the arrow and the milkman, quickly mix in with crowds of identical comrades. We can never be sure whether we will see them again. All the man-boys on each side are equivalent, so all share the same desires and fates as everyone in their group. This condensation of characters into clusters of reverse images of one another simplifies further the thematics of an us-vs.-them drama. There are no individual actions to dilute the linear battle narrative. When one happy gnome forcefully pours milk into a sad gnome near the end, it does not matter whether it involves the initial milkman finally settling his score against the mean archer; all happy gnomes are humiliating all sad gnomes in this synecdochic moment. Thus, every element in the story functions efficiently, moving the plot steadily toward a termination effect, in which all story codes are resolved and the narration closes firmly, with a conventional happy ending reinforcing the ideals and goals of the happy, productive, peaceful gnomes over the mean, aggressive grumps, living in their dim blue world.

Interestingly, these opposing camps of happy and sad gnomes recall the "Joys and Glooms" featured during the mid-1910s in the cartoons by Hearst's International Film Service (IFS). During these earlier cartoons, such as *Feet Is Feet: A Phable* (1915), the tiny figures would appear almost as palimpsests at the bottom of the frame to reinforce whether this was a happy or disappointing moment in the larger cartoon looming above them. Gregory La Cava also animated several bizarre cartoons featuring these figures as the main characters, including *The Joys Elope* (1916). Eshbaugh's gnomes follow the same simple contrast, exploiting teams of identical characters who are only happy or sad, never in between. As Maltin's *Of Mice and Men* reveals, the model sheet for the characters in *The Sunshine Makers* even labels the characters Joys and Glooms, with the former only smiling and laughing and the latter frowning and fretting.[9] In the IFS cartoons there was a very clear-cut moral universe and a definite ending when one group or the other always triumphed, firmly establishing the point of each "phable." *The Sunshine Makers*, too, is a fable with a clear message and resolution. This ending concludes not with a romantic union, as does *The Joys Elope*, but rather with a bizarre sort of successful group play-date. A clear-cut lesson results since the work of the happy, industrious gnomes, who cheerfully overwhelm the child-men and get them to rejoice finally at drinking milk, would parallel the goals of concerned parents in the movie theater, who may have also had to convince a resistant child of the value of drinking his or her milk or eating some unpopular food to grow up strong and healthy. Popeye peddles spinach and individualism; *The Sunshine Makers* promotes milk and collective happiness. By the end, the sad gnomes are all aglow with the warm light of the milk, and their true, repressed (and apparently very gay) selves are allowed to come to the surface in a colorful utopian commune. The film has come full circle, resolving what one assumes has been a long history of antagonism between the two neighboring tribes.

While *The Sunshine Makers* has received very limited attention from historians and critics, compared to more mainstream work by Disney, the Fleischers, and Warner Bros. in the 1930s, the few scholars mentioning the cartoon concentrate on its basic narrative line of two opposing camps. Norman M. Klein provides the most symptomatic cultural reading, inserting *The Sunshine Makers* into his Depression-era melodrama category, as yet another cautiously optimistic cartoon about the need to remain vigilant against disruptive elements that might threaten the community: "A village of happy dairy elves, who all look related, like a family, fight the nasty blue grumpies. Every dark grumpy wears the familiar uniform of the evil fiend (again, like theatrical melodrama: the black suit with tails, and the bent top hat). To make the grumpies smile, the effervescently cheerful elves fire happy milk as artillery, or rather as anti-depressants . . . and the grim Depression gets a lift."[10] For Klein this cartoon is something like Van Beuren's answer to *The Three Little Pigs* (1933), which was also directed by Burt Gillett. The gloomy gnomes of *The Sunshine Makers* are a group equivalent to the Big Bad Wolf. Certainly Eshbaugh's tale does provide a "let's work together and conquer the enemy to preserve our way of life" theme. But it also continues that historical thread of Joys vs. Glooms begun in the comic pages and cartoons of the 1910s.

Similarly, Leonard Maltin writes, "There is something disarming about this jaunty fable that has made *Sunshine Makers* a cult classic for many years. Perhaps it's the elemental conflict of good and evil personified in such a simple and unpretentious manner."[11] Perhaps, but its silly, cloying songs and clearly queer, campy aesthetic may also account for some of its lasting cult appeal today, well beyond the Depression, at a time when a simple faith in good always winning out decisively has pretty much left animation stories. *The Sunshine Makers* remains something of an oddity and something of a surprise from the era of the Production Code and studio animation serials. Gender theorists regularly point out the disruptive function that moments of potential homosexual excess may have on a narrative, sometimes rendering "a spectacle to be enjoyed beyond the narrative."[12] Yet in *The Sunshine Makers,* unlike a feature-length classical Hollywood musical, the campy, theatrical moments are not interludes within some larger narrative set of norms. Happy male gnomes living in harmony form the status quo throughout this narrative.

But one may still wonder to what extent the visual gags—the milk bombs, the bugs used as horses, the sunshine transformed into laughing gas—could be said to disrupt the normal flow of narrative. Does this cartoon prove that the average American studio-era cartoon is simply a loose collection of gags that function much like attractions in the early days of silent cinema? Obviously the story, that one group of comical child-men conquers and transforms another group of similar characters, could be told in many ways, without the use of silly songs, dancing routines, or dragonfly bombers. Each of the scenes in the gradual victory of the happy lifestyle over the aggressively sad lifestyle, however, builds increasingly toward the final resolution. Each scene is more than a clever set of visual gags; it is a micronarrative in itself, opening and closing minor story actions while constructing and finally helping complete the major action code of the happy gnomes teaching the sickly gnomes that being cheerful and drinking milk are better than being sad and inhaling swamp gas.

For instance, our first view of a gloomy gnome is when one ambushes the happy milkman, firing an arrow that pins his hat to a tree. This violent incident provides a cardinal story point, when the happy gnome must decide whether to flee or fight. He replies with the tossed bottle of milk that drives the gloomy gnome back to his village. The visual gag of the disruptive, mean gnome being marked by a glaring white spotlight from the milk is not an isolated comic event. Rather, it is the first sign proving the strong effect milk will have as a powerful weapon over darkness. This confrontation also shows that the nice little gnomes are not passive patsies; rather, they revel in a good fight. While the stricken gnome runs back to the others, the film cuts to the oblivious blue group chanting their tune, "We're happy when we're sad." This slow musical dirge establishes their characters and motivations, thus providing indices informing us of their personalities, setting, and behavior—they are the reverse of the happy gnomes in every way. Next, when the glowing gnome arrives, everyone hides, revealing their lack of a helpful sense of community. The ringing of the gong finally allows the next cardinal story point, when the group grudgingly decides to fight the happy gnomes. Everything here functions for the narrative, and each textual action determines the next scene, paving the way for closure.

Similarly, when the milk cannon hits two dark blue gnomes in their trench, first changing one temporarily and finally transforming them both into a happy, musical male couple, the action moves the entire narrative forward, proving the happy gnomes are gaining ground and that the enemy might actually welcome defeat. The little grumps seem to enjoy being made happy and gay. This sequence, like every scene of the battle, prepares the audience for the final termination point, when all the sad gnomes are happily singing among themselves in their newly restored village square. Interestingly, the magical transformation of the stricken blue countryside into a healthy forest with blooming trees and singing birds also anticipates the comical change in the drought-stricken fields of *Porky the Rain-Maker* (1936), another Depression-themed cartoon. There, Porky's magic pills bring rain to the parched crops, and wilted trees suddenly sprout leaves and fruit. Like many classical Hollywood live-action narratives, *The Sunshine Makers* follows generic and industrial norms, progressing consistently toward a conclusive termination point, with a firmly resolved story and discursive closure devices, despite its lack of a central, goal-oriented protagonist. While *The Sunshine Makers* was produced by the relatively minor Van Beuren, analysis of two Silly Symphonies from Disney, *Music Land* and *Funny Little Bunnies*, will expand our understanding of common cartoon narrative structures and the functions of gags within individual scenes.

In a manner parallel to *The Sunshine Makers, Music Land* quickly establishes two rival camps, here two neighboring island kingdoms, introduced on a map as the Land of Symphony and the Isle of Jazz, separated by the Sea of Discord. The cartoon is as much about competing musical traditions as it is about color contrasts. As Daniel Goldmark has shown, classical music is featured in many studio cartoons, for a wide variety of purposes, often including satire. Some cartoons, such as Chuck Jones's *Long-Haired Hare* (1949), participate in this "struggle between popular music, which was growing ever more popular, and classical music, clinging to its elevated position in the cultural hierarchy." Goldmark also cites *Music Land* as another title in this tradition.[13] The Land of Symphony, a soothing place of waltz music and pastel colors, stands in sharp contrast to the raucous, boldly colored Isle of Jazz. In the former the queen (a viola or cello) slumbers comfortably on her throne, while the daughter (a violin), bored, sneaks away. In the jazz kingdom the king (a saxophone) drums on his metallic body, accompanied by topless, exotic violins hopping and dancing about as if they were showgirls modeled on Josephine Baker. His son (a smaller sax) is also bored. He sneaks away to look across the sea at his apparent girlfriend, the classical music princess. In *Music Land* the prince and princess, who dare to cross the musical and spatial barriers between them, become the protagonists; their families and kingdoms initially remain narrow-minded, content with their own kind, a bit like the opposed gnomes of *The Sunshine Makers*. In cartoon shorthand the prince and princess function as the Romeo and Juliet of this comedy. Norman

Klein dismisses "the small, dramatic plot" as a single gag on "the world is music" building toward an ending.[14] Yet, *Music Land*'s narrative is an efficient miniclassical movie, driven by the two central characters' heterosexual desire (if cartoon characters based on musical instruments can be said to "have" gender). Its central characters also distinguish it from the group dynamics of *The Sunshine Makers*.

The first cardinal story point of *Music Land* occurs when the young prince decides secretly to row over to the Land of Symphony (using a music note as his paddle). The landscapes on both islands offer visual gags everywhere. The fruits on the trees are blue notes, tree trunks are shaped like upright basses, and benches are music phrases. In terms of the audio, the characters emote via musical notes and squawks rather than words. It is a playful cartoon with music dominating every aspect of the visual and audio style. Once the classical queen discovers her daughter running about happily in the garden with the jazz prince, the narrative takes a new turn. Amid the garden games, the prince accidentally kisses the queen, so he is locked up in a prison cell that is also a large ticking metronome, to reinforce the boredom of "doing time." Just past the cartoon's halfway point, the prince sends for help via a musical score delivered by a bird. The score interferes with the king's attempt to kiss one of the dancing violins, developing further the motif of unauthorized kisses. The king quickly calls for an attack on the Land of Symphony, conducting an array of horns, positioned like the big guns on a battleship. They send forth a barrage of red notes that explode against the other island, where the queen then responds with huge organ pipes firing their own musical blasts. The jazz island attacks with rousing swing music, Harline's "The Saxes Have It," while the classical pipes belt out Wagner's "Ride of the Valkyries."

The warring music, with vibrantly exploding musical notes exploiting fully the three-color Technicolor process, takes a toll on both kingdoms. Desperate to stop the folly, the princess climbs into a music-case boat to float out into the sea, wave a white flag, and try to disrupt the battle. The prince, seeing her in danger, escapes from his shelled prison and meets her in the sea just as she begins to sink. Exploding notes rain down on them, as they are nearly killed by "friendly fire" from their own families. Eventually, both parents race to help their children in danger (Fig. 5.2). The parents meet and flirt, leading quickly to a double marriage between children and parents alike. The children have taught the parents a valuable lesson, as is proven by the jazzy version of the Wedding March that accompanies the ceremony, along with the Bridge of Harmony, seen in the final shots, connecting the two worlds. This ending fits easily within American musical genre traditions, as outlined by Rick Altman. "Just as romantic problems are considered definitively solved once they result in marriage, so the resolution of the musical's thematic dichotomies is presented as permanently efficacious."[15] As in many Fred Astaire–Ginger Rogers musicals, two traditions merge happily, and *Music Land* actually concludes with three unions: the children, the parents, and the music.

FIGURE 5.2. *Music Land* (Disney, 1935).

Beyond serving as a sort of happy parable for how opposites and also generations can productively bridge differences, *Music Land* is an instructive example
in Disney story construction. As I have noted, major events arrive at distinct temporal intervals. This nine-and-one-half-minute cartoon is carefully plotted out
temporally like a musical composition. The first two minutes establish sequentially the two perfectly opposed families (the elegant queen slumbers while the
less responsible jazz king parties). At two minutes the two worlds begin to have
a functional connection when the son peers through a clarinet telescope to see
the object of his desire, the classical princess, waving her handkerchief, signaling him it is safe to visit. Her sleeping mother is apparently already opposed to
this union. The following one-and-a-half-minute scene includes the young saxophone's journey and the young couple's carefree romp in her garden. While never
particularly funny, the tale relies on standard, even cliché, comic gags of court-
ship, including the boy chasing the girl around objects as she pretends to resist
his advances, and the boy leaping out to kiss her, only to grab her stern mother
instead. Much of the action, including the forbidden love theme and competing
genres of music, is fairly typical of 1930s live-action musical romantic comedies.
The next ninety seconds deal with the boy's imprisonment and the birds' delivery
of the note that will begin the war. Major story points arrive roughly every ninety
seconds, breaking the film into seven basic scenes: two introductions to the musical families, the flirtation, the queen's punishment of the prince, the beginning
of the battle, the daughter's attempt to stop the battle complete with her rescue,
and the meeting of the parents, which leads immediately to the double marriage.

Thus the use of visual gags in Disney, including the comically sputtering baritone as an outboard motor on the Jazz King's music-case boat or the nervous grooms whose sweat resembles overflowing spit valves, are integral portions of the characterization and action. There is even tighter unity here than in *The Sunshine Makers,* with more repetition. For instance, the princess waves two white pieces of cloth, the handkerchief to signal flirtation, then the white flag to stop the fighting, and the prison metronome returns later to set the tempo for the rowers in the queen's rescue boat. Even the mechanical bluebirds of happiness that fly around the young couple early on will later be essential for delivering the son's "note" of imprisonment. Isolating a gag in contrast to a story element is indeed a fruitless task. Everything functions here to deliver story information in a clear and cute format.

Disney Studios, which hoped to impress the audience with the superior quality of their animation, always strove to create a certain degree of marvelous spectacle and product differentiation to amaze audiences. Spectators should notice the expensive, lush details, such as the prince and princess reflected in her swimming pool, and the cleverness of the prince's xylophone boat, but also the rich color oppositions between the two musical groups and obvious musical refrains used to reinforce the action while signaling the creativity of the soundtrack. The final product shows itself off as a very carefully crafted piece of entertainment. There are also tiny sound-to-image gags that call attention to the materials of animation, such as when the young saxophone prince extends his clarinet into a telescope and simultaneously on the soundtrack a rising musical scale is played by a clarinet, which then reverses itself back down the scale when the prince folds it back up. This is a perfect example of what became known as "mickey-mousing" a soundtrack, providing an immediate sound effect for the visuals. No detail seems too small for the animation team's attention, from the music note roof supports to the purple treble clef vines on the trees. *Music Land* provides another clear example of the value of analyzing cartoons as efficient narratives, much like short stories, rather than as disruptive strings of visual or sound gags.

However, not all 1930s American studio animation can be said to function as such tight examples of classical Hollywood storytelling. One of the refreshing strengths of recent animation histories has been the real strides taken to escape the simplistic tendency to lump all American cartoons together or assume that all Disney, Fleischer, or Warner Bros. cartoons pretty much followed that specific studio's cookie-cutter approach to storytelling. A great deal of variety inheres from cartoon to cartoon, even within the most highly organized and capitalized studios. One cartoon that does allow us to make productive connections between tendencies in Gunning's cinema of attractions and American cartoons is Disney's Silly Symphony *Funny Little Bunnies.* It is important to acknowledge that Disney's output was hardly limited to little "lesson" narratives that taught how to live in a productive community, or how children have something to teach their parents. Not all Disney cartoons were as efficient or closed as *Music Land*. *Funny Little Bunnies* is an important reminder of another prevalent sort of animation during this supposedly consistent epoch of American animation. *Funny Little Bunnies* is a pertinent test case of a cartoon that seems to defy many narrative expectations from Disney cartoons, yet it was recognized at the time as a highly successful Silly Symphony, even winning the best animation prize at the 1934 Venice Film Festival.

Much like *The Sunshine Makers*, *Funny Little Bunnies* has no single central protagonist. However, beyond its lack of a reckless Betty Boop or an adventurous Mickey Mouse, much less a slugging Popeye, or bumbling Elmer Fudd, *Funny Little Bunnies* even lacks a central narrative. Instead of establishing a unified story line, this cartoon provides a series of creative, nearly random scenes of bunnies preparing candy. The cartoon offers a glimpse into a day in the life of this magic land. Disney Studios makes no attempt to develop a linear and compelling *Three Little Pigs*–style narrative during the song. Rather, Disney produces a seasonal product with all the narrative unity of a set of Easter displays in the windows of a Macy's department store. The cartoon was released initially in late March 1934, not long before the Easter holiday. There is a unity of purpose, showing representative scenes of candy being made, but no temporal or spatial organization, and no motivating cause and effect, nor any real conclusion. Several baskets of colored eggs and candy are compiled, and the cartoon ends. There is no urgent push to meet some production deadline for Easter morning and no single organizing Easter Bunny character. The only sort of textual motivation in this cartoon is between the pace of the rabbits' actions and the tempo of the musical accompaniment.

Funny Little Bunnies is built out of twelve scenes that respond only loosely to the lyrics of the Silly Symphony song "See the Funny Little Bunnies," by Frank Churchill and Leigh Harline. The song and ensuing action clearly establish the film as an exhibitionistic attraction, repeatedly inviting the audience to do nothing more than look. The cartoon begins with the song explaining that storybooks say that far, far away there is a land where the bunnies work all year through to make Easter eggs. However, the song delivers very little information that is directly tied to what we see; most scenes are merely accompanied by humming women or instrumental music with sound effects rather than lyrics that dictate or explain the specific actions we see. It never includes words such as "and next they must boil eggs before they can color them." In the opening scene two white rabbits look toward the audience, apparently waiting for the camera, and viewers, to follow them down a secret path to their magical land, and from that point on we are privy to a set of scenes of candy being prepared by what seem to be a number of different teams. These initial rabbit guides are hardly the equivalent of Jiminy Cricket narrating *Pinocchio* to us. The host rabbits quickly disappear.

The basic organization of the scenes is apparently chronological, with the first sequence inside the magic land revealing numerous rabbits gathering their materials at a sort of stockpile of sugar, flavors, and the pile of chocolate bars that are moved about with a crane, as if they were steel girders. From this point on, various stages of candy preparation are shown, beginning with the melting of the chocolate; then different rabbits pour chocolate into molds to shape it into eggs. Chocolate eggs are decorated in a variety of ways in other scenes, and some chunks of chocolate are carved by sculptors into chocolate rabbits. Chickens also lay eggs in time to the music. Eggs are then boiled and decorated before the final scene, in which candy is assembled into baskets and rabbits whisk it off, as the Easter song concludes.

The overall structure of scenes, many of which seem vaguely sequential in the process of candy production, conforms more to the norms of a categorical documentary organized as a series of descriptive scenes than a cause-effect narrative. One synopsis of the cartoon concisely notes that the film is "a tour of a meadow filled with rabbits readying their wares for Easter."[16] Each scene in this tour is chronologically unified (for instance, eggs roll down a ramp into a pot of boiling water, where a rabbit tests each to see whether it is fully cooked before passing it along), but then the plot shifts to several scenes in which other rabbits decorate eggs. And, there is no reason the boiling scene has to arrive before or after the scene showing how chocolate rabbits are sculpted. Thus, the entire film is a collection of attractions; the scenes are all a series of gags revealing various unorthodox ways that candy can be prepared in this magical land. In one of its more famous scenes, praised repeatedly by the Technicolor Corporation's president Herbert Kalmus, rabbits harvest colors from a rainbow that drips paint into their buckets.[17] In another, various patterns are hand-painted onto eggs by a shaky elderly rabbit, and two cross-eyed rabbits unwittingly paint each other's eggs. Blind bunnies weave baskets. Moreover, "butt gags" abound, topped by one rabbit who sits in a bucket of red dye then backs into the waiting eggs to stamp a bright red heart-shape on each (Fig. 5.3). Eggs are also blasted with frosting by firing squads shooting from pastry clothlike guns, and other rabbits mix polka-dot and striped dyes that magically retain their pattern when stirred and brushed on.

Every detail in *Funny Little Bunnies* is carefully crafted in tempo with the musical beat and designed to amuse audiences with the fanciful tactics of candy preparation. Moreover, there is constant movement in the frame, with smooth, elegant virtual camera movement, along with flawless continuity editing in this Disney cartoon, further increasing the fascination factor for children seeing all this huge, colorful candy made in a lush, fanciful setting in time with a silly musical accompaniment. As in *The Sunshine Makers*, food here becomes spectacle. It is also worth noting that during the 1930s most American families would make their own dyed eggs and candy; store-bought treats would have been a luxury. Easter baskets, like May Day baskets, might be homemade as well, so the audi-

FIGURE 5.3. *Funny Little Bunnies* (Disney, 1934).

ence could certainly relate to these kitchen tasks, performed marvelously here in three-color Technicolor. The visual and audio gags generate a set of spectacular effects, even without a cause-effect story. Not all Disney cartoons during the 1930s told efficient narratives or built ineluctably toward a resolving moral message.

I have argued that *The Sunshine Makers,* despite its lack of clearly defined, individualized characters, or protagonists, helps us understand how typical cartoon story structures manipulate and concentrate story construction to maximize the narrative drive toward a solid termination effect, complete with story resolution and narrative closure. *The Sunshine Makers,* with its clever transformations, functional binary oppositions, and surreal humor, allows us to witness the production of narrative clarity that is so essential to classical Hollywood cartoon storytelling. What some might label the visual, comic gags, such as a gloomy gnome being turned into a happy singing gnome by a blast of bright, white milk, only to be returned to his grim state by swamp gas, cannot be considered an interruption in a narrative. Every scene of a cartoon can be filled with clever physical and audio elements that are the story components, its indices, informants, and characters. Whether such cartoons are indeed perceived universally as "funny" is another matter, but comic story structures allow for one set of values to triumph for the apparent improvement of every life in this diegetic world. The termination effect reinforces the condensed narrative's thematic unity and delivers the formulaic, inscribed happy ending that has been lurking beneath the story outline since the opening scenes. That *The Sunshine Makers* leads to a happy union with two all-male groups dancing hand-in-hand may be unusual among 1930s Hollywood cartoons, but this resolution is textually and generically motivated.

A cartoon such as *Music Land* possesses an equally rhetorical, moral-centered, narrative in which compromise between the two factions wins the day, rather than a pure physical victory of one team over another. This Silly Symphony, with its final "Bridge of Harmony," depends on the narrative systems that establish early on the beauty and vibrancy in each of the two opposing musical camps. The final synthesis of classical and popular music is further joined by the double marriages, with a tight generic resolution right out of musical comedy traditions. By contrast, *Funny Little Bunnies* lacks the classical story structure of these two tales with binary enemies. There is no establishing scene to set up any motives for all the labor we see. There seems to be a general need for candy, but unlike so many Christmas cartoons in which Santa is behind schedule and the workshop has to get his sleigh filled by midnight, *Funny Little Bunnies* provides no clear diegetic drama or deadline. This cartoon functions instead as a sort of large descriptive syntagma, presenting example after example of clever, cute instances of candy being manufactured by a smiling cadre of rabbits. Whether painting eggs is their hobby or job is never established; rather, like the thieves in *The Great Train Robbery* (Porter, 1903), who seem to rob various people simply because that is what thieves do, these rabbits and their colorful tactics are placed on display by Disney and Technicolor for our amusement, nothing more.

NOTES

1. Henderson, "Cartoon and Narrative in the Films of Frank Tashlin and Preston Sturges," 155–56.

2. See Gunning, "The Cinema of Attractions"; and Gunning, "Attractions."

3. Crafton, "Pie and Chase," 363 (Strauven edn.). Among more extreme uses of *attractions* see Vincendeau, *Jean-Pierre Melville,* in which Vincendeau considers *Le cercle rouge* an example of the cinema of attractions.

4. Du Pasquier, "Buster Keaton's Gags," 276.

5. See, e.g., King, *Film Comedy,* 27, 31; and Jenkins, *What Made Pistachio Nuts?* 102.

6. For more on sympathy and identification see Smith, *Engaging Characters.*

7. See Carroll, "Notes on the Sight Gag," 30–31.

8. Maltin, *Of Mice and Magic,* 205.

9. Ibid.

10. Klein, *Seven Minutes,* 133.

11. Maltin, *Of Mice and Magic,* 206.

12. Tinkcom, "'Working like a Homosexual,'" 124. For an insightful discussion of "camp" see Dyer, "Judy Garland and Camp," 107.

13. Goldmark, *Tunes for 'Toons,* 115.

14. Klein, *Seven Minutes,* 115.

15. Altman, *The American Film Musical,* 51.

16. Merritt and Kaufman, *Walt Disney's Silly Symphonies,* 143.

17. See Neupert, "Painting a Plausible World," 107–8.

6

Laughter by Numbers

The Science of Comedy
at the Walt Disney Studio

Susan Ohmer

Most of us treasure cartoons for their ability to defy what is considered normal behavior. Roadrunners beep beep, rabbits sing opera, and ducks travel to Mars. Even animated films that don't center on recognizable characters may play with spatial and temporal logic in ways that challenge our usual patterns of thought. Though many cartoons seem to live by their own rules, the ones produced in Hollywood during the studio era circulated within a system that expected the pleasure they produced to yield concrete profits. Whether they operated as independents, like the Fleischers and Disney, or functioned as the offbeat wing of a studio, such as Warner Bros. Termite Terrace, cartoon producers were expected to turn out films on a regular basis to fill exhibition calendars and attract audiences. Producing laughter on schedule and for profit, that was the challenge.

This paradox was especially acute at the Walt Disney Studio during the 1940s because of changes in the company's approach to animation and in the social and economic environment in which it operated. In the 1920s and 1930s Disney built its reputation by producing cartoon shorts that were both a critical and box-office success. The studio won every Academy Award for cartoon shorts between 1932 and 1939, and its characters Mickey Mouse, Donald Duck, and Pluto became iconic figures in popular culture around the world. Inspired by this success and by a desire to improve both its finances and standing within the industry, Disney released its first feature-length cartoon, *Snow White and the Seven Dwarfs,* in December 1937. *Snow White*'s enormous box-office success spurred the company to launch an ambitious program of feature-film production and to expand both its facilities and its budget to accommodate that growth. In 1940 the company opened a new production facility in Burbank that emulated Fordist principles in its efforts to streamline cartoon production. In December 1941, when the United States joined the war against Germany and Japan, Disney placed its resources and talent at the government's disposal, producing films to support war bond drives and the Good Neighbor program in Latin America. These films, and some of the features Disney released during the war, such as *The Three Caballeros* (1945), combined animation and live action, exploring the shifting boundaries between these realms. Thus, by the mid-1940s the animated shorts on which the studio had built its reputation occupied only a small part of a broader media program, and Walt Disney and others began to question what role they should play in the studio's future plans.

Disney's experiences in Hollywood and in Washington during World War II increased its interactions with people and organizations outside of the film industry. During one of his visits to Washington, Walt Disney met George Gallup, the political pollster, and his then assistant, David Ogilvy, who later founded the advertising agency Ogilvy and Mather. Gallup had built on his success in presidential polling to launch a new firm, the Audience Research Institute (ARI), which was designed to carry out studies of public opinion toward films, film stars, and film projects. The ARI had already begun to conduct studies for RKO, Disney's distributor, and Ogilvy tried to recruit Disney as a client as well. The ARI's early surveys on Disney films in 1940 and 1941 served RKO's interests more than Disney's, but in the postwar period the cartoon producer began to use the ARI for its own purposes. In the late 1940s, when Disney began to rethink its approach to animation, the studio used the ARI's services to study every short cartoon it produced, from early story conferences through previews of rough and color reels. At first the ARI used the same procedures it had employed at other studios, but over time the firm adapted its methods to suit the unique requirements of the Disney studio. By 1950 its brand of research had become such an integral part of life at Disney that the studio described its production research as "doing an ARI."

THE INDEPENDENT AND THE MAJOR

Disney's first experiences with audience research occurred within the framework of its relationship with its distributor, RKO Radio Pictures. Like other cartoon producers during the studio era, Disney relied on a major studio to help finance and distribute its films. In March 1936, as Disney was ramping up production on *Snow White*, the company signed a distribution agreement with RKO that provided an advance against negative costs, which would reduce the amount of operating capital Disney needed and provide access to the major's chain of first-run theaters.[1] For RKO the alliance with Disney promised to enhance its prestige within the industry and give it access to popular and more profitable films.[2]

During the 1930s RKO secured many releases by making deals with independent producers for one or two pictures, a strategy that minimized its fixed costs while guaranteeing a steady supply of films. Its 1936 contract with Disney represented one of these agreements. Though it appeared that this relationship would be of mutual benefit to both Disney and RKO, the balance of power between the two companies shifted dramatically over the next few years, and these shifts influenced Disney's use and perceptions of the ARI's research.

Though the initial agreement between the two companies promised to benefit both, the release of *Snow White and the Seven Dwarfs* in December 1937 strengthened Disney's power in the relationship. *Snow White* became the highest grossing film in American history; eight hundred thousand people saw the film at Radio City Music Hall, RKO's flagship theater.[3] Though Disney's distribution contract with RKO did not expire until spring 1939, the two companies began discussing the terms of renewal immediately and announced their agreement at RKO's annual sales meeting in June 1939.[4] The contract represented the zenith of Disney's power in relation to its distributor. Beginning in 1940, control in the relationship began to shift toward RKO.

During these contract negotiations, Disney announced an ambitious expansion program. Inspired by *Snow White*'s success, the studio decided to put four more features into production and to increase its release schedule from one feature every two years to between two and four features each year. Disney had tripled its staff to complete *Snow White* and estimated that it would need several hundred more employees to produce these additional films. To provide enough space for all this activity, Disney built a new studio in Burbank, at a cost of nearly $2 million.[5] *Snow White*'s profits and Disney's merchandising revenues paid many of these expenses, but Disney still needed the financing and distribution that RKO provided to ensure its cash flow.

Disney, however, did not always meet the terms set out in its contract. In an interview from this period Walt Disney admitted, "We never work on a schedule. In that way if we don't like something we can keep working on it until we do like it."[6] The high standards that had garnered so much acclaim conflicted with the demands of a release schedule. By May 1940, one year into its contract, Disney had completed only half the number of shorts specified for that season.[7] RKO's income from short films that year fell $300,000, and executives blamed the drop on Disney.[8]

Disney's feature films also fell behind schedule. Though it had put four features into production, it couldn't guarantee a firm release schedule. When *Pinocchio* was released in early 1940, a few months behind schedule, RKO hoped the film would provide the same hefty profits as *Snow White*.[9] Though RKO marketed *Pinocchio* as if it were the equal of *Snow White*, Disney's second feature failed to match the box-office gross of its first, primarily because of the turmoil in

European markets. Disney earned $2 million in Europe from *Snow White* but realized only one-tenth that amount for *Pinocchio*.[10]

Though *Pinocchio* failed at the box office, it fit within the narrative conventions, visual style, and character types that audiences had come to expect from the Disney studio. Like Snow White, Pinocchio displayed a childlike innocence and was able to survive frightening circumstances before emerging with new wisdom. Visually, *Pinocchio* built on and extended the trend toward naturalistically drawn figures and environments that characterized *Snow White*, with several bravura sequences that highlighted the multiplane camera and the possibilities of Technicolor. *Pinocchio* focuses on a youthful character that endures trials and tribulations with the help of his mentors, an angel and a cricket. Disney's next film, however, did not offer this point of identification. *Fantasia*'s episodic structure and sparing use of marketable characters posed a challenge to Disney's distributor, who called in the ARI to gauge the film's potential market.

PENETRATION AND WANT-TO-SEE

Unlike *Snow White* or *Pinocchio*, *Fantasia* was not based on a classic tale in children's literature and employed a popular Disney character in only one sequence. *Fantasia* also broke with the established Disney tradition of strongly plotted, character-centered narratives to present a series of imagistic sequences that creatively linked images with music. Though several sequences create mininarratives, they are not linked by any overarching structure; instead, as Moya Luckett has noted, the film is driven more by musical contrasts and changes of tone and design.[11] In addition to its unusual visual and narrative form, *Fantasia* also represented an innovation in sound design. The "Fantasound" system invented for the film was one of the first multichannel systems in which the music track was recorded with multiple microphones from within the orchestra and then channeled into four tracks. Each track was then sent through multiple speakers in a theater so that sound appeared to be coming from different directions within the auditorium. The system required special sound and projection equipment, and a theater that screened *Fantasia* had to be shut for one week before opening and one week after to assemble and take apart the equipment, which weighed eight and a half tons and required the services of a supervising engineer.[12] Rather than negotiate these arrangements through RKO, Disney decided to distribute *Fantasia*.[13] Unfortunately, *Fantasia* did not earn enough in its first engagements to cover its budget, and RKO took over distribution of the film in May 1941. RKO then decided to jettison the special sound equipment and compress the multiple channels of sound onto standard 35mm film.[14] Since RKO had become financially responsible for the film, it wanted to know what people thought about the project and commissioned the ARI to carry out some research.

As part of its contract with the ARI, RKO received a monthly "Index of Publicity Penetration" during this period. "Publicity penetration" was designed to learn what percentage of the filmgoing public had been "penetrated" or reached by a film's advertising and publicity campaign. Whether audiences knew about a film depended on many factors, such as the fame of its cast, public interest in a particular story, and the amount of money and length of time the studio spent on promotion. Penetration studies, the ARI asserted, allowed a studio to judge the success of marketing campaigns. Once the ARI determined whether people knew about a film, the company asked whether they were interested in seeing it, and came up with a "want-to-see" score. The ARI developed a formula that used both these numbers to come up with a general estimate of a film's box-office return.[15]

The ARI included *Fantasia* in its indexes for the week of July 26, 1941, and found very high penetration or public awareness for the film. The findings indicated that Disney's efforts to market the film and the press coverage of its technological innovations had succeeded in reaching audiences. Unfortunately, the ARI also found that only 63 percent of the people who knew about *Fantasia* wanted to see it. A follow-up survey on August 12 found that, of those who had seen the film, 48 percent enjoyed it less than they had expected. The public knew about *Fantasia,* but they weren't motivated to see it, and many of those who had seen it did not find the experience pleasurable.[16]

RKO's misgivings about Disney's choice of subjects were reinforced by the ARI's surveys regarding *The Reluctant Dragon.* The film was the first Disney feature to combine live action and animated sequences and, like *Fantasia,* departed from the fully animated, character-driven examples of *Snow White* and *Pinocchio.* The plot features the comedian Robert Benchley making a visit to the new Burbank facility, where he tries to persuade Walt Disney to make a film about the book he is reading, *The Reluctant Dragon.* Before meeting Disney, Benchley wanders through different parts of the studio and observes various stages of the production process. As Benchley learns about the steps needed to create cartoons, we see several Disney shorts and get previews of upcoming releases, including *Bambi* and *Dumbo.* Though Disney marketed the film as its new feature, critics derided its infomercial quality and complained that it was merely a "super de luxe commercial."[17]

In April 1941 the head of RKO's sales department requested that the ARI include *The Reluctant Dragon* in its next penetration report. He also asked if the research firm could determine what percentage of the public knew the film was a feature and not a short.[18] The ARI included the film in its penetration studies beginning the week of June 14, 1941, a week after its premiere, and continued to measure public reactions to it for seven more reports, through July 26. The surveys confirmed RKO's fears, as the ARI found that even as the film was making its debut, its publicity penetration was nine points below average. Only 34 percent of those surveyed knew that *The Reluctant Dragon* was a feature.[19] Among those who knew something about it, *The Reluctant Dragon*'s want-to-see was 4 to 5 percent below average and declined even further after the film opened. As with *Fantasia,* even when people did go to see the film, they were not enthusiastic.[20]

These low numbers triggered a war of blame between Disney and RKO. Under its distribution agreement with RKO, Disney was responsible for the cost of advertising its films in trade papers and magazines.[21] The ARI argued that Disney should have started its promotional campaign for the film sooner, and RKO accused the studio of deliberately holding back so as not to undermine the success of *Fantasia.*[22] Disney changed the release date for *The Reluctant Dragon* several times and did not settle on a final location for the film's premiere until ten days before the opening, which did not allow much time for promotion.[23] One reason Disney did not heavily advertise the film is that it presented a happy-go-lucky view of the studio at a time when most of its staff was on strike. The walkout resulted partly from jurisdictional disputes among the unions that were competing to organize the Hollywood animation studios and from employees' complaints about conditions in the new studio. The strike began in late May 1941 and lasted until the end of July, the time period covered in the ARI's studies. Trade papers carried reports of the dispute in nearly every issue that summer, and in Los Angeles and New York protestors picketed the theaters where the film screened.[24]

As the ARI saw it, audiences wanted to see the kinds of Disney characters and stories with which they were already familiar and were not excited about the innovative forms and subjects the studio was presenting. The validity of the ARI's beliefs was borne out by the success of *Dumbo,* released in October 1941.[25] The critics and the public praised the film as "a return to Disney first principles," with *Newsweek* noting that "Disney is back again where he is at his best."[26] The ARI tracked *Dumbo*'s publicity penetration from the film's opening week through November 8, 1941, and found that the film enjoyed a steady increase in public awareness matched by a strong desire to see it.[27] By returning to its roots, the ARI argued, Disney could continue to please audiences.

During the early 1940s RKO subjected all of Disney's features to the scrutiny of publicity penetration studies. The extra attention Disney received underscores the company's importance to RKO at a time when RKO needed to release quality films to return to profitability. In RKO's view the ARI's research proved that the public did not like the innovations in sound and design that Disney introduced at this time. The cartoon producer should return to his roots and create the trademark films for which he was known. Yet even Gallup admitted that the research might not be able to convey the full complexity of the public's responses to animated films. And Disney could not be blamed for losses caused by the war in Europe. In RKO's hands this research hampered the artistic innovations

Disney was struggling to achieve. When Disney met Gallup on other projects, however, he saw another side to this work and realized that the ARI could help him achieve his goals.

NEW DIRECTIONS

Along with David Selznick, Walter Wanger, and others, Walt Disney belonged to the Society for Independent Motion Picture Producers (SIMPP), an organization formed in 1941 to campaign for legal and economic conditions that would foster creative and innovative filmmaking.[28] The organization took shape at the same time that Selznick was beginning to work with Gallup, and he spoke often to his colleagues about the ARI.[29] Disney also met Gallup himself through his war work in Washington. These experiences led Disney to conclude that, despite his experiences at RKO, the ARI's work could be useful to him.

Disney first met George Gallup in Washington, D.C., in January 1942, when Gallup was conducting studies for the government. The Treasury Department asked Disney to make a film explaining the new laws that would require many Americans to pay taxes for the first time. *The New Spirit* aimed to reach certain economic groups, particularly lower-income and lower-middle-income citizens, who were expected to resist this financial demand.[30] Gallup offered to provide Disney with a demographic study of the film's viewers in order to evaluate its impact.[31] Gallup's assistant, David Ogilvy, also attended the meeting in Washington and took the opportunity to suggest that the ARI might be able to help Disney choose the subject for his next feature film.[32]

Though Walt Disney declined Ogilvy's suggestion, thinking that it might be a while before he made another feature, the ARI went ahead with this idea on its own. In June 1942 Gallup conducted a nationwide poll that presented five titles and asked respondents which they would most like to see as a Disney cartoon. The choices were "Alice in Wonderland," "Peter Pan," "Peter Rabbit," "Uncle Remus," and "Bambi." Disney had already announced plans to film some of these works, but including "Peter Rabbit" was probably the ARI's idea. The survey found "Alice" the favorite by far, with 48 percent of the vote, but "Bambi," which was actually in production, finished next to last, at only 11 percent. Only 24 percent of the public even knew it was in production. At first Ogilvy was afraid to tell Disney this news and asked Selznick to break it to him.[33] The findings did not stop production on *Bambi,* however, and seem to have spurred Disney to think about how he might use the ARI's services in other ways. In September 1942 Disney commissioned the ARI to provide a detailed analysis of the potential audience for his next project, an animated version of Alexander de Seversky's best-selling treatise *Victory through Air Power.* Seversky, a Russian pilot who emigrated to the United States after World War I and had become a leading expert on air warfare, published the book in spring 1942 to promote his idea that the United States needed to upgrade its aviation program. Gallup estimated that 20 million people had heard of Seversky and that 5 million had either read his book or the *Reader's Digest* condensation of it. The ARI noted that the film was strongest among men and boys but drew a great deal of interest generally. Gallup encouraged Disney to make the film but warned that the public's appetite for war films was diminishing.[34] Released in 1943, the film grossed only a little more than it cost to make.[35]

The Disney studio committed nearly all of its resources during the early 1940s to government work, producing training films and films designed to promote "good neighbor" relations with Latin America. In 1943, though, Walt Disney apparently began to consider what other directions the studio might take after the war. During this period he asked the ARI to carry out several studies that gauged public reactions to a range of the studio's films and characters. In a survey carried out on August 11, 1943, for example, the ARI asked a representative sample of Americans which Walt Disney character they liked best. Donald Duck won by a landslide at 64 percent, followed by Thumper with 51 percent, and Bambi with 47 percent. Mickey Mouse ranked lower than Bambi in the public estimation, at 45 percent.[36] A few months later, on November 9, 1943, the ARI queried another cross-section of Americans about which of six subjects it would like to see as a Disney film: "Cinderella," "Peter Pan," "Alice in Wonderland," "Lady and the Tramp," "Uncle Remus," or "Hiawatha." The survey aimed to uncover both positive and negative reactions, how different demographic groups responded, and whether people preferred to see each subject as a live-action or animated film. In general, the public affirmed its affection for Disney, though the surveys revealed distinct differences between men and women in their preference for certain stories.[37]

Disney's sporadic forays into audience research during the war presaged a much stronger commitment to studying public response in the postwar period. When the studio returned to commercial production after 1945, Walt Disney continued to rethink the company's direction and focus. The ARI's studies helped him manage an increasingly complex enterprise even as he ventured beyond animation to live-action and industrial films. The ARI became an integral part of the filmmaking process at Disney after the war, helping the studio both to maintain its traditions in a changing culture and to integrate new ideas.

A MACHINE FOR MANUFACTURING ENTERTAINMENT

Though Disney films dominated American studio animation during the 1930s, after World War II economic, industrial, and sociological factors combined to weaken the firm's position. In the postwar period, cartoons in general became less profitable, and the Disney studio in particular suffered financially. Critical and popular reaction began to turn against Disney in this period, and within the company attention shifted from animation to live-action production. To maintain its output, Disney adopted an industrial mode of organization that emphasized efficiency and productivity. The ARI helped the company manage this shifting internal and external environment.

The production of animated short films declined rapidly after World War II, primarily because of cost: in 1945 the average cartoon short cost $17,000 to produce, but two years later, this had risen to an average of $25,000 per picture, an increase of nearly 50 percent. Labor costs increased by 41 percent in this period, and Technicolor raised the cost of processing color film. Rental income from exhibitors, the main source of revenue for shorts, did not keep pace with these increases.[38] The Disney studio faced additional challenges. Its ambitious slate of animated features would take three or four years to produce and several more to return the studio's investment. In 1948 and 1949 the Disney studio posted losses, for the first time since the beginning of World War II, of $39,038 and $93,899.[39]

In addition to these economic difficulties Disney lost its preeminence among cartoon producers. The mid-to-late 1940s marked the ascendancy of Warner Bros. and MGM cartoons and the new flat style exemplified by UPA (United Productions of America). Although Disney dominated the Academy Awards in the 1930s, the studio failed to win any Oscars at all between 1943 and 1952. MGM swept the awards from 1943 to 1946 and again in 1948, interrupted only by the debut of Warner's Sylvester and Tweetie in 1947, which earned that studio an Oscar as well.[40] UPA's *Gerald McBoing-Boing* won in 1950.

The lack of external recognition may have resulted in part from a lack of attention to animation within the studio as well. During the mid-to-late 1940s live-action films began to displace animated ones in the company's production schedule. Disney's interest in live action developed during the war, when the studio produced documentaries for government agencies and private industry. When the war ended, the company decided to continue producing live-action films to maintain cash flow, since profits returned more quickly for live action than for animation. Where animation did appear in full-length films, it was often combined with live action, as in *Song of the South* (1946) and *So Dear to My Heart* (1949). In June 1946 all the projects announced in the company's upcoming schedule were described as combinations, including *Cinderella*.[41] Even Roy Disney pressed his brother to give up producing animated films.[42]

To meet the demands of this changing environment, Walt Disney introduced a new managerial style that emphasized efficiency and cost effectiveness. In an article published when the new Burbank facility opened, he described the studio as an "entertainment factory" and "a machine for the manufacture of entertainment."[43] The design itself served as a synecdoche for the rationalization and efficiency governing the company. According to its engineers, the new Burbank headquarters aimed to "provide a smooth and efficient ... flow line" for "optimum per capita production."[44] A postwar memo from Walt and Roy Disney to the studio staff demonstrated that this emphasis on efficiency extended to the use of money as well as time and energy. The memo called for "a constructive attitude toward every dollar which goes into developing, producing and selling the pictures." Film production should be planned in advance to avoid uncertainty and save money. "The production schedule should be buttoned up and not changed," the memo said. Animators should also stay within their budgets and bring films "across the finish line" under their projected cost.[45]

During the 1930s Walt Disney had introduced several changes designed to streamline animation production: he instituted storyboard conferences and pencil tests to check films at an early stage of development, and he organized workers into specialized groups similar to the production units employed at live-action studios.[46] In the postwar era he turned to audience research. According to the studio's annual report for 1946–47, Disney's primary motivation for hiring Gallup was to hold down production costs, which had increased 75 percent since 1941. By taking audience reactions into account in the early stages of production, the Disney company believed it would be able to head off potential failures.[47] Undertaking a program of "scientific" research would also enhance the company's status as a serious business enterprise and allay the concerns of its creditors and stockholders, who had become a force within the company after Disney issued its first public stock offering in April 1940. The earlier research that the ARI had carried out served RKO's needs, but in the postwar era Disney realized that it could use research for its own purposes. Disney's reworking of ARI methods illustrates how techniques adapted for other circumstances could be reshaped to meet changing needs.

LAUGHTER BY NUMBERS

The international popularity of Mickey Mouse, Donald Duck, and other Disney characters suggested to some that Walt Disney possessed an almost instinctive understanding of his audience. Yet even in his earliest days as a cartoon producer, Walt Disney made an effort to study people's reactions. Several animators who worked with him recall in their memoirs how they used to go to theaters to listen to audiences' reactions and observe what sequences or types of characters appealed to them. Disney and his colleagues would then gather outside the theater to parse the film's structure, music, drawing, and movement.[48] According to Shamus Culhane, who had worked at other animation studios before joining Disney, Walt Disney was one of the few cartoon producers who was willing to change a film based on audience response. Other studios used everything their cartoonists produced because they didn't want to take extra time or pay for footage that didn't appear in the film.[49] For Walt Disney, however, understanding what audiences liked was as important as good draftsmanship and the ability to develop gags.[50]

In 1945 the studio launched an effort to study audiences more systematically by holding a series of previews for carefully selected groups. Film studios had long held sneak previews for anyone who came to the theater, but the ARI argued that viewers at these screenings did not necessarily represent the American public as a whole.[51] The institute began conducting preview screenings with audiences that were carefully selected according to their representation in the general filmgoing population. Disney modified this technique to fit its production schedule and budget. Instead of going outside the studio, Disney commissioned the ARI to survey Disney's own employees to determine how well they corresponded to the national filmgoing population. The ARI found that, except for viewers over thirty, Disney employees mirrored the majority of American filmgoers pretty well. After learning this, the studio began to hold in-house previews for audiences of forty employees at a time, who were selected to represent the rest of the country in terms of age, gender, and level of education. Participants came from the general office staff and grounds workers, and from the ranks of junior production personnel, such as the women in ink and paint and the men who worked as assistant animators and in-betweeners.[52] Card Walker, the executive in charge of advertising at the studio, arranged these screenings. For the next ten years, until the mid-1950s, Disney submitted all of its productions, shorts and full-length features, to this employee scrutiny. Eventually the group came to be known as the "noncritical" group because it included people who were not professional animators, as well as less-experienced members of the animation staff.[53]

Disney first used these "studio ARIs," as they were called, to study reactions to its short films. The chosen audience would watch a rough cut of a film in production, a reel that combined footage produced by various animators assigned to the project. After viewing the film, the audience completed a form that asked these questions: Do you like this type of cartoon? Which gags or situations did you enjoy most? Least? Are there any parts that are dull or uninteresting, so shortening would help? Were there any gags or situations you did not understand? Any dialogue? Some questions were closed-ended, that is, people were asked to respond with a "yes" or "no"; others encouraged longer and more detailed responses. Most questions focused on clarity and tried to uncover problems that could be solved through reediting. Walker or his secretary typed the responses about which gags were enjoyed most or least on a separate sheet, indicating that this issue received particular attention. Walker sent transcripts of these responses to the director of animation for each film, who reviewed them and recommended appropriate changes to the animators who were working on it. Usually the alterations were cuts designed to clarify the action or shorten the pace of a scene.[54] Walker also sent reports of each screening and summaries of the audiences' reactions to Walt Disney.

From the standpoint of efficiency this procedure seemed to ensure that the most unpredictable variable in a film's success, audience reaction, could be studied in advance and incorporated into the production process itself. The animators' firsthand experiences of audiences in the 1930s were replaced by carefully designed questionnaires that raised issues that could be addressed through existing production procedures. Though the questions were logical ones to ask about a cartoon, they nonetheless narrowed the potential range of audience responses to these films. The surveys asked audiences to focus on the gags and the dialogue and to indicate whether anything confused them. The open-ended nature of some of these questions made them difficult to sum up easily, but Walker soon found a way to convert them into numerical form.

After several months of reporting individual scores, Walker developed a decimal rating for each film, by multiplying the number of "most enjoyed" votes by seven, the next highest level by six, and so on, and then dividing the result by the number of respondents. His memos to Walt Disney and to the animation supervisors began to contain statements such as, "This film received a 5.67 enjoyment rating." Since the studio subjected every short cartoon to this process, Walker also began to tabulate a running average; each project was compared with the overall enjoyment ratings from other screenings. He then compiled long lists that positioned each film in relation to previous ones according to their rating.[55]

During the 1940s corporate executives viewed the control of information as a crucial part of efficient management.[56] By adapting the ARI's idea of sampling audiences for its own purposes, Disney found another tool to rationalize production and maintain control over an increasingly complex environment. The decimal rating system that Walker developed offered a convenient method for evaluating the productivity of animation units and their success at producing humorous cartoons. These ratings strove to quantify pleasure, to develop a precise numerical measurement for happiness. After each meeting Walker, or the production chief, Harry Tytle, sent Disney a summary of the comments, the names of the animators and directors who worked on the film, its decimal rating, and an indication of how the film compared with others that had been tested. Walker also indicated which gags would be changed and how other elements of the story would be altered. "The production unit will snap up the shooting and cut out one scene with the dynamite in the pants."[57] These summaries enabled Walt Disney to keep up with shorts production while he was engaged in other projects, such as the studio's new live-action films set in England. These surveys are both symptomatic of Walt Disney's lack of day-to-day involvement in cartoon short production and his desire to maintain control over that aspect of his studio nonetheless.

THE CRITICAL AND THE NONCRITICAL

While the carefully chosen studio audience was screening rough cuts of works in progress, the animation staff continued the studio's tradition of holding storyboard conferences. Disney pioneered the use of storyboard meetings in the 1930s as a way to evaluate a film's narrative structure and character development before it went into production. Animators drew key scenes, gags, and actions on storyboards that everyone reviewed together, including Disney. The process enabled personnel to plan scenes in detail before committing to the expense of drawing and painting cels. Two years after the studio began holding its in-house previews of rough cuts, Disney began asking the animation staff some of the same questions the studio asked employees during these previews. The animation staff was called the "critical" group and consisted of senior animators, story men, and background and layout artists, many of whom had been with the studio since the early 1930s.

This group's responses rarely questioned the studio's approach to filmmaking but discussed how a film could be made to look more like a "Disney" production. For example, responses to the storyboard presentation of "Common Cold" (released as *Cold War* in 1951) suggested that the cold virus could be developed into a character, "a little railroad bum looking for a soft touch." "Why not have him do more slapstick?" one suggested, while another asserted that "the germ could have more action."[58] The critical group offered perspective on how "the business might be gagged more" and how the personalities of different characters could play off one another.[59] This group noticed when a film explored Donald Duck's character in new ways and complained when a vocal performance did not fit Mickey.[60] Experienced animators steeped in the Disney tradition, the critical group appreciated fresh ideas, original situations, and opportunities for good visual humor.[61]

Before long, however, differences began to emerge between the critical group's view of the storyboards and studio audience's reactions to the rough reels that resulted from those storyboards. With "Pluto's White Elephant," for example, the critical group felt the story was long and complicated, but the noncritical group enjoyed it. The film was put into production anyway because it was thought that the elephant could be developed as a sympathetic character and because there was nothing else in the pipeline in November 1949.[62] In April 1950 the studio began to invite the noncritical audiences to view the storyboards as well, often in back-to-back sessions with the critical group.[63] As with the rough cuts, having the noncritical group look at storyboards was intended to detect problems early in production, even before the rough reels. Usually the noncritical group reacted more positively to the storyboards than did the critical group and even came to serve as a court of appeals for animators who believed that their peers had not evaluated their projects fairly.[64] If the noncritical group gave a storyboard a strong positive response, it often moved into production even if the critical group had reservations about it. For example, the critical group could not agree on the merits of "Two Chips and a Miss." They praised the "nice modern touch" and "good fast pantomime gags" in the project's first storyboard review on June 27, 1950, but four months later disliked the ending and the female lead. The noncritical group, however, enjoyed the film, and it was put into production.[65] At other times the convictions of the critical group could outweigh the negative response of the noncritical viewers. "Lucky Number" limped through several storyboard and rough-cut presentations, earning low ratings each time. Walker wrote Disney that even after many revisions, the basic plot was still unwieldy. Yet the film moved into final production because the unit producing it believed strongly that it could be a success.[66]

Since the studio or noncritical audience was partly composed of junior production personnel, many seized this opportunity to express their own views of how animated films should be handled. These questionnaires then became an arena where tensions within the studio played out, where different groups articulated competing ideologies of animation. As Walker explained, "Most men of necessity come from clean-up and in-between and have fairly definite ideas as to [the] type of cartoon we should make."[67] Respondents often critiqued the classic Disney style and extolled the merits of the cartoons coming out of Warner Bros. or the UPA style of animation that produced the Mr. Magoo series.[68] Viewers who said they disliked some of the sequences in Disney films expressed a preference for more slapstick comedy with noise and speed.[69] They liked Goofy, and new characters such as Chip 'n' Dale inspired more affection than the classic Donald Duck.[70] They also liked references to contemporary popular culture, such as Frank Sinatra in *Pluto's Blue Note*.[71] In the fall of 1947 Disney began screening cartoons from its rivals at MGM and Columbia.[72] Though the practice lasted only a short time because of budget cuts, the animation staff had an opportunity to compare its work to that of their colleagues at other studios. Shortly after the screenings took place, some began to write on their questionnaires that they preferred the "fast-moving, gag-packed cartoons like MGM puts out."[73] As Walt Disney turned to other projects, the company's dominance in cartoon production waned, and the studio's in-house audience research allowed opposing views to emerge. These responses may have supported the shift toward a more modernist drawing style that some animators, such as Ward Kimball, adopted during this period.

Though this preview system was supposed to simplify cartoon production, it soon had the opposite effect. By 1952 the Disney studio was engaged in a veritable frenzy of audience research: not only did the studio audience attend storyboard conferences, but the critical group began to fill out questionnaires at the rough screenings as well. With opinions circulating constantly, films often required two or three storyboard conferences, and as many rough screenings, before they were approved for release.[74] In addition, the time lag between these stages increased, as the studio pulled more animators into feature production for *Cinderella* and *Peter Pan*. In 1950, for example, the year of *Cinderella*'s release, it was common for six to eight months to elapse between the storyboard presentations and rough reel screenings. With these extended delays, sometimes audiences' responses at one screening didn't match their views at all a few months later. Viewers who loved a rough cut in January might hate it when they saw it again in September.[75] Disney began to shelve many short films because the studio could not reach a consensus on their value, and in 1954 it stopped producing them altogether.

Disney's decision to discontinue cartoon shorts can be explained in many ways: the increasing cost of production and decline in revenues from theaters, competition from television, the animators' growing boredom with well-established characters, changes in audience interests and contemporary aesthetic tastes, new styles and characters emerging from other studios, and Disney's increasing interest in other endeavors, such as Disneyland. The breakdown of the studio's system for measuring audience response is symptomatic of the decline of shorts but may also have contributed to it, by providing empirical evidence of the cartoons' failure to please a range of viewers consistently. The system that was intended to measure and track the effects of humorous characters and stories in the end proved how difficult it is to maintain humor within such a tight framework.

The late 1940s marks a critical juncture at the Disney studio, a time when the company began to transform itself from a small cartoon producer to a diversified major with a full slate of short and feature cartoons, live-action films, and documentaries. It was during this period that Disney started to become the entertainment conglomerate that it is today. Many factors contributed to this change, among them the ambitions of its executives, changes within the film industry as a whole, and the effects of World War II. But along with these forces, the Audience Response Institute played a crucial role in Disney's alteration. The decision to hire Gallup signaled a fundamental shift within the company, a desire to adopt the business practices and organizational strategies of a major studio. As this shift took place, the studio's approach to animation changed as well. The opportunities for innovative narrative forms and image and sound design that so inspired Disney before the war came to be seen as elements that required management and measurement. Animation, the cinematic medium with perhaps the greatest potential for humor and transformation, was expected to meet carefully defined corporate goals, and audience research assisted in that process. Yet because of the detailed records that were kept of this research, historians today can trace changing audience tastes and studio attitudes toward Disney films. Strategies that were once intended to manage and control can be used to take apart the structures they were meant to support.

NOTES

1. "Disney-RKO Deal," 4; and Gomery, "Disney's Business History," 72.

2. "President's Report of RKO Board Meeting, July 30, 1940."

3. "*Snow White* Seen Headed for Record," 16.

4. "Disney's 800G Melon," 1, 52; "RKO Radio Signs Pact," 11.

5. "Disney and RKO Discuss," 22.

6. Ibid.

7. "Disney Feature," 18.

8. "President's Report of RKO Board Meeting."

9. "RKO's Budget," 6.

10. "Loss for Walt Disney," 40.

11. See Luckett, "*Fantasia*."

12. See "Mickey Mouse in Symphony," 50–52; Stull, "Fantasound"; Stull, "*Fantasia* Sound," 7–8, 21; and "Disney's 'Revolution,'" 8.

13. "Distribution for *Fantasia*," 6; "Stoki-Disney *Fantasia* Roadshow Plan," 5, 20.

14. "RKO Releasing *Fantasia*," 1, 3; "*Fantasia* under RKO Release," 1, 8; "*Fantasia* Has Grossed," 7; "General Distribution for Disney *Fantasia*," 47.

15. See the ARI's RKO Report no. 69: "When Should Publicity Start?" and Report no. 81: "Introduction to a New Index," in RKO, *Gallup Looks at the Movies*.

16. "Index of Publicity Penetration" for July 31 and Aug. 12, 1941, in "Increasing Profits through Continuous Audience Research" (RKO, *Gallup Looks at the Movies*). A similar survey on Jan. 17, 1942, confirmed these results.

17. "Disney's Self-Trailer," 2; "'The Reluctant Dragon.'"

18. Ned Depinet to Schaefer, April 19, 1941; Schaefer to McDonough, April 20, 1941; McDonough to Gallup, April 21, 1941, all in RKO, ARI Correspondence File No. 2, RKO Papers.

19. Ogilvy to McDonough, April 19, 1941, in RKO, ARI Correspondence File No. 2, RKO Papers.

20. Index of Publicity Penetration, June 14–July 26, 1941, in *Gallup Looks at the Movies*.

21. "Gross Rental from *Snow White*," 46.

22. Depinet to McDonough, June 3, 1941, in RKO, ARI Correspondence File No. 2, RKO Papers.

23. "Draggin' Disney's *Dragon* into N.Y.," 7.

24. "Mediators Hope," 22; "Labor Conciliator Steps In," 22; "Government Holds Off," 23; Bower, "Films: Snow White and the 1,200 Dwarfs," 565; "Disney Film Picketed," 13.

25. "*Dumbo* Gets Earlier Release," 8.

26. "Disney Rides a Baby Elephant Back into Hearts of His Fans," 61; "The New Pictures," 97–98; "Mammal-of-the-Year," 27–28; "*Dumbo*," *Theatre Arts*, 907; Ferguson, "Two for the Show," 537; "*Dumbo*," *Film Daily*, 4; and "*Dumbo*," *Variety*, 9.

27. Index of Publicity Penetration, Oct 11–Nov 8, 1941, in RKO, *Gallup Looks at the Movies*.

28. For more on SIMPP see Aberdeen, *Hollywood Renegades*.

29. David O. Selznick to Gallup, March 31, 1942, "Gallup Poll 1939–1941–1942," Box 3562, Selznick Papers, Harry Ransom Humanities Research Center, University of Texas at Austin (hereafter Selznick Papers).

30. See Smoodin, *Animating Culture*, esp. 168–85.

31. George Gallup, interview with Thomas Simonet, Princeton, NJ, Sept. 1977.

32. David Ogilvy to David O. Selznick, April 4, 1942, "Gallup Poll 1939–1941–1942," Box 3562, Selznick Papers.

33. Ogilvy to Selznick, June 9, 1942, and Selznick to Ogilvy, July 25, 1942, both in "Gallup Poll 1939–1941–1942," Box 3562, Selznick Papers.

34. ARI to Walt Disney, Sept. 2, 1942; Jack Sayers to Perce Pearce, Sept. 24, 1942; quoted in Shale, *Donald Duck Joins Up,* 69–70.

35. Shale, *Donald Duck Joins Up,* 76–77.

36. Walt Disney Studio, *Identification of Disney Characters,* Title Test Binder A–E, ARI Box 10, Walt Disney Studio Archives.

37. Ibid., "Cinderella."

38. "Cartoon Making Kicked Around," 6; and "Cut Cartoon Output," 5.

39. *Film Daily Yearbook,* 1950, 1003.

40. Kausler, Cawley, and Korkis, "Animated Oscars."

41. "Disney Preparing Eight New Features," 35.

42. Peet, *An Autobiography,* 123.

43. Disney, "Growing Pains."

44. Garity and Ledeen, "The New Walt Disney Studio."

45. Kinney, *Walt Disney and Assorted Other Characters,* 145.

46. Thomas and Johnston, *Disney Animation,* 46–85.

47. "The Walt Disney Studio Annual Report" for the fiscal year ending Sept. 27, 1947.

48. See, e.g., Kinney, *Walt Disney and Assorted Other Characters,* 46; Hand, *Memoirs,* 73–74; and Culhane, *Talking Animals and Other People;* see also Ben Sharpsteen, interview by Dave Smith, Feb. 6, 1974, 5.

49. Culhane, *Talking Animals and Other People,* 113–14.

50. Walt Disney, memo to Don Graham, Dec. 23, 1935; repr. in Culhane, *Talking Animals and Other People,* 120.

51. Weaver, "Studios Use Audience Research," 37.

52. Card Walker to Walt Disney, June 21, 1946, *Casey Jones* file, ARI Box 2, Walt Disney Studio Archive (hereafter WDSA).

53. Walker to Harry Tytle, Nov. 5, 1948, "Corn Chips" critical storyboard, ARI Box 3, WDSA.

54. Walker to Charles Nichols, March 9, 1950, "Cold Turkey" noncritical rough file, ARI Box 3, WDSA.

55. Walker to Walt Disney, Jan. 20, 1947, "Pluto's Fledgling" rough preview file, ARI Box 8, WDSA.

56. Smythe, *Dependency Road,* 86.

57. "Two Gun Goofy" rough reel presentation to critical and noncritical audience, May 14, 1951, ARI Box 12, WDSA.

58. "Common Cold," storyboard presentation to critical audience, June 29, 1949, ARI Box 3, WDSA.

59. "Coon Dog," storyboard presentation to critical audience, Aug. 15, 1949, ARI Box 3, WDSA.

60. "Jet Pilot Donald," storyboard presentation to critical group, Aug. 31, 1949, ARI Box 5; and "Plight of the Bumble Bee," rough presentation to critical group, March 8, 1951, ARI Box 8, WDSA.

61. "Cold Turkey," storyboard presentation to critical group, Nov. 11, 1949, ARI Box 3, WDSA.

62. "Pluto's White Elephant," rough reel presentation to noncritical audience, Nov. 22, 1949, ARI Box 8, WDSA.

63. *Two Weeks Summer Vacation* file, ARI Box 12, WDSA.

64. Walker to Disney, July 7, 1949, "Pluto's White Elephant" storyboard, ARI Box 8, WDSA.

65. "Two Chips and a Miss," storyboard presentation to critical audience, June 27, 1950, and rough screening to critical and noncritical audience, Nov. 22, 1950, ARI Box 12, WDSA.

66. "Lucky Number," rough preview to noncritical audience, Jan. 18, 1950, ARI Box 6, WDSA.

67. "Pluto Plays Football," storyboard presentations to critical and noncritical audiences, March 21, 1951, ARI Box 8, WDSA.

68. Walker to Disney, Dec. 6, 1950, "Two Gun Goofy" storyboard presentations to critical and noncritical groups, ARI Box 12, WDSA.

69. "Pluto's Purchase," Sept. 9, 1946, ARI Box 8, WDSA.

70. "Winter Storage," rough preview, June 19, 1947, ARI Box 11, WDSA.

71. "Pluto's Blue Note," rough preview showing, Oct. 31, 1946, ARI Box 8, WDSA.

72. List found in ARI Box 14, WDSA.

73. *Pluto's Heart Throb* file, Jan. 15, 1948, ARI Box 8, WDSA.

74. See, e.g., the numerous studies for *How to Sleep,* ARI Box 5, WDSA.

75. *Grand Canyon Scope* file, ARI Box 4, WDSA.

PART THREE

Retheorizing Animated Comedy

7

"Who Dat Say Who Dat?"

Racial Masquerade, Humor, and the Rise of American Animation

Nicholas Sammond

INTRODUCTION:
WHAT COULD POSSIBLY BE RACIST AND FUNNY?

We shall best understand the origin of the pleasure derived from humor if we consider the process which takes place in the mind of anyone listening to another man's jest. He sees this other person in a situation which leads him to anticipate that the victim will show signs of some affect; he will get angry, complain, manifest pain, fear, horror, possibly even despair. The person who is watching or listening is prepared to follow his lead, and to call up the same emotions. But his anticipations are deceived; the other man does not display any affect—he makes a joke. It is from the saving of expenditure in feeling that the hearer derives the humorous satisfaction.

—FREUD, *CHARACTER AND CULTURE*

When it comes to cartoons, Sigmund Freud's description of humor as the invocation of affect and its diversion speaks well to the existential horror we call the gag. Especially in the short subjects that fairly defined American animation until 1937, and still thereafter provided its bread and butter, life is an eternal cavalcade of pain. Bodies twist, stretch, explode, melt; they are crushed by anvils, pianos, giant mallets, whole buildings; they are sliced and diced by razors and knives . . . and through it all we laugh. Why is it that, faced with such horrific violence and fierce torment, we are amused, tickled, jollified? And why have cartoons in particular linked that mayhem to other degradations—of race, of gender, of sexuality, of ethnicity—harmonizing social and physical violence?

Of the rude shocks that 'toons have taken on our behalf, the brutality of racism is one of the worst. Although the earliest days of American animation were relatively equal-opportunity in their racism—caricaturing with gusto Africans, African Americans, Chinese, Mexicans, Scots, Jews, Irish, Germans . . . and so on, the parody of Africans and African Americans, tied as it was to the vicious histories of slavery and segregation, offered a particularly virulent insult to human dignity and to human bodies. Persons of European descent could look forward to eventual assimilation into a generic American whiteness, and those of Asian descent might be afforded an uneasy accommodation as hardworking, clever, and inscrutable in the eugenic hierarchies of the day (and in more recent racial fantasies). Other ethnic and racial stereotypes have been subsumed slowly in a process of grudging and gradual inclusion, and this has only added further insult to the injury of ongoing white-black racism.[1] This difference is not of degree but of kind, and cartoons have continued to be a place where the cruelty of stereotypes has found fertile ground for the expression of that distinction.

Following Freud's logic, the humor of racist cartoons, based in the turning toward and then away from this history of horrible violence, should be hysterical. Well, it sometimes is. Whether in the antics of Bosko the Talk-Ink Kid, or in the parody of Harlem night life, *Swing Wedding* (1937), brutality is visited upon black bodies, which are physically assaulted or suffer the symbolic violence of grotesque caricature. And yet this violence is in service of the laugh, and in their manic pacing, jokes, and visual ingenuity these cartoons can provoke laughter. The racist stereotypes that inform this sort of cartoon emerged from a specific iconographic lexicon and have circulated as commonplace expressions of contempt that dismiss the harm they express as ultimately harmless: in cartoons no one bleeds, and no one dies. It's all good fun. The intense affect of racism, instead of evincing either vicious malice or utter horror, is turned aside into a joke, a double-take, a gag, a disavowal.

Those gags, as they feed into larger systems of structural and institutional racism, have contributed to human suffering. Still, according to Freud, the affect that informs them, however brutal, may be converted to more felicitous laughter. Yet we generally agree that this laughter is inappropriate and that this conversion does nothing to blunt the racism itself. A historical understanding of race—if not common decency—requires that good people decry this sort of racism and censure their own laughter if they are amused. And since many different people, even the intended objects of these jokes, sometimes find them funny, we are left with another question: can good people see these cartoons as simultaneously racist *and* humorous? Ostensibly good people—people who would not call themselves racist—made these cartoons. Ostensibly good people have watched them and laughed. It's quite possible to watch today and laugh: in their pacing, language, and visual creativity many of these cartoons are funny even as they are racist. In the circuit between their production and their reception (and back again), they convert the venomous horror of racist discourse into something laughable. So another question that hangs here is, laughable for whom . . . and to what end? The impulse to turn away from them, to censor them, to disavow their humor as nothing more than viciousness made commonplace marks an unwillingness to unflinchingly consider what that laughter can tell us about the feeling experience of participating in racist discourse.

Is there a way out of this either/or bind? Freud's notion of humor depends on a universal notion of shared suffering—the endless rude shock of human existence. We all suffer; therefore we all laugh. But racist humor is *specific:* on its surface at least it depends on hurts to particular people. The problem lies in the either/or, and the ambiguous ontological status of the animated character—made yet alive, an object yet with apparent subjectivity—makes it a useful correlate for how black bodies were imagined by American popular and legal discourse at the beginning of the last century. Like the liminal condition of the animated character, "separate but equal" suggested a transit point from the object status of chattel slavery toward a fully universal subjectivity—which one could always approach but at which one would never arrive.[2] This is not to analogize African American historical experience with cartoons. It is, however, to point out the utility of the animated character for expressing and exploring this contradictory tension between subject and object—and the threat to the subject status of nonblack bodies that this tension represented. One approach to it is to consider how well that threat may be accommodated by expressions of empathy or by sympathy. In parsing those different experiences of sympathy and empathy, the necessary tension between a subject and an embodied object is revealed.

In the moment of recognition and empathy, racist parodies become simultaneously injurious *and* funny. They are injurious because they participate in practices designed to inflict real injury and insult on specific people and to implicate others in that injury.[3] They may be funny when we view them, not in the sadistic model that Freud elaborated in his earlier work on humor but from the vantage of his later work on empathy and shared affect.[4] In this view the racist cartoons of the early to mid-twentieth century continue to be funny, not because audiences necessarily choose to continue to practice or suffer the active, overt racism that informed their making but because the social and material struggles that underpin that racism are still very much alive today.

To get at this tension, then, this essay considers how stereotyping found such a prominent place in early animation—both as broad racist caricature and in the subtler codings of race that shaped enduring characters such as Bugs Bunny or Mickey Mouse—and it explores the conventional history within which this stereotyping located those characters and their audience. This requires revisiting the performative and visual traditions of racial masquerade popular at the birth of American animation, particularly that of blackface minstrelsy. For while racist caricatures came to the fore in American animation's embrace of swing music during its transition to sound, the vestiges of blackface minstrelsy—the white gloves, wide eyes, voracious mouth, and tricksterish resistance—informed animation's most popular characters and lived on long after the racist excesses of animation's Golden Age seemed to pass.[5] And so, if this were *Pee Wee's Playhouse,* we would turn to the King of Cartoons and ask him to roll his projector . . .

DISRESPECT

The Betty Boop short *I'll Be Glad When You're Dead You Rascal You* (Fleischer, 1932) doesn't open with the iconic flapper nor with her sidekicks Bimbo and Ko-Ko. Like many of the shorts the Fleischers produced with popular musicians of the early 1930s, it starts with live footage—here of Louis Armstrong fronting a ten-piece jazz ensemble.[6] After Armstrong gets the band rolling, the animated segment begins. Betty, Bimbo, and Ko-Ko are explorers in the jungle, set upon by generic Ubangi-type natives common to the racist imaginary of early twentieth-century America.[7] Betty is kidnapped by the natives, and Bimbo and Ko-Ko attempt a rescue. After a bit of business they escape and flee the village. But one native in particular is dogged in his pursuit, and soon his body morphs into a giant flying cannibal head that, as it chases Bimbo and Ko-Ko, is intercut with a close-up of Louis Armstrong's disembodied head singing the title song, "I'll Be Glad When You're Dead You Rascal You" (Fig. 7.1). Although Armstrong is dressed in a suit in the opening sequence and is carrying a trumpet and trademark handkerchief, in the close-up he wears a black turtleneck, and his shoulders are matted out of the frame. He sings with obvious pleasure and gusto. After a few verses the cartoon morphs him back to the voracious cannibal head, which so terrifies Bimbo that he sweats himself away to nothing (an obvious phallic joke). The cannibal so scares Ko-Ko that a speedometer emerges from his derriere, and, when it passes 120 mph, it reads, in Hebrew, "Kosher."[8] In the end the protagonists (of which Armstrong is obviously not one) vanquish the natives and go free.

The short is so obviously racist that it barely seems worth the ink to say so. In his compendium on racist imagery in American cartoons Henry Sampson named this sort of film "The Animated Safari" and said of it, "Even if these cartoons did not directly incite bigotry, they certainly encouraged disrespect for people of African descent and therefore tended to reinforce the justification of the continued colonization of Africa by Europeans in the minds of the movie going public."[9] The core of this assessment—that this sort of film was racist and colonialist—is quite reasonable. Yet *how* it is racist is also important, how it achieved its humor through its racism. Louis Armstrong was one of the greatest musicians and performers of the twentieth century, and he was noted for the enthusiasm and joy that he brought to his performances (which were some-

FIGURE 7.1. Louis Armstrong is transformed into a ravenous cannibal chasing Bimbo and Ko-Ko in *I'll Be Glad When You're Dead You Rascal You* (Fleischer, 1932).

times criticized as Uncle-Tomming). That pleasure in performance is evident: Armstrong savors the lyrics (which imagine someone cursing out a man who has slept with his wife), at moments performing as if his rival were right in front of him. In the hands of one of the premier animation houses of the time, that relish becomes voraciousness, literalized as a cannibal head—all lips, tongue, and eyes—slavering after his white victims, and Armstrong's pleasure in singing is transformed into a desire to consume them. That Bimbo melts into a puddle of sweat and Ko-Ko's terror causes him to sprout a Hebraic speedometer from his buttocks—as the cartoon mocks their inadequate masculinity—only casts the racial binary in stronger relief: Armstrong's/the cannibal's voracious sensuality is that which reveals Bimbo's impotence and Ko-Ko's anxious (and incomplete) white masculinity.[10]

For all that, though, the Fleischer cartoon is funny, and it is fun. The music is vital and exciting, and the drawing is inventive, lively, and unpredictable. The cartoon is full of the sorts of transformations that Norman Klein has described as the stuff of "nightmarish humor [and] drunken hallucinations."[11] It is funny *and* racist—startling in its monstrousness—and its humor, or the affect behind that humor, is inextricably interwoven with its racism, its demeaning and derogatory portrayal of a great African American man. *I'll Be Glad . . .* is charged with a blend of fear and desire—the fear of Louis Armstrong as a desirable object as much as a desiring subject—that threatens the film's protagonists, emasculating and whitening them at the same time. Bifurcating Armstrong between an ostensibly real self-contained and self-contented man and an idealized fantasy of uncivilized hunger, it points up the relationship between the two, between the real and the ideal.

IMITATION IS NOT THE SINCEREST FORM OF FLATTERY

What marks animation as a substantial expressive form, a place of contentious pleasure, is that at its best it maintains that tension between the ideal and the real. More so than live cinema, animation is produced and regulated as an Other to what is real. Its alterity, its uncanniness, is contained in its very name: to animate is to enliven that which is not alive. It produces an Other that lives but doesn't, an object that threatens to become a subject. But animate characters are not cut from whole cloth. In animation, the real and the ideal vie with each other. For the sake of expediency and efficiency animation has a tradition of drawing on stereotypes for its characters. In the short form of the seven-minute cartoon the stereotype was efficient because it allowed for the rapid recognition of the social hieroglyphic of character type and the designation of its proper social location: Scotsmen were cheap; the Chinese were hardworking and either excitable or inscrutable; the Irish were lovable drunks; Mexicans were lazy, and so on. Just as vaudevillian performers of the time found utility in stereotypes for their short bits, so it was with cartoonists. Where longer narrative forms permitted the emergence of characters over time (better following the modernist ideal of a complex individual with a unique internal psychology), the vaudevillian gag used stereotyping to transmit a dense packet of social and cultural information in a short period of time. Stereotypes were brutally efficient.

In this sense the stereotype is a form of the Marxist commodity fetish, a "crystallization of social and material relations," a way to sell the bit.[12] At the same time, like the Freudian fetish, it is built around a disavowal: the aggressive refusal to acknowledge the object of desire for what it is and the act of replacing it with a substitute container for the affect of that desire and its repression. The stereotype, even as it draws on the necessary social and corporeal substance of persons, is a disavowal of their basic humanity in favor of grossly exaggerated features that represent characteristics both feared and desired by an imagined white audience. And nowhere is this operation clearer than in the figure of the "darky" or minstrel, based as it is on the bodies of slaves—persons denied their basic humanity. In this figure, and in stereotypes generally, the real is necessary and is necessarily repressed in the service of a functional and efficient ideal. The fetish is a shorthand of an experience simultaneously acknowledged and denied.

Just as the disavowal at the heart of the Freudian fetish is a not-so-secret gesture toward one's own fragile integrity, so the mimetic gesture of the comic stereotype—the claim to know the essence of the other—speaks of a struggle between sympathy and empathy. In animation this is all the more true, because the artist puts pen to paper (or now stylus to pad) and feelingly produces the stereotype as a totemic body. From the lightning sketch to the onstage performances of Winsor McCay and Gertie (Fig. 7.2), early animation featured a back-and-forth

a   b

FIGURE 7.2. (a) Bosko the Talk-Ink Kid, initially designed as a blackface minstrel, disputes with creator Rudy Ising in 1930; (b) Winsor McCay displays his creation to fellow animators (and the audience) in *Gertie the Dinosaur* (1914).

between the animator and the animated. Once animated, by tradition that body resisted the animator, and was subjugated by him. This is fundamental to animation's alterity: the animate character's own insistence on its ontological status as a made object creates a relationship between producer, text, and viewer that is fundamentally different from that offered in live-action cinema. The conjuring trick, of course, is in the hand that makes the animated character that resists it, that asserts its own dubious reality in relation to what it has made.

WHO DAT SAY WHO DAT?

In addition to marking a boundary of negotiation between live cinema and cartoons, this proximity/tension between the real and the ideal has also operated *within* the bounds of American animation itself. For while a variety of racial and ethnic stereotypes facilitated the efficient shorthand of the gag in the early studio animation era, particular stereotypes of blackness underpin the very metaphysics of the form. Plainly put, the same racial formations that had positioned black bodies as in transit from the object status of slavery to full personhood—or as occupying both of those contradictory positions simultaneously—informed a logic of animation that saw in a fantastic blackness the means to traverse the boundary between the real and the ideal. This formative quality charges the relationship between the cinematic head of Louis Armstrong and the drawn cannibal head into and out of which he morphs. Racist caricatures such as this—cannibals, mammies, pickaninnies, crap shooters, jitterbuggers—provided a rich and often disturbing palette for the burgeoning animation industry of the swing era. Yet even before that moment a less apparent and relatively more subtle fantasy of

blackness had already helped to shape the metaphysics of the American animation industry: that of the blackface minstrel.

Usually white and always wearing burnt cork or black greasepaint on his face,
dressed in an ill-fitting suit and typically wearing white gloves, the blackface
minstrel was a fixture on the American stage from the early 1800s well into the
twentieth century.[13] The minstrel show's precursor to the performing animator
was the Interlocutor, usually a white man who directed the minstrel troupe and
who interrogated its two central characters, the "end men" Tambo and Bones.
Metonymic for the instruments they played, Tambo and Bones were simple-
minded rural black folk whose sly or confused answers to the Interlocutor's questions displayed both their own rustic ignorance and the Interlocutor's pomposity.
Blackface continued to play a part in vaudeville well into the 1920s, fading as that
form itself gave way to radio and the movies but experiencing a brief renaissance
in the late 1920s and early 1930s with the rise of popular minstrel two-man acts
such as Moran and Mack or Amos 'n' Andy. Yet it is important to note that none
of these forms—minstrelsy, vaudeville, film—was simply replaced by its successor. Their years of popularity overlapped, and one or more of these attractions
could occupy the same stage in the same week, if not the same night. Vaudeville's
famous comedic two-man acts (such as Abbott and Costello, Hope and Crosby,
Burns and Allen, et al.) followed the same formal principles as Tambo, Bones,
and the Interlocutor, and animation borrowed from both.[14]

In minstrelsy the Interlocutor served as the conduit between audience and
minstrel. He addressed the audience directly and interrogated the minstrels in
a quasi-ethnographic fashion about their friends, family, and the current events
of the day. The instigator and butt of the minstrels' mangling of meaning, the
Interlocutor's frequent inability to make them understand his simple questions demonstrated the limits of education and of class superiority in the face
of natural turpitude. Operating at the border between nature and culture, the
Interlocutor performed an always failing regulation of the minstrels' fantastic
minds and bodies. Vaudeville comedians would compress this relation by fold-
ing the Interlocutor into the duo of Tambo and Bones, making one comic more
intelligent and "civilized," while the other remained ignorant and resistant. Just
as Abbott failed to contain Costello, or George failed to make Gracie see reason,
the Interlocutor could not make the end men make sense: they were the conduits
of *non*sense.

Like those end men, the animated minstrel characters—Felix, Mickey, Bugs,
and similar continuing characters that have come to define the form—were
tricksters and interlopers at the boundary between the screen and the real, aris-
ing from a tradition of interplay with the animator and expressing a desire to
escape the bounds of two dimensions.[15] This relationship to the minstrel is more
than a matter of homology: the white gloves, big smile, and wide eyes sat on an

ostensibly racially ambiguous or unmarked body (usually that of an animal) as vestigial markers of minstrelsy. Likewise, the animated minstrel's behaviors—its resistance to both the animator/Interlocutor who created it and to the physical strictures of animate space—underpinned both the fundamental gag structure of many an early animated short and the basic template of the trademarked continuing character.

HOW ARE YOU TODAY, MR. BONES?

American animation shared the vaudeville stage with blackface minstrelsy, where both were performed at the beginning of the twentieth century. Lightning-sketch animators such as J. S. Blackton, Pat Sullivan, and Winsor McCay developed a language of humor and wonder through the apparent free association between one image and the next, the transformation of one thing into another.[16] The repartee between the Interlocutor and Tambo and Bones played on the free association of words and ideas, and the lightning sketch was its visual equivalent. These animation acts were but one of a variety of bits that made up any vaudeville program. Alongside the dog acts, acrobats, dancers, and comics there were also "Dutch" (German), Irish, Hebrew, and blackface minstrel acts. In the race acts an impersonator of one race or nationality put on the stereotypical characteristics of another. In a performance style that had its roots in working-class burlesques, the shared experience of oppression ideally allowed one to laugh at being stereotyped, because in theory everyone in the theater had gone through it.[17] The signal difference, of course, was that the Irish, the Germans, the Poles, and the Swedes could all, in time, assimilate into whiteness.[18] The African Americans who were mimicked in blackface minstrelsy had no such recourse to whiteness, a condition remarked on by more than one history of the form.[19] Or, to put it in Michael Rogin's terms, by putting on the race of the Other, "ethnic" blackface performers gained entrance to the outer precincts of American whiteness.[20] As Bert Williams, a West Indian black man and the most famous blackface performer of the early twentieth century, described it: "this is the only civilization in the world where a man's color makes a difference, other matters being equal. . . . In London I may sit in open lodge with a Premiere of Great Britain and be entertained in the home of a distinguished novelist, while here in the United States, which fought four years for a certain principle, I am often treated with an air of personal condescension by the gentleman who sweeps out my dressing room."[21]

Because minstrelsy traded on access to an imagined blackness for its aura of authenticity (particularly in its early days), it was a performance form built on the free appropriation (i.e., theft) of others' material—first from (real or imagined) African Americans and then from other minstrel troupes—yet it stressed an intimate knowledge of the transitory routes between the real and the ideal. The minstrel show was a peculiar animal, one in which the usually white performers who blacked up claimed that they were reenacting genuine dances and songs that they had witnessed slaves perform on southern plantations.[22] At the same time, the minstrel pointed to the black performer as an object available for (re)use, and this idea circulated beyond the bounds of minstrelsy proper. The real and feigned appropriation of black performance that legitimized minstrelsy also lived on in the assumption of freely circulating cultural goods in both burlesque and vaudeville. One of the central organizing principles in vaudeville was theft: performers regularly poached material from one another and just as regularly complained about that appropriation. And with that appropriation came a practice of marginal differentiation, the changing of a bit or routine just enough to fend off accusations of outright lifting. In this practice the audience's recognition of a bit's origins, conventions, and references was every bit as important as its uniqueness, and the sharing of common cultural information was central to the experience of theatergoing. It provided both legibility and what Henry Jenkins has called "affective immediacy," a hook, an instant identificatory link to the material.[23] Performers built on known tropes—popular songs, current events, hot dances, racial and ethnic stereotypes—and branded the familiar as their own through trademark gestures and tics. Audience pleasure lay in recognition, misdirection, and identification, of knowing the material but not where it would be taken in a given bit. Gesturing toward empirical authenticity, yet free to ignore verification, minstrelsy offered up a fantastic liminal realm between civilization and savagery, one in which animation was happy to lease property.[24]

Yet this did not engender identification *with* a protagonist but *of* the situation and its referents. If the viewer of the classical cinematic apparatus, the one who gazes and is sutured in, is an individual whose interpellation occurs through the repetitive yielding of the individual self, the vaudeville spectator was meant to experience a subordination of self—not to an internalized subjectivity but to a collective appreciation, to the crowd.[25] Rather than withdrawing the viewer from his or her immediate surroundings and into a dream world of (dis)embodied fantasy, the spectatorial practices of vaudeville proffered the wink and the nudge, a collective experience in the here and now.

In terms of an identificatory model based in empathy rather than sympathy, this difference is essential. To identify with(in) the crowd is to locate oneself in a community of practice, and the experience of identification is first with one's fellow audience members and then with the performer onstage (not the character). Even in those instances in which the audience rejects a given performance and boos a performer (for instance), the community of practice (audience and performers) remains whole, bound up by shared convention.[26] On one hand the empathic reaction that comes from watching a member of one's own community (succeed or) fail—and suffer—is possible, even as one perhaps makes a contribution to that suffering (by, say, booing). Sympathy, on the other hand, requires only that the viewer feel for (rather than with) the performer or character. Conventionally, empathy is premised on one person's affective response to another's condition as shared. In this case it is an empathy shared between human commodities, between those whose labor has been expropriated, under the voluntary pretense of freedom of contract or violently through enslavement. But this sort of identification must be consciously chosen: there is no always already interpellated subject, no yielding against one's will to an implacable apparatus. Instead, there is a bifurcation of the self between house and stage or screen.[27] In terms of racist performance, one could laugh and, ending that laughter, say, "Well, that's not right." Both are legitimate expressions.[28]

GENTLEMEN, PLEASE BE SEATED

Eric Lott has described the minstrel's assumption of fantastic imagined black characteristics as an act of "love and theft," similar to what Stuart Hall calls the "ambivalence of stereotype."[29] It expressed (and expresses) a desire for an imagined liberation from social norms perversely found in subjugated bodies and a fear of the raw sensual power of those bodies. Based as it was on a notion of the indolent and shifty slave, minstrelsy replicated a white fantasy of plantation life, of lazy African Americans wallowing in a sensual torpor, almost devoid of higher mental and moral functions. Torture, rape, and forced labor—and all the institutions that they supported and that supported them—were occluded, leaving the rustic domesticity of the slave cabin. Saidiya Hartman has suggested that minstrelsy's playful show of resistance titillated precisely because of the threat of recriminatory violence at which it hinted: "Certainly, the disciplinary vengeance of farce exercised in minstrelsy reproduced black subjection, albeit accompanied by laughter. On the minstrel stage, the comic inversions, bawdy humor, and lampooning of class hierarchies nonetheless operated within the confines of the tolerable, particularly since this transgression of order occurred by reproducing the abject status of blackness."[30]

On the minstrel stage, then, blackness was not only abject but resistant, and these qualities were inextricably linked. In cartoons that resistance was created for the purpose of its regulation. In animation, Christopher Lehman argues, following a revision in the Production Code, "slave figures receive[d] a more humane depiction . . . and no cartoon produced after 1934 showed the whipping of slaves."[31] This generous gesture, of course, didn't apply to the violence inflicted on or by vestigial minstrel characters nor to the implicit violence of stereotype itself. The slave represented the nadir of labor's enthrallment to capital in an era when contract labor was called "wage slavery" to signify its subordinate status. The minstrel figure, once removed from the slave, stood in for labor unchained:

it represented the slave who talked back, who resisted work in favor of carnal pleasures, whose very laziness was work wasted, signifying a passive revolt.[32]

One example of the circuit from minstrelsy to animation is the movement of the work of the blackface duo Moran and Mack ("Two Black Crows"), whose stage show was also featured on radio and made into films such as *Why Bring That Up* (1929) or *Anybody's War* (1930) (Fig. 7.3). One of their trademark routines found its way into a 1936 MGM cartoon called *The Early Bird and the Worm*, which features two crows who not only shun work in typical minstrel fashion but also borrow their dialogue from a Moran and Mack routine:

> Mack: You wouldn't be broke if you'd go to work.
>
> Moran: I would work, if I could find any pleasure in it.
>
> Mack: I don't know anything about pleasure, but always remember it's the early bird that catches the worm!
>
> Moran: Uh, the early bird catches *what* worm?
>
> Mack: Why, any worm!
>
> Moran: Well, what of it, what about it?
>
> Mack: He catches it, that's all!
>
> Moran: Well, what's the worm's idea in being there?
>
> . . . .
>
> Moran: Who wants a worm, anyhow?[33]

In cases such as this cartoon the broad and explicit lines of racist caricature were absent, but the markers of the minstrel were apparent. As Daniel Goldmark succinctly puts it, "Minstrelsy never died—it simply changed media."[34] Live vaudeville shows shared the bill with feature films in the 1920s and then were gradually replaced by the short subject variety films of the early sound era, of which animation was a staple. So, it wasn't just that early animators performed their craft on a stage also populated by minstrels or that animators frequented vaudeville shows (which some did). More significantly, animation developed in a milieu in which creative borrowing was the norm. This provides the backdrop (quite literally) against which to read early American animation's indebtedness to the minstrel show and its use of racial alterity. Animation is related to blackface minstrelsy in its performative history, its visual iconography, and its description of power relations.

Drawn almost exclusively by whites, and in the sound era voiced largely by white talent, animation had its own means of segregation—and its violation. Even in the silent era the visual representation of blackness had followed the conventions of blackface minstrelsy: the large, pale lips, wide eyes, and elastic loping movements of the minstrel.[35] With the coming of sound, the voice followed the same rule: "black" characters spoke with the long, slow, southern, and

FIGURE 7.3. (a) An ad for Moran and Mack in a Paramount/Publix exhibitors' guide, c. 1930. Publix Opinion Collection, Louis B. Mayer Library, American Film Institute; (b) a bill for Christy's Minstrels demonstrates the necessary gesture toward authenticity, the promise of the "Peculiar Characteristics of the Southern Plantation Negro."

stupid cadence of the minstrel. This minstrel trope was also repeated in cartoon music. For example, Disney's *Steamboat Willie* (1928), famous (erroneously) for being the first sound cartoon, featured the rising star Mickey Mouse playing the tune "Turkey in the Straw," formerly known as "Old Zip Coon," very violently on various farm animals' bodies.[36] Even before this moment, with the rise in the 1910s and 1920s of trademark animal and quasi-human characters (Felix, Krazy Kat, Ko-Ko, Oswald), the visual markers of minstrelsy—the mouth, eyes, gloves, and so forth—were combined with the fantastic qualities whites projected onto the minstrel: cleverness, musicality, joy, humor, agility, and resistance to oppression. As with Mickey's choice of music, these vestigial markings didn't necessarily signal blackness directly, yet they were present, as Otto Messmer's explanation of Felix the Cat's origins makes clear: "Pat Sullivan ... had worked with Raoul Barré, see, so he started off on his own, doing his little Negro Pickaninny [Sammie Johnsin]. Which later on became almost Felix, at least in my mind anyway. Same kind of a, only he was a pickaninny. Now that was going along pretty good, but it didn't through the South, that little anti-Negro feeling. They wouldn't run the Pickaninnies."[37] Yet while Messmer may have taken up work already in progress, he also entered into a community of practice in which blackness and slavery signified very specifically, even when they did so indirectly. As a review of *Trials of a Cartoonist* (1916) in *Moving Picture World* put it, "The figures that he draws become rebellious and refuse to act as he wants them to, so he has a terrible time to make them do his bidding. They answer back and say that he has no right to make slaves of them even if he is their creator."[38]

Associated with the native wit of the young "pickaninny," the minstrel trickster, trademark characters such as Felix partook of the qualities of fantastic blackness and their redemptive disregard for the bonds of either social convention or physical reality. With the coming of sound, the more explicitly *negative* qualities associated with blackness (fear, violence, stupidity, etc.) were increasingly assigned to the clearly marked racist stereotypes—such as the jazz maniacs of *Tin Pan Alley Cats* (1943) or *Coal Black and de Sebben Dwarfs* (1943)—and maintained in a largely segregated world. This segregation extended beyond the regulation of spatial relations to the careful parsing of bodily signifiers. Grotesquely exaggerated physiognomy, a simple matter in animation, and the admixture of fear and desire that charged the popular reception of swing, for instance, could be articulated either way. Reading *Swing Wedding* (1937), Lehman notes that "Harman-Ising turned the hip, urban Cotton Club musicians into unsophisticated rural blacks. The studio also caricatured them as frogs; former studio animator Mel Shaw recalled that because of their large mouths, frogs were considered suitable animals to depict as African Americans."[39] When, however, Cab Calloway played opposite Betty Boop, an ostensibly white character, even as his voice and dance moves remained unmistakable, he could be turned "white" (as in *Old Man of the Mountain* [1933]) or rotoscoped onto an ambiguous minstrel character such as Ko-Ko (*Snow-White* [1932]) or a ghostly dancing walrus (*Minnie the Moocher* [1932]).

The common tumult of reappropriated ressentiment offered early vaudeville and film audiences a performative space within which to experience and express similarity and difference, and the pleasure of that common experience was to come from the conversion of the expected sting of oppression into humor.

This was the vaudeville turn, the production of unexpected differentiation, the defamiliarization of the all-too-familiar realities of class and ethnic inequality. Burlesque and early vaudeville inverted structures of power in a carnivalesque celebration of the underdog.[40] The blackface minstrel such as Tambo or Bones referred to the fantasy of the recalcitrant slave who resisted oppression through a combination of inherent jubilation and native cunning. In this carnivalesque, blackness served as a fundamental ground of difference, that which pointed to the possibility of transformation for ethnic others from tinged to white.

Still, at the end of the day, when the house lights came up, as the minstrels wiped the cork from their faces or the screen flashed "The End," the audience left through different doors. Then a different sort of recognition set in, one of enforced and immutable difference, not of commonality. Yet even leaving through those different exits, the crowd dispersed into the same discursive matrix, within which metamorphosis and mutability were inextricably intertwined. The animate minstrel held the power of transformation, and of escaping the confines of the animate space, precisely because it could not escape the larger institutional logic of race. Like his brother on the stage, the cartoon minstrel embodied the guarantee of the melting pot, the promise of changing one's circumstances, only because he was invested with the immutable charge of blackness, the racial alterity that came from alloying the subject with the object, the commodity with itself. Created by the animator, and standing in for him, the animate minstrel enacted a rebellion against its commodity nature that was designed to fail.

The Fleischers, for instance, built this dynamic into the many gags in which their trademark character, Ko-Ko, used the ink from which he was made to foil Max—as when he would splash ink onto Max's white shirt or mix it into his shaving cream to make him inadvertently black up. The animate character was a made object actively resisting the hand of its maker, with the added twist that the maker also created that resistance. The stereotypical blackness of the minstrel became a shorthand marker for the worker resisting his or her commodity status, one imposed on him or her by the seemingly free choice of entering a virtually compulsory labor market.

VIADUCT? WHY NOT A CHICKEN?

So, is such a historical and instrumental explanation of the genealogy of racist practices in animation exculpatory? No, and that's not the point. The point might be, what was the specific historical relationship between racist stereotypes and the humor that some people found in them? According to Dave Fleischer, Cab Calloway fell to his knees and rolled on the ground in hysterics when he saw the Fleischers' rotoscoped rendition of him singing "Minnie the Moocher" as a

ghostly walrus.[41] But his purported willingness to laugh at himself being reproduced as a "spook" is not an absolution, any more than the widespread popular
African American acceptance of Amos 'n' Andy in the late 1920s and 1930s is an
indication of the accuracy or goodwill in its depiction of African American life.[42]

Nor does blacking up indicate, in and of itself, a performer's individual affinity
with or hostility to African Americans. It was possible for Bert Williams to black
up, to complain of racist discrimination at the hands of his dressing-room attendant, and yet to state, categorically, that "the white men who have interpreted our
race in this manner [of blackface] have done us no discredit; they have given apt
expression to our humor and sentiment."[43] In such unresolved contradictions
lurks the intense affect that charges racist laughter—an affect that policing does
not undo. The veteran animator Dick Huemer, confronted with the suggestion
that the crows he had a hand in animating for *Dumbo* (1941) were racist, was
shocked and responded that the "colored" choir that had voiced most of them
"liked it very much and enjoyed doing it hugely. They even offered suggestions,
and we used some of their ideas, lines of dialogue or words, little touches. . . .
I don't think the crow sequence is derogatory. In fact, when someone mentioned
the possibility to me, I was quite taken aback."[44]

The important and meaningful recuperative work in instances such as this—
with their focus on the words or acts of individuals—is based on the commonplace confusion between personal and institutional racism. Eddie Cantor, for
example, was a brilliant comedian who made a name for himself as a blackface
minstrel (among other things), not because he created or even regulated the form
but because he found in it a means for expressing his talent. The same may be
said for his good friend Bert Williams, who, as Louis Chude-Sokei has pointed
out, was a West Indian immigrant who blacked up to create African American
characters—racist stereotypes by which he created an uneasy geographical, cultural, and political distance from African American culture.[45] The intentions of
the individuals in each of these instances are not as important as the discursive
racial matrix within which those intentions and acts became legible. Their acts
were racist, *and* they were funny to many. That humor gained some of its affective
charge not in spite of that racism but *because* of it. Just as Dutch, Hebrew, or Irish
acts used offensive stereotypes to take advantage of their transgressive qualities,
so it was with minstrelsy. The damage didn't happen onstage or onscreen; it happened within and in relation to a world in which black audiences in front of those
stages and screens would most often come and go through separate entrances,
and watch seated separately, with "their own kind." It, and the affective charge
behind the associated humor, happened in the gap between the real and the ideal.

Yet the rationalization and justification around race has been no less true in
animation. One has only to look. Art Spiegelman, recounting how he developed
the graphic novel *Maus* (1986), has indicated that he drew the inspiration for

a   b

FIGURE 7.4. (a) A hunter is blasted into blackface by *Lucky Ducky* (MGM, 1948); (b) idle hands are the devil's workshop: close-up from *Uncle Tom's Bungalow* (Schlesinger, 1937).

his depiction of Nazis and Jews as cats and mice from racial caricature in early cartoons.[46] Also, in conversation, some animation historians have agreed that the white gloves, the broad mouths, and the overly large eyes that are standard on many animated characters derive from blackface minstrelsy.[47] And, a breath later, they will insist that early animators' borrowing from minstrelsy became sedimented in famous continuing characters for purely *practical* reasons. First, there was *contrast:* in the early days of animation, when film stock, cels, and lighting were all of uneven quality, black bodies were easier to read than white ones. (To fully accept this answer, we have to overlook all of the early "white" continuing characters, such as Col. Heeza Liar, Bobby Bumps, or Dreamy Dud, who are less well remembered today.) Second, there was *economy:* white gloves on a four-fingered hand meant less repetitive detail to draw, and hands were hard to draw well (Fig. 7.4). (This, of course, contradicts the argument for contrast, even as it appeals to efficiency.) Third, there was *clarity:* the large eyes and mouths and broad gestures were more emotionally expressive, which was important in the short form.

So, yes, indeed and yes, but: one explanation does not contradict the other. Exploring the forbidden terrain of those images and gags that might be racist *and* funny, it becomes possible to understand that all of those practical explanations are at some level valid *and* that the practices they explain (away) were still grounded in racist discourses. And all of those reasons also support racial formations that see black bodies as more physical than those of whites, black hands as idle, crap-shooting tools in the devil's workshop, and black sensibilities as more emotionally expressive and less rational than those of whites.

But it is sometimes difficult to raise this point, that racist attitudes were the coin of the realm for artists and audiences of the day, because it seems to suggest a maliciously racist intentionality (or duplicity) on the part of the discursive founders of animation. And if that were so, it would require us to disavow those cartoons as wrong, hence not really funny. It would certainly be enough to argue that broad racist caricature and the use of the vestigial elements of minstrelsy point to black stereotyping as underpinning early animation practices. If this is so, then it is more valuable to read the importance of racist discourse to the formation of American animation in discursive, institutional, or structural terms than in personal ones. Whether any specific animator was or was not racist, the practices that animators by necessity entered into were. But a more significant exercise is to explore how racial animus in the cartoon was important to the joke itself, how the "ambivalence of stereotype," the imbrication of intense fear and desire in the same derisive image, alloyed fear of racial difference with desire for that difference.

THE FACT OF LAUGHTER

> *Humor is not resigned; it is rebellious. It signifies the triumph not only of the ego, but also of the pleasure principle, which is strong enough to assert itself here in the face of the adverse real circumstances. . . . By its repudiation of the possibility of suffering, it takes its place in the great series of methods devised by the mind of man for evading the compulsion to suffer—a series which begins with neurosis and culminates in delusions, and includes intoxication, self-induced states of abstraction and ecstasy.*
>
> —FREUD, *CHARACTER AND CULTURE*

In *Character and Culture* (1928) Sigmund Freud was attempting to describe a psychology of what was funny at exactly the historical moment when the animated sound cartoon—with all of its very troubling dynamics of race, class, gender, and sexuality—was exuberantly bursting onto the scene as a popular form of short entertainment. And Freud, in describing humor as a violent rebellion in service (or perhaps honor) of the pleasure principle, knew best the genteel white society of Vienna. This was the same Vienna whose city council in 1928 attempted to bar the scandalously sexual and nonwhite Josephine Baker and her "heathen dances" from its streets and stages for fear of cultural pollution. Jazz, the mongrel music of America, was a worldwide phenomenon, and in Europe the (sometimes celebrated, sometimes abhorred) eruption of the "jungle" into polite, white civilization, threatened/promised to disrupt/accelerate its tidy march into modernity. For ostensibly white audiences—whether in the United States or in Europe—blackness stood, in the guise of jazz, the minstrel, and the racist caricature of the lazy coon, as a rebellion against the strictures of white, middle-class life.

In the United States both jazz and the minstrel seemed to speak back to elite demands for "civilized" behavior in a society overrun with uncivilized immigrants, migrants, and rubes straight from their failing farms.[48] For black audiences, of course, the psychic violence of the civilizing force could signify quite differently. In the era of the Great Migration, the coal wars, and the Scottsboro trials, violence was neither abstract nor necessarily internalized. In many ways the discourse of internalization is beside the point. The simultaneous performance in cartoons of blackness as primally powerful and as pitifully abject seems more fruitfully understood in terms of identification than of internalization, in the interrogation of (one's own) laughter. In the fantasy of blackness that underpinned both racist caricature and the vestigial minstrel, cartoons offered up not a model for behavior as much as a test of affinity. Is it possible to laugh not in sympathy with the violence visited but with empathy for all whose worth is determined by their commodity status?

Yet the distinction between the animate minstrel and broader racist caricatures of animation's "Golden Age" remains important. The trademark minstrel character permitted the image of a safe but violent rebellion against normative social mores and the strictures of rationalization, one in which its race was masked by the plausible deniability of the animal or clown figure. When race was made literal in the racist caricature, it presented the flip side of that desire, the [racialized] punishment of that rebellion. What had been in early animation a pantomime of the creature's rebellion against its creator, and its inevitable failure and punishment, became in the early sound era the literalization of race as rebellion and its necessary repression. For example, this cycle of displacement could be compressed into a single series of actions in a gag repeated in many cartoons: a trickster character, chased by an enraged attacker, suddenly turns and savages that attacker by shooting him or blowing him up. Rather than being reduced to a bloody mess, the attacker is literally blown into racist black caricature, expressing his abject humiliation at the hands of the animate minstrel trickster. In these cartoons characters victimize themselves and each other, and in doing so they stand in as stereotyped fetishes for a complex of social relations. In the aborted chase the motive force of the trickster/minstrel is made manifest: its potency derives from its blackness, and in that moment of violence the complex interplay of appropriation and subjection becomes literalized in the blackening of the desiring pursuer. The gag articulates the danger in the amalgam of fear and desire that is the stereotype: an attempt to fully possess the raw power of the minstrelized object (such as Lucky or Bugs) could blast you into abjection.

The joke literalizes the omnipresent threat: do not desire too much, and do not identify. This is the color bar violently maintained all the way down to the ground, even in cartoons. The "compulsion to suffer" about which Freud speaks (to and from a certain neurotic subject position) could vary both in the degree of its interiority and in its objects. The compulsion to conform to white, middle-class norms of socialization was itself internalized from within a larger set of social and material relations that Rogin described as an avenue to whiteness for ethnic Americans.[49] As has been well remarked for generations, for African Americans that internalization was a path to double-consciousness, a potential violence against oneself, the internalization of oppression, and offered no guarantee of social acceptance or advancement.[50] Even for those making the transition from ethnicity to whiteness, that internalization carried with it the requirement of the repudiation of the object, and real empathy was/is a gesture of historical self-immolation. Yet even careful distinctions between the forms and objects of the social (and sometimes material) relations from which shared laughter erupts leave only the uncertain possibility of a collective empathy overtaking a necessarily failed liberal sympathy. Imagine a segregated audience—whites in the orchestra, blacks in the balcony—laughing together at the same animated caricature or minstrel. Except in the most compassionate and detached abstraction that sees such an audience as a unified whole sharing in the victimhood of racism's violence (in which an injury to one is an injury to all), the meaning of the laughter isn't uniform, any more than is the fabric of struggle and violence that informs it. The threat of empathy in the context of the racist cartoon is that it may rob one of a perhaps precarious subject status. That is, to feel for others—to imagine feeling *as* another—carries with it the risk of becoming as partial and divided as those who are the objects of ridicule. Sympathy is a safer choice that permits the illusion of subjective unity, denying the freedom to laugh *with*, leaving only the possibilities of not laughing or of laughing *at*.[51]

But there is, in the end, still laughter. This is where Marx's gloss on the fetish meets Freud's.[52] Both build their notions on a romantic anthropological conceit that has its roots in a fantasy of an African Other as that which stands in materially for a larger set of historical forces, the avowal of which would fatally disrupt the social order. (And both assume that fetish is the embodiment of an almost willful misconception of those forces.) For Marx that history is social and material/oppositional; for Freud it is cultural and personal/integrative. Usually, Freud is read as describing the production of the fetish as a refusal to acknowledge the difference produced through the violence of (imagined) castration. Yet it is also a refusal to accept the incommensurable tension between difference and similarity. In Freud's example the boy (yes, the boy) witnesses this difference in his mother and cannot face the threat of paternal castration that she represents. He disavows her difference, replacing it first with a scarred similarity so horrible it must be denied, then with an object charged with the emotion behind that disavowal. The situation is similar with blackness in cartoons. The tension that informs the animated minstrel (or the stereotype) is twofold: it requires witnessing blackness as human, but as necessarily and simultaneously less so (primitive, unemployed, and subjugated) and more so (carefree and free from the bondage of labor) than whiteness, and the animated creature as both living and yet handmade. To para-phrase Marx, it addresses an audience that is hailed as self-made but knows (and needs to forget) that it has lost the tools of its own making. And so there is vio-lence. And so there is laughter, the raucous screams of the (perpetually disavowed and disavowing) commodity.

CONCLUSION

In his history of American animation, *Seven Minutes*, Norman Klein suggests that "blacks in musical comedy had so powerful a meaning in American enter-tainment, and they were so often played by whites themselves, they almost transcended the issue of race itself. *Almost*, but certainly never entirely. To say 'almost' merely captures the sense of how important 'blackface' was to the car-toon form."[53] Although Klein admits to the centrality of African American music and dance, and of blackface minstrelsy, in the development of cartoons in the United States, he does not actually explore exactly why race and minstrelsy so deeply informed the art and craft of animation. He doesn't quite explain the incredible tension in his amazing claim—the tension that is contained in that "*Almost.*" Perhaps the beginning of that explanation is in the strange ambiguity hiding in the use of "they" in this passage. At first, it seems that Klein is speak-ing of the incredible influence of actual African Americans on (an implicitly white) American entertainment. Yet as his thought unwinds, we discover that some of these influential blacks were actually whites in blackface. Here, being authentically black is not about race but about performance. As with the fetish, that performance is rooted in the material world, indeed requires it, but leads inexorably away from it. And one direction it leads is toward the hand that draws the minstrel who must turn on that hand but only because it has been made to do so. It is almost real, almost uncontainable in its contradiction. The white hand of the animator created in the animate minstrel a compulsion to rebel against the conditions of its making and destined it to fail in that rebellion. And if that makes for laughter, that laughter is nervous; it is tinged with regret and shame, with guilty pleasure. And it begs the question of who is laughing, and how.

NOTES

Research support for this essay was provided by the Dean of Arts and Sciences and the Connaught Fund at the University of Toronto, and the Social Sciences and Humanities Research Council of Canada. Special thanks to Jon Nichols for the insights into minstrelsy and animation that led to this study, and to Cynthia Chris and Aubrey Anable for their close reading and invaluable criticism. Thanks also to the editors for their patient and constructive criticism, and to my research assistants, Alicia Fletcher, Andrea Whyte, Sarah Barmak, and Agnieszka Baranowska.

1. For an overview of eugenics in the United States see Kline, *Building a Better Race*; and Lovett,

Conceiving the Future. For a eugenic argument see Herrnstein and Murray, *The Bell Curve.* For the ongoing potency of this discourse see Roberts, "A Nation of None and All of the Above."

2. For a discussion of *Plessy v. Fergusson* and the racial formation "separate but equal" see Patterson, *"Brown v. Board of Education";* or Martin, *"Brown v. Board of Education."*

3. For a detailed and fascinating discussion of the comic and alterity, a detailed engagement of which is beyond the scope of this chapter, see Zupančič, *The Odd One In.*

4. Compare Freud, "The Relation of Jokes to Dreams and to the Unconscious" (1905), with Freud, "Humor" (1928), discussed here. For a discussion of this comparison, to which space does not permit a detailed reply, see Critchley, *On Humor.* For the sake of argument, this chapter somewhat collapses humor and joking, considering the similarities more important to the topic than the differences.

5. For an excellent account of animation and swing see Goldmark, *Tunes for 'Toons.* For a discussion of swing, race, and modernism see also Dinerstein, *Swinging the Machine.*

6. For a musicological discussion of this segment see Goldmark, *Tunes for 'Toons,* 86–91.

7. For discussions of African Americans and fantasies of the jungle and of Africanness see Cripps, *Slow Fade to Black;* and Naremore, "Uptown Folks." For a detailed analysis of African Americans in musicals see Knight, *Disintegrating the Musical.*

8. See Holberg, "Betty Boop"; and O'Meally, "Checking Our Balances."

9. Sampson, *That's Enough, Folks,* 81.

10. Of course, this is only a racial binary if we consider Ko-Ko's literalized Jewishness as "white." Otherwise, we are actually dealing with racial triangulation. See Rogin, *Blackface, White Noise.*

11. Klein, *Seven Minutes,* 66.

12. Marx, *Capital,* vol. 1.

13. Generically, minstrels were male, with men in drag playing women's roles. In the twentieth century in particular, some women did black up, the most famous perhaps being Sophie Tucker. See Brooks, *Bodies in Dissent,* 199–204; and Brown, *Babylon Girls,* 68–74, 213–14.

14. Comedians such as Costello or Allen (and the writers who crafted their material) also made heavy use of the sort of wordplay found in minstrelsy's stump speech.

15. The association between minstrels and trademark animated characters is long-standing. Even in the sound era, as Christopher Lehman points out, that relationship continued: "Iwerks also adapted Sambo and company to the animation trends of the mid-1930s. Sambo looks and acts just like Mickey Mouse—hardly a surprise, given that Iwerks helped to create the mouse. The boy is dressed in short pants and huge oval shoes just like Mickey's" (Lehman, *The Colored Cartoon,* 54). See also the discussion of Felix below.

16. See Crafton, *Before Mickey.*

17. By the birth of the movies, however, vaudeville was increasingly catering to middle-class audiences, with the larger entrepreneurs such as Keith and Albee or Tony Pastor creating elaborate theaters and cleaning up raunchier acts in an effort to bring in middle-class dollars. See Lewis, *From Traveling Show To Vaudeville;* Allen, *Horrible Prettiness;* and Slide, *The Encyclopedia of Vaudeville.* At the same time, however, the acts themselves retained a distinctly working-class flavor, and indeed this was part of the allure, the chance for safe class mixing.

18. Louis Chude-Sokei has pointed out that the construction of the notion of the "immigrant" came to signify the European immigrant and necessarily excluded those arriving from the Caribbean and Latin America. See Chude-Sokei, *The Last "Darky."*

19. See, e.g., Roediger, *The Wages of Whiteness;* Lott, *Love and Theft;* and Rogin, *Blackface, White Noise.*

20. See Rogin, *Blackface, White Noise,* 45–120.

21. Hammond, "Cohan Is Too Busy to Resent Appellation."

22. This distinguished early minstrels from other blackface performers who demonstrated dance and vernacular from less exotic locales such as New Jersey. See Lhamon, *Raising Cain*.

23. See Jenkins, *What Made Pistachio Nuts?* 59–95.

24. For detailed discussions of the history of blackface minstrelsy see Cockrell, *Demons of Disorder*; Bean, Hatch, and McNamara, *Inside the Minstrel Mask*; and Mahar, *Behind the Burnt Cork Mask*.

25. This offers a counter to Benjamin's fears of the desire of the masses appropriated by film producers and crystallized in the body of the star. See Benjamin, "The Work of Art in the Age of Its Technological Reproducibility," 34–55.

26. For an overview of the "concept of community of practice" see Rogoff, *Everyday Cognition*; and Lave and Wenger, *Situated Learning*.

27. Discussing comic performance, Zupančič describes this bifurcation from the perspective of the comic actor, pointing out that while epic performance is a narration of relations, and tragic performance the representation of relations, comic performance offers the collapse of performer and character into one imperfect object that performs its lack for us. See Zupančič, *The Odd One In*.

28. For a discussion of problems of cross-racial identification see Ignatiev, *Race Traitor*.

29. Lott, *Love and Theft*, 38–63; Hall, "Racist Ideologies and the Media."

30. Hartman, *Scenes of Subjection*, 29.

31. Lehman, *The Colored Cartoon*, 47.

32. For a discussion of torture and humor in relation to the American conquest of Iraq see Henderson, "Disregarding the Suffering of Others."

33. This tagline was also used in *The Wacky Worm* (Warner Bros., 1941) and is muttered by a crow as he gives up trying to catch a worm. To hear a recording of this routine, visit www.archive.org/details/MoranMackTheTwoBlackCrows-01–10.

34. Goldmark, *Tunes for 'Toons*, 84.

35. Although space doesn't permit a discussion here, the other obvious and significant source for stereotyping in animation were print media.

36. See Goldmark, *Tunes for 'Toons*, 84; see also 77–106, 183n12, and 184–85n21.

37. Canemaker, "Otto Messmer Interview."

38. Quoted in Crafton, *Before Mickey*, 174; originally published in *Moving Picture World*, Dec. 9, 1916.

39. Lehman, *The Colored Cartoon*, 39.

40. For a discussion of the address to the middle class in vaudeville see Allen, *Horrible Prettiness*. Allen bases his argument very much around Stallybrass and White's notion of the carnivalesque, which they in turn build from Bakhtin; see White and Stallybrass, *The Politics and Poetics of Transgression*; and Bakhtin, *Rabelais and His World*.

41. Adamson, "'Where Can I Get a Good Corned Beef Sandwich?'"

42. See Ely, *The Adventures of Amos 'n' Andy*; and Knight, *Disintegrating the Musical*.

43. "Music and the Drama," *Chicago Record*, c. 1910. Needless to say, there are issues of freedom of speech and of permissible discourse that may have shaped Williams's public pronouncements. What we can note here is that in order to protect and further his career, Williams entered into and furthered that discourse.

44. Adamson, "With Disney on Olympus."

45. Chude-Sokei, *The Last "Darky,"* 82–113.

46. See Cavalieri, "Jewish Mice, Bubblegum Cards, Comics Art, and Raw Possibilities." In his graphic retelling of this story, *Breakdowns: Portrait of the Artist as a Young %@&*!*, Spiegelman is more specific, pegging it to insights gained in film classes he took with Ken Jacobs at SUNY in the early 1970s. More recently, Niall Ferguson, with his usual subtlety, compared President Obama to

Felix the Cat, stating that both were "not only black . . . [but] also very, very lucky" (Ferguson, "A Runaway Deficit May Soon Test Obama's Luck").

47. Conversation with Ray Pointer, July 2006; conversation with Jerry Beck, Aug. 2007; Klein, *Seven Minutes*, 192.

48. For a discussion of the production of jazz in dominant discourse and cinema respectively see Gabbard, *Representing Jazz;* and Gabbard, *Jammin' at the Margins.* For a discussion of jazz and modernity/technology see Dinerstein, *Swinging the Machine.* Regarding jazz as produced in contemporary criticism see Gennari, *Blowin' Hot and Cool.* See also Clover, "Dancin' in the Rain"; and Naremore, "Uptown Folks."

49. See Rogin, *Blackface, White Noise.* For critiques of Rogin see Cripps, review of *Blackface, White Noise,* 1462; and Knight, *Disintegrating the Musical.*

50. See Du Bois, *The Souls of Black Folk;* and Fanon, *Black Skin, White Masks.* For a detailed historical analysis and critique of this idea see Wright, *Becoming Black,* 66–110.

51. For a useful discussion of identity and subjectivity around injury see Brown, *Babylon Girls.* While Brown's discussion of wounded identity is by no means exhaustive, it does frame issues of race, gender, ability, and sexuality in terms of the regimes of legitimation and avenues to power that have grown around and within racial formations in the United States over the last two centuries.

52. Rogin, in *Blackface, White Noise* (182–89), makes a similar move to link the Freudian and Marxist fetish in the act of blacking up. But Rogin makes this link primarily in the context of the Oedipal dynamics he locates in the Jewish use of blackface and soon after drops it. Žižek suggests that the Marxian and Freudian fetishes are different because the Marxian fetish stands in for a positive network of social relations, while the Freudian replaces a lack (see Žižek, *The Sublime Object of Ideology,* 49). Although space does not permit a detailed discussion of this supposed difference, see below for a brief clarification.

53. Klein, *Seven Minutes*, 192.

8

"I Like to Sock Myself in the Face"

Reconsidering *"Vulgar Modernism"*

Henry Jenkins

Published in *Artforum* in 1982, J. Hoberman's "Vulgar Modernism" represented a benchmark in critical discussions of "popular art." Hoberman constructed the case for the formal innovation and artistic importance of a range of popular artists who were seemingly locked out of the canon on the basis of their low cultural status, even as their work continued to influence a broad range of modern and postmodern artists.[1] Hoberman described "vulgar modernism" as "the vulgar equivalent of modernism itself. By this I mean a popular, ironic, somewhat dehumanized mode reflexively concerned with specific properties of its medium or the conditions of its making." He suggested that this "sensibility . . . developed between 1940 and 1960 in such peripheral corners of the 'culture industry' as animated cartoons, comic books, early morning TV, and certain Dean Martin/ Jerry Lewis comedies" (33). Hoberman devoted the core of his essay to individualized discussions of the animator Tex Avery, director Frank Tashlin, cartoonist Will Elder, and television performer Ernie Kovacs, yet his introduction made clear that the concept of "vulgar modernism" extends more broadly, speaking to a particular relationship between popular culture and high art during this postwar period.

Although Hoberman did not originate the analogy between a certain tradition of popular humor and modernism, he helped to expand the debate from auteurist studies of individual artists, often described as distinctive or idiosyncratic within their own medium, to offer an account of a larger artistic project that took shape across and between media in the postwar period. There is still a lot we do not know about these artists and how they might be related, but it is increasingly clear that Hoberman's intuitive sense of their fit with each other reflected some behind-the-scenes collaborations. Let's take, for example, the musician Spike Jones. Jordan R. Young's biography of Jones, *Spike Jones off the Record: The Man Who Murdered Music*, traces his migrations across different media (stage, radio, live-action and animated cinema, comics, television, and records), as well as his collaborations with a range of other artists often associated with "vulgar modernism": Jones sought advice from Tex Avery and Frank Tashlin on gags for his various film and television performances, contributed material to Ernie Kovacs's television series, and published pieces in early *Mad* magazine.[2] All signs are that these artists knew each other socially and professionally, were informed by each other's work, drew on the same aesthetic roots, and, in every other sense, constituted what we might describe as a circle.

While we have a tendency to deal with animated and live-action comedy as separate traditions, vulgar modernism blurs the boundaries between the two. Live performers adopted larger-than-life personas that stretched their bodies beyond human limits; they occupied worlds that continually call attention to their constructed nature through their use of reflexive gags or their deployment of signs and other background elements that signal their departure from the constraints of mundane reality. Indeed, when I show my students the works of Spike Jones or Olsen and Johnson, they often remark how much they resemble American cartoons of the same period. This may reflect in part the fact that the animated versions of vulgar modernism are more widely shown today, yet these performers are often viewed as "cartoonish" even when they are appearing onstage in front of a live audience. By the same token, Tex Avery could turn a character like the wise-cracking Screwball Squirrel into a vaudeville performer, tapping all of the cornball and flamboyant elements of that performance tradition to disrupt the conventions of the animated short subject, turning to the camera, disrupting the action, and simply making fun of the situations he finds himself in much the same way the Marx Brothers did a decade or so earlier. All of them were drawing inspiration from Madison Avenue with their reliance on signs, billboards, and slogans as devices for comic commentary on the action. And the kinds of amplification of the body, literalized metaphors, and silly sounds we associate with cartoons were spilling over into the stage, radio, and recorded sound performances of Spike Jones, suggesting that vulgar modernism could, at least sometimes, operate purely on the level of sound-based media. In short, vulgar modernism was a period of cross-pollination between comic traditions, between media, and, if Hoberman is right, between high art and popular culture.

Above all, the artists I am calling vulgar modernists deploy these techniques to produce laughter as opposed to the shock and displeasure that often surrounds reflexivity within the modernist tradition. Indeed, much of the humor here is generated through breaks with conventional modes of representation or by the introduction of a metalevel that comments ironically on the depicted action. In some cases such devices are not in and of themselves funny, but they may create a comic climate where we can laugh at the actions being depicted. In others, what we find comic is the sheer density of information and flurry of activity or the exaggeration and amplification of human emotion. At the same time, the comic dimensions of these works—the sense that they were not going to be taken seriously—may have given the artists sufficient expressive freedom to break with classical and realist conventions being enforced elsewhere in their medium.

Over the past decade or so, many of the artists associated with vulgar modernism have been rediscovered, with new books published on Will Elder and Jack Cole, a recent coffee-table book reprinting sketches and published works by Basil Wolverton, and the reissue of some long-lost television and radio performances of Spike Jones on DVD. This chapter draws heavily on this new material to reconsider the vulgar modernists, attempting to offer a more systematic mapping of their shared aesthetic traits and their specific place in the history of American comedy. I will expand the group of artists labeled as vulgar modernists, define what this group shared, and suggest why it is productive to draw comparisons between works produced across such a broad array of different media. Hoberman's essay still provides a good starting point for discussing these artists, especially insofar as it foregrounds their complex relationship to both modernism and popular culture. If anything, Hoberman's core claim that they constituted something like an artistic movement is strengthened by the recently available material. Almost three decades later we still lack an adequate critical language to discuss this distinctive style of popular art—and, indeed, one could argue that the turn toward cultural studies has further displaced aesthetic considerations from our understanding of these works. We still seem blocked by established cultural hierarchies from being able to meaningfully engage with what's most interesting in these "funny pictures."

I write this chapter in the hopes of sparking further evaluation rather than making a definitive statement. My focus is going to be on Tex Avery, Spike Jones, Olsen and Johnson, Will Elder, Jack Cole, and Basil Wolverton. For space considerations I am not taking on Bob and Ray, Ernie Kovacs, Frank Tashlin, and many others who would also belong in a more thorough discussion of vulgar modernism. My focus here is primarily formal, though there are important ideological questions, having to do with their representations of race, gender, sexuality, wartime propaganda and postwar advertising, censorship and regulation, and so forth, which will need to be confronted in any larger discussion. In short, this chapter opens a can of worms, hoping more people will pay attention to these artists and their contributions to American culture. But then, comedy is always messy business.

MODERNISM?

Read today, Hoberman's essay feels more timid than it did a few decades ago—an attempt to negotiate with the sensibilities of a high-art readership (and thus preserve entrenched cultural hierarchies) even as it rescues certain key popular artists from the margins of critical consideration. We see this exceptionalism in the speed with which the essay labels such works "para-art" (by the start of the second paragraph) or the ways in which it borrows authority through analogies to already acclaimed modern artists, describing Tex Avery, for example, as "the Manet of vulgar modernism" (33). In short, some artists rise above the "muck" that surrounds them, to reference another analogy in Hoberman's essay. To this day, his almost oxymoronic coupling of *vulgar* and *modernism* sparks controversy from those celebrating popular art and those defending high culture alike; we still have a long way to go before we resolve the vague discomfort that comes from applying formalist criticism to what we call popular culture more often than we speak of popular art.

Modernism operates in Hoberman's argument as a very broad and loose signifier of twentieth-century high art (and it has become even more elastic as developed by subsequent generations of critics informed by his interpretations). What linked these popular artists to "modernism" for Hoberman was their interest in foregrounding the materiality of their medium and the conditions of its production and reception, their embrace of reflexivity and intertextuality. Consider, for example, his description of what Will Elder brought to early *Mad* magazine: "His best pieces are collage-like arrangements of advertising trademarks, media icons, banal slogans, visual puns, and assorted non-sequiturs.... As *Mad*'s leading formalist, Elder allows internal objects to tamper with the boundaries of a panel, breaks continuous vistas into consecutive frames, offers visually identical panels with wildly fluctuating details, and otherwise emphasizes the essential serial nature of his medium" (37). In short, Hoberman was interested in these popular artists' refusal to produce a coherent, consistent, or classically constructed diegetic world, openly displaying their own authorial interventions. Hoberman, in that sense, was inspired by *Screen*'s attempt to generate a Brechtian mode of film theory in the 1970s and by the French rediscovery of Frank Tashlin and Jerry Lewis. Both sources of inspiration rested on arguments that self-reflexivity and intertextuality shattered the codes and conventions of classical cinema.

Hoberman's project has been most vigorously taken up by the cartoonist and cultural impresario Art Spiegelman, who has used these artists as a missing link between the gutter art of the Tijuana Bibles of the 1930s and the underground comics of the 1960s and art comics of subsequent decades.[3] Spiegelman has, in the process, broadened the canon of the vulgar modernists by, for example, reprinting works by Basil Wolverton in his influential *Raw* anthologies, writing a book focused on the modernist sensibilities of the comic book artist Jack Cole (*Plastic Man*), or, for that matter, designing an album cover for *Spiked: The Music of Spike Jones,* bringing this once cornball performer to the attention of new hipsters.[4]

Hoberman's vision of "vulgar modernism" was very different from the concept of "cartoon modernism" being promoted in a recent book by Amid Amidi.[5] Amidi is interested in the design aesthetic introduced into American animation in the 1950s by cartoonists such as Ward Kimball, John Hubley, Maurice Noble, and Ernie Pintoff, among others; these artists explicitly drew inspiration from trends in contemporary art. Amidi's focus is on simplification, stylization, abstraction, the flattening of depth perception, and the expressive and nonnaturalistic use of color, among other properties. If Hoberman linked the vulgar modernists to Brecht's concepts of distanciation, Amidi defines his cartoon modernists in relation to Picasso, Matisse, Miro, Klee, and bebop jazz. Tex Avery would be an interesting figure for closer consideration because he is the one crossover between these two very different conceptions of the relationship between American animation and modern art, having embraced aspects of this design aesthetic in his final few years of work (see, for example, *Symphony in Slang* [1951]).

VULGAR?

Hoberman provided only a vague sense of what was "vulgar" about vulgar modernism. *Vulgar* might imply untutored or ignorant, suggesting that we might approach such works much as the art world deals with outsider and folk artists. Yet this argument is less than persuasive when we consider how many of these artists received formal training (and thus were exposed to twentieth-century art movements), experimented on the side with producing works that more fully met high art criteria, and often directly and explicitly parodied various modern artists and movements throughout their work (witness the recurring theme of "smashing the classics").[6] These guys studied side by side in art school with people who would go on to careers within the art world; they had the technical skills to do work that would have met the art world's criteria of evaluation, but they opted to pursue their careers in other spaces, creating different kinds of works for different kinds of audiences. They enjoyed their own marginality and often made fun of the pretensions and obscurantism of more exalted forms of artistic expression.

We might use the term *vulgar* in a descriptive sense, to describe the relatively low cultural status granted their work at the time it was being produced; we might deploy the term *vulgar* to refer to certain intentionally distasteful aspects of their representation of the body and sexuality, their deployment of everyday materials including advertising as the inspiration for their own artistic production, though in that sense, they prefigure where art has gone in the postmodern period. Can we rescue *vulgar* by redefining it in terms of transgressions committed both against the institutional practices of mainstream media and the world of high art, or are the class politics of *vulgar* so deeply entrenched that it resists reappropriation on this level?

We might also see these figures as "vulgar" in much the same way that Miriam Hansen has spoken of "vernacular modernism" (here, drawing heavily on slapstick comedy as a primary reference point) and its relationship to classical cinema: "the term vernacular combines the dimension of the quotidian, of everyday usage, with the connotations of discourse, idiom and dialect, with circulation, promiscuity and translatability."[7] Like Hoberman, Hansen welcomes the productive tension between popular art and high culture. I am holding on to Hoberman's term *vulgar modernism* for much the same reasons: it generates discussion of the relations between the two terms, discussion that needs to occur if we are not to simply naturalize old assumptions about the relations between high art and low.

I want to move away from Hoberman's easy deployment of the concept of "para-art" and the implication that these works are not quite art, worthy of aesthetic consideration but not perhaps the ultimate recognition given to "true artists." I start from the assumption that popular art needs to be evaluated on its own terms, that it needs to be understood in relation to its own aesthetic goals and circumstances, and that no apology need be made for popular artists simply because they work in institutional settings other than the art world. In framing the concept of vulgar modernism, Hoberman signaled a need to step outside of the popular tradition in order to explain the reflexiveness found in these works. Hoberman may not fully appreciate the degree to which early comic strips or vaudeville sketches were already calling attention to their own conventions, were already taking pleasure in their nonrealistic properties, and were already making fun of the line between high and low culture. We need to understand vulgar modernism both as part of the process by which modernist art devices were popularized and as part of the process by which popular art remained true to its own transgressive impulses.

CARTOONUS INTERRUPTUS

Let's begin with a consideration of one of the emblematic moments from Tex Avery's oeuvre, the opening sequence from *Screwball Squirrel* (MGM, 1944). The streetwise protagonist hijacks "the picture" from his cloyingly rendered counterpart, Sammy. Sammy's big eyes, fluttering eyelashes, baby talk, and coy gestures, accompanied by sentimentalized music, stand in sharp contrast to Screwball's aggressive manners, broad gestures, nasal voice, slangy language, elastic body, and slapsticky gags. Sammy and all of his "cute little furry friends in the forest" are no match for Screwball, who takes the sissy squirrel behind a tree and knocks the crap out of him, turning to the camera to explain, "You wouldn't have liked that picture anyway," and promising "funny stuff" is coming soon.

Animation scholars have correctly identified this moment as a critical confrontation between two schools of American animation, though most of them have incorrectly aligned Sammy with Walt Disney. In the context of Tex Avery's then-recent move from Warner Bros. to MGM to take over the animation division, it is more likely that the immediate reference point was to Hugh Harman and Rudy Ising, his predecessors. We can read the gesture as acknowledging the changing of the guard at Metro, much as Avery began his first MGM cartoon, *Blitz Wolf* (1942), by offering a syncopated version of the MGM lion's opening roar. Both moments signal that nothing was going to be taken seriously in the Avery era.

Perhaps more broadly, we can see the vulgar modernists as taking on what Mark Langer has called the West Coast school of American animation with its middle-class ideology, middlebrow taste, and classical aesthetic, in favor of a style that saw itself as more "adult" at a time when American cinema in general was reinventing itself to reflect the sensibilities of a postwar audience. Langer contrasts the West Coast school with the New York school, which he associates with the Fleischer brothers. Many of the defining traits of the New York school carry over to this postwar generation of artists, including a focus on transgression of social norms, an emphasis on the artificiality of the characters and their drawn nature, the use of "exaggerated effects" that call attention to the "artificial" and "manufactured" nature of cartoons, and a "polyphonic and heterogeneous" mixture of elements.[8] Langer's discussion of the "New York School" gives us a way of situating the vulgar modernists in a much older history of cartoons and animation, rather than reading them as a modernist disruption of the realist or classical cinema.

Many of the "vulgar modernists," however, come from the middle parts of the country, not from the coastal cities, and felt outside both urban sophistication and middle-class propriety. Yet, like the Fleischer brothers, their work was informed through borrowings from vaudeville, where so many of them got their start. Indeed, there is a long tradition of confusing the kinds of transgressions of the practices of the legitimate theater found in vaudeville with devices associated with modernist distanciation, but it's worth remembering that the devices are deployed here to very different effect: to intensify rather than diminish our emotional experience.

We might understand the opening of *Screwball Squirrel* in relation to a widespread vaudeville trope, the interrupted act. In another essay, which traces this motif across Buster Keaton's film career, I describe the functions this device played in variety entertainment: "The interrupted performance was a common act structure within the vaudeville tradition, seeming to hold open the prospect of onstage action as spontaneous, unrehearsed, improvisational. Vaudeville sought to maintain the illusion—and it was only partially an illusion—that the audience's responses shaped the performance. In a theatrical tradition described by one Chicago critic as 'the field of the expert,' there was a certain pleasure in watching a performance go awry, witnessing events disrupt and threaten the performer's mastery over stagecraft, only to see order restored once again."[9]

In their stage show *Hellzapoppin,* Olsen and Johnson took this principle of the interrupted performance to the absolute limits, building a long-running Broadway show on the promise of the unexpected and the spontaneous:

> During *Hellzapoppin,* the audience had bananas, beans, "pottie-seats," eggs, and live chickens hurled at them; loud shots exploded; planted hecklers raised a rumpus; a ticket scalper cavorted up and down the aisles with tickets for a rival show; a clown tried to extricate himself from a straightjacket for the show's duration; an elderly woman, outraged that her dress had been lifted by a trick gust of air from under the stage, attacked the entire cast with her umbrella. . . . A woman persisted in bellowing "Oscar, Oscar"; the audience was bombarded with rubber snakes and spiders; and a whirling madness of cacophonous pandemonium and blatant boorishness engulfed the theater.[10]

Universal brought the production to the screen as one of the last gasps of the 1930s anarchistic comedy tradition, resulting in what Hoberman described as "an alternative universe as might have been scripted by Victor Shklovsky under the influence of mescaline" (33). The opening sequence literally pulls the floor out from under a high-class musical number, sending a chorus line, dressed in fine evening clothes and singing about heaven, falling gracelessly toward the pits of hell. The film concludes with Olsen and Johnson's elaborate attempts to disrupt the performance of a play within a play, destroying a ballet sequence, for example, through the tactical deployment of sneezy powder, sticky paper, men in bear suits, and thumb tacks.

While some of the running gags carry over from the stage, *Hellzapoppin* (1941) also finds cinematic equivalents for the play's disruptions of the theatrical experience, introducing, for example, an ongoing battle between the characters in the film and a projectionist (played by Shemp Howard), who grumbles about being forced to become an onscreen actor, mixes up the reels, and, in a gag that confuses the role of cameraman and projectionist, refuses to pan to follow the action but prefers to remain focused on a bathing-beauty extra. In one sequence a fight in the projection booth jolts the projector, causing the characters to bounce uneasily on the screen; their attempts to restore balance by adjusting the frame line throws the image further off kilter, bringing the film itself out of alignment.

At one juncture Olsen's head gets slammed against the frame bar repeatedly as the two try desperately to right themselves. Eventually, the characters are thrown into another film altogether, a western inadvertently spliced into the middle of their reel. This transposition forces them into battle with Indians, before they finally arrive back in their proper place in the film.

Hellzapoppin represents a particular inflection of what Steve Seidman and Frank Krutnik have described as the Comedian Comedy tradition.[11] In most works in this genre the focus is on the formal and social transgressions of a core performer or team; these transgressions are typically resolved through the comedian's normalization and social integration in the final reel. In *Hellzapoppin* formal transgression is dispersed across a range of different performers (here, including not just Olsen and Johnson but also Shemp Howard, Martha Raye, Hugh Herbert, and others). A woman crying out for "Oscar" interrupts Olsen and Johnson so many times that they demand someone do something about her, a request accompanied by offscreen sounds of a gunshot and then silence. Hugh Herbert bombards Olsen, Johnson, and Raye with arrows during one particularly exposition-heavy conversation, with characters nonchalantly dodging or pluck-ing away the projectiles whizzing all around them. Just as disruption of the stage performance of *Hellzapoppin* could come from any direction and could exploit any aspect of stagecraft, the film version promises us a world where "anything can happen and probably will."

This interrupted performance structure was also the stock and trade of Spike Jones. The literary modernist Thomas Pynchon emphasizes these elements: "Spike's preferred structure was first to state the theme in as respectably main-stream a manner as possible, then subversively descend into restatement by way of sound effects, crude remarks, and hot jazz, the very idiom Spikes [sic] Jones and his Five Tacks had begun with back in high school, to the great displeasure of their parents."[12] Jones and His City Slickers produced a range of fractured recordings of classical music but also directed these auditory challenges at folk songs and middle-brow lounge music, as might be suggested by his best-known work, "Cocktails for Two." One widely circulated recording of the song opens with a few bars on the piano and a humming chorus, gradually complemented by strings and a male vocalist who valiantly tries to maintain his decorum as the band adds gunshots, clinking glasses, slide whistles, kettle drums, fire bells, gasps, coughs, hiccups, and belches. It is a classic showdown between music, which defines the high, and noise, which defines the low.

Many modern listeners know the audio recording of "Cocktails for Two," which was a favorite on the *Doctor Demento* radio show, but the stage perfor-mances relied as much on sight gags as on comic sounds, including the use of drunken midgets, two-headed or headless men, acrobats, and a range of other activities that upstage and engulf the soloist (as can be seen on recently reissued kinescopes of the television series). Members of the Spike Jones troupe always emphasize the highly structured nature of these comic disruptions—describing how they had to be taught to burp with the beat, if not in tune with the music. The DVDs give us access to multiple versions of "Cocktails for Two," each sharing common elements but each also including novel additions, suggesting a structured but still open space for improvisation within each performance.

From "Cocktails for Two" it is not hard to find our way back to Tex Avery's *The Magical Maestro* (1952), which depicts the showdown that occurs when a carnie magician knocks out an orchestra conductor and takes his place, waging war on an opera singer who is offering a fairly straight rendition of a classical aria. The malevolent maestro does everything he can to distract his high-class rival, including magical transformations of his identity, turning him into, among many others, a ballet dancer, a football player, an Indian chief, a convict, a blackfaced minstrel, a South Seas Islander, and a Chinaman. These disruptions include both visual gags (proliferating rabbits) and sound-based gags, such as abrupt shifts in musical genre (including hillbilly, Hawaiian, and minstrel performances). While the film offers a narrative frame for the interrupted act, disruptions, as in *Hellzapoppin,* also occur from outside the narrative space, such as hair that seems to get caught up in the film's projector and lingers until the opera singer plucks it away. Once again, the interrupted performance structure allows for the pitting of high culture against low, music against noise, and professional polish against liberating improvisation.

CHICKEN FAT

If Avery used the opera singer and the magician as comic stand-ins for the text's struggle between norms and their disruptions, the aesthetics of early *Mad* magazine can be read through a more literal conflict, or at least competition, between the writer Harvey Kurtzman and the artist Will Elder for the attention of the reader. Elder liked to cram his panels with what he called "chicken fat," extraneous gags and signs that pulled our attention from story actions in the foreground to seemingly irrelevant background details. As Elder explained, "chicken fat is the part of the soup that is bad for you, yet gives the soup its delicious pleasure."[13] For the most part these background gags were Elder's own additions, not dictated by Kurtzman's script, though some have suggested Kurtzman increasingly created opportunities for such elements. At other times the writer expressed frustration when these gags overwhelmed the basic building blocks of his narrative or upstaged his verbal humor. Readers would linger on a single panel, scanning for more comic elements rather than following the forward momentum of the plot.

One frequent form of "chicken fat" was advertising signs or graffiti, texts that often annotated the action or offered conflicting ideological perspectives

FIGURE 8.1. *(top)* Panel from "Starchie," *Mad* magazine, June 1954.
FIGURE 8.2. *(bottom)* Panel from "Shadow!" *Mad* magazine, April-May 1953.

on the events. Throughout Elder's "Starchie," background details hint at a much harsher social milieu than depicted in the Archie Andrews comic books. Yet Elder cannot resist putting a Burma Shave rhyme on the butts of a series of background figures in one panel (Fig. 8.1). A scene from "Shadow!" showing a young woman falling down a flight of stairs places a different advertising slogan on each step, while the natives in "Ping Pong" defend themselves with the Blue Shield Knights of Pythias icons, playing cards, Parcheesi boards, roulette wheels, and surf boards (Fig. 8.2). Such images need not be consistent from frame to frame, as in "Sooperdooperman," where a different icon appears on the chests of battling caped crusaders in each panel, further undermining any conception of a coherent or consistent fictional world.

Elder's contemporary, Basil Wolverton, is similarly known for his use of background details and signs. Consider the range of different signs depicted on the cover of a single issue of *Powerhouse Pepper*: "Fighters: Don't mope on the rope," "Seconds don't count. The referee does!," "Don't pile in this aisle!," "Tonight: Powerhouse Pepper vs. Doug Slugmug," "Next Week: Rush Crushmush vs.

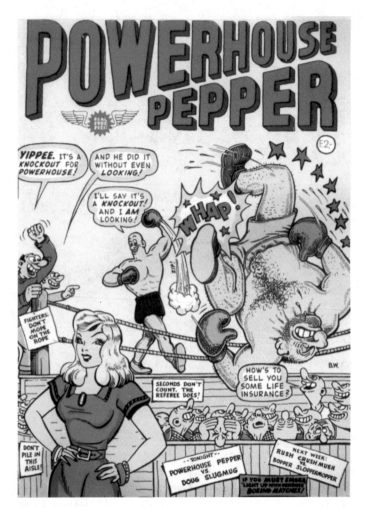

FIGURE 8.3. *Powerhouse Pepper* cover, July 1948.

Bopper Sloppermopper," "If you must smoke, light up with genuine boxing matches." A heckler from the crowd asks via a word balloon, "How's to sell you some life insurance?" while the protagonist is distracted from punching down his oversized opponent by a shapely woman walking down the aisle (Fig. 8.3). A semiotician would have a heyday interpreting the various functions of such signs (promotional, regulatory, informative) within the fictional world, as well as the ways that their language, especially the rhyming slang that was Wolverton's trademark, becomes a source of pleasure in its own right.

Wolverton similarly deploys sound effects graphics as a source of pleasure in and of themselves, often using them to distract from rather than reinforce the main action. One illustrated essay, "Acoustics in the Comics," captures the cartoonist's fascinations with sound effects. Wolverton begins the essay describing his uncertainty as he tries to figure out the best way to graphically convey the sound of a horse stepping on someone's head (in a way that preserved his desired comic effects).[14] Responding to critics of his often wild and crazy images, Wolverton embodies such criticisms through the figure of an editor who insists on "realistic" sound effects. Across a series of misadventures, he depicts the cartoonist as trying to identify the precise sounds required to represent a range of unlikely experiences, so that "flop" represents the sound of "dropping your uppers on a gob of putty," "Jworch" as the sound of a safe falling on a man, "Koyp" as the noise a skin pore makes when it snaps shut upon contact with cold air, and "sop" as the sound of "a[n] octopus tentacle slapping a bald bean" assuming the head is round (though it makes a "spoip" sound if the head is flat). These acoustic gags play on the ways that Wolverton's art refused to abide by realist expectations, as the artist preferred to draw his readers in more zany and improbable directions. Wolverton was interested in the ways that wacky or unlikely sounds might disrupt the norms of a classically constructed text; many of his best graphics engulf his frazzled protagonists with textual representations of their disruptive and distracting sonic surroundings.

CORNY GAG, ISN'T IT?

Tex Avery's cartoons similarly exploit our fascination with background details, though the linear nature of cinema makes it much harder for us to linger over and savor such elements. (One probably has to watch *Screwball Squirrel* many times before spotting the painting of a fire hydrant hanging on the wall of the dog's quarters.) Rather, they unfold in front of the camera, one gag at a time. Consider a few examples from his first MGM film, *Blitz Wolf* (1942). A Good Humor truck appears alongside a tank battalion. A sign pops out of the top of a flame thrower promising, "I don't want to set the world on fire." The Hitler-like Big Bad Wolf steps out of a truck that bears the label "Der Fewer (Der Better)" and holds up a sign to the camera, "Go on and Hiss! Who cares!" (which gets pelted with tomatoes ostensibly lobbed from the picture house audience). When the Wolf's Der Mechanized Huffer und Puffer blows the little pigs' house down, it reveals a sign reading "Gone with the Wind" before the camera pans to show a second sign, "Corny Gag, isn't it?" An endless tilt up the barrel of an aligned weapon pauses long enough to let us read the words on yet another sign: "Long darn thing, isn't it?" And when the weapon fires, it wipes out a graphic representing Japan and yet another sign drops down from offscreen space informing us that "Doolittle

Dood it!" Again and again, such signs destabilize our relations to the represented actions, sometimes suggesting that the characters are themselves aware that they are appearing within a cartoon that we are currently watching (as in the wolf's direct address to the audience) and to which we may respond (as in hurled fruit) and other times speaking on behalf of an unseen narrator, who feels compelled to comment on the depicted actions (including labeling gags as "corny").

Avery also often based gags on the disjuncture between sound and image. Consider three examples from *Screwball Squirrel*. In the first example Screwball closes the door to a phone booth before letting loose with a prolonged raspberry, a sequence designed to call attention to the act of censorship, which represses some of his more bodily humor. (This particular rude noise is specifically prohibited in the Production Code.) In the second example the camera pulls back from the canine antagonist rolling down the hill in a barrel to show that the musical accompaniment is not nondiegetic, as we might have initially imagined. (Instead, it has its source in the fiction: Screwball is making appropriate sounds using drums, timpani, and bird whistles.) At another point, as the dog relentlessly chases the squirrel, we begin to hear repeated noises on the soundtrack, and the image gets caught in a loop, which suggests the recycling of stills that goes on routinely in animated shorts. The image freezes, and the squirrel steps away, hits the needle of a phonograph, gets the music on track, and then steps back into his place in the chase. In all three cases Avery refuses to allow us to take the relations between sound and image for granted, suggesting that what we hear is controlled by arbitrary regulations and constraints; alternately, he blurs the line between diegetic and nondiegetic sounds. Like Jones and Wolverton, Avery sees noise as the source of comic disruptions and interruptions of the well-constructed text, finding pleasure in the breakdown of normal codes and conventions.

Terry Gilliam has described what he values most about Elder's work: "the way he filled every inch of the thing with, just stuff, . . . jokes on jokes on jokes."[15] Such visual clutter and comic density is especially visible in the expanded panels that open many of Elder's *Mad* parodies. One such panel for "Is This Your Life?" tries to engulf all of 1950s American culture into a single crammed and cramped image, including fictional characters (the Lone Ranger, Donald Duck), newscasters (Edward R. Murrow), and political personalities (Nikita Khrushchev, Richard Nixon), television and film stars (Groucho Marx, Bing Crosby, Marilyn Monroe), and brand icons (Aunt Jemima; the Smith Brothers; the Quaker Oats man; Snap, Crackle, and Pop; on and on). The opening of "Starchie," shows Blondie and Little Orphan Annie as another two students attending Riverdale High, while Annie carries a textbook, "Freud is a Fraud by Freed," which pulls us into another discursive field altogether.

Such plays with intertextual references are also common to the work of Tex Avery (see *Who Killed Who?* [1943], where Santa Claus pops out of a closet and pulverizes the protagonist for failing to respect a sign warning him not to open the door before Xmas) or in *Hellzapoppin* (where Johnson bumps into a sled marked Rosebud and mumbles that he thought they had burned that thing or where the Frankenstein monster pops out of the audience and hurls Martha Raye back onstage during the disrupted ballet sequence described earlier). All of this suggests that what Hoberman described as the "encyclopedic" nature of Frank Tashlin's comedy, "an elaborately cross-referenced Bartlett's of mass media quotations," or the "collage-like" qualities of Will Elder's comics might be extended to describe the tradition as a whole (37). These artists borrowed freely across media, genres, modalities, and niches within the cultural hierarchy in a promiscuous play with intertextuality.

Moreover, these artists saw visual density as a source of pleasure in and of itself. Often, the specific details are less funny than the sense of their accumulation, of so many unlikely things occurring in the same space at the same time. We can't take it all in. No two readers see the same thing. And, indeed, part of the pleasure is the promise of comic effects beyond comprehension. The Hell sequence at the start of *Hellzapoppin* powerfully demonstrates the ways visual density can be deployed for comic effect: we see acrobats leaping and flying in every direction, with people walking in between jugglers hurling flaming sticks back and forth, with elements thrust into the frame from every possible offscreen space, and with gag elements appearing and then vanishing again with no real explanation. The introduction of Olsen and Johnson gets heralded by a menagerie of chickens, ducks, sheep, goats, and dogs, in a scene that includes everything but the kitchen sink (which, have no fear, gets brought in for comic effect in one of the film's later scenes). At the risk of a bad pun, this "devil may care" attitude reflects a sense of old vaudeville, burlesque, and joke-book gags, being pulled out of mothballs, for one last play, with everyone involved recognizing how tired or hokey these devices may be individually but hoping that if they throw enough things at the screen at once, something will produce a laugh or a sense of wonderment. And when the wordplay gets too bad, one can just step outside of the joke altogether: "corny, isn't it?" These comic artists flag their jokes the way Babe Ruth pointed out his home runs: we know where they are going to go, but it's still amazing to watch them get there.

FORMS STRETCHED TO THEIR LIMITS

In this intensified comic atmosphere, bodies—whether those of live comic performers or cartoon characters—were, as Spiegelman observes of Jack Cole's creations, "forms stretched to their limits."[16] Vaudeville's performer-centered mode of production and its emphasis on constant novelty and heterogeneity pushed its stars to develop a range of performance skills and to exploit as many of them in any given performance as possible. This push toward intensification resulted in such specialties as the protean or quick-change artist who might transform his identity dozens of times in the course of a performance, trying to play all of the parts in the enactment of a Shakespearean drama or an adaptation of *War and Peace*. It also resulted in the tradition of the eccentric dancer, whose performance would include back flipping acrobatics and rubber-legged dance moves, which often defy our normal assumptions about human anatomy. One can see remarkable examples of this tradition in the preserved segments from Spike Jones's TV work.

In "I Like to Sock Myself in the Face," Peter James, a regular member of Jones's stock company, sings a rapid patter song that proclaims the masochistic pleasures of self-directed violence. The clown, dressed in an oversized checkered suit that defies every piece of advice ever given about what to wear on early black-and-white television, races onto the stage, hurls himself up the curtains, and bobs up and down in rhythm to the music, before proceeding to slap and kick himself in the face, run circles around the bandleader, wind up his legs and kick in all directions, turn back flips, and fling himself on all fours, bouncing up and down on the floor. All of the above is performed live by the breathlessly enthusiastic entertainer and unveiled for us in a series of long takes, which makes it clear that there is no trickery involved.

Such a performance might well be called "cartoonish," and that's precisely the point—it offers us the illusion that a live performer's body may be as elastic and protean as that of a cartoon or comic book character. There is little separating Peter James's proclaimed joy in socking himself in the face and the prolonged sequences of Wolfey's equally intense gyrations and contortions in response to Red Hot Riding Hood in Avery's cartoons. Wolfey gets shown going stiff as a board, stretching his arm across the auditorium to pull his beloved off the stage, banging himself in the face with hammers, whistling and pounding on the table, popping his eyes out of his head, and shooting himself in his desperate and uncontrollable expressions of erotic desire. These hyperbolic reactions became the primary source of comedy for extended sequences in the film, and such displays are often what people remember most vividly about Avery's cartoons.

Spiegelman finds a similar fascination with hyperbolic extensions of the human body in Jack Cole's most famous creation, Plastic Man: "Plastic Man had all the crackling intensity of the life force transferred to paper. . . . Plas literally embodied the comic book form: its exuberant energy, its flexibility, its boyishness, and its only partially sublimated sexuality."[17] The pleasure of reading a Cole comic was watching his protagonist stretch and pull in all directions, changing shape and identity at will, often anchored only by our recognition of the red, black, and yellow coloring of his costume. In yet another analogy to modernist art, Spiegelman argues that the character "personified Georges Bataille's notion of the body on the brink of dissolving its borders," suggesting a sexual charge to images of Plas's bulbous head at the end of his extending flaccid or erect neck or at the suggestion that any body part might take any shape at a moment's notice.[18]

The same might be said of the characters depicted by Basil Wolverton, whom the art critic Doug Harvey has linked to a much larger tradition of grotesque caricature, again drawing on references to surrealism, expressionism, and dada: "Wolverton's obsessively detailed images of impossibly distended organs, alarming proliferations of extra limbs, seething oceans of twisted, sagging, and diseased integument, and traumatic and impractical fusions of man and machine in which man inevitably got the painful end of the stick.... His work has a singularity of focus and vertiginous sense of exhilaration that verges on nausea, and it has continued to be vital and grown increasingly relevant, from the days of vaudeville through to the post-McLuhan mediascape. And if it makes your sister puke, it's done its job."[19]

Spiegelman has emphasized the kinetic qualities of Cole's artwork, tracing the ways that Plas moves from left to right, top to bottom, from panel to panel, forcing the reader to scan rapidly from place to place within the frame. Wolverton achieves a similarly kinetic quality within single images as mouths, eyelids, hair, wrinkles, all seem on the verge of drooping and sagging, like so much meat ready to fall off the bone. A man might tie his neck into a knot to avoid the temptations of drink, or another might attach a fan to his nose to disperse the stench of his buddy's garlicky breath. One character may be all mouth, another all nose; another might have four or five chins, each so butt-ugly that we stare at the page like rubberneckers at a car accident, unable to take our eyes away even as we feel mounting disgust.

There was an inherent tension between all of this frantic activity and any sense of spatial orientation. Jack Cole's Plas zigzags across the page. Wolverton's Powerhouse Pepper makes expressive use of speed lines that seem to swoop upon us from all sides. Peter James races, leaps, and tumbles around every corner of the stage. Olsen and Johnson walk through a series of movie sets with each match on action revealing them wearing a different period costume. A chase scene in Tex Avery's *Who Killed Who* shows multiple versions of the same characters racing around different parts of the space at the same instant. Another gag shows the detective falling down a trap door in the bottom of the frame and then falling into the same shot from above. Don't expect spatial relations to make sense; don't expect the world to cohere; just sit back and watch as they rip the frame apart and put it back together again.

THE LIMITS OF VULGAR MODERNISM

We can celebrate the formal inventiveness, the giddy excitement created by such unfettered movements, the expressive graphics, yet we also have to acknowledge how much of this humor was directed at women—literally, in the case of Avery's representations of the wolf's pyrotechnic desire, or figuratively, in the ways that the works associate all of that ballet, opera, and classical piano music I've described with a feminized realm of high culture. For the most part the "vulgar modernists" were misbehaving schoolboys, running amuck, seeking to shock their teachers, mothers, and sisters with their willingness to transgress norms of taste and decorum. All of this comes out in Harvey's nostalgia for the way Wolverton's cartoons made his sister wretch.

In a world where men display phallic energy through their ability to extend their bodies in all directions, women are often depicted as fixed and static—witness the use of rotoscoping to give Red a much more realistic appearance than Wolfey in the Avery cartoons. There are exceptions, such as Martha Raye's character in *Hellzapoppin,* who shows an ability to freeze the frame and reverse the action in one particular musical number. Yet, for the most part, male characters enjoy much greater freedom of movement and fluidity of identity. One could argue that such male-centered pleasures are consistent with the analogies to modernism, given how often, say, critics have pointed to the masculine assumptions that shaped artists as diverse as Pablo Picasso and Jackson Pollock.

We should not be surprised, then, that alongside Hoberman, the most famous patron of the "vulgar modernists" was Hugh Hefner, who sought to recruit many of those discussed here, including Jack Cole, Harvey Kurtzman, and Will Elder, to work for *Playboy.* While the temptation is to talk about the "no holds barred" nature of their postwar work, we can see the kinds of invisible constraints that shaped their work if we look at the much more sexually explicit work Elder and Kurtzman did on "Little Annie Fannie" for *Playboy* a decade or so later. Biographers describe the cartoonists' discomfort with the erotic imagery and subject matter Hef expected them to produce for his men's magazine, even as he provided them more creative freedom to fill panels with "chicken fat" gags, to introduce intertextual elements, or to shatter the frame borders. (The recent reprinting of *Little Annie Fannie* includes an extensive set of annotations in the back trying to explain the topical pop culture references that ran through the series.)[20] In the end we don't know whether the sexuality was sublimated in their postwar works or whether the sexual explicitness of their later work was forced in their efforts to remain relevant to the sensibilities of a different generation.

Basil Wolverton's grotesques informed later underground comic book artists like R. Crumb. A famous self-portrait of Crumb, his legs twisted and tangled, bears unmistakable similarities to a Wolverton drawing showing a similarly contorted male figure (Fig. 8.4). Crumb would give the grotesque elements of Wolverton's work a political charge: Crumb used images of contorted human figures to push back against what he and others in the counterculture saw as the state's repressive control over their bodies, offering up much more aggressive

FIGURE 8.4. Basil Wolverton
self-portrait.

representations of racial difference as a challenge to a sexist and racist society (in effect, taking the "innocent" ethnic types found in the earlier work and shoving them back into the shocked faces of a generation that had been too complacent about racial inequalities). Reading the "vulgar modernists" alongside Crumb, one sees just how good-natured and complacent the early comic artists were, how much they observed limits and respected norms, even as they sought to enact their disruption and transgression.

While the comedy rests on our acceptance that they hold nothing sacred, there is, in fact, much that remains sacred and protected within the humor of the 1940s and 1950s. While Kurtzman and Gaines faced rebuke before the Kefauver committee for their role in creating E. C. horror comics, *Mad* was seen as a safer alternative to which they retreated in the aftermath. If it was not exactly exalted, it never faced government scrutiny. None of these clowns or comic artists were blacklisted during the McCarthy era; their formal transgressiveness and sublimated eroticism was acceptable in the context of their times in a way that overt ideological critique would never have been.

Hoberman was drawn to these artists at a time when politically engaged filmmakers and cultural critics saw reflexivity as a way out of the illusionism of classical Hollywood cinema: writers such as Hoberman understood the shattering of textual codes and conventions as the beginning of a different kind of relationship to spectators. When they looked at the films of Tex Avery, say, they could find many examples of this kind of formal transgression. Avery's films sent characters flying outside the frame or showed them straddling a line separating black and white and Technicolor. The character at the start of *Who Killed Who* is reading a book "based on the cartoon of the same title." He turns to the audience and explains that if the cartoon is anything like the book, he's about to be murdered. As Dana Polan notes in an essay focused primarily on another "vulgar modernist" text, Chuck Jones's *Duck Amuck* (1953), there is a difference between reflexivity as a formal practice designed to defamiliarize various textual codes and conventions and reflexivity as a political practice designed to critique real-world institutions and practices.[21] One takes pleasure in pulling the rug out from under Hollywood conventions, while the other teaches us a new way to see the world or offers us new perspectives on the realm beyond the movie house.

These artists might have been the last generation of American humorists who could transgress wildly and yet still hold a place within the consensus culture. They were, in short, marginal but not outside mainstream values.

Canons often get defined in terms of the lasting impressions and continued influence of an artist's body of work, and by those criteria these artists continue to exert a strong influence on our culture down to the present day. As Doug Harvey writes in regard to Wolverton, "Generations of comic creators, from Will Elder, Gahan Wilson, R. Crumb and Gary Panter to Peter Bagge, Drew Friedman, and Charles Burns, have been influenced by his meticulous technique and pictorial audacity. Artists from the world of 'fine' or 'high' art, such as Mike Kelley, Jim Shaw, Kenny Scharf, Peter Saul, Jim Nutt, and many others turned Wolverton's pop-culture monstrosities into museum-worthy artifacts."[22] Similarly, Tex Avery's influence is explicitly acknowledged in Jim Carrey's performance in *The Mask*, the opening sequences of *Who Framed Roger Rabbit*, and throughout *Tiny Toon Adventures, Ren and Stimpy,* and *Animaniacs*. It is equally difficult to conceive of the world depicted in *The Simpsons* or *South Park* in the absence of Will Elder and Harvey Kurtzman.

Hoberman's essay ends with the suggestion that "what was once oppositional in vulgar modernism has largely been co-opted by the culture industry" (pointing to the then-contemporary examples of *Mary Hartman, Mary Hartman* or *Saturday Night Live*). I have argued the opposite here—that their containment within commercial culture muted any overt political statements they might have made and that subsequent generations, following their example, have often pushed their transgressiveness much further. Perhaps these later works are consistent with Hoberman's closing call for a "vulgar postmodernism" though I will leave to someone else the always thankless task of policing the borders between modernism and postmodernism. That these works are a living presence in our culture makes the project of revisiting Hoberman's essay and reassessing this body of work that much more urgent.

We have been able only to start the project of a comparative or cross-media analysis of "vulgar modernism" and its place in American culture. Hoberman's intuitive grouping of these artists proves rewarding whether we address the question in terms of biographical details or close textual analysis. These artists were fellow travelers in an artistic project none of them articulated but all of them demonstrated. It was a project whose roots could be traced back to vaudeville but that has been read in relation to a range of modern art movements, caught eternally in a struggle between competing claims of lowbrow audacity and high-art respectability. Calling them vulgar may oversell their transgressiveness, and calling them modernist may overstate their avant-garde impulses; the reality lies somewhere in the tension between the two. Whatever we want to say about them, they were artists who experimented with the basic building blocks of their respective media and taught a generation a new way to look at the world around them.

NOTES

1. Hoberman, "Vulgar Modernism." All subsequent discussions of this essay will be referenced in the text (where pagination refers to the reprint). For a fuller discussion of the history of the concept of popular art see Jenkins, *The Wow Climax.*

2. Young, *Spike Jones off the Record.*

3. See Spiegelman, "Those Dirty Little Comics."

4. See Spiegelman and Kidd, *Jack Cole and Plastic Man.*

5. See Amidi, *Cartoon Modern.*

6. See, e.g., Geisel and Sendak, *The Secret Art of Dr. Seuss;* or Groth and Sadowski, *Will Elder.*

7. Hansen, "The Mass Production of the Senses," 333.

8. Langer, "Polyphony and Heterogeneity in Early Fleischer Films," 65–87.

9. Jenkins, "'This Fellow Keaton Seems to Be the Whole Show,'" 35. For further elaboration of the vaudeville aesthetic see Jenkins, *What Made Pistachio Nuts?*

10. Franklin, *Joe Franklin's Encyclopedia of Comedians,* 258.

11. Seidman, *Comedian Comedy;* Krutnik, "The Clown-Prints of Comedy."

12. See Pynchon, "Mindful Mindlessness."

13. Groth and Sadowski, *Will Elder,* 44.

14. Wolverton, "Acoustics in the Comics," www.animationarchive.org/2007/08/comics-basil -wolverton-on-cartoon.html; many of the graphics drawn for the essay can also be found in Bray, *The Original Art of Basil Wolverton.*

15. Quoted in Groth and Sadowski, *Will Elder,* 51.

16. Spiegelman and Chip Kidd use the phrase as the subtitle of their book about Jack Cole; see *Jack Cole and Plastic Man: Forms Stretched to Their Limits.*

17. Spiegelman and Kidd, *Jack Cole and Plastic Man,* 29.

18. Ibid.

19. Harvey, "The Closer You Look, the Prettier It Ain't," 21–22.

20. Hefner, *Playboy's Little Annie Fannie.*

21. See Polan, "A Brechtian Cinema?"

22. Harvey, "The Closer You Look, the Prettier It Ain't," 22.

9

Auralis Sexualis

How Cartoons Conduct Paraphilia

Philip Brophy

THE CARTOON CORPUS

If cartoons were flesh, pornography would have to be reinvented. Pornography uses the body—its aura, its texture, its materiality, its morphology—to choreograph physical possibilities imagined through the dormant state of the inert (repressed) corpus. In this sense pornography animates the body into heightened states of arousal, erection, and expulsion. It actualizes all that can be desired of the body. Cartoons similarly employ the body to explode with latent libidinal energy, choreographing physical impossibilities imagined through the actual state of the innate (expressed) corpus. Yet cartoons perform this function all the while refuting the body's fleshiness. Indeed, the hypergraphic flatness of cartoons diverts the erotic gaze to the razed ground of flat-painted blocks of color devoid of depth. Flesh is depicted as if to claim that there is no body onscreen: just a shape, its outline, and its shadow.

The depiction of the human body in western cartoon form seems predicated on this fundamental contradiction—one that is firmly lodged in the ideology and ontology of the cartoon form. Procedures like compositing live actors or rotoscoping have consequently been deemed transgressive and have tended to be viewed as corruption or abuse of the animation art form. The implication is that the body is to be drawn and imagineered rather than photographed and actualized. Linked to nineteenth-century ideals of Romantic mimeticism, the human form is to be evoked, idealized, and posed like the painted nude. This critical standpoint replicates the most conservative of binaries: that showing something through the act of photography is a blunt strategy compared with the suggesting of something through any nonphotographic act. This mantra brackets bourgeois ideals of aestheticism from eroticism (nonpornographic sensualism) to drama (nonviolent action).

Cartoons—irrefutably evidencing their lowbrow genealogy in every squiggly move—repulse Romantic mimeticism. Forgoing the poetic for the ribald, they have consistently and strategically mocked the purer pursuits of form. Cartoons are not, however, exempt from the sexual semiotics of their apparition. The history of American classic cartoonography is rooted in an aversion to any actuality of the body's corporeality. Looking at many an apparently innocent cartoon from the first half of the twentieth century, one can see the human form swathed in a voluptuous rendering. The sexual lacing of flora, fauna, and machina abounds, from the pulped fluidity of their physics to the paragynecological extremes of their motion dynamics. It remains hard to reconcile the flagrant aura of these scenarios enjoyed by children and families. And even though it is easy to discern all sorts of aberrant textuality in cultural flotsam from bygone eras, the faux-retro viscosity of gleaming CGI Hollywood blockbuster animation behaves in identical fashion. The CGI grail for realism paradoxically sends it screaming from rendering any flesh in its kiddie cornucopia, yet it evidences eerily tactile precision in its texture-mapping of plastic, fur, jelly, and other faux materials born of twentieth-century petrochemical development. Indeed, the material headiness of a sex shop stocked with purple silicone dolphin dildos and neon-pink fur-lined crotchless panties looks remarkably similar to the candy plasticity of contemporary CGI family animations.

The fact that cartoons are comical and hysterical merely creates a noisescape of interference to distract from their sexualized base. All bodily figuration invokes the registering of one's own form, and the practice of animation necessitates one confronting oneself with how one will engineer a form for the self. The body not only has to be drawn; it also has to be rendered, mobilized, and voiced. Far from practicing any animistic doctrine, cartoons sublimely create the most artificial projection of the self—all the while capturing the neurological and psychosexual vibrations of the body more than any photo/cine-camera could achieve. In this sense their relation to the body is akin to choreographed dance. Just as dance creates physical metaphors of how the earthbound might escape gravity, cartoons dance with equivocal transformative energies. In doing so, cartoons arguably abstract the body into an inhuman reflexive contortion of what could be termed "animamorphism": rather than imbue animals and objects with human traits and behavior, they convey animalistic states of existence in humans through refusing recognizable codes of identification.

The cartoon corpus is thus the form born of such a state. Its near-century's worth of imagery has consistently foregrounded a sexual tonality in the form's handling of its materials, leaving it open to a wide array of erotic interpretation and application. This arises sometimes from manifest bodily depiction, sometimes from latent surface associations, and other times simply from mimetic supposition. Most important, it is in the cartoon's realm of lightly dismissive, ephemeral sensationalism for family-oriented consumption that the psychosexual connotations of its imagery have established an amazing meld of bodily hysteria and sexual denial. This brief introductory discussion of how the human body appears and moves in cartoons is postulated to consider the sexual connotations and implications of how the human voice performs under these conditions of corpulence.

THE EMASCULATED SCREAM

Elsewhere I have discussed the explosiveness of the Warner Bros. cartoon shorts from the 1940s and 1950s as exemplars of the celebratory noise welcomed by their soundtracks.[1] That explosiveness largely characterizes the aural compaction of the classic American cartoon: it has always been a loud, raucous, bombastic affair; hyper-Vaudevillian, self-mocking, antibowdlerizing. Here I will discuss how the voice is implicated in such a field of noise and will directly link it to how the bodily status of the cartoon corpus impacts the role of voice in cartoons.

The most apparent feature in Western cartoon vocalizations is the level of screeching. One can feel the threshold of distortion being reached as the actors' heads turn as red as the overloading display of the recording meters. It's a mania endemic in many forms of comedy the world over, where the scream of the comedic performer conveys its own level of humor irrespective of the words being screamed. This performance is predicated on a palpable loss of control, veering into aberrant modes of address, from the ranting of the possessed voice to the raving of the transcended voice. The cartoon screech (irrespective of its accent, impersonation, or mimicry) connotes how the voice signifies a transformative state as the human becomes something other than its normal controlled being. Like the way its form dances, and like the way its flesh appears, the cartoon voice is pushed into a zone of wild metamorphosis, freed from stable or mannered illustration.

In the most perfunctory of psychoanalytic terms, the scream signifies a variety of ways in which the self is transfigured. From denial to catharsis to pain, the scream signposts trauma at its most exposed. Yet its contralinguistic expression does not exclude it from numerous symbolic connotations. Foremost, the Western cartoon is rarely accepted as a site for workshopping trauma of any kind. This locates the screaming cartoon voice within the cartoon body's "animamorphism" and its various reversals of depiction: the screaming voice comedically references trauma that it then performatively quotes in a scenario where sexual trauma is connoted nonetheless.

To wit: classic Warner Bros. screamers like Daffy Duck and Yosemite Sam (each sharing a nemesis in Bugs Bunny) project hilarious audiovisualizations of neck-stretching, eye-popping, tongue-bulging screams, yet their wound-up voices are uncannily akin to the outbursts of violent male behavioral disturbance. Created prior to World War II, Daffy Duck and Yosemite Sam portray a definitive American aggressiveness, synching to the bravura rush of a patriotic era (at times mixed with anarchistic fall-guy humor and maverick frontier ruthlessness). Yet the darker undercurrents to their testosterone-fueled stance is more audible than perceivable. While the image of their bodily spasms will always appear comedic even without its soundtrack, the voice of that same image when heard in isolation will waver between comedic and traumatic. Most of their extreme vocalizations arise from slapstick physical pain and desperate frustration, testifying to the notion that humor is granted at the expense of someone else's pain and misfortune. Daffy Duck and Yosemite Sam are not likable characters per se (though this does not extinguish their charm), and their voices, more than the visage, typify their ravaged and destabilized composure.

The Warner Bros. cycle of Wile E. Coyote and Roadrunner shorts (notably occurring in the postwar period from 1949 through the following decade) provides the perfect symbolic inverse to the screaming pantheon. The Coyote is entirely mute; the Roadrunner is capable of only a fixed phoneme (the famous "Beep! Beep!"). There is something frighteningly repressive in their devoicing. The Coyote is never allowed an authentic howl—the prairie/desert cry of the wild where the animal howls with nature—and the Roadrunner is disallowed the expanded vocabulary of sonic signage that defines each bird species with its language. Specifically, the Coyote has been barred access to the soundtrack, while the Roadrunner has only restricted access to it.[2] Of course, their cartoon scenarios are wonderfully enriched by all sorts of sonic and musical bombast, but the erasure of their performative character voices symbolizes darker things.

Some may find this reading too fanciful, but their voicelessness can be read as a sign of the postwar American male: traumatized, declassified, reinstated, emasculated. Working from such a base, the hunger instituted within the Roadrunner suggests a certain sexual character, as the scowling emaciated primal male of the Coyote becomes both predator and scavenger in his desperate pursuit of the feminized Roadrunner. The Beckett-like absurdism is striking: there appears to be only one Roadrunner in this cosmos; the Coyote will never catch it; even if he did, it would be unlikely to fill his stomach for long; and yet he never dies of hunger from not catching the bird. This all points to the chase being an archly symbolic affair, which allows a sexual interpretation such as I'm peddling. More so, the Coyote and Roadrunner pessimistically invoke the collapsed postwar marriage, where codependency breeds all kinds of unspeakable trauma unleashed by America's involvement in World War II. Their vocal silence on the soundtracks links to all that is unsaid in the marital bed, all that is silenced by the return to normal domestic routine, and all that is undisclosed in regard to their military past. While a TV show like *The Honeymooners* (1955–56), with its sharp scripting and acute social typing, has long been championed as a terse embodiment of the marital discord typical of the postwar period, the Coyote and Roadrunner cycle of cartoons similarly sculpts a partly figurative, partly abstract study of the same. The latter's symbolic distortion may be in heavy contrast to the former's sociological semblance, but the employment of silenced cartoon animals engaged in a ravenous battle waged in a wasteland governed by transdimensional physics positions the Coyote and Roadrunner cycle to be read as acerbic reductions of gender conflict of its time.

The headiness of World War II and its compound effects on the male sexual psyche are not the prime focus of this brief chapter. While the notions discussed here may appear to generalize such a complex area of study, I remain engaged in a semiotic reading of how the Warner Bros. characters betray inflections of the psychological composition of the postwar American male—specifically by noting the sexual, erotic, and fetishistic extensions of their rendering in cartoon form. In a sense I am auditing their classic cartoons through the collective voicing of male sexual frustration in other cultural modes of expression from the time, from bleak film noir to violent abstract expressionist painting to psychotic rockabilly records. In all these and more cultural forms, the maddening swirl of sexual frustration, violent desire, morbid predilection, and aberrant pathology constitutes the planetary gravitational pull for the views propagated here.

THE ABSENTED VOICE

And so we arrive poised in front of Tinker Bell. First employed by the Disney Studios in *Peter Pan* (1953), Tinker Bell is a fascinating emblem of the postwar era and thus of classic American cartoonography. Using the method I employed to tease out issues of voice in the Warner Bros. cartoons, I will first consider Tinker Bell's semiotic morphology—how she appears, how she is formed, and how she moves—and then move on to interrogate her voice.

In one concise figure Tinker Bell embodies all the problems of figuration in cartoon morphology. While her petite frame and miniaturization allude to a vaguely puerile state, her slight pointy breasts indicate her sexualized status. Those quaint mammarian pinnacles also aid in distinguishing her from Peter Pan. Both have foppish blonde bangs, perky noses, doe eyes, and lithe limbs, and both are dressed in forest waif chic. Peter Pan's and Tinker Bell's similarity is such that each could be the other in drag. Only Tinker Bell's gossamer wings declare her femininity with some assurance. If only she could talk, we could then have her gender confirmed for us every time she opens her mouth. But her silent smile and fluttering eyelids leave much open to interpretation. Suffice it to say, Tinker Bell is a delicious confusion of sex and gender—and sexuality rears its hydra-head whenever its depiction is vague, bipolar, or multiple. She may be mute, but the visuality of her sex is deafening. She speaks through her sex, defining the peculiar substance to her muteness.

Tinker Bell's emblematic stature is proven by the brand status she assumes for the Disney corporation—starting in the immediate postwar televisual era, via her appearance in the *Disneyland* (1954) TV show's opening and closing credits. In this latter guise Tinker Bell is like a medicating angel, sprinkling "pixie dust" across the sky, sending all traumatized victims into an induced somnambulistic state. Her fanciful flight semiotically evokes similar sexy yet pixielike scantily clad girls emblazoned on the breastlike turrets of World War II bomber planes. In this respect her cartoon appearance is less part of established Disney caricature and more part of the complex merger between the wartime cheesecake pinup and the postwar saucy burlesque dancer. Tinker Bell also connotes a bomber plane herself in the *Disneyland* opening, raining fire bombs in a spray of destruction against the Axis. Ironically, she showers the kingdom of Disneyland in cascades of sparkling glitter, in a mute symbolic attack on the Bavarian architecture so beloved by Hitler and so embraced by Disney and America's pre–World War II infatuation with European grandeur. The Tinker Bell addressed and undressed here is not the pure English vessel of J. M. Barrie's creation in *Peter and Wendy* (c. 1911) but the reconstructed Disney figure designed for family entertainment during the postwar period, when so much cultural exchange was predicated on healing the horrors created by America's involvement in the war.

While the Roadrunner is always out of reach owing to supersonic speed, Tinker Bell comes dangerously close, flirting with the viewer. Her phallic wand, her magic dust, her fluttering wings all stand for ways in which tactility can be suggested. Scantily attired, she wafts like the smell of Woman, hovering and floating through space without actually touching anything, yet making her presence felt as a "phantom tactility."[3] Everything about her suggests the act of touching, yet like the ungraspable Roadrunner, she will never be held. The vulgarity of these words is in keeping with Tinker Bell's flirtation, for what is she but a caricature of Betty Grable pretending to be a prepubescent lady-boy, seducing the unwitting viewer engaged in consuming family entertainment? Again, the silencing of Tinker Bell's voice amplifies this reading, in that its removal is a salient symbol of the repressive consequences of her manifestation.

Here, we can best outline the concept of how cartoons "conduct paraphilia." *Paraphilia* is the umbrella term used to account for varying degrees of fetishistic engagement. But more than recycle the modus operandi of fetishistic mechanics (e.g., a man obsessively fondling women's shoes, etc.), paraphilia clinically and—more importantly—theoretically allows for querying definitions of "normal" sex. Epicentral to this querying is the posthuman phenomenon of a human being completely satisfied sexually with the most nonhuman, unhuman, and inhuman manifestations and objectifications. While clinical analysis of a paraphiliac might be concerned with the dysfunction caused by the paraphiliac's integration into society, a theoretical consideration of the same can widen the narrowed channels through which human sexuality is deemed operable and sustainable. Paraphilia and its attendant pornographic formulations confront us with an expansive field, stretching well beyond our location and comfort (the Latin of the term means "beyond love"). To venture across that field is to realize that "where sex isn't is where sex is."

Essentially, Tinker Bell's eternal escape from the viewer's grasp unleashes the prime impulse of pornography, and in doing so creates a fetishized object (a paraphiliac token) for the viewer. The fact that Tinker Bell is so clearly not a hardcore image is of crucial consequence. Pornography is never to be read literally or figuratively despite its maddening photographic veracity and paralegal documentation of its actions. Rather, to consume the onscreen pornographic body is to consume its absence. Its form becomes its own "phantom tactility" in that one engages with its body knowing that it is not there. This is not simply the mechanics of desire, for the abject materiality of the body's depiction in pornography consequently establishes its own iconography and vocabulary. The surface of its rendering and the composition of its forms in a sense overtake the body and—just as in the cartoon's "animamorphism"—constitute a transfigured state of the body. This corpus then becomes the clear object of desire, which unlocks the paraphiliac realm.

And here is where Tinker Bell—bi-gendered multiaged taliswoman of the postwar Disney franchise—augurs the dark shadows of her illuminated dance. Accepting that she has been sexualized, and that both her tactile appearance and beckoning movement invite sexual co-option, what exactly is invited by her as she erotically cajoles the viewer into submerged identification with her childlike body? The sleaze implicit in this rhetoric is intentional: a Tinker Bell syndrome exists as strongly as the Peter Pan syndrome.[4] A Tinker Bell syndrome would allude to grown (and overgrown) men attracted to diminutive doll-like girls, often young enough to be their daughters. Tinker Bell's cartoon corpus facilitates this, whereas faded photos of Betty Grable more likely invite the ennui of impotence. Betty is real and hence prone to the same destitution as the aged veteran who desires her. Tinker Bell is unreal: like Peter Pan she is ageless and thus excites the male sexual drive beyond its limits. Wielded like the conductor's baton, her magic wand reverses impotency, configuring the member much like the imagined limb of the amputee.

Following this obtuse linkage from bomber turret to miniature breasts to impotent phallus to severed limb, we can finally append Tinker Bell's absented voice. If Tinker Bell bore an actual voice, she would embody a human corporeality, presenting her illustrative image as being the vessel for that human characterization. To elaborate: the recorded human voice audited solely as sound (such as in a live radio play, a recorded song, a live or recorded phone call, or even coming from behind a closed door) is already noncorporeal. Its nonvisual representation is its material aura: its sound effect is its sound broadcast/recording/generation, which in turn is the sound it makes. This "hypermateriality" is noticeable in many people's aversion to the sound of their voice: it sounds too "actual," too "present," like a specter of themselves hovering too close for comfort. Generally, people can be more comfortable with their mirror image or photographed or videographed self, because the human image is largely read by humans as a form of signage that allows the slightest but integral distance between oneself and one's "self." Cartoons densify this visual signage of the human self (contrary to the perception that they simplify), creating greater distance in the recognition of the depicted body as a result of the immaterial layering that the drawn image and cartoon form accrues. The screaming Warner Bros. males have a potency driven by Mel Blanc's inimitable vocal characterizations, imbuing his characters with an aggressively societal demeanor in contrast to their inhuman figuration. By comparison, Tinker Bell creates a hole by discounting the formula of binding human voice recording with drawn human body, and as such she retains a wholly nonhuman corporeality.

This is why Tinker Bell's absented voice is central to a discussion of paraphiliac propensity, because the presence of an actual voice diminishes the nonhuman aura of the quasi-pornographic cartoon corpus. The complexity of this finely attuned distinction can best be demonstrated by comparing Tinker Bell with Holli Would, the sexy cartoonization of Kim Basinger's body in Ralph Bakshi's *Cool World* (1992). Kim Basinger's voice openly states her sexuality. In fact, it decodes her diagrammatic body, reminding us and Brad Pitt that even though she appears as a cartoon, she is very real and wholly sexual. Unlike Robert Zemeckis's *Who Framed Roger Rabbit* (1988), which pits the impotent male rabbit against Jessica's parody of female sexual enticement, *Cool World* perversely plays with the swirling sexualization born of a less iconic and more pornographic body via Holli's rotoscoped presence. In its joining of voice to body, however—of human encoding to figurative rendering—*Cool World* parlays an imagined Kim Basinger to be the agent of sexual allure. Tinker Bell has no such real-world referent. Like a silent siren she is anchored in the sea of paraphiliac desire, where real physical sex is subjugated by a fetishization of unreal imagined sex.

THE PEDOPHILIAC CRY

Paraphilia remains a form of sexual practice, despite the clinical assignation of its being "beyond love" and outside the parameters of normative sexual interaction. The idea of having sex with anything but a fellow human is the bracing notion of fetishism, with paraphilia conceptually covering all fetishistic practices. Yet the sexual attraction to cartoon images is grounded in a long history of prephotographic forms of protopornography, from the illustrated Kama Sutra to pulp-printed Tijuana Bibles. Consequently, cartoons not intended for such consumption are not exempt from that historical legacy, and it doesn't take much for something like Tinker Bell to make that legacy potent and viable. While Daffy Duck, Yosemite Sam, and Wile E. Coyote have been discussed here as graphic memes of male sexual pathology, and the Roadrunner and Tinker Bell as triggers for the same, Gerald McBoing Boing (1951) is an embodiment of the outcomes of those characters' symbolic audiovisualization.

Scripted by Dr. Seuss, the first self-titled *Gerald McBoing Boing* short from 1955 functions as a social allegory advocating acceptance of a child's difference in a normalizing social world. Gerald is inexplicably born with no recourse to speech save for his marvelous ability to produce sound effects from his mouth. While this is an inventive gag, let us first consider its technical ramifications. Incapable of even the most primal vocal utterance, Gerald has a voice that is "metadiegetic" in that its source is not even from within him but from the mechanical beyond of the animatic apparatus. He literally "speaks soundtrack" by synchronizing lip movement to recognizable sound effects. This makes Gerald a rarity in the cartoon cosmos because he is wholly devoid of human corporeality (as distinct from Tinker Bell, who only attains a similar status by emitting no sound whatsoever through her voice box). Gerald's illustrative mode eschews mimetic form, plus his lexicon of sound effects tersely opposes the grammar of any spoken speech, making him a synesthetic meme. Moreover, he lives his complete life in acceptance of the fomented terror that besieges Daffy Duck in Chuck Jones's *Duck Amuck* (1953) when the extradiegetic nemesis first erases (literally) Daffy's beak, then replaces his speech with offscreen sound effects.

Although it is a progressive positivist text couched within a humorous tale, *Gerald McBoing Boing* does not block a reading of how Gerald's voicelessness enacts trauma. He is the archetypical traumatized child because of that voicelessness, recalling mute photocine innocents in Jean Negulesco's *Johnny Belinda* (1948), David Miller's *The Story of Esther Costello* (1957), and Arthur Penn's *The Miracle Worker* (1962). But whereas such socially concerned films can openly elicit sociological value, *Gerald McBoing Boing*'s cartoon status would seem to preclude those types of analysis. My contention, as indicated previously, is that unvalidated cartoons are equally capable of embodying such value, at least at the level of proactive interpretation. And what more appropriate place to consider the symbolic codes of childhood trauma than in a children's cartoon. Elsewhere I have discussed various modes of catatonia in relation to the representation of women's voice in the cinema.[5] Here I will extend this to meter voicelessness in the child, using Gerald as a sonic gauge.

The child who does not speak implies multiple causes for his or her malaise that require various diagnostic measures. Babies who seem disconnected from the world around them early on may be deaf, or their inability to register aural activity might be a simple matter of sensory overload, considering the expanded frequency range bombarding the infant's ear drums after formative months of low-frequency massaging in the mother's womb. The child who shows a marked absence of vocalization may or may not be deaf, but he or she could potentially be mute. Lack of speech could also suggest a retardation in developing speech facility. And finally (though not comprehensively), the child who deliberately refrains from speech may be hiding an unspeakable experience. All these inabilities to speak—from the physiological to the psychological—invoke catatonia. While catatonia is not exclusively an inability to speak, its freezing of forward social momentum through the refusal to speak points to the primacy of interactive speech in ascertaining well-being. So how might we diagnose Gerald McBoing Boing? His parents are depicted as comforting and caring adults, despite their goofy panic typical of 1950s child-rearing clichés. They seek various professionals to explicate and rectify Gerald's situation, but none can provide the occupational therapy needed to empower Gerald to handle his orality in social situations. In fact, he is mostly able to communicate quite well to others; only his barking manner and raucous address upsets others. In *Gerald McBoing Boing* Gerald finds his role in society by providing the live sound effects for broadcast radio drama. Thus he is socially integrated and sonically subsumed by having his speech acknowledged as "spoken soundtrack."

Still, the surrealist advent of his vocal disposition—which in the cartoon shifts from affliction to talent—is never qualified. This in some measure replicates what would take decades to be read as a sign of child sexual abuse. Everything will appear normal on the surface of the social world, save for some inexplicable behavioral quirks in the child—none of which would be immediately traceable in clear linear fashion to incidents accepted as causing trauma. The child who is antisocial and/or self-destructive is deemed an overt problem rather than a symptom of a covert problem. Sonically, this also describes Gerald: his refutation of language makes him antisocial, while his loud sounding in social environments destroys his position within that space.

Interpreted this way, *Gerald McBoing Boing* is eerily tragic because the protagonist's traumatic disposition is socially accepted. Today that would amount to giving self-cutters special discounts at knife stores rather than interrogating why they behave in such a self-debilitating way. This is not in any way to condemn *Gerald McBoing Boing*. In fact its semiotic palimpsest is perfectly archived. Once its social allegory is peeled away, we are left with a child whose difference is not coded by look, appearance, or form but through the uncontrolled and unexplained repression of his voice as an instrument for a common language. Gerald's sound effects are a subcutaneous language, speaking not at the level of grammatical denotation but at the level of pathological connotation. Our close auriscopic analysis of his vocal demeanor and linguistic disposition has been genealogically traced through paternal garrulity and maternal taciturnity, to declare his voiceless cry as a repressed sign of pedophiliac trauma.

THE SYNESTHETIC DUMBNESS

Gerald's status as a device for producing wacky "cartoon sound effects" when he intends linguistic speech ensures both his iconic appeal and his fateful ability to be a total cartoonographic being devoid of human corporeality. Having covered how his "voice" is synchronized to his graphic form, we can now consider ideas of synesthesia in relation to his and others' audiovisuality. Synesthesia has long been dreamt as an ideal in audiovisual practice, as well as in wishful theories of film music. A century of music is now straddled by the heroicizing of Richard Wagner at one extreme and the asceticism of Carsten Nicolai at the other. From the music of planetary spheres to the sound of machinic glitches, experiments in "intertranslational" aurality abound as composers seek to alchemically unlock an exact sonomusical correlation of optical manifestation. But unlike those gilded artistes, Gerald is synesthetic beyond choice. To this extent he reinstates synesthesia as an affliction: an inability to not register a converse symbolic framework organized by sensory correlation when presented with a primary linguistic framework (such as uncontrollably tasting lemon while hearing flutes, etc.). For some, then, a synesthetic propensity is discomforting and relentless.

Trapped by his own signage, Gerald spirals in pathological patterns typically associated with victims of abuse incapable of breaking the cycle of their traumatic experience. Pedophiles are often the victims of child abuse themselves, and their behavior can be encoded within their psyche like grooves in an analog record. Again, this marks Gerald as an uncanny figuration of abuse as a result of his phonographic oracularity. So here we turn our attention to the "abuser"— to the potential figure who on one hand is implicated in the cause of Gerald's trauma and on the other hand has suffered enough to have instigated a cycle of abuse. It must be remembered, though, that this connection results from a textual operation, as have most of the notions forwarded here. Plus, the linkage will be primarily through oral and aural means, centered on a semiotic reading of a character's cartoon voice.

Thus parenthesized, the stage is set to introduce the character of Mister Magoo, star of numerous shorts between 1950 and 1959, followed by the *Mister Magoo* cartoon TV series (1960). Across these collected shorts, Magoo is a septuagenarian with bad eyesight and diminished hearing who blithely goes about his daily activities ignorant of his misreading of their entailed situations, such as intending to go to the movies but instead catching a plane. The ongoing gag is based around Magoo's never realizing he has done the wrong activity in the wrong place with the wrong person using the wrong object. In the TV series Magoo often causes havoc and chaos, which results in his believing he has encountered an inefficient device or a disrespectful attendant. This leads him to rant and rave in a comedic stereotype of a grumpy old man. Taking this formulaic setup into account, Magoo provides an interesting contrast in synesthetic composition to Gerald. Just as Gerald's voice contains the metadiegetic key to his audiovisual figuration, Magoo's hoarse harangue indicates the extent of his blindness and the degree to which he lives an imaginary existence constructed equally by his lack of sight and lack of sound. Synesthetically, his audiovisuality is controlled by equivocal inequities in his sense of sight and sound: he is as blind as he is deaf. And though Magoo is afflicted with debilitated senses, their proportional decay defines his synesthetic dumbness.

Most important, Magoo is never undone, chastised, or corrected. If Gerald is a token of the powerlessness of the child, Magoo is a token of the omnipotence of the father. In relation to the raging prewar characters of Daffy Duck and Yosemite Sam, and the emasculated postwar character of Wile E. Coyote, the elderly Magoo is a terse caricature of the final throes of patriarchal hysteria. He is the worst a father can be: from another era, unused to lack of control, presumptive of all around him, and incapable of any sustainable dialogue with his environment. He depicts the pathetic demise of the male psyche in complete denial of his social impotence. Deaf and blind to a degree that should forbid him from public intercourse, Magoo nonetheless barges through the world oblivious to dangers brought upon himself and others. This further enhances his patriarchal contrast to Gerald's puerility, in that Magoo is allowed his transgression while Gerald has to fight for acceptance. Magoo wields the symbolic power of the abuser, whereas Gerald is a symbolic retainer of that abuse.

If Gerald's future is a mystery, so is Magoo's past. Magoo may be a widower or a divorcee, but he is now clearly the eternal bachelor, drowning in his own delusional conquests as a paramour. This largely results from his old-world courteousness and his poetic appreciation of pulchritude in forms he presumes to be women. Excited in their presence, time lines merge in his ramblings, in that he may be addressing a past lover or a new flame. Just as the Coyote's hunger is driven by the Roadrunner's imaginary status as food, Magoo's interest is driven by an imaginary Tinker Bell. As a cartoon character he bears lineage to the great pantheon of lustful wolves baying at the smell of female. Magoo, however, is distinguished from those fevered characters by virtue of his outward impotency. As such he clarifies the latent sexual crisis signposted by exaggerations of virility and expulsions of arousal. Wile E. Coyote, for example, transfers the wartime wolf lust in Tex Avery's *Red Hot Riding Hood* (1943) to a domesticated husband forced to provide a meal for the table, such as when Coyote hilariously obeys culinary protocol while eating a tin can in *Guided Muscle* (1945). Magoo's poetic mumbling is a sign of the collapse of the predatory into the domesticated. Trapped in a cycle of endless courting, his chivalry directed toward store mannequins and wash mops indicates an ineffectual drive and harmless flirtation. Compared to the emasculated Coyote (as mentioned, a classic symbol of postwar male sexuality), Magoo is neutered—not castrated, just quietened.

Accordingly, Magoo is accidentally yet intensely paraphiliac. In his synesthetic state of reading everything through disconnected corollary triggers, he engages in social intercourse with (mostly) inanimate objects. The sexual subtext here again might seem a phantasm considering the innocuous nature of many *Mister Magoo* shorts, but in considering paraphilia we must at least momentarily allow that "where sex isn't is where sex is." Harmless as he seems, Magoo essentially penetrates the world. His meandering forward journey is predicated on his pushing and thrusting himself into situations. Like the chauvinism of the explorer hacking his way through virginal growth, Magoo charges onward, wielding his umbrella like an Arthurian sword. And Magoo's world is mostly a realm of domestic objects, utilitarian tools, and consumer commodities—all the province of postwar affluence in the United States. Thus, he is an impotent senile old man forever bumping into and handling things. The confirmed paraphiliac has no interest in humans nor any use for the markers of their socially accepted sexuality. Magoo is truly "beyond love": reduced to a demented dry-humping sociopath, he is incapable of any form of physical sex bar that of his form interacting with the inanimate plethora that constitutes his imaginary world.

A FINAL DIAGNOSTIC

To perceive how cartoons conduct paraphilia—how a graphic figurative form like the cartoon symbolizes a sexual practice like paraphilia, which is based on being attracted to objective signs rather than physical beings—a circulatory analytic method is necessitated. I have spun here analytic lines around three distinct modes by which the cartoon corpus is assembled: (1) "animamorphism," (2) "inhuman corporeality," and (3) synesthetic constitution. Between their joined lines, we have seen how resulting forms of the cartoon corpus belie their innocent intentions and activate semiotic interpretation. And as the cartoon corpus is a bodily construct, it is inevitable that pornographic fabrication and sexual configuration are raised by this assessment of how the cartoon body is imagineered. Finally, my focus has been on classic American cartoonography and, as such, has gravitated to determining factors from the pre- and postwar epochs that provide a sociological and psychological grounding to the semiotic interpretations sounded here.

A select group of cartoon characters has been chosen and proposed as emblematic figures in both the definition of the cartoon corpus and the means by which cartoons conduct paraphilia: Daffy Duck, Yosemite Sam, Wile E. Coyote, the Roadrunner, Tinker Bell, Gerald McBoing Boing, and Mister Magoo. Pertinent to this chapter's contribution to studies in film sound, the performance of these characters' voices has been crucial to comprehending how screaming, voicelessness, catatonia, dubbing, and rambling generate the soundtrack to the cartoon corpus. Through the process of auditing their vocalization, we are left holding an *auralis sexualis:* a forensic manual for diagnosing how cartoons conduct paraphilia.

NOTES

1. See Brophy, "The Animation of Sound."

2. According to the voice commentary on the DVD release of *Looney Tunes Golden Collection Volume 1,* Paul Julian remarks that he provided the vocal sound and that sound effects editor Treg Brown manipulated the recordings of only a few takes. Treg Brown also mentions that the Roadrunner's tongue flipping was produced by a finger being inserted into and quickly withdrawn from a bottle.

3. For more on "phantom tactility" see Brophy, "The Body Horrible."

4. A populist sociological treatise, Dr. Dan Kiley's *The Peter Pan Syndrome* discusses the rise of aging baby boomers in the United States and their unwillingness to accept their maturation through various means of clinging to childhood nostalgia.

5. See Brophy, "I Scream in Silence."

PART FOUR

Comic Inspiration

Animation Auteurs

the comedian is described as an "imperturbable inventor" who actualizes "delirious conceptions . . . obeying nothing but the logic of a dream."[2] The British film
critic Raymond Durgnat next takes up Bowers's cause in his 1969 study *The Crazy
Mirror: Hollywood Comedy and the American Image,* describing the comedian as
"one of the silent cinema's innumerable research problems" and complaining that
even the titles of his movies were, in some cases, unknown—powerful evidence
of the obscurity in which Bowers had come to languish.[3] Forward to the present:
we now know the titles, but, still, it is as a research problem that Bowers's legacy is
defined. Who was this comedian who found his greatest champion in a European
surrealist before lapsing into decades of obscurity? What sense can be made of
a career that took Bowers from the forefront of film animation in the 1910s, as
director on the Mutt and Jeff series, to writer, star, and producer of "novelty"
films combining live-action slapstick and stop-motion animation for FBO (Film
Booking Office) and Educational Pictures in the 1920s, to his final years as a
children's illustrator in the 1930s and 1940s? The problem is not only that Bowers
is unknown but that his career followed a path whose logic belongs to so seemingly alien a cultural imaginary—truly, as Borde put it, a "dream logic," binding
invention to animation to slapstick, where the boundaries separating science from
sleight of hand, mechanics from magic appear so imperfectly fixed.

It is my contention that the "Bowers problem" nonetheless opens on to larger
issues in the cultural history of American comedy, for Charley Bowers was hardly
the only comic filmmaker whose career traced such a path. One thinks obviously
of Buster Keaton, a self-confessed "mechanically inclined" boy, whose slapstick
form was stamped with the imprint of a fantastical mechanics; of Snub Pollard,
whose comedies for Hal Roach similarly exploited little inventions, systems of
pulleys and strings for household tasks; of the comedian Larry Semon, a former
cartoonist, like Bowers, with a penchant for costly trick stunts; or even of Walter
Wright, a director for Mack Sennett in the 1910s whose experiments with in-
camera effects and sensation scenes won him a reputation as "the Keystone's
'trick' director," before he departed filmmaking for a career as an inventor in the
1920s.[4] Bridging the nineteenth and the early twentieth centuries, this fascination
with invention and entertainment (of invention *as* entertainment) had fueled
many aspects of popular culture—not only in cinema—ranging from the *New
York Sun*'s famous "Moon Hoax" of 1835, in which a powerful new telescope was
reported to have revealed flying people on the moon, to Rube Goldberg's famous
"invention" cartoons almost a century later. Yet Bowers provides perhaps the
ultimate expression of this form of humor in motion pictures, a filmmaker whose
comedies unfold a delirious *mise-en-abyme* of mechanical spectacle both at the
level of content—in comic plots populated with inventors and bizarre contraptions—and at the level of technique—in Bowers's use of stop-motion animation
to depict anything from "eggs hatch[ing] Ford cars" to "oysters div[ing] into

soup."[5] It is, indeed, the very range of Bowers's activities as an artist and film-maker that marks his work as a unique occasion for the analysis of cultural forms, a crossroads where animation, slapstick, and even children's literature reveal a shared lineage in semimagical regimens for figuring technology. Part of the purpose of this chapter, accordingly, is to use Bowers to trace the vestiges of magical thinking—what I will call the "art of diddling"—within American culture's encounter with technology and to examine those playful diddlings as a way of rethinking slapstick and animation's complexly intertwined genealogy.

Still, in order to make an unknown comedian known, we need to begin with the basics: once again, who was Charley Bowers?

"BETWEEN FANTASY AND EXACT KNOWLEDGE": BOWERS AS INVENTOR AND TRICKSTER

A first answer: Charley was an inventor. At least, that's how he described his occupation in the 1930 census report.[6] That, too, was how he was presented to the industry in 1926, when, after a decade directing the Bud Fisher Film Corporation's *Mutt and Jeff* cartoons, he moved into live-action comedies for FBO, shortly after Joseph Kennedy's takeover of that organization. "Charles Bowers, inventor of the new 'Bower's [sic] Process,'" reported *Film Daily* in May, "claims that . . . his invention permits of the manipulation of the film after the camera has done its work." Bowers "makes the following claims for his process," the report contin-ued: "that he can photograph anyone and then show him doing anything imagin-able, such as walking a tightrope, sitting atop the dome of the Capitol, or flying from a skyscraper in New York to the new bridge in Philadelphia [the Benjamin Franklin Bridge, opened to traffic that year]. The inventor further states that he can make the Statue of Liberty bow to the Leviathan as she steams into the harbor, or tie the Washington monument into a knot."[7] What was here described as a single invention—the "Bowers process"—was, in fact, an imaginative assem-blage of effects ranging in practice from stop-motion animation to combinations of live-action footage and animated sequences, skillfully contrived by Bowers in collaboration with his technical partner, H. L. Muller.[8] Still, it was Bowers's willingness here to claim the impossible—as though he had actually developed a magic camera capable of severing cinema's indexical bond to the real world—that is the notable point. What was being perpetuated here—and, as will be seen, in much other discourse on Bowers—was a tradition of the technological marvel that had preceded the professionalization of early twentieth-century mechanics, a tradition looking back to the fantastic impostures of an earlier generation of showmen and hucksters who were an important legacy for Bowers's own career.

This also allows a second answer to our question: who was this man? Namely, Charley was a liar. Perhaps Bowers's most widely circulated film, *Now You Tell*

One (1926) concerns a search for a champion liar undertaken by a "Liars Club"; the independently produced *It's a Bird,* the film so admired by Breton, offers a "program of tall stories, dedicated to the great American whopper," with an introduction by the radio personality, and tall-tale aficionado, Lowell Thomas;[9] and Novelty Pictures' *Believe It or Don't* (1935) offers "strange news and odd facts from faraway places," including a report from a "Follywood" nut farm, where "they train peanuts to act in the movies." The Bowers's process was itself often described as disproving the axiom that "the camera never lies" ("every [Bowers] short . . . proves the camera is a monumental liar," noted one ad);[10] and the man himself was, in his personal relations, a near-compulsive falsifier. In the only firsthand reminiscence of Bowers to come down to us, Dick Huemer (an animator on the *Mutt and Jeff* films) remembered him as a "bodacious crittur," claiming that "nobody abhorred the truth as much as he did" and that "gaudy falsification of almost any subject afforded him more pleasure than the bald truth." Bowers was, Huemer recalled, practiced in the art of the "whopper," whether amusing his staff with tall stories of how he had once walked a tightrope between skyscrapers or in his proclivity for "financial peccadilloes" and what Huemer enigmatically described as his "bilking" of Raoul Barré.[11] Studio-published biographies of the filmmaker similarly strained credulity: early publicity for his live-action comedies told of the Iowa-born son of a French countess who learned tightrope walking at age five; joined the circus at six; returned home two years later to the surprise of his father, who died from the shock; then supported his mother by mowing lawns, jockeying horses, packing pork, printing menus, and writing history—all before he "animated one hundred reels of cartoons, worked out the Bowers process, invented a camera and—grew up."[12]

The figure that emerges, then, is that of the confidence man; and, if I choose that phrase over its synonyms, it is precisely to evoke the title of Melville's 1857 novel and to suggest, once again, Bowers's relation to an earlier cultural imaginary. It was Lewis Mumford who wrote that "Between fantasy and exact knowledge . . . there is an intermediate station: that of magic."[13] And the confidence man, a trickster figure for the industrial age, belonged precisely to this regime.[14] The roots of Bowers's creativity may thus be said to lie firmly within the comic tradition of the tall tale, the same tradition that, according to Constance Rourke, marked the dawning "consciousness of native [American] humor" in the nineteenth century and that, in Bowers, became a template for the comic reimagining of twentieth-century technologies.[15] Throughout Bowers's career his work would play on the nexus of invention and deception, of machinery and magic, of fabrication in the twofold sense of *making things* and *making things up.* His short-lived series of daily cartoons, *Life's Little Phonies,* published in the *Chicago Tribune* for four months in 1916, explicitly linked telecommunications technologies with new opportunities for lying, turning on the playful ambiguity in the term *phony* to

FIGURE 10.1. Two of Charley Bowers's *Life's Little Phonies* cartoons, from the *Chicago Tribune*, May 5 and 13, 1916.

associate phone users with deception. Each of the single-panel cartoons depicts talking heads for whom the anonymity of modern telecommunications prompts all manner of white lies: "Why, certainly, I'm master in my own home," claims a balding man over the phone, while his battleaxe wife shrieks "WHAT!" In another, a dentist's assistant reassures a prospective patient, "You need have no fear. The doctor's methods are absolutely painless," while "Dr. Yank N. Drill" is visible in the background operating with a hammer and chisel (Fig. 10.1). In his live-action comedies of the 1920s, Bowers's onscreen persona straddled a related dialectic, linking technology not to lying per se but to a broader realm of magic and fable. Here, he appeared simultaneously as both inventor and magus, both engineer and creator of cutesy golems. In *A Wild Roomer* (1926), for instance, Bowers's character designs a mammoth console for controlling household chores: in a remarkable, five-minute stop-motion sequence the machine sprouts robotic arms, designs a doll on which it performs a heart transplant, clothes the doll (now living), and feeds it a banana. The sequence ends with the doll riding off on the back of a squirrel, predictably. The magical productivity of modern mechanics was also conveyed in star discourse on the comedian, where Bowers's identity as camera technician and inventor frequently shaded into that of wizard: "he is Aladdin and the camera is his lamp . . . a MASTER of camera wizardry," ran one promotional piece; "More amazing than Aladdin's lamp of the magic genii are these mysterious creations," claimed another.[16]

"NOVELTY AND MYSTIFICATION": BOWERS, THE SHORT SUBJECT, AND THE OPERATIONAL AESTHETIC

What one starts to glimpse in Bowers's films, then, is how native traditions of buncombe and the tall tale could be reconfigured as magical modes of imagining technology.[17] But this is hardly the only relevant context for these films. Shifting to issues of industrial history, one finds that Bowers's work emerged during a major transformation in the American film industry's configuration of its short-subject output; and this, too, helps account for the films' surprising qualities. The mid-to-late 1920s marks an era of major boosterism within the short-subject field, as the major studios began adding shorts to their feature programs, resulting in a jockeying for prominence between independent short manufacturers and majors alike. Organizations such as the "Short Feature Advertising Association" aggressively campaigned to raise the short's profile among exhibitors, launching innovations such as "National Laugh Month" (which one exhibitor described as a "great move to impress the importance of short subjects on the public").[18] The trade journal *Motion Picture News* lent its hand to these campaigns, establishing a monthly "Short Subject Service Guide" in the spring of 1927 to provide "a specialized and dignified form of service" to the short film, which it described as the "life-blood of the successful theater"; around the same time, both MGM and Paramount announced their move into short-subject distribution, prompting the *News* to predict "a great year for Short Subjects."[19] Indeed, both distributors of Bowers's live-action comedies were at the leading edge in ballyhooing the short subject, Film Booking Office declaring that it would "lay particular stress" on its short-film output at the beginning of the 1926–27 season, while E. W. Hammons's Educational Pictures was, of course, exclusively a distributor of shorts, the leader in the field, having edged out Pathé.[20]

Technical novelty, apparently, was the key to success. Beginning in the mid-1920s, the short subject took over a number of functions banished from features, with many foregrounding achievements in the medium's technological base in ways that the illusionism of the feature film could not have sustained. The landmark innovations of the Vitaphone and Movietone shorts need no comment here; less commonly noted, however, are the frequently bizarre confections of technical effects to be found elsewhere, in, for example, Red Seal's Marvels of Motion series (each one of which exploited the medium's ability to manipulate time—as, for instance, in reverse footage of an egg being "unfried" and then leaping back into its shell); in Lyman P. Howe's Hodge Podge films (in which, as *Film Daily* described them, "unusual views . . . [were] depicted, interspersed with animated bits, art embellishments and a few nonsensical ideas"); or in Alvin Knechtel's "mystery" segments for Pathé Review.[21] The field of the "novelty short" became a major venue for technical showmanship, exacerbating tendencies toward mechanical spectacle already well established in other short-subject genres, such as slapstick and animation. "Only the limits of the camera," commented one trade journal, could stop the "remarkable" technical feats of the recent short subject.[22] And, certainly, no comedies were so consistently sold in these terms as those of Charley Bowers. Advertisements promoted his work as

FIGURE 10.2. Advertisement for *Egged On* from *Motion Picture News*, June 5, 1926.

"the industry's greatest novelty" (Fig. 10.2), promising "camera miracles" that marked "an epoch in novelty-comedy production."[23] "Novelty, novelty, novelty—that's . . . Bowers," commented *Motion Picture News*, which elsewhere praised his films for "just the right amount of novelty and mystification."[24]

This juncture of technical "novelty and mystification" was in fact characteristic of many slapstick films from the 1920s. As I have argued elsewhere, slapstick's ascendancy as a form with cross-class appeal had, in part, entailed a drift from an aesthetics of popular realism—in which comedy rested on the working-class clown's contestations of cultural hierarchy—toward a "mode-of-production" or "operational" aesthetic predicated on technological display and spectacular stunts whose exemplars included Keaton, Larry Semon, the directors Del Lord and Walter Wright, and others.[25] At the level of critical discourse, too, slapstick's disrepute as a comic form associated with the traditions of workers and immigrants had been superseded by a new appreciation that focused on the *mechanical* aspect of comic action, what the musical comedy playwright George M. Cohan termed the "mechanics of emotion."[26] Henri Bergson's mechanistic definition of comedy—according to which laughter erupts whenever someone behaves in a mechanical way, like a wind-up person—is well known; but this was only part of a developing mechanistic discourse whose other symptoms included scientistic attempts to adjudicate the success of gags with "laugh recorders" and pseudo-medical essays on comedy as a "safety valve"—note the mechanical metaphor—for ensuring the smooth-running of the mental faculties.[27]

In a real sense Bowers's comic style marks an extreme in this development, a point at which the spectacle of physical slapstick is fully subsumed beneath the display of mechanical process. Bowers's comedies depended on a single master plot—and that master plot was simply the process of invention itself. Typically, Charley portrays an inventor who must demonstrate a machine; he designs the device (e.g., a system for perfecting a nonslip banana peel in *Many a Slip* (1927), a labor-saving device for restaurant management in *He Done His Best* (1926), the aforementioned console from *A Wild Roomer*); and that machine is either successful or not. At the center of these films comes the spectacle of mechanical process in elaborate sequences that, like Rube Goldberg's contemporaneous "invention" cartoons, invite viewers to trace absurd, nonpurposive chains of cause and effect through the image of the machine—an "operational spectatorship," as it might be defined, focused on technological means rather than technological ends. The main invention sequence from *Many a Slip* may serve as a representative example. "After some meticulous tests with the infinite enlarging Bowerscope," a preliminary title explains, "Charley finally succeeded in isolating the *iskaytelos*, a slippery germ."[28] The sequence commences with Charley climbing atop a ladder and peering down through the giant Bowerscope (Fig. 10.3a); a cut to his point of view and we are shown an animated germ skating around on the microscope slide (Fig. 10.3b). Charley next applies various solutions to banana skins, each of which he carefully attaches to the arms of a giant centrifuge. A lever is pulled, turning a large windmill on the side of the house (Fig. 10.3c) and causing the centrifuge to rotate (Fig. 10.3d). The banana skins are removed, each one tested for slipperiness on a flight of steps that Charley drags in from the side of the lab (Fig. 10.3e). After numerous banana-skin pratfalls, Charley finds one peel that fails to slip; he examines it through the Bowerscope, sees that the

FIGURE 10.3. Charley inventing nonslip banana peel in *Many a Slip* (Bowers, 1927).

iskaytelos is dead—a wreath of flowers on its inert body—and declares, "I've discovered iskaytocide!" (Fig. 10.3f). As reviews of the time observed, it was the sheer spectacle of mechanical process—as opposed to the (nonexistent) logic articulating those processes—that provided the film's main point and appeal: "The various machines which he invents for diverse purposes function and accomplish something, but just what really does not . . . matter because you are fascinated watching the inventor set them in motion, watching the various wheels and belts revolve and do something or other."[29] Or, as an ad for a later Bowers film put it, "Don't ask us how the darn thing works. That's Bowers' secret process idea."[30]

"TO DIDDLE IS HIS DESTINY": BOWERS, ANTIMODERNISM, AND THE ART OF DIDDLING

It is perhaps not wholly accurate to describe Bowers's aesthetic as one of means rather than ends. Ends remain important, even while—or even *because*—they are absolved of all practical possibility. Unlike Goldberg's cartoons, which linked their spectacles of process to everyday—indeed, mundane—tasks ("Simple Way of Hiding a Gravy Spot on Your Vest," "How to Tee Up a Golf Ball without Bending Over"), Bowers's machines were more notably linked to the production of wonders (from unbreakable eggs in *Egged On* [1926] to ostriches made of old clothes in *Say Ah-h* [1928]). As such, and to return again to a previous point, these films belonged to an earlier imaginary in which technological progress had accustomed the public to a belief in the continued appearance of mechanical marvels, a magical conception of technology that had preceded the famous decay of "aura," of magic and metaphysics, a decay that Walter Benjamin associated with the era of mechanical reproduction. Wonder had, of course, been a central figure in the American response to the machine age, the decisive emotional and intellectual experience in the presence of technological possibility; but it was also an experience that generated the mechanical hoax as part of a vernacular tradition of popular technology, whether in any number of sham "perpetual motion" machines, in the flagrant humbug of a P. T. Barnum, or in the string of elaborate tall tales perpetuated in New York's antebellum popular press (including the aforementioned "Moon Hoax" as well as phony reports of transatlantic balloon crossings and the like).[31] The growth of industrial technologies had thus been accompanied, from the mid-nineteenth century on, by a structuring of implausibility through those very same technologies, establishing the art of the lie—what Edgar Allan Poe termed the "exact science" of "diddling"—as an essential component of the aesthetics of machinery. As Poe wrote: "A crow thieves; a fox cheats; a weasel outwits; a man diddles. To diddle is his destiny."[32]

It is arguably within this orbit of technical "diddling" that stop-motion animation and slapstick find their shared heritage. The earliest examples of stop

motion appealed to a similar spirit of inquiry provoked by Barnumesque humbug, making their reception a form of intellectual exercise centered on puzzling
out how the illusion was achieved. The first famous instance was Vitagraph's
1907 *The Haunted Hotel*, a film whose European success was followed by the
publication, in the French weekly *L'illustration*, of two articles exposing the
stop-motion technique, in turn prompting an indignant response from Georges
Méliès, who proposed a code of filmmakers' confidentiality as a remedy for future
breaches.[33] Yet one does not have to look abroad, nor only to animation, to find
equivalent dramas of cinematic secrecy and exposé; the history of live-action
slapstick abounds in them. In late 1917, for instance, a publicity agent for the
Paramount Pictures Corporation sent out a press release injudiciously explaining
the camera trickery employed in one of Paramount's new line of Mack Sennett
comedies—live-action, of course—prompting a furious letter from Sennett himself: "We do our utmost here to keep any and all of our mechanical contrivances
a studio secret," Sennett insisted. "Can you imagine, as an illustration, a magician
explaining to his audience how a trick is done and then going ahead and doing
it? Naturally there ceases to be the required illusion; therefore it is of no interest
to the spectators whatever."[34] Regardless of the differences in the techniques
employed, slapstick and stop motion evidently shared a stock-in-trade in baffling
illusionism.

It is possible, in fact, to see in these parallels something of stop motion's
specificity as a "diddling" technique of animation, in contrast with other techniques like cutouts, drawing, and rotoscoping. For what stop motion shared
with slapstick's aesthetic of fantastic machinery was precisely a foundation in
profilmic reality, a direct bond to three-dimensional objects recorded "out there"
in front of the camera (*direct* here being used to distinguish stop motion from the
more mediated bond in rotoscoping). The stop-motion image preserves a world
of real objects that have been reworked to behave in unreal ways, much as in the
wire-assisted stunts and double exposure spectacles of slapstick's own world of
crazy machines and uproarious inventions. The rationalization of vision built on
the putative veracity of the camera ("the camera never lies") was thus studiously
assaulted in stop motion as in other in-camera effects, whose unique property
was to generate an indexical record of an apparently "impossible" objectivity.
This, surely, is why contemporary critical discourses tended to gravitate toward
the language of deception in accounting for these techniques and why Bowers
acquired a reputation for proving the "camera is a monumental liar." (Perhaps
Bowers's own *Believe It or Don't* put the point more succinctly: "The eye of the
camera never lies," declares a voice-over narrator, while stop-motion peanuts
arrange themselves onscreen to respond "AW NERTS.")

That Bowers operated within this aesthetic of deceptive vision was no doubt
part of his appeal for European modernists, whose own fascination with the

perceptual instabilities of modernity must have prepared the way for Bowers's enthusiastic reception by Breton in the 1930s ("our eyes opened to the flat sensory distinction between the real and the fantastic"). In the U.S. context, however, such an aesthetic spoke rather to fundamental fault lines in the American imagining of technology, contrasting sharply with discourses of industrial rationalization and scientific certitude. This sense of a contradiction between fantasy and reason, between diddling and professional science, welled up nowhere more powerfully than in the field of popular culture, where the "impossible" pleasures of mechanical mystery vied increasingly against more secular representations that tilted the rhetoric of invention in line with a Taylorist emphasis on efficient productivity. The growing primacy of positivist expertise is clear, for instance, in Susan Douglas's study of the amateur wireless-radio hobbyists of the 1910s and 1920s. The "radio boys" were urban middle-class youth who pursued not magic but an entrepreneurial culture of technical expertise, following in the footsteps of Thomas Edison and the Wright Brothers.[35] In children's fiction, meanwhile, the more rationalized paradigm was supplied by the Tom Swift series, which was introduced in 1910 with the stated goal to "convey in a *realistic* way the wonderful advances in land and sea locomotion" and which turned repeatedly on the less-than-marvelous theme of patent rights.[36] *Tom Swift and His Airship* (1910), for instance, contains the following passage:

> Tom's task was to arrange the mechanism so that, hereafter, the rudder could not become jammed.... This the lad accomplished by a simple but effective device which, when the balloonist saw it, caused him to compliment Tom. "That's worth patenting," he declared. "I advise you to take out papers on that." "It seems such a simple thing," answered the youth. "And I don't see much use of spending the money for a patent. Airships aren't likely to be so numerous that I could make anything off that patent." "You take my advice," insisted Mr. Sharp. "Airships are going to be used more in the future than you have any idea of. You get that device patented." Tom did so, and, not many years afterward he was glad that he had, as it brought him quite an income.[37]

Contrast this, for instance, with Bowers's own first foray into the world of children's literature, *The Bowers Mother Goose Movie Book* (1923), a nursery rhyme flip book whose cover blurb bestowed a quasi-animistic quality to its pages: "FLIP THE PAGES . . . THE PICTURES LIVE!"[38]

What must in addition be reckoned with here is a further, overarching distinction pitting an alienated experience of technology, as emblematized in modern industry, against a nonalienated one, as embedded in the premodern notion of magic. For what in the Tom Swift series is a commitment to technology in relation to the capitalist logic of profit and exchange—whereby invention ultimately becomes investment—is in Bowers a vision of technology as a vehicle for realizing and giving concrete form to the workings of fantasy itself. Bowers's comedy is thus not that of the assembly line—it is not the comedy of Chaplin's *Modern Times* (1935), in which the clown's body is subordinate to the relentless onrush of cogwheels, factory belts, and pistons—but rather that of the workshop, as a secluded space of invention that recurs over and over again in his comedies and that links his own labor as an animator and inventor to that of the characters of his films. The workshop appears in *Egged On,* in the form of the old barn where Charley assembles his system for making unbreakable eggs; it is the kitchen in *He Done His Best,* which he redesigns as the control room for a fully automated restaurant; and it is the apartment lodgings in *A Wild Roomer, Fatal Footsteps* (1926), and *Many a Slip,* all of which become impromptu laboratories in which Charley's fanciful contraptions are incubated and brought to term. A pocket of stasis, the Bowers workshop can be thought of as a kind of enclave within which fantasy can operate—in some sense akin to Johan Huizinga's vision of the "ideal playground," a "temporary world within the ordinary world" where "special rules" apply.[39] One thinks of the fascination that other, similarly secluded, enclaves have exerted in modernity's imagination of technology, those subterranean spaces and high-tech caverns that supplemented the efficient organization of modern industry with a more ancient fascination with mystic underground realms.[40] The technological regime of these films thus rests on a combination of elements excluded from the more obviously hegemonic spaces of modern industry: where the idea of the factory, for example, is that of a mode of production in its rationalized and public guise, the idea of the workshop configures technology according to a more private imaginary, its bonus of pleasure residing not in the utility of the product but in the autonomy of productivity itself. The operative dialectic here—factory vs. workshop, or industry vs. magic—seems, moreover, to correspond to a tension Fredric Jameson has identified as fundamental to modernity's representations of technology; and this is the tension, drawn from Coleridge, between Imagination and Fancy, Imagination designating that architectural faculty of the mind that shapes new worlds in the image of the machine versus the more purely local and decorative pleasures of Fancy.[41] As an illustration of Fancy's private dimensions, Jameson notes a well-known scene from Jean Renoir's *La règle du jeu* (1939): "the nascent embarrassment of Dalio as he exhibits his heart's desire, . . . an immense mechanical orchestra, which, in full animation, leaves its owner to blush and prance awkwardly in imitation alongside it."[42] One only wishes to add that the path from here to the factory as a space divorced from the home and the craftsman's shop exemplifies the logic of disembedding that is characteristic of modernity, a "lifting out" of technology from the realm of private fantasy and its restructuring across social space—an observation to which I will return.[43]

The methodological point, at any rate, is that the aesthetic of fantastic machinery sustained in Bowers's comedies—grist for the mill for scholars who have related early slapstick to the technologies of turn-of-the-century modernity[44]—is perhaps best seen through the matrix of pre- or even antimodernism, a retreat from the rationalization of modern science toward earlier, less alienated imaginings. In an era of unprecedented technological advance, the idea of technology's magical productivity—Bowers's idea—could hardly be other than *residual,* as a representation not only formed in the past but marginalized within the present as "comic" or nonserious, suited best to the realm of slapstick, of cartoons, even of children's literature, to name the major areas of Bowers's creativity.[45] It belongs, that is, to a moment preceding the recognition of industrial modernity as a system in its own right, when it was still possible to consider uses for technology that were not already assimilated to a vision of productive labor. What has been described by Miriam Hansen as slapstick's "vernacular modernism" may, in other words, have emerged paradoxically as a *withdrawal* from the modern.[46] But if this is so, then it becomes easier to discern something of slapstick's ambiguity, as a form that not only "play[ed] games with the violence of technological regimes" but that, in doing so, ultimately marked a major accommodation to those regimes.[47] As the historian T. J. Jackson Lears has written, the paradox of turn-of-the-century antimodernism was that, in its quest to recover irrational and vitalist forces in the face of the banality of modern life, it helped ease an acceptance of that very banality, smoothing the path for more secular and corporate modes.[48] Magic may have been opposed to rationalized science in its celebration of mystery, of the impossibility of connecting cause to effect; yet such an aesthetic also assumed an important ideological role, as a highly charged site of pleasure, in making tolerable the growth of corporate industry. Perhaps nowhere was this functioning more dramatically clear than in the closing phase of Bowers's career; and one of the last of his films would also be the most obvious in its structure of accommodation.

"SOUNDLY SOLD ON THE COMPANY": BOWERS, THE OIL INDUSTRY, AND THE NEW YORK WORLD'S FAIR

Whatever the reason, Bowers did not remain with Educational, or with any Hollywood firm, after 1928. Early that year, E. W. Hammons's organization fumbled its transition to sound—a short-lived attempt to back the unreliable (and scarcely less short-lived) Vocafilm disc system—complicating the programming of Educational's forthcoming season.[49] When that program was announced in May, Bowers's name was nowhere to be seen. According to census records, Bowers soon relocated to the East Coast—first to Connecticut, later to New Jersey—where he seems to have devoted much of his time to illustrating, turning out children's books, and contributing cartoons for the *Jersey Journal.*[50] Increasingly spotty, his film output was, after 1935, exclusively in the field of stop-motion animation (including what appears to have been two entries in a planned series on a family of mice for release through Paramount, *Wild Oysters* and *A Sleepless Night,* both 1940), before a serious illness terminated his creative career in 1941, bringing death five years later.[51] Still, his work found one last moment of acclaim, not in picture theaters but at the New York World's Fair of 1939, for which, in collaboration with first-time director Joseph Losey, Bowers contributed a promotional short for the oil industry, *Pete Roleum and His Cousins.* With its theme of "The World of Tomorrow," the New York Fair made unprecedented use of motion pictures, the ideal vehicle for the combination of education, entertainment, and promotion that made up most of the fair's commercial exhibits. And of the more than six hundred films testifying to the "scope and importance" of cinema as "one of the seven modern means of communication," *Pete Roleum and His Cousins* won the highest plaudits—the "fairest screen fare at the Fair," according to Walter Winchell.[52]

Of course, this would not be the last time that the oil industry would hire a liar to publicize its product; more surprising is that this was not Bowers's first association with that industry. Back in 1926, when he had first entered the field of live-action filmmaking, it was reported that Bowers had recently completed a noncommercial "six-reel picture for one of the big oil companies using [the Bowers process] for gushers and other effects."[53] Certainly, the qualities of Bowers's operational aesthetic were attuned to the promotional rhetoric of modern industry. Historians of the 1939 World's Fair have noted how several companies marketed their product precisely by fusing technology with the spectacle of magic, as in General Electric's House of Magic exhibit (in which, according to *Business Week,* "tricks . . . with thyratons and stroboscopes" left audiences "thrilled, mystified, and soundly sold on the company").[54] Planned as a demonstration of enlightened engineering, the fair thus became what *Life* magazine described as "a magnificent monument by and to American business," and Bowers's picture was part of the hard sell—a "fantasy" film, as it was described, featuring a drop of oil as a "new hero."[55]

The film unfolds as a history of technological advance in which oil is celebrated not only as a lynchpin of industry and transportation but also, increasingly, for its benefits to an American consumers' republic. As the narrator proclaims early on: "Oil turns the wheels of industry! Of pleasure! Of comfort! It cools and heats! Builds cities! Makes a paradise on earth!" The slippage here from "wheels of industry" to an air-conditioned, comfortable "paradise on earth" is replicated over the course of the film: the picture's initial focus on heavy industry shifts into the realm of consumer goods as Pete Roleum introduces products like chewing gum, suntan lotion, and nail polish. The film's visual aesthetic further reinforces these consumerist associations, corresponding to what the historian William Leach has described as a "commercial aesthetic" in which "color . . .

and light" functioned as the principal "visual materials of desire."[56] Filmed in Technicolor, *Pete Roleum and His Cousins* recalled in its color design "some of the scenes in 'Snow White'" in the opinion of one reviewer, who also noted how the film's exhibition at the fair created an immersive environment that, not unlike a vaudeville show or cabaret act, broke down the barriers separating audience and spectacle. "A 'Hellzapoppin' touch is added by having two interlocking sound tracks on the film, one of which carries, through an amplifier in the back of the hall, derogatory statements and questions from a heckler addressed to Pete the central character. As in all good acts, Pete always gets the last word or last laugh."[57] Refiguring technology as entertaining, multisensory spectacle, the film culminates in a musical extravaganza—penned, bizarrely, by Oscar Levant and Brecht's former collaborator Hanns Eisler—in which a chorus line of oil drops declares, "Muscle and strength have we! We're the spirit of energy! . . . We're the modern musketeers! The oil men!"

Inescapable here is a structural shift in the imagination of modern technology; and we may speak of something like a recathecting of Bowers's filmmaking in accordance with the ideological imperatives of industry and commerce. From the opening image of the world turning, to subsequent scenes envisioning a planet desolate without oil, *Pete Roleum and His Cousins* projects a global and systemic perspective—the oil industry as a framework for modernity itself. Yet this, in turn, entails a dissociation of Bowers's animation techniques away from the more private terrain of fantasy—away, that is, from the representational regime of the workshop—and effaces that properly magical productivity in which Bowers's earlier diddlings had found their material. There is nothing "fantastic" about the products celebrated in this film; we are no longer in the realm of unbreakable eggs and metal-eating birds. Instead, fancy shifts its center of gravity from the level of the product to that of representation, the aura of the magical surviving only in a consumer sense, to the extent that stop motion supplies an appealing gloss on the products themselves. Diddling thus reaches its limit as the source of an alternative conception of technology, and industry finds its meaning as the loss of magic.

In conflating magic and consumerism, comic process and corporate promotion, *Pete Roleum and His Cousins* nonetheless provides an appropriate conclusion to this chapter, a testimony to the shifting and unstable role of comic mechanics as an anarchic supplement to industrialization. "Our ability to lie," Jacques Derrida once wrote, "belongs among the few obvious, demonstrable data that confirm human freedom."[58] Certainly, there could be no history of American humor in general—and no histories of slapstick or animation in particular—outside of the particular creative freedom afforded by the diddling arts. The same, too, could be said of the history of American corporate advertising, which, as several historians have observed, emerged from its own tradition of preposterous humbug and snake-oil salesmen in the patent medicine era.[59] In straddling all of these vectors, Bowers's career thus speaks to the remarkable prevalence of the tall tale as a resource through which individuals in diverse fields negotiated their transition to modernity. But it also signals the precariousness of that resource—its evasiveness, even its complicity—in the face of the twentieth century's dominant technocratic idiom. In a society committed to industrial progress and control, Bowers's resurrection of the art of fantastic machinery, of the art of mechanical deception, attained a fetishistic charge as a refusal of rationalization; yet the appeal to the irrational was always recuperable as appealing fantasy, the mystery of technology as mystification. And no wonder, for, by proving the camera "a monumental liar," Bowers only intensified mechanization's allure, charting unexpected relations linking slapstick to surrealism, animation to commercial ideology.

NOTES

Versions of this chapter were delivered at the 2007 Society for Cinema and Media Studies conference in Philadelphia and at the "Space Matters: Reframing Early Cinema and Modernity" symposium at the University of Michigan in 2009. I am grateful for the responses and comments I received there. I am also grateful to Charlie Keil for his editorial assistance and suggestions and to Inie Park for her many and patient read-throughs.

1. Breton, "Note sur le cinéma à propos du film *It's a Bird*," 1206–7 (my translation).

2. Borde, "Le mystère bricolo," 62; quoted in Durgnat, *The Crazy Mirror*, 98.

3. Durgnat, *The Crazy Mirror*, 98.

4. Keaton and Samuels, *My Wonderful World of Slapstick*, 41; "Three-Minute Visit to Keystone Studio." Information on Larry Semon's father is derived from "Prof. Semon at the Bijou." I am indebted to Brent Walker for information on Walter Wright's post-Keystone career.

5. The quotes are from an advertisement for FBO's 1926–27 release schedule in *Motion Picture News*, May 22, 1926, 2425–29.

6. U.S. Census Bureau, *The 1930 Federal Population Census Microfilm*, 27.

7. "New Process," *Film Daily*, May 30, 1928, 14.

8. Very little is known about Harold Muller, Bowers's longtime collaborator, and even less about the exact division of labor between the two filmmakers. According to his entry in the 1923/24 *Motion Picture Studio Directory*, Muller's early film career had included work with color and synchronized sound technologies (as cinematographer at Charles Urban's Kinemacolor and the Talking Motion Pictures company, respectively). Evidently a skilled and inventive technician, he was credited as director and cinematographer on the majority of Bowers's live-action comedies and up until the fully animated *Wild Oysters* (1940). See clippings file, Billy Rose Theatre Collection, New York Public Library for the Performing Arts. I am grateful to Steve Massa and Richard M. Roberts for this information.

9. In 1931, the year following the release of *It's a Bird*, Thomas published *Tall Stories: The Rise and Triumph of the Great American Whopper*. The exact relation between Bowers's film and the publication of this book is unclear. Three years later, however, in 1934, Bowers and Thomas seem to have entered into a more official collaboration when it was announced that a series of Lowell Thomas "Tall Story" comedies was to be produced with the "world famous Bowers Process." According to

early advertisements, the series was to be backed by a multimedia campaign involving "the Lowell Thomas daily broadcasts," "tens of thousands" of members of Thomas's "Tall Story Club," and nine new editions of the *Tall Stories* volumes. Evidently the collaboration was unsuccessful, since none of the proposed series ever made it to release. See "Bowers Plans Comedy Series with Thomas," *Motion Picture Herald*, Feb. 24, 1934; and the advertisement for Lowell Thomas "Tall Story" Comedies, *Film Daily Yearbook 1934*, 116.

10. Advertisement for Educational Pictures, *Photoplay*, Feb. 1928, 13.

11. Huemer, "Humoresque."

12. Advertisement for Educational Pictures, *Photoplay*, Feb. 1928, 13.

13. Mumford, *Technics and Civilization*, 36.

14. See Halttunen, *Confidence Men and Painted Women*.

15. See Rourke, *American Humor*, 60. Rourke proceeds to list some famous nineteenth-century whoppers: "An old gentleman was so absent-minded that he tucked his pantaloons into bed one night and hung himself on the back of his chair, where he froze to death. Another had whiskey so good that when he drank it he spoke broad Scotch. A man was so tall that he had to get up on a ladder to shave himself. There was the immemorial oyster, so large that two men were required to swallow it. . . . Such tales were told throughout the century and perhaps have never died. Their lineage is long; they appear in shy forms on the New England frontier of the eighteenth century. . . . [But it] was in the West that these tales took on their final inflation; and from the West they spread over the country" (60–61).

16. Advertisement for Educational Pictures, *Photoplay*, Feb. 1928, 13; review of *Whoozit? Motion Picture News*, March 17, 1928, 896.

17. Rourke's *American Humor* accounted for the emergence of the tall tale in the nineteenth century as a way of coming to terms with the "expansive effect" of the western frontier. That tradition survived in Bowers, I am beginning to suggest, as a way of playfully negotiating the no less "expansive" impact of turn-of-the-century technological change. See Rourke, *American Humor*, 61.

18. "Exhibitors Lining Up for Laugh Month," *Motion Picture News*, Dec. 18, 1926, 2429.

19. "Short Subject Service Guide," *Motion Picture News*, April 15, 1927, 1335; "The Week in Review," *Motion Picture News*, March 25, 1927, 1024.

20. "F.B.O. Has 54 for 1926–27," *Motion Picture News*, May 22, 1926, 2458a. On Educational see Richard M. Roberts, "'Mixed Nuts' and Educational Pictures," *Classic Images*, Jan. 1992, 26–28.

21. "Expansion of Short Subjects," *Film Daily*, May 30, 1926, 16.

22. Ibid.

23. Advertisement for *Egged On, Motion Picture News*, June 5, 1926, 2645; advertisement for *Now You Tell One, Motion Picture News*, Dec. 4, 1926, 2112–13.

24. Review of *Hop Off, Motion Picture News*, June 23, 1928, 290; review of *Whoozit? Motion Picture News*, March 17, 1928, 896.

25. See King, "'Uproarious Inventions.'" The terms "popular realism" and "operational aesthetic" are drawn from, respectively, Oberdeck, *The Evangelist and the Impresario*; and Harris, *Humbug*.

26. On Cohan and the "mechanics of emotion" see Jenkins, *What Made Pistachio Nuts?* 32–37.

27. On the "laugh recorder" see "'Laugh Recorder' Try Out in Los Angeles," *Motion Picture News*, March 31, 1928, 1029; on comedy as a "safety valve" see Bisch, "What Makes You Laugh?"

28. The quoted titles are taken from the Image DVD release (2004), which translates back into English the title cards from the surviving French release print (in which the slippery germ is named *patynhos*). The original English titling does not survive.

29. Review of *Many a Slip, Motion Picture News*, Jan. 21, 1927, 235.

30. Advertisement for *Say Ah-h, Motion Picture News*, Feb. 25, 1928, 609.

31. The principle of "perpetual motion"—that a machine might run continually without any source of power beyond its own momentum—was much debated during the late nineteenth century, giving rise to many humbug inventions.

32. Poe, "Diddling Considered as One of the Exact Sciences."

33. See Crafton, *Before Mickey*, 17–18, 29–30.

34. Mack Sennett to Adolph Zukor, Dec. 13, 1917, Correspondence folder (1915–1919), General Files, Mack Sennett Collection, Margaret Herrick Library, Academy of Motion Picture Arts and Science. Sennett's "outrage" here was perhaps more than a little specious: his own publicity staff made a habit of revealing tidbits of technical information, even including an exhibitors' slideshow the previous year. See "Start a Lecture Campaign in Your Theatre," *Triangle*, April 22, 1916, 1, 6.

35. See Douglas, *Inventing American Broadcasting, 1899–1922*.

36. Appleton, *Tom Swift and His Motor Cycle*, dust jacket (italics added).

37. Appleton, *Tom Swift and His Airship*, 66–67.

38. *The Bowers Mother Goose Movie Book* (1923) has recently been reprinted by Optical Toys of Putney, VT (opticaltoys.com).

39. Huizinga, *Homo Ludens*, 8–10; quoted in Nasaw, *Going Out*, 80.

40. See Williams, *Notes on the Underground*.

41. See Jameson, *Archaeologies of the Future*, 42–56. On the dialectic of factory vs. workshop see n. 43 below.

42. Jameson, *Archaeologies of the Future*, 47. The sequence is also cited in Jacques Lacan's 1958 seminar "Le désir et son interprétation."

43. I am here paraphrasing Lewis Mumford, *Technics and Civilization*, 138: "It was the existence of a central building, *divorced from the home and the craftsman's shop*, in which large bodies of men could be gathered to perform the various necessary industrial operations with the benefit of large-scale co-operation that differentiated the factory in the modern sense from the largest of workshops" (emphasis added). Readers of Marx's *Capital* will know, however, that the relation of the factory to the workshop is more complex than Mumford's metaphor of "divorce" might suggest; for, as *Capital*'s chapter on modern industry explains, industrial work processes *incorporate* older systems of production rather than *supersede* them, a phenomenon evident in the continued presence of artisanal workshops within the early twentieth-century factory. Thus, while the phenomena of factory and workshop may be juxtaposed in theory, that opposition must be understood as neither a rigid historical nor a spatial separation but rather a mixed development. See, on this issue, Samuel, "Workshop of the World." On "disembedding" see Giddens, *The Consequences of Modernity*, 21–29.

44. See, e.g., Gunning, "Crazy Machines in the Garden of Forking Paths"; and Rabinovitz, "The Coney Island Comedies."

45. I am using *residual* here in the precise sense suggested by Raymond Williams: "The residual, by definition, has been effectively formed in the past, but it is still active in the cultural process.... Thus certain experiences, meanings, and values which cannot be expressed or substantially verified in terms of the dominant culture, are nevertheless lived and practiced on the basis of the residue—cultural as well as social—of some previous social and cultural institution or formation" (Williams, *Marxism and Literature*, 122).

46. See Hansen, "The Mass Production of the Senses," esp. 70–71.

47. Ibid., 70.

48. Lears, *No Place of Grace*, 58.

49. On Educational and Vocafilm see "Educational Acquires Vocafilm," *Motion Picture News*, Jan. 14, 1928, 121; "Vocafilm Busy Preparing New Acts," *Motion Picture News*, Jan. 21, 1928, 201; Gomery, *The Coming of Sound*, 84.

50. See "Charles Bowers; Pioneer in Film Cartoons; Jersey Writer, Director and Producer's Career Began at 6 on Tightwire."

51. *A Sleepless Night* seems never to have been released, since it survives only without a soundtrack.

52. Crowther, "Films for the Fair"; Winchell, "Walter Winchell on Broadway."

53. See "F.B.O. Has New Comedy Series," 2260.

54. Quoted in Susman, "The People's Fair," 224.

55. *Life* magazine, quoted in Susman, "The People's Fair," 223; see also "Oil Industry Movie Presents New Hero."

56. Leach, *Land of Desire,* 9.

57. "Oil Industry Movie Presents New Hero." On the stage production of *Hellzapoppin* see Henry Jenkins's contribution to this volume.

58. Derrida, "History of the Lie," 95.

59. See, e.g., Lears, *Fables of Abundance,* esp. part 1; and Marchand, *Advertising the American Dream,* chap. 1.

11

Tex Avery's Prison House of Animation, or Humor and Boredom in Studio Cartoons

Scott Curtis

I've done it all a hundred different ways. I'm burned out. I just don't think the stuff is funny anymore.

—TEX AVERY

There is a thin line between comedy and tedium. Anybody who has seen several Tex Avery cartoons in a row is probably very familiar with this boundary. The film critic Jonathan Rosenbaum once wrote, "To be sure, if you see as few as half a dozen Averys at a stretch, you're likely to notice repetitions of gags and certain recurring obsessions . . . and as many as a dozen together is an experience promoting migraines and nervous exhaustion."[1] The Avery scholar Floriane Place-Verghnes agrees: "Seeing that these cartoons should be entertaining, it may seem paradoxical to say that watching them for two hours (that is, the average duration of a movie) is an extremely tiring exercise as far as the concentration of the audience is concerned."[2] Even Joe Adamson, who otherwise praises Avery's work, recognizes the dangers inherent in it: "But, like any freedom, the freedom of the animation medium brings with it its own responsibility. The stylization, the exaggeration, the free-wheeling disregard for earthly reality, are all liberating enough for a scene or two, but it's a thrill that can wear out pretty quickly, unless it's given a steady guidance beyond the momentary."[3] It's a theme in the literature about Avery's cartoons: even the best examples walk that razor's edge between the sublime and the boring.

To be fair, a Tex Avery cartoon is not the only thing that walks that line. Comedy itself inches toward monotony. If Henri Bergson's theory of laughter is correct—that comedy depends on the invocation of the mechanical—then there is something in the very nature of comedy that is circular and, hence, evokes the specter of boredom.[4] Comic routines that depend on repetitive gags or the constant inversion of roles (e.g., hunter and hunted) have a circular energy that can go on like a perpetual motion machine. Gags can be endlessly repeated and varied, roles constantly reversed. The gag can take on a life of its own, studiously unconcerned with character or plot. And if, as Bergson argues, what's funny always amounts to the intrusion of the mechanical into life—what makes us laugh, in other words, is the recognition of, say, mechanical rigidity or thingness in humans—then this very tendency toward the mechanical is part of the soul of comedy but also carries with it the threat of tedium.

Bergson does not deal with failed comedy. He does not discuss why something that tries to be funny is *not* funny. In fact, no one who writes about Avery dwells on his sometimes listless stabs at humor. For good reason: trying to explain why one cartoon is funny and another isn't is rather futile. Nevertheless, Avery cartoons lend themselves especially well to what we might call a "Bergsonian" analysis. On one hand, if we want to understand the thin line between comedy and boredom, Bergson's theory of laughter is an excellent starting point. On the other hand, if we want a great example of the constitutive relationship between humor and tedium, we need look no further than a typical Tex Avery cartoon. What critics have recognized as Avery's tendency toward monotony hints not only at a "mechanical" approach to the task but also points toward something deeper and sadder. We see this in a number of places. First, we have the cartoons themselves, which are structured in such a way that they are almost perfect examples of Bergson's ideas about comedy and the mechanical. Second, Avery's cartoons constantly reference the monotonous yet intermittently funny process of image production during the era of classical Hollywood studio animation. From these references we can almost see Avery coming to grips with the grind and glee of his art form. Finally, we have Avery's biography, which is a tale of perfectionism, obsession, frustration, and despair about the drudgery of studio animation and also, perhaps, about the meaninglessness of it all.

Bergson's thesis on comedy is not the only one out there, of course, and it may seem rather perverse to think of Avery's cartoons in light of a theory of laughter written in 1900. But there is something about each that resonates with the other. Avery's cartoons are certainly very funny, yet, taken as a whole, there is also something sad about them. The very thing that sets them apart from standard studio animation—the frenetic accumulation of gag after gag—also reveals their dependence on inherently mechanical comic structures. Ultimately, I want to explain how Avery cartoons can be very, very funny and yet very sad or even boring at the same time. They are undoubtedly exuberant—no one who has seen the Wolf's reactions in *Red Hot Riding Hood* (1943) could say otherwise. But we must also admit that there is something slightly cold and mechanical about these very same cartoons. Taken individually, some cartoons sing with sparkle and energy, while others might tackle their individual gags with relish but without much conviction about the value of the project as a whole. Looking closely at some of Avery's cartoons with Bergson in mind might help us understand Avery's tragicomic, almost nihilistic, world.

UNDERSTANDING AVERY

Born Frederick Bean Avery in 1908 in Taylor, Texas, "Tex" Avery graduated from North Dallas High School, where he enjoyed drawing cartoons of school activities for the yearbook.[5] He hoped to sell a comic strip but had no luck in Dallas, Chicago, or eventually Los Angeles, where he migrated in the late 1920s. In 1930 he got a job as an inker and painter at Charles Mintz Studios, then at Walter Lantz Studios, where he moved up to become an animator's assistant. At Lantz, Avery found the opportunity to direct; he also found his wife, an inker named Patricia Johnson. It was also at Lantz Studios that he lost his left eye as the result of an office gag gone awry. In mid-1935 Avery left Lantz for Warner Bros. Along with fellow team members Chuck Jones and Bob Clampett, Avery changed the pace and style of humor in Warner Bros. cartoons. He created Daffy Duck, and his versions of Porky Pig and Bugs Bunny became definitive. Avery made more than sixty films in his six years at Warner Bros., before moving to MGM in September 1941. The animation historian John Canemaker makes this assessment: "There, at Hollywood's grandest and wealthiest studio, he reached his apogee as a director by intensifying the pacing and exaggeration of the cartoons and elaborating on themes, character types, and humor that he first explored at Warners."[6] Avery worked there in the division opposite William Hanna and Joseph Barbera, who made MGM's Tom and Jerry cartoons, until 1954, when MGM shut down Avery's animation unit. He then went back to Lantz Studios for a year, making only four cartoons, and eventually settled at Cascade, a small Hollywood studio where he directed animated television commercials in relative obscurity for twenty years. In the last three years of his life he worked for his former rivals at Hanna-Barbera Studios; he died in 1980. This chapter will focus on his MGM period, arguably the richest vein in a mother lode of comedy.

Let me begin with a typical Avery cartoon. *Droopy's Double Trouble* (1951) is not one of his best, but it's not one of his worst, either. It's the eleventh Droopy cartoon out of a total of sixteen over twelve years; Droopy was probably Avery's best-known character (other than Bugs Bunny or Daffy Duck, of course), the one that had the best chance for the brand-name recognition that Tom and Jerry or the Warner Bros. characters enjoyed. While Droopy was undoubtedly popular, he didn't catch fire and sweep the nation in the same way that Mickey Mouse,

Bugs Bunny, or even Tom and Jerry did. Avery's inability to create a truly mer-
chandisable character was something of a frustration for the cartoonist; he tried
a number of different characters during his years at MGM, but his particular
comic approach was more gag-oriented than character-oriented.[7] Of all his MGM
characters, Droopy hung around the longest.

Droopy, of course, is a comically unimposing, overweight little bloodhound
with the sad-sack voice of Wallace Whimple from the *Fibber McGee and Molly*
radio show.[8] Often pitted against the treacherous bulldog Spike or the opportu-
nistic Wolf, Droopy carries out his task unruffled by the various plots they mount
against him or by their wildly frantic reactions as their plans backfire. Droopy
is, as Adamson so eloquently put it, "an imperturbable semicolon surrounded
by exclamation points."[9] In *Droopy's Double Trouble* the head butler, Theeves,
has left sub-butler Droopy in charge of the mansion: "While I'm away with the
master, you'll need a bit of help around the house. Locate a reliable person and
have him report to me for instructions," Theeves says. This gives Droopy the
opportunity to hire his twin brother, Drippy, who apparently just hangs out at
the gym all day. "That's my brother. He's strong," Droopy says to the audience
as Drippy gratuitously punches holes in the front door. Theeves offers only this
instruction to Drippy: "No strangers are permitted on the premises." Meanwhile,
Spike (sporting his best Victor McLaglen Irish brogue) plays a bum who has
befriended Droopy for the handouts Droopy kindly offers. Running to the back
door to meet Droopy in the kitchen, Spike is astonished by the welcome Drippy
gives him: a powerful punch that sends him flying into a hammock, which in
turn sends him slamming back into the door. Drippy exits and Droopy now
opens the door to find dazed and bruised Spike waiting. He brings him in, sets
him at the table, and starts to feed him but exits to get something, leaving the way
open for Drippy to follow orders once again, Spike never recognizing that Drippy
and Droopy are two different hounds.

This situation sets up the gags that follow: unbeknownst to Droopy or Spike,
Drippy switches places with Droopy in order to carry out his orders and clobber
Spike in a variety of ways, then recedes once again. The basic gag is always the
same; the interest lies in the way in which the clobbering is administered and how
Spike reacts. This is one of two basic comic structures in Avery cartoons of the
MGM era. Both structures follow a "variations on a theme" pattern. In *Droopy's
Double Trouble* and others, after the initial setup the same gag is repeated over
and over with variations on the same action. *Rock-a-Bye Bear* (1952) provides
another example: Spike is hired to keep things quiet for a cranky hibernating
bear. He can't make any noise, or he'll be fired. His rival wants his job and so
tries to make him squeak by inflicting pain, but Spike holds in his cry of pain,
runs outside to the top of a hill, and lets go with a yelp. Repeat. An even better
example is *Bad Luck Blackie* (1949), a masterpiece of this genre: all a little kitten

must do to protect himself from Spike's cruelty is ring a bell, after which the eponymous black cat will walk in front of Spike and something will automatically fall out of the sky onto Spike's head. The rest of the cartoon is a series of escalating gags repeating the same action with variations.

In other Avery cartoons, such as *Homesteader Droopy* (1954), which is set in the Old West, or *One Cab's Family* (1952), about a family of anthropomorphic taxicabs, or *The Shooting of Dan McGoo* (1945), based on Robert Service's famous poem,[10] the *setting* is stable and the gags vary. The different gags are based on the filmmaker's and audience's shared knowledge of the setting and its clichés. If taxis could have children, for example, what jokes would that setting or situation create? This is not to say that action variations like those described above cannot find their way into a setting-dominated cartoon, or vice versa. In *The Shooting of Dan McGoo*, for example, the sultry singer from *Red Hot Riding Hood* puts on a show, and the same repeated action that we saw in that film—the Wolf reacting to her wildly and with much fanfare—takes up a couple of minutes of the cartoon. Still, this repeated gag is not the motivating structure of *The Shooting of Dan McGoo*. Instead, the structure hinges primarily on a series of different gags deriving from the setting or situation, in this case, the retelling of the Service poem. In *Dan McGoo* the gags range from what John Canemaker calls "literalizations"[11]—literal visualizations of a colloquialism, such as "Drinks are on the house, boys," and everybody rushes to the roof for a drink—to reaction gags to "metagags" that comment on the action (a sign in a rowdy bar reads, "Loud, isn't it?").[12]

Generally speaking, then, there are two common patterns in Avery's MGM cartoons: a comic structure that revolves around a repeated gag with variations and a comic structure that creates different kinds of gags out of a single setting or situation. These options are not exclusive, and they can be combined. *Screwball Squirrel* (1944), for instance, appears to alternate gags that derive from a setting or situation (the chase) with variations on a single kind of gag, the metagag. But even if cartoons often combine structures, usually they tend to lean one way or the other. Close examination of *Screwball Squirrel*, for example, reveals that nearly all the gags are variations of the single-gag option—that is, almost every gag is a metagag, a commentary on the conventions or process of animation, from the famous "skipping-phonograph-creates-a-skipping-image" gag to the more subtle use of the frame line as a way of restricting and revealing point of view (I will discuss this gag in more depth later in the chapter).

The main point here, however, is that this two-option pattern explains and emphasizes the importance of *repetition* for the typical Avery cartoon. Things happen over and over again in Avery's world. In individual cartoons gag structures are repeated, and settings and stories are repeated across cartoons. Individual gags are never repeated within cartoons, but they often recur in different cartoons. In *Señor Droopy* (1949) the Wolf guides a charging bull into a cellar and closes the door, then folds the door into ever smaller units until it is the size of a matchbook. He then tosses the item away, at which point it unfolds and the bull charges out again. The same gag appears in *Homesteader Droopy* (1954). Sometimes even footage is repeated: the live-action footage in *TV of Tomorrow* (1953) is used again in Avery's very next cartoon, *The Three Little Pups* (1953). Sometimes whole stories are repeated: *Little Johnny Jet* (1953) is exactly the same story as *One Cab's Family* (1952); only the type of family (taxicabs, airplanes) has changed. At the level of style certain devices are always at Avery's disposal, such as the frame-line trick I noted above (the camera "pans" to reveal someone who has appeared just outside of the frame). Characters, stories, gags, setups, openings, endings, reactions, backgrounds, voices, sound effects, musical cues, stylistic techniques—everything in Avery's arsenal is reused at some point.

AVERY MEETS BERGSON

I am not criticizing Avery's work. This kind of recycling is fairly typical in the animation industry and in comedy in general. Cartoon backgrounds, for example, are often repeated to save time and money. And as Donald Crafton writes about silent film comedy, "Slapstick cinema seems to be ruled by the principle of accretion: gags, situations, costumes, characters and camera techniques are rehearsed and recycled in film after film. . . . Nothing was discarded in slapstick."[13] Indeed, perhaps more than brevity, repetition is the soul of comedy. This is the thesis of Bergson's treatise on comedy, *Laughter*. As I noted earlier, Bergson argues that what we find funny is basically the intersection of the human and the mechanical. When someone does something funny, Bergson maintains, we can find something machinelike in those actions: "The attitudes, gestures and movements of the human body are laughable in exact proportion as that body reminds us of a mere machine" (79). A comic body is machinelike, according to Bergson, not only for its movements but also for its qualities: it becomes something that is not fluid and adaptable but rigid, inelastic, and objectlike. It is the superimposition of these qualities on more flexible, malleable, "human" qualities that creates humor and laughter: "Any arrangement of acts and events is comic which gives us, in a single combination, the illusion of life and the distinct impression of a mechanical arrangement" (105). Hence repetition, to the extent that it reminds us of the automatic functioning of the machine, is comic when it pertains to human action. "Wherever there is repetition or complete similarity, we always suspect some mechanism at work behind the living . . . in a word, of some manufacturing process or other. This deflection of life towards the mechanical is here the real cause of laughter" (82). Those familiar with Bergson's other philosophical works, such as *Matter and Memory*

(1896) or *Creative Evolution* (1907), will recognize his interest in vitalism in this essay on laughter:

> Life presents itself to us as evolution in time and complexity in space. Regarded in time, it is the continuous evolution of a being ever growing older; it never goes backward and never repeats itself. Considered in space, it exhibits certain coexisting elements so closely interdependent, so exclusively made for each other, that not one of them could, at the same time, belong to two different organisms: each living being is a closed system of phenomena, incapable of interfering with other systems. A continual change of aspect, the irreversibility of the order of phenomena, the perfect individuality of a perfectly self-contained series: such, then, are the outward characteristics—whether real or apparent is of little moment—which distinguish the living from the merely mechanical. (118)

Given this definition of "life"—continuous change, irreversibility, individual uniqueness—it is not too difficult to guess what Bergson ascribes to "the merely mechanical": *repetition, inversion,* and what he calls the *"reciprocal interference of series"* (118). Each of these, as it turns out, is a common comic device that Bergson recognizes in French theatrical comedy but that we can also see in Avery cartoons.

Let us examine *Droopy's Double Trouble* in light of Bergson's ideas. First, Bergson counts as mechanical not just processes, such as repetition, but also certain characteristics, such as rigidity or inelasticity. But it seems counterintuitive to call a Tex Avery cartoon, especially, "inelastic"; cartoon characters are nothing if not *elastic*. For example, when Droopy introduces his extra-strong brother Drippy to Theeves the butler, Drippy shakes his hand and painfully renders it a stretched out, springy mess—a predictable cartoon gag that takes advantage of the ability of drawn animation to stretch objects beyond their "realistic" dimensions (Fig. 11.1). But Bergson would argue that it is not the stretchiness of the hand that makes it funny; the elasticity of the hand is secondary to what Bergson would count as the primary comic quality: its "thingness." That is, Drippy turns Theeves's hand into *an object,* and this is what strikes us as funny (or at least what Avery assumed would be funny). In fact, the elasticity of cartoon bodies invariably indicates the thingness of those bodies; it is precisely because they can stretch that they fall under Bergson's category of "the mechanical." Silly putty stretches; hands or dogs or ducks do not.

We must therefore think of "rigidity" in broader terms. Even though cartoon characters stretch, the source of the amusement comes from the imposition of "mechanical," "rigid," or "objectlike" qualities—which includes, in this case, the ability to stretch—onto human or anthropomorphic characters. The same holds for live-action comedy. If someone makes a funny face, according to Bergson, it is funny because it "will make us think of something rigid" (76). Even though the

FIGURE 11.1. Drippy turns Theeves's hand into an object in
Droopy's Double Trouble (MGM, 1951).

funniest face might require extraordinary flexibility of the muscles, what's funny
about it is the sense that "the person's whole moral life has crystallized into this
particular cast of features" (76). The funny face becomes a *mask* that does not hide
but instead reveals one aspect and holds it, maintains it, and presents it as a per-
manent and dominant feature of that personality. Like a caricature a funny face
brings out and reduces the personality to a single feature; the normally mobile
and fluid quality of the face or personality becomes static. This is the "rigidity"
or "mechanical inelasticity" to which Bergson refers. This rigidity also applies to
personality itself. Single-mindedness, the inability to adapt flexibly to changing
circumstances, can be very funny, for example. Drippy's function in the cartoon
is to carry out his instructions without question or doubt, and this makes him
a comic character. Spike, too, pursues his goal without regard to consequence,
even though most would be on their way after the first punch. Droopy also has a
comic function: he is not allowed to notice the events going on behind his back.
Absentmindedness, then, is another comic characteristic because it implies an
automatic quality to the action. The absentminded character is on "autopilot," so
to speak, or more precisely, is unconscious of him- or herself. This brings out the
"mechanical" aspect of the character, which is the source of the comic. With his
stress on "automatic" qualities, Bergson pursues a distinctly modern definition
of comedy that emphasizes the tension (and reciprocity) between the human
and the mechanical. We may disagree with the historically contingent nature
of this definition, but it rings true when we think of modern comic characters:

"In one sense it might be said that all character is comic, provided we mean by character the ready-made element in our personality, that mechanical element which resembles a piece of clockwork wound up once and for all and capable of working automatically. . . . It is comic to wander out of one's own self. It is comic to fall into a ready-made category. And what is most comic of all is to become a category oneself into which others will fall, as into a ready-made frame; it is to crystallize into a stock character" (156–57). In Avery's cartoons, at least, we constantly encounter this "ready-made," "automatic," *mechanical* aspect of character. To summarize: "The comic is that side of a person which reveals his likeness to a thing, that aspect of human events which, through its peculiar inelasticity, conveys the impression of pure mechanism, of automatism, of movement without life" (117).

So "automatism" applies to both character and process. Repetition, as we have seen, is a part of the comic repertoire that happens to evoke the automatic quality of machines. Even if the action is constantly repeated, even if we know that it's coming, we laugh. Why? "Because I now have before me a machine that works automatically. This is no longer life, it is automatism established in life and imitating it" (81). Similarly, Bergson names another comic process: *inversion*. Take, for example, the inversion of roles one might find in any given cartoon. Screwy Squirrel and the dog may perfunctorily take on the roles of hunted and hunter, but these positions are inverted throughout the cartoon: Screwy, always in charge, allows himself to be hunted for the sake of the plot, while the dog often involuntarily surrenders his typical role of hunter. Back and forth they go, and these turnarounds are a source of humor in the cartoon. Such inversions imply a reversibility and interchangeability that is both mechanical and comic. But the concept of inversion can also explain more subtle reversals in the Avery universe, such as the metagag. Why are metagags funny? Some argue that such gags rely on a "comic distancing" effect that reminds the viewer of the process of production and thus provokes laughter. Place-Verghnes writes, "When watching a cartoon, we have an impression of reality because we accept its codes from the start. However, if the said codes are questioned and if the 'set of strings' is uncovered, the effect is comical. Tex Avery uses various means to lay the structure of the cartoon bare, the leitmotiv clearly being: 'never forget you are watching a cartoon.'"[14] So, according to this argument, the metagag is a comic reminder that we are watching a cartoon, as if we forgot, and the reminder provokes surprise and laughter. But explaining laughter in terms of "surprise" or "distancing" or "incongruity" is insufficient, since these could equally apply to any number of cases that do not provoke laughter at all. Thinking about it in Bergsonian terms, we could argue instead that the metagag is *an inversion of diegetic and nondiegetic worlds.*

For example, in order to evade Meathead the dog in *Screwball Squirrel,* Screwy ducks into a hole in a tree and reemerges through another hole above it. Meathead is in hot pursuit, but at the last second Screwy reaches down and actually *moves the first hole* up so that the dog slams into solid wood (not quite solid, since it takes on the shape of his head). What's going on here? How can there be one set of laws in which a hole is movable and another in which the tree is solid? Both can exist at the same time in animation, but what makes this a gag (and not science fiction) is that the laws *do not* exist at the same time. Instead, there is a momentary inversion of the two sets of laws, one pertaining to a fictional world of squirrels and dogs and trees, another pertaining to the nondiegetic world of animators. That is, there is one set of laws that apply to a "normal" fictional space (as in live action) and another that derives from the endless possibilities of drawn animation. This inversion implies their equivalence and reversibility; the role of cartoon character and that of animator can be inverted at any moment. We may be surprised and pleased at the gag, but surprise is not the comic element; instead, the comic element is, again, the transposition of human (animator) and mechanical (cartoon). We see this inversion of cartoon and animator again and again in Avery's world: a visible line between color and black-and-white reads "Technicolor ends here" (*Lucky Ducky,* 1948), or a voracious goat literally chews up the scenery (*Billy Boy,* 1954). In each case the gag depends on an inversion of one set of rules for another. It is also noteworthy that this inversion is often tied to character. Some have argued that there are no consistent laws of physics for an Avery cartoon, nothing defining the difference between real and unreal; the laws seem to be different for hunter and hunted, rascal and victim.[15] But that is precisely the point: the laws *are* different for each character. What we might call good luck or good karma or good timing in the real world is codified in comedy according to character. Buster Keaton gags, for example, often revolve around Keaton's uncanny ability to escape harm: recall the famous *Steamboat Bill, Jr.* (1928) gag in which a falling facade of a house appears about to crush him; only he occupies the one spot where an open window allows him to stand unscathed. Nature works differently for some. The same principle applies in animation, except that there are two distinct laws of physics at play and some characters have access to both.

There is one last Bergsonian comic device to explore before we move on: the "reciprocal interference of series." This is a series of events that can be interpreted in different, sometimes mutually exclusive, ways, depending on the point of view. In *Droopy's Double Trouble* we could say that there are at least three series or three interpretations of the events: Droopy sees a bum who needs a handout, Drippy sees an intruder who needs to be expelled, and Spike sees a single Droopy who is alternately gracious and vicious. Then there is the actual series of events that the audience sees: there are twin Droopys. The comedy comes from the collision of these series, resulting in mishap for Spike. There are two keys to this device: absentmindedness and point of view. Spike must be so inattentive that he does not notice the switch of Droopy for Drippy. The audience sees this switch, however, so our point of view creates a new interpretation of events. So we could simplify to say that there are only two series: the events as the protagonist (Spike) imagines them and the events as the audience actually sees them. As Noël Carroll explains with regard to similar silent film gags, "The actual situation or event interferes with the protagonist's imagined picture of the event, with the net effect that the protagonist's expectations have been reversed."[16] Spike's expectation is that Droopy will be kind to him, but we see the switch and expect the disaster that follows. Spike's limited knowledge of the events leads to his confusion and eventual madness—at the end of the film he is carted away by an ambulance as a "mad dog," having been driven insane by Droopy's apparently bipolar behavior. This collision of imagined versus actual events is what Bergson means by the "reciprocal interference of series."

With this particular device, absentmindedness is used to restrict point of view. The gag doesn't work if Spike sees everything the audience sees; staging the switch so that it escapes his attention is an easy way to ensure that he doesn't. Avery has another device that restricts point of view in the same way—what I will call "the frame-line reveal." The first Droopy cartoon, *Dumb-Hounded* (1943), has many examples of this technique. In this cartoon the Wolf is an escaped prisoner trying to elude Droopy, who slowly but surely tracks him down. The Wolf (and the audience) thinks he has left Droopy long behind as he races up the stairs to an apartment. He enters the apartment and closes the door. He turns screen right and the camera pans right as he walks. Suddenly, the pan reveals Droopy to have appeared out of nowhere (Fig. 11.2).[17] In this gag the frame line acts as a limit for both the Wolf and the audience. There is an even bolder example in *Screwball Squirrel*. Meathead, the dog, has chased Screwy up a tree. In a medium two-shot Meathead backs Screwy onto a branch. Screwy backs out of frame right, leaving Meathead alone in the frame. Meathead proceeds forward, the camera tracking slowly to follow, he suddenly registers surprise and the camera pans quickly right to reveal a sign at the end of the branch: "Sucker!" Even though Meathead should be able to see beyond the frame—if this were a live-action film—he does not; the frame almost forces his inattentiveness. It functions the same way for the audience: we cannot see beyond the frame either, so the "reveal" inverts our interpretation of the events, which we share with Meathead. So this technique shares some features with the "reciprocal interference of series" device in that it relies on restricted point of view and reversed expectations. This could also be considered a metagag, since we have a similar inversion of diegetic rules (he should be able to see beyond the frame) for nondiegetic rules (in drawn animation, nothing really exists beyond the frame until it is created by the animator). It is indeed a versatile gag, and Avery used it liberally.

FIGURE 11.2. The "frame-line reveal" in
Dumb-Hounded (MGM, 1943).

THE PRISON HOUSE OF ANIMATION

Bergson's theory of laughter is useful because it emphasizes comic devices "that consist in looking upon life as a repeating mechanism, with reversible action and interchangeable parts" (126). Comedy, in other words, can be a very mechanical business. No one would know this better than a studio animator. A typical cartoon could require up to ten thousand drawings. Studio animation units were designed to make this work as efficiently as possible by creating an

intricate division of labor among directors, head animators, character animators, in-betweeners, backgrounders, inkers, and painters.[18] Even with all these
people working on a single cartoon, the film would go through various stages,
from initial storyboard to exposure sheets to pencil tests to final film. So the
tally of eight thousand to ten thousand images required for a finished film does
not count all the storyboards and drafts and tests. Any way we look at it, that's
a *lot* of images—generating images, one after the other, is a constant feature of
the job. There are positive aspects of this division of labor, as Adamson notes:
"Though the final result seems to be the reduction of the animator to one solitary post on an assembly line, the intended and usually effected outcome was
to allow the creative aspect of animation to be separated from the mountainous
drudgery."[19] Indeed, Avery recognized early that he would not have been able
to take on the job of animator: "They [animators] get new scenes all the time,
but it's a monotonous thing, in a way. I couldn't do that for twenty-five years.
I'd get tired of it. But I never got tired of directing cartoons. It was always a new
challenge."[20]

Nevertheless, even as a director Avery could not escape the daily grind.
Coworkers remarked on his legendary perfectionism and his inability or unwillingness to delegate. One Warner Bros. story man, Michael Maltese, says in an
interview,

> Tex is a hard man to work for; he's a perfectionist to this point: that even when
> he's ready to turn out a good cartoon, it's still not as good as he wanted to make it.
> Another director will say, "All right, it came out great. That's fine. I'll take my bows,
> and next time we'll see what else we can do." I think nobody worried and suffered
> to make a great cartoon more than Avery did. It was never good enough for him. I
> told him, "You proved yourself already," but he'd think, "No, it's got to be better."
> And he worried himself to the point where it got to be too difficult for him.[21]

Likewise, the MGM story man Heck Allen recalls, "Tex never had anybody. He
laid the pictures out for the goddam background man; he did everything for the
so-called character man, who draws the models of the character. Tex did it all,
the guy just cleaned up after him."[22] The pressure to produce images, along with
the self-imposed pressure to produce perfect cartoons, even forced Avery to take
a year off between 1952 and 1953:

> Oh, I got too wrapped up in my work. I tried to do everything myself. Normally
> a director will rough the scenes out and time them, and then check over the com-
> pleted scenes and make changes for the boys. But I attempted to put so much on
> paper, the way I saw it and the way I wanted it, pinning it right down to the frame,
> that it required a lot of work—Saturdays, Sundays—to keep up to schedule. I was
> doing all the technical stuff: pans, and getting a character in a certain spot at a
> certain time. I enjoyed it, but it got too rough for me.[23]

There were other pressures as well. Canemaker paints a darker picture of Avery's career than we normally see in portraits of him. His vision of his films clashed with that of the Production Code Administration, so "he spent considerable time and effort thinking of ways to avoid offending" that office.[24] His producer at MGM, Fred Quimby, was a humorless ex-salesman who didn't understand most of Avery's gags. And Quimby seemed to favor Avery's rivals, Hanna and Barbera, which was another source of irritation and insecurity.[25] Heading this list of frustrations is the incident at Lantz Studios: an office gag with a flying paper clip cost Avery his left eye and his confidence. Canemaker concludes from interviews that Avery changed after this event and "became less expansive, more closed, and focused on the insular world he was creating in animation."[26] But even this world had its limitations, and Avery grew increasingly unhappy with his own gag formulas. A fellow MGM animator, Michael Lah, recalls Avery's sad assessment: "I've done it all a hundred different ways. I'm burned out. I just don't think the stuff is funny anymore."[27]

The year off helped, but the MGM cartoons from 1953 to 1955 are not Avery's best work. There are some inspired moments—*Deputy Droopy* (1955) takes the central gag of *Rock-a-Bye Bear* to sublime heights—but generally, they lack the earlier spark. Avery's fatigue is most evident in his last MGM cartoon (which, admittedly, he codirected with Michael Lah), *Cellbound* (1955). In this film an inmate takes twenty years (from 1934 to 1954, approximately the number of years Avery spent in the studio system) to dig himself out of prison by the spoonful. Once he escapes, twists and turns of the plot find him inside a television set destined for the warden's home, where he must now improvise and impersonate various TV shows if he is to remain undetected. It is an uninspired cartoon, full of lame gags and leaden timing, but its narrative movement from one prison to another is remarkably prescient of Avery's career. Even in the earlier films, however, the usual exuberance is sometimes tinged with boredom and despair. Avery's MGM cartoons, it seems, speak to the Bergsonian tension between automatism and spontaneity in comedy. That is, the energy of even the best Avery cartoons is often balanced by sly asides about or rehearsals of the drudgery of studio animation. The liberating power of drawing cartoons for a living often finds itself cancelled by the capriciousness of fate and its swift reversals of fortune. It's enough to drive anyone mad, as it does Spike in *Droopy's Double Trouble*. Sometimes, bemused resignation is the only option left.

To conclude, let us look at another Droopy cartoon. *Northwest Hounded Police* (1946) best illustrates this ambivalence between novelty and repetition. It is the fourth Droopy cartoon, basically a remake of the first, *Dumb-Hounded*.[28] Both films feature Droopy implacably pursuing the Wolf, who has escaped from prison (prison seems to be a theme in Avery's cartoons). The gag is that Droopy inexplicably shows up no matter how far or how quickly across the planet the Wolf runs. Droopy is *always* there. So both films are, structurally speaking, examples of Avery's single-gag formula. Variations come from the Wolf's reactions, the lengths he goes to escape, the way Droopy is revealed, and the occasional metagag. *Northwest Hounded Police* begins at a version of Alcatraz called "Alka-Fizz Prison," where "No Noose Is Good Noose." The Wolf is in his cell when he produces an extra-large pencil and draws a crude door on the wall outside his cell. Drawing is power: the Wolf opens the door and starts his ingenious escape to Canada. At Mounty County Police Headquarters, where "We Aim to Police," Droopy (as Sgt. McPoodle) is volunteered to track down this vicious criminal. As the Wolf runs across the Yukon territory, he finds a series of Burma-Shave signs:

> Don't Look Now
> Use Your Noodle
> You're Being Followed
> by Sgt. McPoodle.

The Wolf looks and the camera pans left to find McPoodle on his little blue horse. Thus begins the gag, which consists of variations on the frame-line reveal. The Burma-Shave jingle hints at the cartoon's themes of invisibility/visibility ("Don't Look Now") and omnipresence ("You're Being Followed"). The Wolf runs, but he can't hide.

The Wolf runs immediately to a cabin and shuts the front door—and another on top of that, and another, and another . . . (there are eight in all), just to be extra sure. Frame-line reveal right—Droopy is in a chair by the fire, reading the comics. Reaction, then reopening each of the doors to reveal Droopy again. Reaction, bust through the back door, open it, Droopy there again. Reaction, escape to a bird's nest at the top of the highest mountain—"He'll never find me here"—Droopy cracks out of the egg. Reaction, dive to a lake below—Droopy is in a passing school of fish. And so on. Sometimes the reaction comes before the reveal, sometimes after, but even though the audience can always expect the reveal, Avery plays with expectations. At one point, the Wolf finds himself on a tiny atoll in the middle of the ocean. Flanked by two rocks, the Wolf, like the audience, has by now caught on: "Yeah, I know. He'll probably be right under that rock." But no, Droopy appears under the other, smaller rock. This reduces the Wolf to tears of frustration and copious self-flagellation before he swims to New York and runs into a movie theater (in a nice metagag he takes a turn too quickly and nearly runs off the edge of the film). What's playing? An MGM cartoon, of course, and Droopy says from the screen, "Hello, Joe." The Wolf finds a plastic surgeon, only to receive Droopy's face. The doctor changes it back but is then revealed to have Droopy's face himself. The Wolf decides to end it all by throwing himself to the lions, but he even finds Droopy inside the belly of the beast. Finally, he mercifully ends up back in prison. "Well, I'll be," he says matter-of-factly, "he finally got me.

But there's just one thing that's bothering me. I wonder if there coulda been more than one of them little guys?" Quick pan right to reveal hundreds of Droopys saying, "What do you think, brother?" End, fade out.

The moral is clear: the power of the pencil may appear to be liberating, but you really can't escape. Droopy's omnipresence could be read as an allegory for the thousands of drawings of him that went into the making of this very cartoon. He and the other characters were everywhere in the animators' lives. After drawing Droopy several hundred times in a day, even going to a movie might not provide the escape one hoped for. The final shot of hundreds of Droopys is only a logical literalization of the truth that the Wolf discovers but that studio animators already recognized: the number and ubiquity of images is mind-boggling and inescapable. The pencil, in this case, is a double-edged sword, a promise and a curse.

In one sense, then, this is a very sad cartoon. It clearly indicates that the emancipatory potential of talent or creativity is an illusion. Idealistic or romantic notions of the creative power of authorship are eventually overwhelmed by the sheer number of images one is forced to produce as a studio animator. Making one image after the other, over and over again, is a monotonous job, but there are moments of inspiration and laughter. This is a theme in this cartoon, but this rhythm is rehearsed in its structure as well. Each gag is a brilliant variation on the last, but one can't help but notice the essential *sameness* of it all. The individual gag may be different, but the rhythm and structure of the gag are the same as all the others. Yet we laugh. Somehow, this cartoon rides that thin line between spontaneity and boredom. This is the line that studio animators walked every day: How do you maintain a sense of improvisation in a cartoon that is built out of thousands of drawings and dozens of tests? How do you keep laughing in the face of drudgery and setbacks? How do you separate what's funny from mechanical, automatic repetition? The wonder of this and other Avery cartoons is that they do not try; instead, they reveal the mutual reliance of humor and repetition and use it to great effect. But perhaps precisely because of this, Avery felt the tension between laughter and ennui most keenly of all.

NOTES

1. Rosenbaum, "Dream Masters II."

2. Place-Verghnes, *Tex Avery*, 139.

3. Adamson, *Tex Avery*, 27.

4. See Bergson, *Laughter*, 66ff.; subsequent references to this source are cited parenthetically in the text.

5. This biographical sketch is drawn from information in Adamson, *Tex Avery*; and Canemaker, *Tex Avery*.

6. Canemaker, *Tex Avery*, 16.

7. Ibid., 52.

8. Bill Thompson (1913–71) was the voice of both Droopy and Wallace Whimple (and many other characters on *Fibber McGee and Molly*).

9. Adamson, *Tex Avery*, 73.

10. The poem, "The Shooting of Dan McGrew," is included in Service, *Songs of a Sourdough*, 50–54.

11. Canemaker, *Tex Avery*, 159.

12. The term *metagag* is first used with regard to Avery cartoons in Scheib, "Tex Arcana."

13. See Crafton, "Pie and Chase," 107 (Karnick and Jenkins edn.).

14. Place-Verghnes, *Tex Avery*, 157. Ronnie Scheib makes a similar argument.

15. Place-Verghnes, *Tex Avery*, 169.

16. Carroll, "Notes on the Sight Gag," 30.

17. I use *track* and *pan* throughout with the knowledge that such techniques are simulated in drawn animation.

18. Not to mention writers, composers, producers, and others who did not actually draw images but were vital to the cartoon.

19. Adamson, *Tex Avery*, 22.

20. Quoted in ibid., 157.

21. Quoted in ibid., 134–35.

22. Quoted in ibid., 141.

23. Quoted in ibid., 180–81.

24. Canemaker, *Tex Avery*, 17.

25. Ibid.

26. Ibid., 13. This list of pressures does not include the turn for the worse that Avery's life took after he left MGM, with the death of his son and the dissolution of his marriage.

27. Michael Lah interview, *Tex Avery*, television documentary (Turner Broadcasting/Moondance, 1988); quoted in Canemaker, *Tex Avery*, 18.

28. And *Dumb-Hounded* reworks the central gag from an Avery Warner Bros. cartoon, *Tortoise Beats Hare* (1941). In that one, however, the "trick" of Cecil Turtle's constant presence and duplication is "naturalized" by a plot device: he calls his family to help him win the race against Bugs Bunny.

12

Tish-Tash in Cartoonland

Ethan de Seife

If the name "Frank Tashlin" is recognized today, it is generally for the reason that the trajectory of Tashlin's filmmaking career is characterized by a couple of unusual swerves. Once a print cartoonist, Tashlin parlayed his drafting skill into a career as an animator and then as a director of animation; once a director of animation, Tashlin parlayed his gag-writing and shot-composition skills into a career as a director of live-action, feature-length films. It is this latter, midcareer turn on which rests whatever Tashlin's reputation as an *auteur* may be: inasmuch as he is known, it is as the director of live-action features that purportedly resemble cartoons and/or as a director of cartoons that purportedly anticipate the techniques of live-action filmmaking.

One cannot overstate how pervasive is this assumption: virtually everything ever written about Tashlin refers to the apparent likeness between his cartoons and his features. The opening sentences of the animation historian Dewey McGuire's piece on Tashlin's cartoons provide ample evidence of how this assumption defines an understanding of the director: "There are two things everyone knows about Frank Tashlin. One, he made animated cartoons using the language of live-action features. Two, he made live-action features using the language of animated cartoons."[1]

The problem, though, is that none of the many critics who hold this view articulates what this "language" is. Numerous authors have attempted to forge this connection on the grounds of particular stylistic devices: "unusual" camera angles, rapid editing, and the like. Before I suggest an alternative framework for understanding Tashlin's work, let me provide a brief survey of these arguments.

In the mid-1950s Jean-Luc Godard (at *Cahiers du cinéma*) and Roger Tailleur (at *Positif*) first advanced the notion that Tashlin's features resemble "live-action cartoons." In the half-century since New Wave critics wrote so excitedly about Tashlin, few advances have been made in the field of Tashlin studies. Most critics hold, very simply, that Tashlin's cartoons resemble features and that his features resemble cartoons and that these facts serve to explain Tashlin as a director, Q.E.D.—rather too pat and teleological a conclusion to be of much value to the historian.

We can trace the predominance of this argument to two sources. In the last major interview he granted before his death in 1972, Tashlin discussed with Mike Barrier his days at the Leon Schlesinger Unit. "Wherever I am," said Tashlin, "wherever I'm working at the time, my mind and heart are ahead, somewhere else. I'm never where I'm at. When I was doing cartoons, I was concerned with one thing: doing feature motion pictures. I remember I did the first montage they ever did in a cartoon; I was always trying to do feature-type direction, with little animals. And then when I was doing films, I started thinking of doing plays."[2] Tashlin flatly states here that his ambition as a cartoonist was to be a director of features, but the sole specific tactic he mentions—montage—is more than a little vague; "feature-type direction, with little animals" is also, alas, pretty imprecise.

The other source is the influential animation historian Leonard Maltin. In an oft-cited passage Maltin writes of Tashlin's unusually rapid editing style with reference to his 1937 cartoon *Porky's Romance*. Maltin analyzes a six-second sequence in which Petunia Pig, after having turned Porky away from her door, notices that he had brought her a huge box of chocolates. This prompts her to change her mind, rush out the door, and whisk the delighted but confused Porky into her parlor. Maltin correctly counts ten shots in this sequence, for an Average Shot Length (ASL) of two-thirds of a second, for this sequence only. For this and other reasons Maltin argues that Tashlin was an unusually innovative animator. "Tashlin's strongest suit was his interest in the cartoon as *film*. . . . Even in his early period he toyed with the possibilities of camera angle, cutting, montage, and other cinematic devices at a time when some of his colleagues were still taking more prosaic approaches to their work."[3]

Maltin overstates the importance of this one sequence, which accounts for all of one-seventieth, or 1.4 percent, of the film's running time. A burst of rapid editing does not necessarily an innovator make. In fact, the overall ASL of *Porky's Romance* is 8.77 seconds, and the average ASL for Tashlin's cartoons is 6.43 seconds, meaning that this film, taken holistically, is edited significantly *less* rapidly than Tashlin's norm. The clip Maltin selects is too brief and unrepresentative to support claims as strong as this one.

Maltin also errs in divorcing Tashlin's work from its generic context. In Maltin's example, for instance, Tashlin uses rapid editing for a very particular *purpose*: to enhance the humor of the scene. The gag is about the rapidity with which Petunia changes her mind about her suitor once she sees the box of sweets. The rapid-fire editing is a *comic* device, here employed to convey both frantic pace and female fickleness. In this and most other cases Tashlin's stylistic decisions are best understood by considering them in the context of the comic effects they produce.

A study of thirty-seven Warner Bros. cartoons made between 1935 and 1940 reveals that the studio's animators worked within a fairly wide range of ASLs. (The average ASL of all thirty-seven films is 10.07 seconds.) Certain cartoons by other directors are cut just as quickly as, or more quickly than, Tashlin's. Chuck Jones's *Sniffles Takes a Trip* (1940), for instance, has an ASL of 5.08 seconds; Tex Avery's *Daffy Duck in Hollywood* (1938) has an ASL of 5.29 seconds; Fritz Freleng's *Boulevardier from the Bronx* (1936) clocks in at 5.5 seconds.

On the other end of the spectrum, Jones, Avery, and Freleng all made films with double-digit ASLs in this period, as well, respectively: *Daffy Duck and the Dinosaur* (1939), 17.92 seconds; *Believe It or Else* (1939), 18.54 seconds; and *He Was Her Man* (1937), 10.45 seconds. The Tashlin cartoon with the longest ASL, and the only one with an ASL exceeding ten seconds, is *Porky's Spring Planting*, at 10.15 seconds. Deeper analysis may reveal these directors' differing strategies in using editing for comedy and would likely yield finer-grained comparisons.

Maltin makes another strong claim about Tashlin's cartoons. He holds that, since Tashlin used such devices as rapid editing, montage sequences, and unusual camera placement, his cartoons were more *filmlike* than those of his contemporaries. But Maltin overlooks an essential fact that one might think would weigh heavily on the minds of animation historians, whose field of inquiry has been rather severely marginalized within film studies. Animation *is* film. It is no more or less "cinematic" than live action. No matter whether a moving image is shot in a studio or painted onto cels (or even transferred physically onto the emulsion, as in Man Ray's 1923 film *La retour à raison*), it is still a work of cinema. A film that features unusual camera placement and rapid editing is no more "cinematic" than a film shot in a single take with a static, chest-high camera.

In a similar vein the animation historian Greg Ford is determined to forge links between the animated work and the live-action work:

> Tashlin's taste for the language of feature films was evident from the very beginning in his first stint as an animation director at Warners in 1936. Tashlin's first Warners cartoon, *Porky's Poultry Plant* (1936), contains delirious high and low angled shots (and rapid-fire editing) of a daredevil aerial dogfight with a marauding buzzard. He employs elaborate montages of bugles blown and bayoneted rifles raised high in . . . *Little Beau Porky* (1936). . . . *Little Pancho Vanilla* (1938) utilizes simulated "camera movement" that was quite unusual for animated films of the period; . . . *Wholly Smoke* (1938) opens with a fancy "tracking shot" . . . [and also] incorporates atmospheric "dissolves" that chronicle Porky's mounting cigar sickness and tobacco-bred hallucinations.[4]

It is unclear how the techniques that Ford enumerates are peculiar to the realm of live-action cinema or how Tashlin's use of them in his animation is evidence that he was directing his cartoons in a featurelike style. The tools that Ford identifies are just that: tools, and they have long been available to filmmakers in both live-action and animation.[5] Whether these techniques were unusual for animation *of the time* is an entirely different claim, the proof of which would require a great raft of supporting evidence.[6]

Ford tries to force the connection in other ways, as well. He argues that the famous scene in Tashlin's live-action feature *Will Success Spoil Rock Hunter?* (1957) when Tony Randall steps out of character to address the audience has its roots in such Tashlin cartoons as *Porky's Romance,* in which Petunia Pig introduces herself to the audience in a similar way. As well, certain repeated gags, Ford claims, strengthen the connection between the cartoons and the features. He points to a gag in *Porky's Railroad* (1937) in which a snail outruns a locomotive; the same joke shows up decades later in Tashlin's 1964 feature *The Disorderly Orderly,* in which a snail outpaces a crawling, straitjacketed Jerry Lewis.

Ford's example of the snail gag does not have much to say about the connections between animation and live action. It is, simply, a joke; it does not belong unequivocally to either animated or live-action filmmaking. The only conclusions we might tease out of this observation is that snails have long been comic shorthand for "slow" and that Tashlin, like many directors, recycled his gags every now and then.

Ford's claims about direct address are equally ahistorical. This device has a long history in American stage and screen comedy. Tashlin *does* use it in several cartoons—and so do Tex Avery and Bob Clampett, to cite just two proximate cases. More pertinently, direct address may be found in any number of films starring Buster Keaton, Charlie Chaplin, the Marx Brothers, Bob Hope, and scores of other comedians whose styles descend, ultimately, from the vaudeville tradition.[7] That this device occurs in both Tashlin's cartoons and his features speaks *not* of the identity of the films of those two modes but of the deep, insoluble connections between American comic traditions and American animation traditions.

Those cited above are just a few examples of the overwhelming tendency in the critical literature on Tashlin: the assumption of a slippage between the animated work and the live-action work. But such claims are groundless: no stylistic device lies exclusively within the domain of one or the other of these large modes of cinema practice.

If we are to make a connection between Tashlin's cartoons and Tashlin's features, the way to do it is not by focusing on the specific stylistic fillips that may exist in both his cartoons and his features nor by assigning undue value in general to his unusual career path. Rather, the linkage between the films of the two "realms" of Tashlin's career is far more straightforward than this and yet has not really been acknowledged in the rather scant body of literature on Tashlin: the genre of comedy.

Tashlin was a comic artist. His print cartoons; his animated cartoons; the gags and scripts that he wrote for such artists as the Marx Brothers, Red Skelton, and Laurel and Hardy; the live-action features that he wrote, directed, and/or produced—all of these are very strongly identified as works of comedy. By understanding how Tashlin both adhered to and deviated from the conventions of this (admittedly capacious) genre, and by studying the techniques by which Tashlin crafted his visual-comic style, we may gain insight into the director's style.

The curious case of Frank Tashlin raises any number of questions that pertain to the focus of the present volume. *How* are Tashlin's films funny, and are they funny in ways that are particular to either live action or animation? What are the "throughlines" of comedy that connect Tashlin's cartoons and his live-action features? What, ultimately, is the connection between Hollywood animation and Hollywood comedy, and how may we see Frank Tashlin as representative of it? Tashlin is a filmmaker who cannot be "explained away" by the fact that he happened to make a move from director of cartoons to director of live-action features. Indeed, this fact explains relatively little about him. Far more surprising is that so few other directors made similar moves from one of these realms of filmmaking to the other. (In Tashlin's time the only other director to make such a career transition was Gregory La Cava, best known for live-action features such as *My Man Godfrey* [1936] and *Stage Door* [1937], less well known for his cartoons, including many in the 1910s through the 1920s Katzenjammer Kids and Happy Hooligan series.) Because of his distinctive career arc, Tashlin has provided an all-too-convenient, one-man crystallization of the ways in which cartoons and live-action features are ostensibly similar. Instead, we should reconsider Tashlin's contributions to American comedy: the single genre in which he worked provides a framework for understanding how the techniques and conventions of that genre find expression in both animation *and* live-action.

For this reason Tashlin provides an excellent opportunity to ask questions about the generic identity of Hollywood animation. Animation, as a cinematic "mode" or "realm," is by no means restricted to a single genre—and yet the great majority of American animation, especially that made within the studio era (roughly 1920–60) and including every animated film Tashlin himself made, does indeed fall within the genre of comedy. Other national animation traditions are not so generically restrictive. Japan's large anime industry—which for decades has produced comedies, as well as works of science-fiction, horror, and melodrama, to list only some of the best-represented genres—is probably the clearest counterexample, but Canada's, France's, and China's animation industries, to name a few, are also relevant here. Why, then, are most American cartoons comic, and can a study of Tashlin's cartoons help us understand anything about this correspondence?

Ontologically, animated and live-action films diverge from, but also overlap, each other. Without initiating the book-length study that this topic merits (a subject that has not yet been satisfactorily addressed in the scholarly literature on animation), suffice it to say that the key difference between animation and live action is that the former is made one frame at a time. This difference, though seemingly small, generates far-reaching ontological disparities, all of which are rooted in the same thing: that animation affords a far greater degree of *control* over the filmed image than does live-action filmmaking.

To be strict—and pedantic—about it, it is true that even live-action film is made one frame at a time, in that each frame of film does indeed spend a stationary split-second behind the taking lens so that a blur-free image may be exposed. In real-world terms, however, no live-action film is made by counting, monitoring, or adjusting each individual frame as it pauses momentarily for exposure. In animated films, movement is simulated, one frame at a time, by animators; in live-action films the movement is still simulated, but this simulation is provided by the rapid, motorized movement of the film through the camera.

Because an animator may spend minutes, hours, weeks, or more on a single frame of film (some single-frame, computer-generated images are so complex as to require hours or even days to render), he or she may thus exert a degree of control over the image far more precise than any live-action filmmaker can. This essential difference is highly significant. A live-action filmmaker cannot, for instance, control the complex ways in which a breeze riffles a tree's five thousand leaves, nor the behaviors of animals in a scene that takes place at a zoo, nor the pinpoint reflections of a light source off of a multifaceted glass building, but each of these levels of control is within the grasp of a (patient) animator.

Another matter that separates animation from live action is that, in the former, even such tools as cinematography and editing become subsumed within the domain of mise-en-scène: the arrangement of elements in the frame. All camera movements are simulated by changes within the mise-en-scène, not by the manipulation of an actual camera. As well, depending on one's perspective, there are either zero cuts in an animated film or a cut every twenty-fourth of a second. But both of these perspectives render the term *editing* trivial: it does not make sense to speak of the expressivity of editing if the cuts are either nonexistent or so frequent as to render them meaningless. A "cut" in animation is merely a wholesale replacement of one composition with another, even though this transition is not qualitatively different from those that separate any given frame from its two adjacent frames within the film. While the *effects* of both cinematography and editing are identical in animation to the effects of these tools in live-action filmmaking, these devices in and of themselves are folded into the dominion of mise-en-scène when they are deployed in animated film.

What this means is that, on a visual level, animation is a near-totalizing mise-en-scène experience,[8] and, moreover, those animators who are skilled mise-en-scène artists have the potential to command great expressive power from this realm of filmmaking. Frank Tashlin was one such gifted mise-en-scène artist. I propose that the principal skill that Tashlin carried over from animation to live action was a fine-tuned control over all elements of mise-en-scène. Moreover, since the American animation industry, during Tashlin's animation career, made far more comedies than films of any other genre, Tashlin had ample opportunity to employ his mise-en-scène skills in the service of comedy. Indeed, Tashlin's mastery of mise-en-scène is the very quality that elevates his live-action comedies above the mass of midcentury comic films made by journeyman directors, a topic I will address below.

Of necessity, Tashlin, as an animator, crafted all of his gags by deploying his mise-en-scène talents on a frame-by-frame basis. Such prolonged experience with the minute mechanics of visual comedy gave Tashlin an advantage when he moved into live-action film, but it does not mean that Tashlin simply "transferred" his animation technique to his live-action films or that his live-action films are in some way "cartoonlike." As it happens, the principal comic influences on the Warner Bros. animators (as well as those at other American animation studios) are the same as the principal comic influences on the creators of most American comedian-centric comedies of the studio era: vaudeville performers and the American slapstick tradition. That we can detect some continuities between Tashlin's cartoons and his live-action features should not come as a surprise: they derive from the same tradition, and their creator spent the early part of his film career observing, replicating, and modifying—on a precise, frame-by-frame level—a certain style of visual comedy. This is decidedly *not* the same thing as saying that Tashlin's features are cartoonlike or vice versa. Commentators who state that Tashlin made cartoon-like features seem to be operating under the misapprehension that animated and live-action comedy derive from two separate traditions—a perfect example, incidentally, of the ghettoization of animation within film studies as a whole.

To say that Tashlin's features contain gags similar or identical to gags in his cartoons is merely to acknowledge that animation is likely a fine forum for the development of gag craft, especially the crafting of gags that depend for their humor on visual devices. It is for this reason that it truly is surprising that so few American animators made the leap to the realm of live action: much of the live-action comedy made at the time benefited (or would have benefited) from the work of skilled visual-comic stylists. Though some of Tashlin's live-action features *do* engage in the kind of physics-defying humor that, for many writers, exemplifies a "cartoonish" live-action style, this type of comedy is not unique to Tashlin. Rather, it is Tashlin's visual handling of comic material that characterizes his style—specifically, it is his reliance on mise-en-scène as a comic device that offers the strongest links between his cartoons and his live-action features.

TASHLIN'S VISUAL-COMIC STYLE

Rather than understand Tashlin as a director whose cartoons employ the "language" of live-action cinema or whose live-action films somehow resemble cartoons, we would do better to understand Tashlin as a comic artist who found multiple forms for the expression of his visual-comic style.

One of the most important scholarly books on American film comedy, Henry Jenkins's *What Made Pistachio Nuts? Early Sound Comedy and the Vaudeville Aesthetic,* argues for the dominance of vaudeville as an influence on early film comedy and closes with a throwing down of the gauntlet, of sorts.

> Though the period of its greatest influence ended in 1934, the vaudeville aesthetic left a strong imprint of *[sic]* screen comedy. . . . On the margins of the studio system, in poverty row productions, short subjects, and animated cartoons, anarchistic comedy remained a viable alternative to the more integrative styles of comedy preferred by the majors. Works like *Hellzapoppin* and *Never Give a Sucker an Even Break* [both 1941] suggest the possibility of anarchistic comedy even in the face of the relative conservatism of late 1930s and early 1940s comedian comedy. The whole vocabulary of anarchistic comedy was inherited by the character cartoons of the 1940s, with Bugs Bunny's humiliation of the stodgy Elmer Fudd a pleasurable reworking of the earlier confrontations between Groucho Marx and Margaret Dumont. . . . By the late 1940s, Hollywood again embraced the more reflexive and performance-centered style of comedy associated with the vaudeville aesthetic. The films of Hope and Crosby, Danny Kaye, Martin and Lewis, and others build upon the formal traditions of early sound comedy.[9]

Though Jenkins's book is often cited and much admired, the suggestions he offers for further inquiry seem to have been largely ignored. I refer to his point that animation (specifically Warner Bros. cartoons) is one of the chief inheritors of the vaudeville style of comedy, a style that also found great expression in the comedian comedies of Bob Hope, Bing Crosby, Danny Kaye, and Dean Martin and Jerry Lewis. It is no coincidence at all that all of these stars appeared in Tashlin films. Jenkins argues, in no uncertain terms, for a comic tradition that unproblematically shapes both animated and live-action films. Indeed, from the perspective of the tradition itself, there is no gap: a comic film is a comic film.

What, then, is this vaudeville-derived style of comedy, and how might we use Tashlin's oeuvre as a way to understand comedy in American animation? The following section describes several of the more pertinent stylistic features of vaudeville-based comedy and argues for a continuation of these features in Tashlin's animated work. As a way to present an argument for a continuum of comic influence, brief mention is made below of some of Tashlin's live-action features that employ similar or identical comic methods.

Nearly all of the literature on vaudeville insists that the form was, above all, modular. A typical vaudeville show consisted of perhaps a dozen or more brief acts and "bits" strung together with nothing more than the lowering of a curtain—if that.[10] The economic benefits of such a structure were many. Brooks McNamara puts it succinctly:

> The variety structure found in [vaudeville entrepreneur Tony] Pastor's show was replicated countless times in other types of popular entertainment. Its absolute simplicity made the structure especially appealing to managers. In essence, the format of the show generally amounted to the presentation of one or more specialty acts by each entertainer on the bill, plus several bits and sketches in which a number of entertainers—or perhaps the whole company—performed. The resulting show was relatively cheap and efficient to run in comparison to legitimate theatre, in no small part because it could be varied considerably according to the available performers and their particular talents.[11]

Audiences did not attend vaudeville shows to watch the unfoldings and resolvings of classical narratives. However, the "socko finish" was de rigueur. The vaudeville historian Joseph Laurie stresses the importance of the "belly laugh" and laments the eternal problem of the lack of good "curtain lines" in vaudeville comedy.[12] Jenkins, too, says that climax was far more important than closure and that the audience's final response to a performer was the most important, as it would form the basis of any lasting impression.[13] Even more important, this structure exerted a very strong influence on the *kinds* of gags that were employed in vaudeville-style comedy. Not only did a joke or skit have to end with a bang, but brief gags were generally more highly valued than long ones, a fact that has great significance for comic timing. Moreover, broader gags were essential for summoning the requisite belly laughs, thereby privileging certain styles of joke-telling and -writing over others. The relationship, in vaudeville, between structure and form is a strong one.

While it is certainly possible to develop, sustain, and resolve a coherent, classical narrative in even the seven minutes allotted to most American cartoons, a great many cartoons abide by no such structure. Rather, the American cartoon is one of the great cinematic repositories of disconnected, modular, near-narrativeless structure. Several of Tashlin's films, especially those from the 1930s, exhibit this structure; in many of them he simply makes no attempt to present anything resembling a coherent story. Such cartoons as *Speaking of the Weather* (1937), *Have You Got Any Castles?* (1938), and *You're an Education* (1938) are little more than strings of disconnected gags.[14] The first five minutes and forty seconds of *Have You Got Any Castles?*, for instance, consists of a series of brief, one-off gags, most of which refer to elements of popular culture: Benny Goodman as the Pied Piper, a Cab Calloway caricature, quick bits featuring William Powell, Charles Laughton, and Greta Garbo, among others. The thinnest possible story is tacked on in the film's last fifty-six seconds and is little more than a chase scene.[15]

By no means, though, did Tashlin exclusively make nonnarrative cartoons. Several of his cartoons present more fully developed narratives, such as *Porky's Double Trouble* (1937) and *Little Pancho Vanilla* (1938). Around this same time, Tashlin directed the key transitional film *Cracked Ice* (released under the Merrie Melodies banner), which features a hybrid narrative structure. The film's first section is plotless: it consists of a series of disconnected, vaudeville-style blackout jokes, here centered on the whimsical actions of ice skating animals: a pair of Russian wolfhounds (identified by their fur hats) dance with folded arms; a skating pelican opens its bill to reveal a miniature frozen lake on which skates a single fish. At precisely the halfway mark Tashlin introduces an elaborate gag that serves as the basis for the simple narrative (with a complicated setup) that dominates the remainder of the film. In this portion of *Cracked Ice* an inebriated pig uses a magnetized dish of soup bones to trick a St. Bernard into surrendering some of the liquor in his neck-mounted barrel, but, when pig and dog collide, the magnet falls into the water, where it attaches itself inextricably to a passing fish. The fish swims through the stream of seeping liquor, instantly becomes drunk, and begins darting crazily about under the ice. In short order the magnet attracts the metal blades of the pig's skates, causing him to career wildly about on the ice. The topper to the whole scenario is that the pig's frantic movements win him first prize in an ice skating contest, but when he fills his victory chalice with liquor, the magnetized fish passes beneath it and the cup zips away. The magnet gag takes up the entire second half of the film. This two-part narrative structure— also found in *Porky's Poultry Plant, Porky in the North Woods* (both 1936), *Porky's Road Race* (1937), and *Porky's Spring Planting* (1938)—allows Tashlin to develop the rudiments of a story with a beginning, middle, and end. It is in films such as these that we may see Tashlin moving from a modular, vaudeville-like structure based entirely on disconnected gags to a more integrated structure in which character traits and plot complications assume greater importance.

Tashlin's increased use of more narrative-centric gags should not be seen as an "evolution," as if he were graduating to a more sophisticated form of comedy. Such a claim would be not only teleological but ahistorical, as many of Tashlin's later, more narrative-dependent, cartoons feature equally thin, gag-punctured narratives.

Tashlin's 1940s cartoons often include gags that break with narrative logic. *Plane Daffy* (1944) is an excellent example. Daffy, pursued by gun-toting *oiseau fatale* Hatta Mari, hides inside a refrigerator. Before Hatta Mari can shoot him, Daffy quickly sticks out his head to say, in a weird, high-pitched voice, "Well, whaddya know? The little light—it stays on!" He then zips out of the fridge and escapes. Another gag in the same film has Daffy racing across the room, a blur of orange and black. Then, unaccountably, he happens upon a platform with a staircase at each end. When he reaches the first step, the blurring instantly ceases, and

Daffy walks daintily up the steps. Reaching the plateau of the platform, Daffy zips along, once again a blur (Fig. 12.1); upon reaching the top of the other staircase, he daintily tiptoes down the steps, then resumes running. Just as the refrigerator appears solely as an opportunity for Daffy's offhand joke, the stairs appear solely to interrupt his pace; in both cases Tashlin temporarily halts the progression of the fairly thin narrative (little more than a chase scene, at this point in the film) to make a joke. A notable gag in *Swooner Crooner* has absolutely nothing to do with the story. In this film Porky Pig plays a poultry farmer who notices that all of his chickens have gone missing. He frantically searches his entire farm, at one point uprooting a water pump, only to discover that inside of it is a water cooler.

Sight gags such as these point not only to Tashlin's skill with comic mise-en-scène but to the fact that his films frequently express a certain disdain for tidy narrative. Indeed, this is one of the marks of anarchic Hollywood comedy and, furthermore, is one of the strongest indicators that American animation and American live-action comedy derive from the same tradition. As remarked above with regard to Greg Ford's assessment of Tashlin's comic style, jokes that apparently interrupt a cinematic narrative—via direct address, for instance—are not the exclusive provenance of either animated or live-action comedy. The fact that we find many such gags in his feature comedies indicates not that Tashlin was making "live-action cartoons" but that he found that both comic animation and comic live-action features were suitable venues for irreverent comic devices such as this one.

And, again, Tashlin is by no means the only director of live-action comedies to include moments of diegetic rupture or interruption; such moments are even *more* common in the films of such workmanlike directors as Norman Taurog, Hal Walker, and Norman Z. McLeod—and yet these directors' films (inasmuch as they are considered at all) are not said to evoke animation. In fact, the presence of such anarchic, fourth-wall-rupturing comedy is almost entirely dependent on the presence of such vaudeville or Borscht Belt veterans as Bob Hope, Danny Kaye, Jerry Lewis, and others who fit into Steve Seidman's "comedian comedy" tradition. Though a fuller discussion is somewhat outside the scope of this chapter, the fact is that such performers' personae are permanently associated with this form of narrative breakage. We find this deliberate rupturing of narrative cohesion in Tashlin features such as *Son of Paleface* (1952), *Artists and Models* (1955), *The Geisha Boy* (1958), *The Alphabet Murders* (1965), and many others; but we also find it in such non-Tashlin comedian comedies as Walker's *At War with the Army* (1950) and *Road to Bali* (1952), McLeod's *Road to Rio* (1947) and *Casanova's Big Night* (1954), and Taurog's *The Stooge* (1953) and *Pardners* (1956), to name a scant few.

The distinction between Tashlin's feature comedies and those of Walker, McLeod, and Taurog is not one of order but of kind. The *type* of jokes that Tashlin employs is no different from the *type* of jokes that the other directors employ. The distinction lies in the fact that Tashlin's gags are almost always more graphically

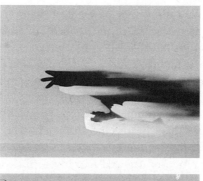

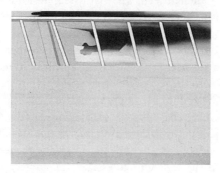

FIGURE 12.1. The humorous contrast
of Daffy's pace in *Plane Daffy* (Warner
Bros., 1944).

sophisticated and better designed. It is only in that animation provided Tashlin
with a proving ground for his graphic and comic talents that we may consider it
as a device that separates Tashlin's work from those of his contemporaries.

Any of Tashlin's eight films with Jerry Lewis provides ample evidence of the
director's penchant for an episodic, gag-centric structure that either diminishes
or is at odds with any degree of narrative unity; *Cinderfella* (1960), possibly the

most uneven of Tashlin's films, may be the best example. In this film Tashlin relies heavily on showcase scenes: isolated moments of performative comedy that highlight his star's talents but that have only tenuous connections to the film's plot. Such scenes are a hallmark of the performer-centric style of vaudeville comedy, as described by Jenkins. In showcase scenes from earlier in his live-action career (such as the massage-table in *Artists and Models,* described below), Tashlin maintains a balance: he highlights his performer's special talents but still fits the scenes, even if tenuously, into the film's narrative matrix. The showcase scenes in *Cinderfella,* however, represent a trend in Tashlin's later films toward the diminished integration of gag and narrative—indeed, toward the kind of structure we find in so many of his cartoons. Were the showcase scenes to be removed from *Cinderfella,* the film's plot would barely be affected. In fact, nearly all of the humor in the film is to be found in the showcase scenes; few of the scenes that advance the narrative are also comic. Put another way, the showcase scenes serve a key generic function: without them, *Cinderfella,* already a strange hybrid of comedy and melodrama, could not properly be considered a comedy at all. One scene in particular illustrates the film's relatively low level of gag-and-narrative integration and highlights the shared heritage of Tashlin's cartoons and his features.

By himself in the kitchen, Fella (Lewis) listens to a radio broadcast of the Count Basie Orchestra. The gag is Lewis's elaborate mimicry of the actions of nearly all the members of the band: with only his face, body, and vivid imagination, he plays drums, saxophone, piano, and other instruments. This is one of the purest instances of a showcase scene in all of Tashlin's films, since it has absolutely nothing to do with the rest of the story—it is plainly designed to highlight Lewis's gifts for timing and mimicry: performative sight gags.[16]

The structure of *Cinderfella*—as well as that of most of the other Tashlin-Lewis films, most prominently *The Disorderly Orderly* (1964)—alternates somewhat uneasily between scenes of narrative advancement and scenes of isolated, modular visual comedy. In the style and content of the comedy ("impossible" gags, visual puns), as well as in their structure, these features *do* resemble Tashlin's cartoons. But they do so only insofar as the films of the two types possess a shared heritage. That is, they do not so much resemble each other as they resemble the structure and style of the "parent" form that spawned them both.

Another important vaudeville skill was brevity. Vaudeville's modular format meant that each act had only a limited time in which to gain favor with the audience. To this end, Brett Page, in his 1915 manual on how to write for vaudeville, stressed that "compression" (i.e., brevity) is as valuable a quality as the Aristotelian ideal of unity of character. Page also encouraged the would-be vaudeville writer to sketch his or her characters clearly and efficiently and to introduce each new comic point as clearly and briefly as possible. Efficiency, he argued, is of the utmost importance.[17] Though good advice for a writer in any field, it nevertheless points to the unusual time pressures under which vaudevillians worked. Jenkins reaches the same conclusion, stressing that the reliance on easily recognizable ("eccentric") clothing, props, accents, and stereotypes were useful shorthand devices that contributed to the "economy of gags."[18]

Again, the standardized, economically determined seven-minute duration of the Tashlin-era Hollywood cartoon links it to the comic traditions of the vaudeville stage. Films with durations as short as those of the "Golden Age" cartoon could hardly afford to devote significant screen time to complex characterization. To this end cartoon characters were nearly always designed so that their phenotypes strongly suggested character and comic traits. A great many Warner Bros. cartoons from the 1930s and 1940s depend quite heavily on caricatures of pop-culture icons: singers, movie stars, and the like.[19] Tashlin (as well as other Warner animators) made several cartoons that, by using this technique, "piggyback" on established personae, thus avoiding the issue of characterization altogether: *Have You Got Any Castles?*, *The Woods Are Full of* Cuckoos (1937), *A Hollywood Detour* (1942), and several others.

Caricature is one method of quick visual characterization. Most of Tashlin's cartoon characters, however, were not caricatures; they were designed with no specific real-world referent in mind. Tashlin was a skilled character designer; by studying his design of Porky Pig, the Warner Bros. character with which he worked most often, we can see the visual strategies Tashlin employed for the purposes of efficient and effective visual characterization.

Porky Pig was a key character for the Leon Schlesinger Unit. He was the first animated Warner Bros. character to "catch on": the first in whom animators detected the possibility of a recurring role. At the time of Porky's debut (1936), Warner animators were struggling to keep up with Disney, whose massive commercial and artistic success set the bar high for their competitors. One element that Disney had but Warner Bros. lacked was a roster of recurring characters with strongly defined traits. The main advantage of such a roster was that the consistencies in the characters' personae would encourage audience attachment and, thereby, repeat business. (Indeed, this is the purpose of any star system.)

However, the mere fact of Porky's recurrence did not guarantee him a consistent appearance. It was not until August 1939, with the promotion of Robert McKimson to the position of head animator, that Warner's animated characters would remain visually consistent from film to film. As Michael Barrier writes, "Until 1939, there wasn't much reason to worry about consistency in how the characters looked because there were so few continuing characters, and most of them were used by only one director apiece. . . . But when characters like Elmer Fudd and the early Bugs Bunny began to appear in different directors' films, the case was made for a head animator who would . . . smooth away the imperfections in others' more creative work. McKimson was ideally suited for such a job."[20] Tashlin's 1930s Porky Pig cartoons were made without official design strictures; like his colleagues, Tashlin could and did make changes to Porky.

In Porky's first film, Friz Freleng's *I Haven't Got a Hat* (1936), the pig's appearance is significantly different from that of his familiar modern incarnation. In the first definitive model sheet for the character, Porky is quite fat and round, with squat legs, bulbous cheeks, and a snout whose height is about a third of that of his head. On this 1936 model sheet the height of Porky's head constitutes just less than one-third of his total height. The Porky of *I Haven't Got a Hat* is nearly spherical, so heavily did Freleng emphasize the pig's porkiness. The only hints of sharp or straight lines anywhere on Porky's body are some nearly unnoticeable ones that delineate his hoof and a notch in his eyeball; every other line is round and soft, imbuing the character with cuteness, friendliness, and jollity.

A model sheet from Tashlin's 1937 film *Porky's Romance* shows that, if anything, Tashlin made the character rounder still. In Tashlin's model sheet Porky's cheeks are not small and kidney-shaped but so round as to be nearly spherical. Similarly, the pig's legs in the 1936 model sheet were already fat and round, but his thighs, knees, and calves are all nevertheless distinguishable. In Tashlin's model sheet, Porky's legs are little more than small circles attached to the larger circle of his body. Tashlin even rounds out such details as Porky's eyeballs—on Freleng's sheet the pupils are notched; on Tashlin's they are solid, rounded dots. As well, Tashlin made Porky's mouth less wide, and his ears smaller and rounder. The result is a character that is even more bulbous and spherical than he was under the pen of Freleng. More to the point, in rendering the character so globoid, Tashlin communicated Porky's amiability, innocence, and eagerness, as well as the naiveté that would become the character's most prominent trait. These traits, and their visual-comic framework, were apparent to the viewer at a glance; it is a fine example of Jenkins's "economy of gags" in action.

IMPOSSIBLE COMEDY?

Many of the arguments for the cartooniness of Tashlin's features refer to "impossible comedy," the idea being that Tashlin, in breaking the laws of physics, turns his films into "live-action cartoons." One of the many examples of impossible humor in Tashlin's live-action films is the scene in *Artists and Models* in which Lewis, through the aid of a none-too-convincing prop table, is stretched like so much taffy by a merciless masseuse (Fig. 12.2).

The problem with such an argument is that this type of humor is one of the stalwart mainstays of American comedian comedy. To use an example from Lewis's own work, an editing-based gag in *The Bellboy* (1960) has Lewis's character arrange into neat, even rows hundreds of chairs within the space of a couple of

FIGURE 12.2. An elastic Jerry Lewis in *Artists and Models* (Paramount, 1955).

seconds. To cite another example—nearly at random—from midcentury Holly-wood comedy, *The Road to Rio* (Norman McLeod, 1947), the fifth entry in the Bob Hope–Bing Crosby "Road" series, contains a gag in which the two comic leads sway on a ship's deck as if their feet are nailed to the deck: their entire bodies dip and rotate at impossible angles. Later in the same film, a cleaning woman accidentally knocks Hope's trumpet into a tub of sudsy water. When he performs on the ship's stage moments later, he brings down the house when bubbles issue forth from the bell of his instrument.

The fact that we can find this form of comedy in many, many films *not* directed by Frank Tashlin should be, in itself, sufficient grounds for dismissing the "live-action cartoons" argument. This kind of impossible comedy is utterly common-place in midcentury American comedian comedies, and it ultimately derives from and is an intensification of old slapstick routines. It is quickly and easily grasped and so ludicrous as to nearly guarantee a belly laugh; in these ways, such humor plainly derives from vaudeville tradition.

Similar arguments have been made for Tashlin's use of Jayne Mansfield—specifically, her unusual physical proportions—in her two films for Tashlin. Greg Ford, for instance, pushes the cartoon/live-action connection again in comment-ing on the apparent influence of Hatta Mari, the curvaceous spy in Tashlin's cartoon *Plane Daffy*, on the physical appearance of Mansfield in her Tashlin films—as if Tashlin could physically mold a living human to conform to a pheno-typic ideal; as if Tashlin could somehow have predicted the existence and appear-ance, six years before her public debut, of Jayne Mansfield; as if Mansfield wasn't already plenty curvaceous before she ever met Tashlin.[21]

What Tashlin *did* do—and what her other directors generally failed to do—was to depict Mansfield in such a way as to draw humorous visual attention to her voluptuousness, a quality Tashlin found inherently funny. He clad her in absurdly form-fitting clothing, even going so far as to affix a tassel to each of her buttocks in *The Girl Can't Help It*; he had her sprawl her curvy body across a massage table that occupies the great majority of a CinemaScope frame in *Will Success Spoil Rock Hunter?* For Tashlin, Jayne Mansfield was but another potentially humorous facet of mise-en-scène.

To return to the subject of the specific types of gags common to the vaudeville stage, the historian Joseph Laurie provides a useful rundown. Among others, he identifies ethnic humor, double entendres and parody, cross-dressing (for performers of both genders), and "blue" humor as especially prominent.[22] Though none of these forms of humor originated in or were peculiar to vaudeville, they constituted, according to Laurie, a comic backbone for the medium.

Risqué humor is a controversial subject in accounts of American vaudeville, and it merits a small digression. Certain writers see vaudeville as the epitome of "clean" entertainment. Charles W. Stein, for example, writes, "[Vaudeville] was clean, wholesome, respectable entertainment, suitable for the entire family. . . . No off-color language was permitted."[23] Page's vaudeville-writing manual backs this up: one of his many "themes to avoid" is the "blatantly suggestive."[24] Other writers, including Laurie, steadfastly insist that the humor of the vaudeville stage was far racier than its official chroniclers would have it. He and Abel Green list a number of popular "naughty songs" banned by Chicago police in 1910, including "Without a Wedding Ring" and "Her Name Was Mary Wood but Mary Wouldn't."[25] In the introduction to his book on the collected jokes of the vaudeville writer and performer Ed Lowry, Paul Levitt goes so far as to characterize vaudeville's blue humor as "pervasive." "Make no mistake about it," Levitt writes, "blue humor [in vaudeville] existed—and thrived."[26]

Clearly, *two* strains of vaudeville comedy—the Clean and the Blue—coexisted, in much the way that a "family-friendly" comedy like *Marley & Me* may play on a multiplex screen adjacent to one showing a foul-mouthed comedy such as *Role Models* (both films were released in late 2008). At no time was there a single, monolithic vaudeville tradition. What *is* clear, however, is that Tashlin took delight in borrowing from the "blue" tradition: his cartoons—and, to a much greater extent, his features—brim with double entendres and other sexual gags. Moreover, such gags are often communicated visually.

One of Tashlin's finest visual gags of any kind appears in the first shot of his 1942 Columbia cartoon *Cinderella Goes to a Party*. We see, in silhouette, Cinderella's wicked stepsisters, dressing for the ball on either side of an ornate vanity. As they speak about the prince, the fat one cinches up her torso inside a girdle, and the skinny one stuffs a pillow inside her slip. Then the women

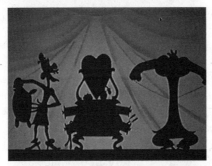

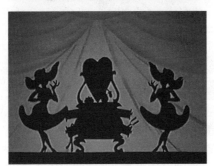

FIGURE 12.3. The wicked stepsisters prepare for the ball in *Cinderella Goes to a Party* (Columbia, 1942).

simultaneously yank identical dresses over their heads, their movements perfectly synchronous and symmetrical. The result: they look identically slender and lovely—in silhouette, at least (Fig. 12.3). This gag is a terrific synthesis of beautifully timed movement, excellent character design, sharp use of silhouette to strengthen the joke (and reduce visual clutter), and social/sexual satire.

Tashlin's most sustained animated dabbling in risqué humor occurs in the four cartoons he made in the Warner Bros. Private SNAFU series, which the studio produced as its contribution to the war effort.[27] The Warner Bros. style of humor, which already occasionally pushed at the limits of propriety, was further unleashed in the SNAFU films, whose intended audience was the men of the armed services. The cartoons never venture into out-and-out vulgarity, but they come closer than anything the Production Code Administration would have approved for general release.

In Tashlin's SNAFU cartoon *The Home Front* (Nov. 1943) the narrator says, "It's so cold it would freeze the nuts off a Jeep." Though this joke is literalized by two hexagonal pieces of metal falling from an icy military vehicle, the double entendre could not be clearer. Seconds after this joke, Tashlin cuts to the interior of Snafu's Quonset hut, the walls of which are covered with pinup girls in various states of undress. A short while later, we see Snafu's grandfather, back home, take in a burlesque show that goes on far longer and with far more jiggling than is required to complete the gag. Later, a horse gaily distributes its own manure across a field; after massive crops spring instantaneously from the soil, the horse says to the camera, "This stuff sure makes things grow, don't it?"

The Home Front is a fascinating film because Tashlin's inclusion of these, and other, off-color jokes nearly steers the film away from its intended purpose. The SNAFU films have a standard structure: in the first part Snafu complains about or shirks his duties; in the second the dire repercussions of this shirking unfold— usually death for Snafu or defeat for Allied forces; in the third, if he survives, Snafu realizes the error of his ways. Since these films were designed as behavior instruction for soldiers, the third section is vital: without it Snafu might come across as merely humorous rather than dangerously foolish. *The Home Front* is so packed with gratuitous, off-color jokes that the third act is actually absent. In the first section Snafu complains about how he is cold and miserable, and how he is certain that, back home, everyone he knows has it easy. To counter his assumptions, "Technical Fairy, First Class," a military fairy godfather character who recurs in the series, shows him what his friends and family are actually doing on the home front: building tanks, planting victory gardens, and the like. By the time the second act is complete, the film is at the 4:20 mark and quickly draws to a close, forsaking any scene in which Snafu explicitly learns his lesson. In other films he is transformed into a horse's hindquarters; here, he merely marvels at how wrong he was. Arguably, *The Home Front*'s lack of a "moral" section undermines the film's effectiveness. It is the only one of the SNAFU films *not* to contain some sort of lesson, either explicit or implicit, for an intended military audience.

Just as other Tashlin cartoons also employ sexual comedy, so do other Warner Bros. animators engage in this type of humor. Tashlin was not unique in this regard; indeed, the modern, racy edge to Warner's cartoon comedy is one of its strongest marks of distinction. Neither, of course, was Tashlin unique among

1950s and 1960s live-action comedy directors in his use of blue humor: this technique was a staple of such directors as Tashlin's contemporaries Billy Wilder and Blake Edwards; as well, it was an inevitable component of any film that stars performers such as Bob Hope or Harpo Marx (not to mention Mae West), whose deviant sexualities were "built-in" to their personae. This is another way of saying that this element of Tashlin's style does not "come from" his animated work, nor did his animation style "become" his live-action style. Rather, and at the risk of repetitiveness, this ingredient of his style may be traced to a larger, deeper comic tradition that informs both Tashlin's cartoons and his live-action features.

It is the rare Tashlin feature that does not contain one or more risqué jokes; indeed, it is one of the strongest marks of his style, as well as the technique for which he is perhaps best known. Nearly any Tashlin feature illustrates the importance of blue humor to his style: the many likenings of bananas to penises in *The First Time* (1951); Tony Randall stressing the first syllable of *titular* while a near-naked Jayne Mansfield stands nearby; the magically "erect" tail on Jerry Lewis's giant mouse costume, as his character is summoned to the boudoir of Zsa Zsa Gabor; there are many, many more. The strong presence of risqué humor in both Tashlin's cartoons and his features points to a shared lineage—in this case, one that derives from the "bluer" incarnations of vaudeville.

It must be noted that, while vaudeville is surely a major influence on Tashlin and other American animators of the 1930s and 1940s, it was just as surely not the *only* influence. Vaudeville's legacy in Tashlin's work is well worth exploring, but space prohibits a fuller examination of, for instance, the impact of early animation, college humor magazines, or even jokes Tashlin heard in his office. There is no way to determine the relative degrees to which certain strains of comedy influenced Tashlin, nor is there a way to say for certain which comic ideas sprang solely from his imagination.

Tashlin did once remark on the connections between Warner Bros. animation and the vaudeville tradition. In a 1971 interview with Mike Barrier he says:

> A lot of our humor came from Jack Benny, and I'll tell you how. Jack Benny was on [TV] Sunday nights, when Jack was very, very big. We'd come in Monday morning, all of us were talking about Jack. Jack had running jokes—there'd be a knock on the door, Mr. Kitzel would stick his head in the door and say one line. That rabbit [Bugs Bunny] started doing that—"What's up, doc?" Bing, door closes, out. We'd get all of this from Jack Benny. We really stole from all over, and perhaps, as it came out from the assembly line, put some originality into it.[28]

Benny, of course, enjoyed great success in radio, television, and film, but his career began in vaudeville. Other Warner Bros. animators have made related claims. Chuck Jones, in discussing his art, refers to his admiration for Buster Keaton and Charlie Chaplin, and he likens Bugs Bunny to "a cross between

Harpo and Groucho."[29] Tex Avery, though specifically discussing his later MGM work, could just as well be speaking of his Warner Bros. films when he says, "The real problem [in directing humorous cartoons] was to build up to a laugh finish. . . . If you build up to a point and then the last gag is nothing, you've hurt your whole show, audience-wise. So in all of them we attempted to be sure that we had a topper."[30] Avery uncannily echoes Jenkins's characterization of vaudeville structure, which holds that shows were designed to have "socko" endings.

I have gone to some lengths to identify the various traditions to which Frank Tashlin's comic style belongs—to situate his films historically, rather than simply accepting them as unique, since uniqueness is not a particularly useful analytical concept. But this is not to say that there is nothing special or different about Tashlin's films. In the larger work from which this chapter is condensed, I discuss at length the specific interests and devices that Tashlin employs regularly, and the ways in which he combines and recombines these interests and devices to forge his own style.[31] By making such auteurist arguments, my take on Tashlin owes much to those of the first critics to take him seriously: Jean-Luc Godard and Roger Tailleur, who, in the 1950s, staked a claim for Tashlin's authorship partly on the grounds of his skillful mise-en-scène. The cinephile critics at such journals as *Positif* and *Cahiers du cinéma*, at least in the late 1950s, valued mise-en-scène above other cinematic devices. (Essays that illustrate this point include Alexandre Astruc's "What Is *mise en scène*?" and Jacques Rivette's "The Age of *metteurs en scène*," among others.)[32] In the half-century since Godard and Tailleur wrote appreciatively of Tashlin as a master of mise-en-scène—and, therefore, as an auteur—numerous other critics have distorted their sensible central idea to make claims about the essential similarity of the director's cartoons and features.

But what *is* it, exactly, about Tashlin's mise-en-scène that is so distinctive? Not even Godard or Tailleur addresses this question with any degree of precision. If his films' systems of mise-en-scène really are their most outstanding elements, how may we use this to carve out a place for Tashlin as an auteur? What is it about Tashlin's mise-en-scène that differentiates his live-action comedies from those of, for instance, Norman Z. McLeod and Norman Taurog?

Generally speaking, Tashlin's visual (i.e., mise-en-scène-based) humor is richer, more intelligent, and more challenging than the visual humor in the films of "the Normans." Having mastered comic mise-en-scène as an animator, Tashlin takes visual comedy to higher levels in many of his features by crossbreeding it with his career-long interests in sexuality and satire, comic modes present to lesser degrees in the films of McLeod, Taurog, and others.

For instance, a rather saucy sight gag from *The Girl Can't Help It*—in which Jayne Mansfield holds two milk bottles in front of her ample bosom—takes on a far more complex meaning. It works on its own as a sight gag, to be sure, with Mansfield's breasts "doubled" by the bottles. Beyond the obvious sexual component of the joke, Tashlin slips in some sly social satire, in having Tom Ewell's character, Tom Miller, who has just spent a drunken night of cheap thrills with a cigarette girl, quiver when faced with such self-assured femininity as Mansfield's. The joke cuts two ways: Mansfield's voluptuousness, in and of itself, is played for laughs, but the real butt of the joke is Miller, whose sputtering confusion lampoons the empty bravado that hides the sexual immaturity of the modern American man.

This very ambiguity characterizes much of Tashlin's best visual comedy and is one of the principal means of separating his work out from those of his more workmanlike colleagues. Importantly, such moments of complex sexual and social satire not only distinguish Tashlin's style but are rooted in mise-en-scène, a cinematic means of expression that he mastered as an animator. In this regard Tashlin's cartoons *did* influence his live-action features quite strongly, but, again, this influence was not a simple process of "transferring" his skills from one mode to the other. Rather, Tashlin, as an animator, achieved such a level of command over mise-en-scène that he was able to combine those visual and comic skills, as a live-action director, with other complex strains of comedy; in so doing, he forged his own cinematic style. The seeds were sown in his years as an animator, but his style was articulated most strongly and convincingly in his tenure as a director of feature films. The films of Frank Tashlin provide a fine opportunity for an investigation into the generic structures of American animation but not because Tashlin borrowed uncannily from or presciently anticipated live-action filmmaking techniques. Rather, his films make for a good case study because the director was unusually committed to the muse of comedy. With but two small exceptions (the bizarre 1947 animation *The Way of Peace* and the toothless 1958 live-action would-be comedy *Say One for Me*), Tashlin did not wander from the genre of comedy. He was a comic artist who found success in multiple realms of artistic expression. In this way he is similar to such undisputed comic mainstays as Groucho Marx, Jack Benny, Red Skelton, Ed Wynn, Bob Hope, Danny Kaye, and many others who found comic success in multiple media: stage, radio, film, television. (Indeed, Tashlin himself dabbled in all of these media, in some more successfully than in others.)

For some reason, however, the general trend among scholars and historians who have considered Tashlin is to tacitly argue for a disconnect between animated and live-action film. As we have seen, animation and live-action are perhaps best considered as two distinct but overlapping modes or realms of filmic expression, and one of the many areas of overlap is, in fact, genre. Claims for Tashlin's uniqueness have been overstated—which is not to say he did not possess his own particular directorial style. On the contrary: a Tashlin film reveals itself as such fairly readily to even a minimally trained eye; his cinematic style, as I have detailed it here, may be traced by careful study of its recurring elements and the ways in which he varies and permutes them. Tashlin *is* an unusual case but for a different reason: his work

The Fox and the Grapes:	5.16 sec.
The Tangled Angler:	7.73 sec.
A Hollywood Detour:	8.96 sec.
Under the Shedding Chestnut Tree:	5.48 sec.
Dog Meets Dog:	5.48 sec.
Concerto in B-flat Minor:	5.08 sec.
Wolf Chases Pigs:	7.46 sec.
Cinderella Goes to a Party:	5.88 sec.
A Battle for a Bottle:	4.55 sec.
Woodsman, Spare That Tree:	4.63 sec.
The Bulldog and the Baby:	4.38 sec.
Song of Victory:	5.08 sec.
Porky Pig's Feat:	6.28 sec.
Scrap Happy Daffy:	5.36 sec.
The Goldbrick:	9.30 sec.
The Home Front:	5.67 sec.
Puss 'n' Booty:	5.56 sec.
I Got Plenty of Mutton:	6.68 sec.
Swooner Crooner:	5.14 sec.
The Chow Hound:	5.25 sec.
Censored:	4.30 sec.
Brother Brat:	6.41 sec.
Plane Daffy:	8.31 sec.
Booby Hatched:	6.65 sec.
The Stupid Cupid:	7.08 sec.
The Unruly Hare:	5.63 sec.
Behind the Meatball:	6.22 sec.
A Tale of Two Mice:	5.54 sec.
Nasty Quacks:	6.11 sec.
Hare Remover:	6.45 sec.
Average duration:	6:43
Range of duration:	4:12 *(The Chow Hound)*–
	8:15 *(The Tangled Angler)*
Range of ASLs:	4.30 sec. *(Censored)*–
	10.15 sec. *(Porky's Spring Planting)*

NOTES

1. McGuire, "Well, what do you know?" 1.

2. Barrier, "Interview with Frank Tashlin," 156.

3. Maltin, *Of Mice and Magic,* 231, 234.

4. Ford, "'Cross-referred Media,'" 79–80.

5. Of course, there are no camera movements or high-angle shots per se in animation: such effects are simulated by the animator's hand. Throughout this chapter, for the sake of clarity, all such devices are understood to be, in animation, simulated, though they are discussed using the same terms as for their live-action analogues.

6. To be clear, Ford does not argue for the nonexistence of these techniques in pre-Tashlin animation; he may be correct that they were unusual. Still, they *do* occur in pre-1936 American animation. A single 1933 Popeye film, *Blow Me Down,* for instance, provides an example of a high-angle shot of Popeye leaping up a saloon stairway, as well as an example of simulated camera movement: Popeye dispatches a couple of dozen thugs in quick succession, and the camera "cranes" around the saloon to show us the locations where Popeye's mighty punches deposit seven of them. (I thank Rachel Walls for calling this film to my attention.)

7. For a definitive study of the techniques of these and other vaudeville-inspired comedians see Steve Seidman's landmark work *Comedian Comedy.*

8. Obviously, the manipulation of the soundtrack in an animated film does *not* fall under the mise-en-scène umbrella.

9. Jenkins, *What Made Pistachio Nuts?* 281–82.

10. See Jenkins, *What Made Pistachio Nuts?* 78–81: "'No Time for Plot': The Structure of the Vaudeville Act."

11. McNamara, introduction to *American Popular Entertainments,* 19.

12. Laurie, *Vaudeville,* 51–52.

13. Jenkins, *What Made Pistachio Nuts?* 79.

14. Relevant here is a brief summary of the differences between Warner's two cartoon series, Merrie Melodies and Looney Tunes. Though now "Looney Tunes" is used as a catchall term for Warner Bros. animation, the two series were, for years, distinct. Merrie Melodies, as the name suggests, were designed to emulate the successful formula of Disney's Silly Symphonies, which were plotless cartoons designed around a piece of well-recognized music: characters would "act out" the lyrics to the song. Merrie Melodies were designed to exploit the vast Warner Bros. music catalog. At first, Looney Tunes were different only in name from Merrie Melodies, as they also were designed to showcase the songs of Warner's music library. In the mid-1930s, however, Looney Tunes became the Schlesinger Unit's forum for experimentation with recurring characters and more narrative-driven cartoons, while Merrie Melodies remained music-focused.

Speaking of the Weather, Have You Got Any Castles?, and *You're an Education* were all made under the Merrie Melodies banner, meaning that Tashlin is only partly responsible for their plot-lessness. It was by studio decree that these and other Merrie Melodies were little more than strings of disconnected gags: they were never intended to present stories but to promote pieces of popular music. All of Tashlin's Porky Pig films, however, are Looney Tunes. See Barrier, "Interview with Frank Tashlin," 158–61; and Maltin, *Of Mice and Magic,* 226–29.

15. Of note is the film's framing device, in which a caricature of Alexander Woollcott, as the Town Crier (his popular radio character), provides a brief prologue and epilogue. The two Woollcott scenes—which total about eighty seconds—were trimmed from the film for its 1946 "Blue Ribbon" rerelease. See Prouty, "Filmography," 200.

16. The scene does, however, foreshadow a later event of minor narrative value: the unexpected appearance of the Count Basie Orchestra in the climactic scene at the ball.

17. Page, *Writing for Vaudeville*, 73, 124, 127.

18. Jenkins, *What Made Pistachio Nuts?* 70.

19. For a fine, detailed account of the functions of caricature in Warner Bros. animation see Crafton, "The View from Termite Terrace."

20. Barrier, "Interview with Frank Tashlin," 363.

21. Ford, "'Cross-referred Media,'" 81.

22. Laurie, *Vaudeville*, 81, 83, 88, 93, 286.

23. Stein, *American Vaudeville as Seen by Its Contemporaries*, xiii.

24. Page, *Writing for Vaudeville*, 81. Though overt sexuality was taboo, ethnic humor was not; the book provides an extensive list of stereotypical ethnic characters and their best-known traits (117), demonstrating, if nothing else, that standards of acceptability are forever in flux.

25. Green and Laurie, *Showbiz from Vaude to Video*, 102.

26. Levitt, *Vaudeville Humor*, 8.

27. The studio made twenty-five SNAFU cartoons (three were made by other studios), of which Tashlin directed four; Jones, eleven; Freleng, eight; and Clampett, two.

28. Barrier, "Interview with Frank Tashlin," 156–57.

29. Ford and Thompson, "Chuck Jones," 25, 36.

30. Quoted in Adamson, *Tex Avery*, 173.

31. See de Seife, *Cheerful Nihilism*.

32. Both essays originally appeared in *Cahiers du cinéma*: the Astruc piece in October 1959; the Rivette piece in January 1954. Both are anthologized, in English translations by Liz Heron, in Hillier, *Cahiers du cinéma, the 1950s*.

PART FIVE

Beyond the Studio Era

Building on Tradition

13

Sounds Funny / Funny Sounds

Theorizing Cartoon Music

Daniel Goldmark

Discussing the various means of showing speed in a cartoon, Kristin Thompson describes a device in which Daffy, in *Conrad the Sailor* (1942), moves so quickly that when he stops suddenly, several Daffys are used to show his movement across the frame, catching up to him, one at a time, as the director, Chuck Jones, makes explicit his means of suggesting speed.[1] Music's understood place in cartoons, as with most film music, precludes it from commenting on its own subjectivity; it in fact remains one of the few constants in the animated universe typically immune to any character's machinations yet at the same time responds seamlessly and immediately to whatever happens in the narrative at any given moment. Even in such a reflexive cartoon as Jones's *Duck Amuck* (1953), in which every convention of the animator's table is forfeited for the sake of Bugs Bunny's joke on Daffy, the music plays along: when Daffy says "Let's finish this!" he asks for an end to the torture he has endured, and since the deus ex machina has been taking him quite literally so far, the soundtrack accommodates his request by playing the appropriate musical tag for the end of the cartoon—even though the cartoon is far from over.

How is our understanding of cartoon sound, and especially the music, affected when we consider the fact that the soundtrack—like the entire process of animation—is understood to be unnatural, a fabrication? What happens when the cartoon soundtrack turns its all-seeing, all-mimicking musical voice on itself and either becomes a self-parody or lets us go behind the soundtrack and see/hear how it's really done? And can cartoon music ever be anything more than a melodic tracing of the physical antics that audiences most remember from cartoons? These questions get at the heart of how cartoon music "works": that is, what the creators and (passive) consumers of cartoon music expect from it, how these expectations arose, and how they are met.

Work on cartoon music so far has been largely limited to genre studies (jazz, classical, opera), biographies (Stalling, Bradley), and historical surveys (1930s, 1940s, late 1920s). Underpinning all of this music, however, is the audience's expectations for it, the things that are seen as inherent, obvious, or even somehow natural to cartoon music. Nothing just is a particular way, of course; in this case, cartoon music is coming out of the practices of early film composers, comic film, vaudeville, and other discourses present in the 1920s and 1930s.

Besides the prominent place of musical performance in cartoons throughout animation's Golden Age, music's role can vary from being placed in ironic relief to the characters themselves to making explicit commentary on the musical score. By outlining the approaches taken to music in relation to comedy, I will show that the diverse scoring styles at the Hollywood studios have much to do with the various studios' storytelling styles and approaches to humor (visual, verbal, slapstick) and ultimately help define the cartoons, not purely on images but on a constructed notion of what "sounds" funny.

I've spent enough time in earlier writing to establish that the expectations for cartoon music are different from those for live-action feature scores.[2] But it seems difficult to discuss how some cartoons foreground, confirm, or frustrate the expectations of cartoon music when those very assumed qualities have never been quantified. I'm not proposing a definitive list of what cartoon music "does"; such a list would not only be impossible to compile (or justify) but would likely become immediately obsolete. I would like, however, to consider briefly a possible range of what the music can or should do in a cartoon.

The title of Claudia Gorbman's discipline-defining book *Unheard Melodies* plays on the long-standing perception of film music with the film industry that scores should not be listened to but simply heard. The music should never be so obvious as to get in the way of the narrative or, God forbid, the dialogue. Cartoons are willfully antinarrativistic at times, consisting of extended strings of related (or unrelated) gags. Cartoons also complicate the belief that film music should be heard on a functional (read psychological and emotional) plane but not actively listened to unless absolutely necessary. As with practically all studies of film music, Gorbman does not address cartoon music, and justifiably so: the history of animated cartoons, and the practices of scoring animation, lie so far outside mainstream film history so as to constitute an almost entirely different field. Yet the composers for the major animation studios—Carl Stalling (Warner Bros.); Scott Bradley (MGM); Joe DeNat and Eddie Kilfeather (Columbia); Frank Churchill, Leigh Harline, and Oliver Wallace, among others (Disney)—worked within a production system that had evolved over many years to accommodate the needs and idiosyncrasies of composers for *live-action* films, the same composers who won Academy Awards for film scores and were known to the general public (as much as film composers could be known, that is).[3] We need to keep in mind, then, that cartoon composers were groping about in the early days of film sound just as much as the composers of live-action films.

We can find a fairly typical description of cartoon music from the mid-1940s, at the height of the output from the major Hollywood studios:

> Certainly the brightest use of music in shorts is in the cartoon, where it is an indispensable part of the action. Its purpose usually is to act as a sort of commentary on what's going on, sometimes using tunes whose titles or words are pertinent to the subject in hand, in the manner of the movie-theater's pianist in the silent days of the film. Since a cartoon has little or no dialogue, its score is far more than mere background, and must emphasize effects in its continuity and reinforce its impact. With the exception of the occasional theme bits, cartoon scores are original and represent some of the most sparkling of screen composing. Philip A. Scheib of Terrytoons, Carl Stallings [sic] of Vitaphone, Scott Bradley of Metro have been doing outstanding work for years in this exacting field.[4]

Lauding the work for cartoons as the "brightest" among all film scores, the critic makes her case largely by enumerating the ways that cartoon scores are like feature scores: "commentary on what's going on," "using tunes whose titles . . . are pertinent to the subject in hand," "cartoon scores are original," and so on. Granted, the writer also points out the key difference, as she sees it, from feature-film music, that the "score is more than mere background, and must emphasize effects in its continuity and reinforce its impact." Save this one difference, however, it seems that there is little to differentiate music for the two forms.

The comparison to film music has always been cartoon music's undoing: no matter how "outstanding" the composer or "indispensable" the music, it is never considered on its own terms but always in relation to its more mainstream relative. Gorbman provides a rough list of what was expected from or otherwise associated with Hollywood film scoring, many items of which are to be found in cartoon music as well: invisibility, "inaudibility" (that is, not being overt or explicit), signifier of emotion, provider of continuity, etc.[5] For cartoons, however, there is the ever-present ability for self-critique and outright satire that leaves no subject, even the film's own technology, safe from ridicule. And thus another of music's functions in cartoons becomes evident: as a target for comedy.

SEEING THE MUSIC

The Hollywood animation studios did few things better than mock themselves and every studio, live-action and animation, in the industry. The Van Beuren

FIGURE 13.1. How cartoon music is made: *Making 'Em Move* (Van Beuren, 1931).

short *Making 'Em Move* (1931) is an excellent example of the behind-the-scenes story, giving the viewer the inside scoop on how cartoons are made, particularly the factory-like system that dominated theatrical animation in the 1930s. Practically every imaginable gag drawn from the process of animation and filmmaking appears, beginning with a veritable zookeeper, snoozing outside the door to the cartoon studio, who is there to make sure none of the animators escape. The repeated use of the seemingly ubiquitous "Mysterioso pizzicato" as the keeper escorts into the studio a woman, who has "always wondered how they were made," sets up a false sense of foreboding before reaching the (suddenly jauntily scored) lunacy inside.[6] What sets the story apart from other reflexive shorts like *You Ought to Be in Pictures* or *Duck Amuck,* however, is that the animated figures in the studio are making films of . . . animated figures. We see funny animals drawing funny animals, with a small musical ensemble on a bandstand playing to keep the animators moving, not unlike the man who beats out a rowing rhythm on a prison barge.[7]

Recording the music in the cartoon proceeds thusly: after an anthropomorphic movie camera shoots the animation (with each animator simply hand-flipping his animation drawings in front of the camera), it attaches the film (from its film magazine/head) to a reel and sets a phonograph needle/horn on top, which is picking up the sounds of a band playing in an adjacent room. The phonograph horn in the room in which they play is more like a sonic vacuum cleaner, sucking up all the musical notes that the musicians produce and, eventually, the musicians themselves! (Fig. 13.1). Despite that last bit of comic flair, music's place in the studio seems fairly straightforward and not at all mysterious. By leaving out the tremendous amount of work that goes into the composing, recording, and editing of a cartoon score (at least at some of the studios), *Making 'Em Move*

FIGURE 13.2. Scoring the villian: *Making 'Em Move*
(Van Beurén, 1931).

essentially minimizes the music's role in the animation process to a few gags and
some corny melodies.

Perhaps in keeping with the idea of animals animating animals, there is a
telling moment during the screening of the studio's latest cartoon, titled "Fables
Animals Present Little Nell." When the stereotypical villain walks onscreen, he is
underscored with the same cue we heard earlier in the film, the traditional "bad-
guy" cue of the "Mysterioso pizzicato"—except that he's accompanying himself
on the saxophone, with each note of the melody mickey-mousing each of his
footsteps (Fig. 13.2). I'll discuss later the significance of the mickey-mousing gag,
but for now, suffice it to say that what little music there is for the cartoon within
the cartoon dwells on the most stereotypical, generalized notions of cartoon
music, insinuating that the human creators of this cartoon thought little of the
music in their own shorts.[8]

Only a few years later, Warner Bros. produced two cartoons that went behind
the scenes: *You Ought to Be in Pictures* (1940) and *Porky's Preview* (1941). The first
showed Porky and Daffy on a live-action stage at the Warner studio, while the
second, completely animated, featured a youngster Porky (he says that he's seven
years old) showing his homemade cartoon to a paying audience. As with *Making
'Em Move,* the fun lies in watching the cartoon within the cartoon. Porky's artistic abilities are minimal, so all the people he animates are stick figures. Musically,
composer Carl Stalling provides a brilliant parody of his own scoring style for
Porky's short, with a simplistic, amateur sounding version of "The Merry-Go-
Round Broke Down" playing during Porky's credits (including a repeat of the

same five notes several times in the middle to suggest a skipping record), and a litany of Stalling's favorite pop songs ("La Cucaracha," "Aloha Oe," "The Old Gray Mare," "The Latin Quarter," etc.). Stalling and Avery both poked fun at the by-now-formulaic nature of studio cartoons: Avery's jokes are his usual string of blackout gags, rendered in almost flip-book style animation, and Stalling dredges up his most familiar tunes to characterize each joke in turn.

Poking fun at how cartoons were made was clearly an easy task; the animators and writers could simply focus their wit on themselves. Less common—but just as revealing—is when animation's normally invisible machinery makes a conspicuous entrance for the sake of a gag.[9] An excellent example comes from the Columbia studio in *The Herring Murder Mystery* (1943). The unnamed proprietor of Ye Olde Fish Shoppe (Marinating a Specialty) is abducted by several large fish, including one smoking a calabash pipe (his business card reads "Sherlock Shad, Homicide Division"), and taken to the bottom of the ocean, where he is put on trial for his life. The format of the trial is largely a spoof on the popular radio quiz show *Information, Please.*

The first hint of the cartoon's more elastic approach to the plot comes after the first of many instances of the fish jury singing (to a slight variation of "Here We Go Round the Mulberry Bush"):

> There's something on the end of the hook
> The end of the hook, the end of the hook
> There's something on the end of the hook
> And it's shad roe, shad roe, shad roe to me!

At this point the judge pulls out a dictionary to look up the term, which viewers see defined as

> Shad Roe ... falsehood,
> fabrication,
> fiction.
> "OR JUST A LOT OF
> BALONEY ... "

The characters stop being simply silly and move into the realm of the reflexive when the owner of the fish shop is asked by the district attorney (stereotypically depicted as a shark), "Where were you on the night of January 13th?" The defendant's response is not heard; while his body clearly gesticulates and his mouth moves, no sounds are heard, prompting the judge to ask, "Is anything wrong with the soundtrack?" The camera pans left, exposing the edge of the frame, the film's spoke holes and the thin, black line of the soundtrack running in between the two. If this rupture of a typically invisible barrier weren't enough, the soundtrack

FIGURE 13.3. The soundtrack talks back: *The Herring Murder Mystery* (Columbia, 1943).

itself then gets into the act. The wavy line on the side jumps out into the shape of a head and responds to the still unanswered question, "No, nothing's wrong with the soundtrack. Just speak a little more distinctly, stupid!" (Fig. 13.3).

The device of visually depicting the soundtrack—to say nothing of conversing with it—means that the cartoon's creators recognized a typically invisible part of the mechanics of animation. And this wasn't the first time; in fact, this soundtrack gag is very possibly a spoof of a similar setup in *Fantasia* (1940).[10] Following the film's intermission, the host and narrator, Deems Taylor, returns to the stage (breaking up some impromptu playing amongst the musicians that is dangerously close to devolving into an all-out jam session) and introduces "somebody who is very important to *Fantasia*. He's very shy, and very retiring. I just happened to run across him one day at the Disney Studios. But when I did, I suddenly realized that here was not only an indispensable member of the organization, but a screen personality whose possibilities nobody around the place had ever noticed. And so, I am very happy to have this opportunity to introduce to you—the soundtrack."

Taylor's language emphasizes the manner in which the writers sought to personify and even anthropomorphize a technical component of the film, without changing its fundamental appearance: it is shown as a straight line that changes according to whatever sound it produces. And sure enough, Taylor proceeds to have a conversation of sorts with the soundtrack; he asks the soundtrack to show the viewing audience what the sound waves of instruments of various timbres look like, and the wave obliges. The wave is little more than another obedient member of the onscreen orchestra, not there to perform as a soloist but as part of the ensemble, and certainly does not talk back to Taylor like the soundtrack in *The Herring Murder Mystery*. Disney extends to the soundtrack the same respect he gives all the music in the film.

MICKEY-MOUSING: THE UNFUNNIEST MUSIC?

These examples of sound effects and music run amok tell us something about the expectations of the cartoon soundtrack, but they are ultimately exceptions when compared to how things work in "normal" situations. Building gags on the audience's grasp or ignorance of cartoon sounds means that a degree of understanding is necessary to appreciate the humor, whereas most cartoon music works on a more implicit and even subliminal level.[11] The responsiveness of the cartoon soundtrack is fluid and immediate: we see a character move or begin to speak, and the music reacts instantly. It's an outburst from the soundtrack, almost a character unto itself, one with feelings and reaction times. Yet the viewer never questions these responses, which are far more rapid and tailored to the actions than in live-action film. From this point of view many musical interactions in cartoons have the potential to be disruptive, or at least jarring—yet they are not.

When music underscores a scene in a cartoon, there is always a secondary layer of meaning. Besides providing an emotional barometer, establishing setting—all the attributes mentioned earlier—the music also serves as a veritable timekeeper. Practically every studio composer, at one time or another, timed the action to the very beat or at least accented or "caught" certain actions, effectively drawing the score *into* the story so that it was no longer simply *under*scoring the sequence. Exceptionally overt parallelisms like this, especially when synchronized exactly, are usually called mickey-mousing.

While the exact provenance of this term is unclear, we might consider one possible theory as to how its meaning shifted in the early years of sound. When the industry began to take sound seriously after *The Jazz Singer* in 1927, many films using the new technology featured musical numbers—audiences wanted to hear their favorite singing/musical stars—and thus had little or no underscore. Cartoons were one of the few (if only) mediums to use continuous underscore. We can probably make a case for cartoon music's providing an example for early feature-film composers as to how underscoring might sound in the sound era.[12] Once fully scored films begin to appear in the early 1930s (by Steiner et al.), the term "mickey-mousing" comes up as a way to compare the feature scores to the most prominent, fully underscored films on the market: cartoons.[13]

The common belief regarding mickey-mousing is that it is a negative thing when heard in live-action films, belonging more properly in the realm of (less seriously regarded critically and therefore less important) animated films. For live-action films no one put their vitriol more solidly on the table than the composer and author Irwin Bazelon, who wrote the following regarding Max Steiner:

> Steiner had a special weakness for this practice, which often vulgarized the scenes he was scoring. Using highly illustrative music to echo the action and mood of

the film, he translated into musical terms the very movements depicted on the screen—sometimes in precise synchronization. This redundancy—the viewer already sees the action unfolding before him—acts as a distraction, amplifying its own musical shortcomings. By constantly calling attention to itself, the Mickeymouse score becomes offensive and tiresome. Whereas the typical background score made no dramatic contribution to the film at all, being practically irrelevant, the Mickeymoused score went to the other extreme, accentuating the obvious. Mickeymousing stressed the cleverness of the composer rather than the dramatic mood of the moment.[14]

Fred Karlin and Rayburn Wright's *On the Track: A Guide to Contemporary Film Scoring,* for many years the guidebook and authority on how to write scores for practitioners, does not even mention the term *mickey-mousing,* let alone warn against its use, which might imply a complete repudiation of the technique, a refusal to acknowledge its very existence in the world of competent film composers.[15]

And yet mickey-mousing, while explicit and self-referential in live-action films and often seen as a sign of an unskilled or lazy composer, was in no way suppressed in animation. The term itself seems to exist more for live-action folks to describe music that sounds "cartoony." The perception certainly exists, however, that mickey-mousing somehow *belongs* in cartoons. Roy Prendergast writes in passing that "'mickey-mousing' is appropriate, even expected, in cartoons . . .'"; and in a review of Gail Kubik's score for *Gerald McBoing-Boing* (1951), Frederick Sternfeld describes the tendency for music to trail the action as "customary."[16]

Cartoon composers themselves weren't thrilled with the pejorative nature of the expression. MGM's Scott Bradley had no love for the technique, saying in a lecture, "Some years ago, when cartoons were new, it was easy to follow a character up the steps with an ascending scale passage and down again when he ran down. But these patterns soon became too obvious, and we had to dress them up in new fashion."[17] Just two years later, a critic in *Film Music Notes* reported the Disney composing crew's disdain for the term: "But it seems that Oliver Wallace, Charlie Wolcott, and the rest of the eminent and talented staff of Walt Disney productions, object most strenuously to this term. Their argument is quite valid. As they say, the score in cartoons, or rather animated pictures, now makes just as much use of mood music, entirely unrelated to physical action, as does the score of the average picture using live actors. Therefore, they say, the term 'Mickey Mouse' music does not represent solely physical music, and should no longer be used in this sense."[18]

Were not the early Mickey Mouse cartoons praised for, among other things, their extraordinary synchronization of sound and image? Part of this adulation might have come from the still novel technology of sound, but I think just as much the very idea of developing a musical shorthand or analogy for cartoon antics was a cause for wonder and celebration. The very thing about it that was (is) so offensive in live action—its complete lack of subtlety by telegraphing a person/animal/thing's exact movements—is seen as totally normal and expected in cartoons. And why? Is it because music based on exact timings is, in cartoons, a form of mickey-mousing? Put another way: almost all studio cartoon music from this period was written to correspond with some level of the action, from a single note (a realization cue ["Boing!"]) to a long melody (tracing the descent, for instance, of a leaf wafting through the sky on a breezy day). If mickey-mousing describes this synchronized interpretation of the action through the music, then almost all cartoon music is, in some form, mickey-mousing.

Of course, I'm being fairly obtuse in my use of the term here, as most people (myself included) would argue that mickey-mousing isn't *just* synchronized action: it's a deliberately explicit, even idiosyncratic, scoring style that calls attention not just to the music (unpardonable scoring sin no. 1) but to the action as well. By the time the term surfaced, it had only a negative connotation, probably because the term (supposedly) arose to describe what live-action composers should *not* do in their films.[19] This association with feature-film scoring is one reason why I think applying the term to cartoons is largely useless. Combined with the idea that almost all cartoon music is mickey-mousing of a sort, and is meant to be that way, the result is a term that has little or no value in describing cartoon music.

Michel Chion's approach to the term fortunately does not take on the simple pejorative connotations of film scoring practices. As he does with many of his typologies and categories, he tries to explain the music's purpose as it appears in the larger context of the film. When addressing mickey-mousing in detail, he writes that "this device . . . has been criticized for being redundant, but it has an obvious function nonetheless. Try watching a Tex Avery cartoon without the sound, especially without the musical part. . . . Sound helps to imprint rapid visual sensations into memory. Indeed, it plays a more important role in this capacity of aiding the apprehension of visual movements than in focusing on its own substance and aural density." Ultimately, Chion points out that the strategic use of sound in cartoons can inject into any story a sense of what he calls "reality."[20] Chion gets to the essence of what mickey-mousing in cartoons can achieve—reifying the physical impact of visual action in a made-up world—without getting caught up in evaluating the technique's effectiveness or status among composers.

MODERN MICKEY-MOUSING

The idiosyncrasies of mickey-mousing are so ingrained in approaches to scoring practices that we can find plenty of examples of television animation since the

1990s (during the renaissance of television animation, which Linda Simensky refers to in this volume as the Second Golden Age of Cartoons) that use mickey-mousing to achieve a new, latter-day effect: evoking cartoons of the 1940s, particularly Warner Bros. and MGM cartoons (those that were most associated with the sound). It's not that mickey-mousing suddenly became acceptable; rather, the directors and writers that grew up with Tex Avery and Bob Clampett cartoons applied a sense of irony to the indebtedness their own cartoons have to the earlier directors and styles. Since the composers can't just use mickey-mousing indiscriminately, it often shows up in the context of stories that deliberately work outside the show's traditional fictional narrative or diegesis.

The annual Halloween episode for *The Simpsons* offers an excellent example of a recurring nondiegetic convention. Normally the twenty-two-minute show would offer a traditional sitcom exposition of a single story (or, in more recent years, several stories dovetailing with each other). For the yearly horror fest each of the show's three acts offers a story that not only does not connect to the others but also ignores the show's typical standards for violence and fantasy: people die at the tentacles of space aliens Kang and Kodos; Bart finds he has an evil twin brother; Homer runs amok as a gargantuan green eating machine. The Halloween episode also offers the show's creators a chance to have fun with current pop culture (seen in spoofs on the Harry Potter series, on *I Know What You Did Last Summer,* and on *Bram Stoker's Dracula*) and classic tales of horror or suspense (*The War of the Worlds, The Island of Dr. Moreau,* "The Most Dangerous Game") without being beholden to changes to the übernarrative during the rest of the season.

In "Nightmare on Evergreen Terrace," a send-up of the slasher franchise *A Nightmare on Elm Street,* Groundskeeper Willie takes the place of Freddy Krueger in the dreams of Bart, Lisa, and their friends. As the story opens, we see Bart playing with his greyhound, Santa's Little Helper, but something is off: Bart looks inexplicably different,[21] and the music is unusually responsive and playful. Alf Clausen's original music for *The Simpsons* is typically limited to interstitial cues that join scenes, occasional short cues for dramatic moments, and musical numbers. The music playing through this scene, then, calls attention to itself by its mere presence. It becomes clear that we're meant to see this scene as taking place not in the usual animated diegesis: Santa's Little Helper speaks to Bart (with a British accent); when Bart is hit on the head a huge bump appears and is immediately surrounded by chirping birds, while the words "NO SALE" momentarily replace Bart's pupils; Bart reacts to Willie's appearance with a Tex Avery eye take (eyes stretching far out beyond his body); and Bart's realization of Willie's intentions garner a minimalist response of a small sign Bart holds up that reads simply "YIPES!" (à la the Coyote and Roadrunner). When Bart finally wakes from his nightmare, things return to normal (except for Bart's injury, that is).

Perhaps the writers' joke was that when sitcom cartoon characters dream, they dream of a zany cartoon life. Whatever the intent, the effect—completely shifting the stakes of the diegesis to that of a different cartoon universe—is achieved largely through the soundtrack, including some overly conspicuous sound effects, the use of "Pop Goes the Weasel" for when Bart and his dog play, "Listen to the Mocking Bird" for the head/chirping birds gag, and several moments of mickey-mousing (especially when Bart gets hit by a Frisbee, and when he notices Willie). The marked difference (mickey-mousing and pop tunes) from the scores Clausen provides for normal *Simpsons* episodes signals the viewer that a joke is being played.

While *Family Guy* also follows the basic rules of sitcoms, the show typically doesn't do special episodes, opting instead for extensive cutaway (imaginary or fantasy) sequences within its normal weekly episodes. And yet in its first network run (seasons 1 through 3) the creators produced "Family Guy Viewer Mail #1," where supposedly viewers' story ideas were turned into three short stories. The first of these, "No Bones about It," involves Peter's receiving three wishes from a genie. After first asking to see what Kelly Ripa is like off-camera, Peter says, "I wish I had my own theme music." At first nothing happens, but when the genie admonishes Peter to "Get up. Try it out!," the music begins to play, synchronized exactly with each of Peter's movements. Over the next minute we see Peter in a variety of situations—getting up in the morning, walking down the street, encountering a destitute homeless man, about to have sex with his wife, and riding on a bus—each of which generates a new musical theme. The cues that the composers Ron Jones and Walter Murphy write for each of these situations are working versions of library cues, music meant to evoke a general mood. Such cues first appeared at large in animation during the earliest days of television programming, with music for the early *Huckleberry Hound* and *Yogi Bear* shows provided by various mood music libraries owned by Capitol Records, among others.[22] By the 1990s such music was more common in Saturday-morning fare; *The Simpsons* led the way for original scoring to be standard for prime-time animation. Thus, the gag comes not just from Peter's every movement being mickey-moused but from being set to vaguely familiar sounding tunes that have no outstanding features. The writers even acknowledge the music's history as stock music: during the bus scene, when someone complains about the music, Peter replies, "That's classic traveling music! Try to enjoy it."

Sometimes the joke on musical conventions can be much more subtle—or at least restrained. Music in *The Powerpuff Girls* derives largely from the world of dance music and industrial, manufactured beats. In almost every episode, however, there comes a moment when something is said that garners a double take. In this moment all sounds and movement cease as the camera holds on the image of a character (or characters), who stare for a moment before blinking.

This normally unseen reflex is magnified in the absence of any other actions or sounds, doubly so when combined with a few select hits on a xylophone, whose timbre has been tied to animation practically since the first time Mickey played a makeshift xylophone on a cow's teeth in *Steamboat Willie*. The eye-blink take is very obviously mickey-mousing, which plays right in to the overarching narrative of *The Powerpuff Girls* being a self-aware and satiric mélange of superheroes, girlie animation (i.e., *Care Bears* or *Rainbow Brite*), and anime. With the help of just a few notes the characters can step out of themselves momentarily and mock an especially corny joke or silly idea.[23]

CREATING FUNNY MUSIC

There are plenty of other examples we might discuss, but I believe the point should be clear: as much as the close synchronization of music and image will always be a part of cartoons, for dramatic and technical reasons, the idea of mickey-mousing is so closely tied to animation as to provide a new, ironic read on what music's role can be in a cartoon.[24]

So the very notion of mickey-mousing has become a source of humor in some cartoons, rather than a means of amplifying the humor in a verbally based gag or physically based take. Nothing about the music is inherently funny, but then, why should it be? Humor has so much to do with context and a person's own take on the world as to make explaining it, if not difficult, then at least extremely daunting. Chuck Jones typified the inexplicable essence of comedy in "Music and the Animated Cartoon," jibing that, "One producer asked his artist to use lots of purple in the backgrounds because, as he put it, 'purple is a funny color.' Well, I think G-flat is a funny note."[25]

What remains to explore is another fundamental question about the place of sound in cartoons. Directors, writers, and editors in cartoons at one time or another came onto the bright idea of integrating unintentional or even forbidden sounds into the soundtrack and even the narrative. How, then, do cartoons surmount the idea of having music, or any sounds, that we are not meant to hear and, furthermore, that we logically know we *cannot* hear?

Consider the rise of sound technology for film in the late 1920s and the explosive popularity of the crooner, particularly performers like Bing Crosby or Russ Columbo, who were catapulted to fame because their singing styles worked so well with the recent advances in microphone technology. Rather than having to project or even yell, crooners could sing softly into the microphone, knowing that their voices would still be heard, creating a new intimacy that made these singers attractive to many and a menace to others. Rick Altman discusses how the new technology affected even as notorious a vocal powerhouse as Al Jolson, who, in *The Jazz Singer*, sings to large rooms and large audiences, as well as to his long-suffering mother in her own parlor, thus giving audiences one of sound's important new additions to the feature narrative: hearing the sounds of intimacy and privacy (ironically enough, projected into a room filled with people). Thus, in Jolson's conversation/performance of "Blue Skies" for his mother "in the privacy of the family living room, however, the amplifying technology operates in spite of and against Jolson's quiet demeanor, thus changing us spectators from the destined audience of a self-conscious performer to a group of auditory voyeurs intent on hearing *sounds that are not meant for us.*"[26] I might thus modify Gorbman's term "unheard melodies," when applied to cartoons, to "unhearable melodies," which provide an impassioned, carefully synchronized soundtrack to guide us on our journey though the cartoon universe, whether or not we ever stop to listen.

NOTES

1. Thompson, "Implications of the Cel Animation Technique," 116.

2. See Goldmark, *Tunes for 'Toons.*

3. *Pinocchio*'s win in this category in 1940 was a rare exception until another fully animated film won *(The Little Mermaid),* long after the Golden Age of Hollywood cartoons had ended.

4. Hamilton, "Music and Theatrical Shorts."

5. Gorbman, *Unheard Melodies,* 73.

6. This short cue comes from the 1914 collection of stock mood music, the *Remick Folio of Moving Picture Music,* by J. Bodewalt Lampe.

7. True, Bugs is drawing and redrawing Daffy in *Duck Amuck,* but he is shown as being out of place, an animated character sitting in a live-action world, whereas everything in *Making 'Em Move,* animators and drawings, exists in the cartoon diegesis.

8. The idea of cartoon music written to sound like bad cartoon music would reappear a half-century later when *The Simpsons* began showing the "Itchy & Scratchy" cartoons on Krusty the Clown's show. Once more, the cartoon within the cartoon simultaneously makes light of and derides the contemporary animation world, complete with a hackneyed score filled with sound effects and slide whistles. The difference is that the music here is all original and written by Alf Clausen to sound derivative.

9. The sudden appearance of a film's mechanics occurred often enough that it wasn't terribly jarring. Ending the story before the big finish or having the bad guy win for once were ways in which the Warner Bros. cartoons, for instance, frustrated Hollywood narrative norms. Some of the twists simply toyed with dramatic conventions, while others took useful advantage of the animated medium and did the impossible: for instance, in Jones's *My Favorite Duck* (Warner Bros., 1942), Porky is about to catch a fleeing Daffy and give him a well-deserved beating when we actually see the film break! Daffy walks on to explain, had the film continued, we would have seen how he turned the tables on Porky, until Porky, too, walks on and clobbers Daffy, ending the cartoon. The film breaking (at Bugs's hands) also brings an end to Bugs Bunny's boxing film *Rabbit Punch* (Warner Bros., 1948). Tex Avery became known for consistently directing against the grain, writing outrageous gags and plot twists that exceeded each before it. A gag showing Avery's prototypical wolf running off the edge of the film into white space occurs in *Northwest Hounded Police* (MGM, 1946).

10. Thanks to Mark Kausler for reminding me of this scene.

11. For more on humor in film music see Smith, "Popular Songs and Comic Allusion in Contem-

porary Cinema"; and Goldmark, *Tunes for 'Toons,* esp. chap. 1, "Carl Stalling and Popular Music in the Warner Bros. Cartoons."

12. There were, of course, special original scores written for films during the presound era.

13. See Handzo, "Appendix: A Narrative Glossary of Film Sound Technology," 409–10.

14. Bazelon, *Knowing the Score,* 24.

15. See Karlin and Wright, *On the Track.*

16. See Prendergast, *Film Music,* 228; and Sternfeld, "Kubik's McBoing Score with Excerpts of Score," 8.

17. Bradley, "Music in Cartoons," n.p.

18. Dubin, "News Items," n.p.

19. Several films of the 1940s have brief musical underscoring to punctuate a visual—or, more often, spoken—pun taking place. Witness Cary Grant being physically kicked out of his house at the beginning of *The Philadelphia Story* (Cukor, 1940) or Orson Welles mocking his own wealth to his former guardian, Mr. Thatcher, in *Citizen Kane* (Welles, 1941). The music in these cases isn't always strict mickey-mousing (in the *Citizen Kane* scene there is no physical action to mimic melodically), yet the brief fragments of melody, often on woodwinds, ensure that a feeling of irony underpins whatever is happening. Even in the quickest of melodies, the brief bit of mickey-mousing has the same effect as if the characters broke into song: a known musical convention, with all the implied meanings and associations it carries, has taken hold of the narrative.

20. Chion, *Audio-Vision,* 121–22.

21. To make the dream look more like a studio-era cartoon, Bart is drawn with a heavy black outline and bright colors as usual, but the backgrounds do not have the heavy outline, giving them a more subdued tone that resembles Golden Age–era cel animation.

22. See Lanza, "Rhapsody in Spew."

23. I'm not suggesting this take originates with *The Powerpuff Girls;* one of the bits of mickey-mousing in "Nightmare on Evergreen Terrace" is a similar blink gag scored by xylophone. The difference is that in *The Simpsons* such a gag takes place only in the alternate universe of the Halloween episode, whereas it is commonplace in the Powerpuff Girls' dimension.

24. The episode "Pipe Down!" of *The Fairly Odd Parents* involves Timmy's wishing for "complete and utter silence" so that, until he can undo the wish, the only sounds in the cartoon come from Guy Moon's original score—essentially six minutes of mickey-mousing.

25. Chuck Jones, "Music and the Animated Cartoon," 94 (citation refers to the reprint).

26. Altman, "The Sound of Sound," 69.

14

The Revival of the Studio-Era Cartoon in the 1990s

Linda Simensky

In the history of the animation business there are two eras that stand out in terms of quality of animation and volume of production. The first is the Golden Age of Cartoons, which came out of the studio system in Hollywood; the second is the era that came on the heels of (and perhaps contributed to) cable television's ascendancy to mass popularity. Not surprisingly, the Golden Age of Cartoons turned out to be the main influence on the most successful television cartoons of the 1990s. Here I will examine how the theatrical cartoons made in the 1940s and early 1950s went on to inspire and impact the television animation directors of the 1990s.

My own involvement in animation began during the late 1980s, when I worked in the Programming and Scheduling department at Nickelodeon in New York. I went on to help form the Animation department at Nickelodeon in 1990 and became Director of Animation for the department, where I oversaw the development of series and pilots until 1995. I left in late 1995 for Cartoon Network in Atlanta, Georgia, to be Director of Programming and ultimately became Senior Vice President of Original Animation. I oversaw the development and production of pilots and current series for the network until I left in late 2003. Through these positions I had a unique vantage point for watching this second golden age of animation unfold. I also had a chance to work with a number of animation directors and creators. All the artists at one time or another brought up the artists or directors from earlier eras who had influenced their work. At both Nickelodeon and Cartoon Network, artists were encouraged to speak of their influences, and fans, historians, and reviewers were able to refer back to these as they wrote about the series and their creators.

THE IMPORTANCE OF INFLUENCES

What has been interesting to animation historians and animators has been the variety of animators and styles that influenced each creator. It was fairly evident as early as the first three Nicktoons series that each creator had some director or style he or she was emulating. For example, as Gabor Csupo was from Hungary, *Rugrats* was influenced by Eastern European independent animation, particularly Russian and Hungarian design. Peter Chung, who directed the *Rugrats* pilot, brought in extreme anime-influenced angles to the pilot, such as a particularly strange angle from inside a character's mouth. Jim Jinkins had done work as a writer and illustrator in New York, and the animators he worked with had backgrounds in the New York animation and advertising worlds, as well as in independent animation. The show *Doug* had the marks of these influences with an illustrated, storybook feel and color styling, and classic storytelling. *The Ren & Stimpy Show* was purely a Hollywood cartoon and certainly the most authentic throwback to the days of Looney Tunes that had turned up in kids television in decades. The cartoon was part Clampett Looney Tunes, part Hanna-Barbera parody, and part underground cartoon with some B-movie flavor mixed in.

The approaches used to make these cartoons borrowed much from the Golden Age process, as most younger directors emulated particular directors from earlier eras. By looking at two directors from the 1990s and their animated series, as well as their very different approaches to comedy, we can see the manifestation of this influence.

THE LEGACY OF THE GOLDEN AGE OF CARTOONS

There were several elements that the animators of the 1990s borrowed from the first Golden Age of Cartoons. To begin with, the making of cartoons required a leader or visionary at the helm—the director. In the earlier era, directors were expected to have their own styles and visions and were expected to be able to build and guide teams of artists. The directors were given a certain amount of freedom to have their own ideas and their own sensibility to make their cartoons, as long as what they did worked for audiences. And the teams of craftspeople who worked on these cartoons were equally aware of the teamwork involved with animation. While some of these artists came from solitary professions such as fine arts and illustration, they understood that working in animation required teamwork, as well as a certain amount of luck to work with the animators, voice artists, and background and color stylists who shared or understood the director's vision and were able to carry it out, while still contributing enough of their own vision to feel fulfilled.

Also, production involved the creative skills and input of the entire creative and production team. The process of storyboarding was particularly crucial. A director would usually work with one or two writers to work out the beats of an outline for a story, perhaps with some key bits of dialogue or phrases. The director would then sit with storyboard artists to work out the story, and these board artists would then draw out the story in a storyboard, a series of what looked like panels from comic books. Sometimes scenes or expressions would be acted out. These storyboards would be tacked up on the wall for story sessions, and the storyboard would be pitched and then tweaked until it was funny enough. The writers who participated in this process often had art backgrounds but generally excelled in the area of story, such as Michael Maltese, a writer at Warner Bros. during the 1940s and 1950s. These writers didn't write scripts and then hand them over to the director and the animators, however. The writer sat with the storyboard artists and the directors and worked on the gags and plussed the dialogue.

According to Tom Sito, an animation director and author, this system worked because it forced everyone to be funnier, and it functioned as a first test audience. "A strange dynamic takes over when you have your board up on a wall and you have to defend it," said Sito. "Some jokes that you thought were hilarious just don't work and some scenes juxtapose in a certain unexpected way that makes everyone laugh." He also commented that it was in story sessions that others could point out duplicated gags or suggest stronger placement for a gag.[1] This system strengthened the communication between the different departments and tended to keep everyone focused on the same goals for the film.

As Sito pointed out, however, the story pitching sessions had their downsides. Tempers would flare as board artists would get more defensive. The costs of the short could increase if there were story problems. Any problem could impede the flow of the production process, and if there was an issue with the story, this could cause production to stop.[2] Nevertheless, the story session was clearly a crucial part of the creative process.

SHIFTS IN THE ANIMATION INDUSTRY

The introduction of television into daily life in the 1940s and 1950s had a major impact on cartoons. Although people didn't stop going to theaters to see films, they did stop depending on movies for newsreels and other short subjects. Theaters were not screening as many shorts, so the production companies stopped ordering them. As Leonard Maltin notes in *Of Mice and Magic,* at that time the animation industry was starting to shift. In the late 1950s the costs of cartoon production were rising, and the studios, starting with Walt Disney, began to curtail short-subject production, pointing out that there was not enough return on investment for a short. Maltin adds that other studios that were cutting back on shorts and could handle mass production turned to television as a destination for their productions.[3] Many of those animators went to work either in commercial production or in television production.

Television programmers began to acquire or produce kids' programming to run Saturday mornings or after school or in syndication packages. Although there were many opportunities to sell animated series, budgets for television were much smaller than film cartoon budgets. In *My Life in 'Toons* Joe Barbera writes that in 1957 "it cost between forty thousand and sixty-five thousand dollars to make a single Tom and Jerry (theatrical) cartoon. Screen Gems was offering the sum of $2,700 for five minutes" for a cartoon for television.[4] Where a theatrical cartoon would have used twenty thousand or thirty thousand drawings, the limited animation process designed by Bill Hanna and Joe Barbera would use about three thousand drawings for a cartoon of the same length.[5]

Since many of the directors and animators were the same people who had worked on theatrical animated shorts (for instance, Hanna and Barbera, as well as Friz Freleng), continuing to produce animation for television required a radical change in the production process to get the costs down. Producers making animated shorts for television figured out how to cut expenses by focusing on the dialogue in scripts rather than on complex visual gags with fluid animation. Hanna and Barbera simply looked to UPA, a film studio that I will discuss later in this chapter. Guided by the types of artistic shorts, particularly UPA's shorts, where limited animation was an artistic choice rather than a requirement, animators created simple character and background designs that could work in limited animation, devising formulaic characters and stories and limiting voice talent and numbers of characters. These shortcuts in the production process naturally had an impact on the quality of the animation. At best, some studios took up the challenge of limited animation and wrote some of the sharpest and wittiest dialogue of the day, such as the Jay Ward studio, which produced *Rocky and His Friends* (1959–61) and *The Bullwinkle Show* (1961–64). Other studios, such as Hanna-Barbera, emphasized quantity and speed over quality.

At the same time, humor in cartoons went from funny, gag-driven, and/or character-driven shorts made for theaters to formulaic shorts made for an audience that executives believed would watch any cartoons. The cartoon characters of the time often were given one personality trait or goal to guide all the stories about that character. This allowed writers to think less about the character arc and the character's motivating aspects and more about some variation on a basic situation or plot. The process of a team working together on the production and story beats was gone. The assembly-line process took over, and often the different departments had little or no interaction.

While some cartoons broke out of the pack, most animated series of that era were cheaply produced and visually not as intriguing as the Looney Tunes, Disney, and UPA shorts. Most of the kid-oriented properties of the era suffered from dull writing, uninspired animation, and lack of character development. Yet innovation on the production side did continue. There was still visual innovation throughout this era, mostly in graphic arts, underground comics, and other popular culture movements. Independent animation, internationally and domestically (but outside the studios and Hollywood), became a dominant force in moving the animated medium forward.

All the while, certain animators who were fans of the animated shorts of the 1940s and 1950s attempted over the years to recreate the Golden Age of Cartoons or at least to bring back some of the processes that had worked for the better cartoons of earlier years. Chuck Jones teamed up with MGM and created a series of specials rather than attempting series production. Ralph Bakshi hired a Canadian animator, John Kricfalusi, and went on to set up *Mighty Mouse: The New Adventures* in the late 1980s. These animators were attempting to gain a little more control over the process of television animation with a system they knew worked for making funny cartoons.

CABLE TELEVISION AND THE 1990S

The 1990s brought many changes in television viewing. Cable television, which developed and spread in the 1970s, became much more widespread throughout the 1980s. By the late 1980s and early 1990s, most established cable channels were pushing to add their own original productions to become more than networks that ran reruns, music videos, and imported series. Channels were becoming more focused and specialized and were proliferating rapidly.

Cable television, the "new medium" of its era, also attracted a different kind of employee, people who worked in diverse areas such as education, music, advertising, radio, art, and publishing and were drawn to cable by its promise and its newness. Those who worked in cable seemed to have more attitude, and the executives were often younger than their counterparts in broadcast, as well as slightly more rebellious. On the rare occasions when there was enough funding, cable producers were encouraged to experiment and find shows to acquire that were unusual and brand-defining. There was a sense that discerning viewers could find surprises and hidden gems on cable.

As for animation in this period, there were signs of life. In 1988 Robert Zemeckis directed the film *Who Framed Roger Rabbit,* which put classic animated characters back in the collective consciousness. Consequently, people began talking about the classic animated characters they had loved as kids. The Saturday morning series *Pee Wee's Playhouse* featured animation as well as a very retro vibe that attracted adults. A sketch show on the Fox network, *The Tracey Ullman Show,* featured short animated pieces between sketches, and these interstitials included a cartoon family created by the cartoonist Matt Groening that would eventually go on to become the hit series *The Simpsons*. MTV ran animated music videos, as well as a wide variety of brilliant animated station IDs. Disney Feature Animation released the feature film *The Little Mermaid*, which was extremely successful at the box office.

Cable television was staffed with a number of employees who had grown up watching Looney Tunes after school and were acknowledged fans of animation. They tended to see the cable world as fertile ground for experimentation, and animation was part of that experimentation. Eventually, two of these channels, Nickelodeon and Cartoon Network, the two basic cable channels that focused on kids aged two to eleven, would have the biggest impact on television animation in the 1990s.

CABLE TELEVISION AND NICKELODEON

Over time, Nickelodeon and Cartoon Network would transform television animation from a creative backwater to one of the more inventive forces in the history of recent animation. Nickelodeon, which had premiered in 1979, was the first network for kids and currently is one of the most successful cable channels in the entire cable universe.[6]

Nickelodeon became involved in animation production as the network became more successful in the late 1980s and the head of programming, Herb Scannell, became convinced that the time was right for Nickelodeon to start developing animation of its own. Until that point Nickelodeon had not made any deals to acquire new series from any of the existing animation companies. Executives at Nickelodeon did not feel a connection with many of the popular companies of the time (such as DIC, Hanna-Barbera, and Marvel), which were focused more on selling series than on producing quality shows. The only way to produce something that would fit the Nickelodeon brand, Scannell believed, was for the Nickelodeon team to find its own series and oversee the production themselves. Executives and producers at Nickelodeon believed that the network could resurrect the auteur process for cartoons and find creators who were visionaries with unique sensibilities and senses of humor that were compatible with Nickelodeon's.[7] Nickelodeon would search for creators with animation backgrounds, who had unique design styles, sensibilities, and a sense of timing and gag-telling. These creators would see their series through the entire process, from inception through production and, in essence, would produce the animation the same way it had been produced in the 1940s. Nickelodeon declared that the shows would be character-driven, gag-driven, and funny. Just like the rest of Nickelodeon, these shows would be gender-blind, and each series would need to work for girls and boys equally. The main difference would be that instead of producing theatricals, Nickelodeon's creators and producers would use the same process to produce for television.

Another major difference was that Nickelodeon would produce short pilots first, complete shorts with a story and characters that could be tested with audiences. This piloting process is now the norm for animated series development, but at the time it was a surprising development that added time and expenses to the entire series process. The other networks looked on dismissively, and most assumed that like many other similar proclamations that proposed to "fix" animation for the better, this would not work.

In 1990 Nickelodeon used this process, which we now refer to as "creator-driven," to produce the first of the new generation of funny cartoons, and the network did it in part by referring back to the first golden age. After eight pilots, three shows were chosen to go to series: *The Ren & Stimpy Show,* from the creator John Kricfalusi of Spümcø; *Rugrats,* from the creators Gabor Csupo, Arlene Klasky, and Paul Germain of Klasky-Csupo; and *Doug,* from the creator Jim Jinkins and the newly formed Jumbo Pictures.

In this process Nickelodeon reinvented series animation. John Kricfalusi—an animation director, creator, longtime advocate of the unit process of the Golden Age of Cartoons, and a student of cartoons from that era—and his series, *The Ren & Stimpy Show,* would breathe life into the process of creator-driven production. Kricfalusi and his team would have to try to make this approach coexist with the cable network television production process, which came complete with network executives, deadlines, budgets, and the broadcast standards department.

As a division of MTV Networks, Nickelodeon did have the advantage of being part of a huge media conglomerate, Viacom, affording the children's channel Viacom's vast resources and the ability to amortize their expenditures to make animation production affordable. Nickelodeon's ultimate goal was to build a library of titles developed by the network for the network, titles that Viacom would ultimately own. This process would be the first step in creating the product for future new channels. Nickelodeon's other goals were smaller in scale but equally important to the future of television animation. The network wanted to make fun, funny, and smart cartoons; to improve the quality of animation for kids on television; and to have series with characters who acted, and more important, who were funny, empathetic and meaningful. What the network was not trying to be was Disney. If anything, Nickelodeon was protesting the status quo by trying to be something that all other network and production companies were not.

Ultimately, the cartoons now known as the first three Nicktoons did quite well, with all three getting Emmy nominations in their first year; *Rugrats* won Emmys three years in a row. Nickelodeon was successful in this endeavor for several reasons. The channel was able to put in the time, money, and effort to get the shows to work, through careful development and selection of creators and series, through focus groups and through working with artists who were passionate and knowledgeable about cartoons. At this time, the directors on the series had a fair amount of freedom for television producers as a result of the creator-driven process.

JOHN KRICFALUSI AND BOB CLAMPETT

The Ren & Stimpy Show's creator, John Kricfalusi, was open about his influences and proudly declared that his biggest influence was Bob Clampett, the animation director best known for his frenetic Looney Tunes cartoons in the 1940s. Years later, talking about Clampett on his weblog, Kricfalusi noted, "I think he was the most influential and greatest of the classic cartoon directors. He was the looniest of all the Looney Tunes animators and was largely responsible for their success and style."[8]

Robert Clampett began his career in animation working at Leon Schlesinger's studio on the Looney Tunes and Merrie Melodies shorts. After Hugh Harman and Rudolf Ising left, Schlesinger set up a new unit run by Fred "Tex" Avery on the Warner Bros. lot known as "Termite Terrace." Clampett was hired to work as an animator with Avery and, in this capacity, worked on the first cartoon featuring Daffy Duck, *Porky's Duck Hunt*, in 1937. He went on to become one of the "big five" Warner Bros. animation directors and had his own unit through 1946.[9]

Each of the Warner Bros. directors had his own directing style. Avery was known for his gags, whereas Chuck Jones was known for his clean, intellectual style and his ability to create psychological conflict or sympathy for the characters. Clampett, considered the brashest of the directors, created or refined a number of gags or stylistic innovations, such as the extreme squash and stretch movements, frenetic timing, and exaggerated takes that now distinguish the Warner Bros. shorts.

What also differentiated his shorts from others of the time was the crazy energy and wild surrealism Clampett injected. His most notable shorts, all directed between 1941 and 1946, include *Tortoise Wins by a Hare* (1943), *A Corny Concerto* (1943), *Book Revue* (1946), *Baby Bottleneck* (1946), *Kitty Kornered* (1946), *The Great Piggy Bank Robbery* (1946), and the rarely seen *Coal Black and de Sebben Dwarfs* (1943).

Much of what we think of as hallmarks of the Looney Tunes shorts are actually the trademarks of a Clampett short. Clampett was known for holding on extreme poses, wild in-betweens that could not necessarily even be seen in a typical viewing, and the distortion of character designs to show extreme emotion or over-the-top reactions. His cartoons had a sense of frenzied urgency, and the characters sometimes exhibited a craziness that was not necessarily motivated. Daffy Duck in particular was given to fits of neurotic behavior.

Unlike many other directors of the time, Clampett used film to have fun. He often broke the fourth wall, allowing his characters to toss off snide comments to the audience ("Funny situation, ain't it?"), and he worked in parody and numerous popular culture references to movies, radio shows, and popular personalities of the day.

Character integrity was not always as important to him as were gags. For instance, he did not seem to be as interested in sticking to or developing Bugs Bunny's personality in *Tortoise Wins by a Hare* but instead took Bugs somewhat out of his (at the time, still-developing) character to be the butt of jokes. In addition, Clampett was drawn to raunchy and overt sexuality and attacks on good taste, and his shorts could often be tasteless, odd, and unsettling, as evidenced in *Coal Black and De Sebben Dwarfs* and *An Itch in Time*.

CLAMPETT'S INFLUENCE

Bob Clampett's shorts were not part of the post-1948 package of Looney Tunes that was sold to television stations through syndication, so his work was not as well-known to viewers as many of those directed by Chuck Jones and Friz Freleng. However, his shorts did manage to have a major impact on the animators of later generations, who were amazed by his in-betweens, his takes, and his timing. John Kricfalusi is probably the most prominent animator to be influenced by Clampett. As Mark Langer has noted, "One only need look at the playful violation of taste norms, hip references to classical animation, and use of stretchable-bendable characters by directors like John Kricfalusi to see a Clampett sensibility."[10]

"Why do I like Clampett so much?" posted John Kricfalusi on his weblog. "Because he, like me is open to a wide variety of influences and incorporates so many different ideas and skills into his cartoons. He is the least imitative of other animators and was the most imitated outside of Disney during his reign."[11]

Kricfalusi began his career working on Saturday morning cartoons such as *The Jetsons* revival in 1985 before going to work for Ralph Bakshi on the Rolling Stones' 1986 music video, "Harlem Shuffle." His most well-known work at the time was on Bakshi's Saturday morning series for CBS, *Mighty Mouse: The New Adventures,* which ran from 1987 to 1989. Kricfalusi was a longtime advocate of the Hollywood cartoon studio system with separate units run by specific directors. In a 1988 interview for *Animato* with Harry McCracken, he noted, "I've been trying to do that ever since I got into the business. As soon as I found out how compartmentalized the industry was, I realized, 'Well, no wonder cartoons are so bad.' . . . Even the actual direction duties are split up between about eight different guys. One guy records the voices, another guy times the storyboard, another guy times the sheets, one guy is the story editor. All these jobs should be covered by the director. None of these guys talk to each other."[12]

Besides pushing the unit system, Kricfalusi advocated emphasizing posing, expressions, and design to cope with the limitations of movement in television cartoons. He thus tried to make the point that what he believed would improve the quality of cartoons would be the funny drawings and the characters' reactions rather than fluid animation or animation done just to keep movement on the screen.

Kricfalusi then went on to found his animation studio, Spümcø, with his fellow animator Jim Smith, where Kricfalusi created the series *The Ren & Stimpy Show*, which he sold to Nickelodeon in 1989. *The Ren & Stimpy Show* premiered on Nickelodeon in 1991 and immediately became a hit for viewers and a fascinating curiosity for animation fans. Although he had some freedom on *Mighty Mouse*, when he was finally in charge of his own creation, Kricfalusi was able to set up production exactly as he had wanted.

The Ren & Stimpy Show featured two main characters, Ren Hoek, an asthmatic hound with a Peter Lorre voice, and Stimpson J. "Stimpy" Cat, a simple and slightly dopey but good-natured cat. The other characters in the series included Mr. Horse, George Liquor, Muddy Mudskipper, and Powdered Toastman, and such items as the History Eraser Button, rubber nipples, the Happy Helmet, Log, and the game "Don't Whiz on the Electric Fence."

The series was notable for a variety of reasons. It brought back the structure of classic cartoons. In the same way that Bugs Bunny, Daffy Duck, and Porky Pig showed up in different situations or jobs in cartoons, Ren and Stimpy were similarly more like actors in plays than they were actors in a situation comedy. The characters turned up in a variety of situations, playing not only themselves in their various domiciles or out looking for work but also performing as actors in space-themed B movies, as hosts of a nature show, and as Royal Canadian Kilted Yaksmen.

But what separated Kricfalusi from most of his contemporaries was his ability to channel Bob Clampett and the Looney Tunes, not to mention some of Hanna-Barbera's more ridiculous moments. The Ren & Stimpy cartoons revived cartoony exaggerated movements, silliness, squash and stretch, and surrealism, all on a television budget. Kricfalusi's appreciation for poses and reactions led to a different kind of direction for television cartoons, with long holds on humorous visuals and reactions, sometimes longer than necessary, leading to what seemed like fairly unusual timing. Often, the animation seemed to hold on the most extreme in-betweens rather than on the key poses, leading to holds on bulging eyes or over-the-top reactions at times.

Understanding Kricfalusi's appreciation of Bob Clampett makes it easier to see the origin of many of these quirks. Kricfalusi has spoken many times of how he would make the animators at Spümcø look at Rod Scribner's in-betweens in Clampett's *The Great Piggy Bank Robbery* to see the exaggerated drawings. On the DVD commentary of *The Great Piggy Bank Robbery* Kricfalusi notes that the cartoon's drawings were about feelings, not about sticking to model sheets. He noted that this cartoon had everything a cartoon should have—it was "fast, super lively and what it is that makes cartoons different from every other medium."[13] Naturally, a studio of animators who appreciate the most extreme in-betweens might want to try holding more on funny drawings, no matter how it might impact the overall timing.

The author and animation historian Michael Barrier noted to Kricfalusi in an interview, "Like many other people, I've grown accustomed to thinking of your Ren & Stimpy cartoons as Clampett-flavored theatrical cartoons that have been squashed inside TV budgets. You've relied on 'acting' through outlandish draw-ings, rather than through the comic movement of the kind that made Clampett's cartoons unique."[14] Without a doubt the budgets, schedules, and overseas ani-mating of television cartoons make it much harder to recreate the older cartoons. Nevertheless, whether or not an animator recreates or comes close to recreating the earlier cartoons seems irrelevant if the end result is something that attracts an audience.

In addition to being inspired by Clampett's emphasis on acting, posing, and his ability to create a range of human emotions in a cartoon, Kricfalusi was also greatly influenced by Clampett's darker side. The same tastelessness that would crop up in Clampett's shorts turned up in Kricfalusi's work, although often in a more extreme, even seditious manner. The same unsettling, anxious, and mildly disturbing sense that one might feel after a particularly intense Clampett short is there in the Kricfalusi shorts as well. The *Ren & Stimpy* short "Space Madness" probably left most viewers wondering why Ren was so angry and what he was talking about as he sat in the bathtub.

Kricfalusi became so well-known for his appreciation of Clampett that he wrote an entire weblog posting, "The Importance of Having a Lot of Influences," to detail *other* animators and illustrators who had an impact on him, as well as to pontificate on why animators need to see the work of other animators, past and present.[15]

The Ren & Stimpy Show and John Kricfalusi himself were much-analyzed and much-copied in the early 1990s after the series premiered. Kricfalusi went on to do several Yogi Bear shorts for Cartoon Network and a series of Flash-animated shorts for the web, as well as the series *The Ripping Friends* for Fox Kids. In 2003 he reinvented *The Ren & Stimpy Show* as *Ren & Stimpy Adult Party Cartoon,* an older-skewing cartoon for Spike, a Viacom network targeted to young adult males.

THE EMERGENCE OF CARTOON NETWORK

A few years after Nickelodeon premiered its first three original animated series, Turner Broadcasting added Cartoon Network to its stable of cable television networks, which included TBS, TNT, and CNN. Turner already owned the pre-1941 Warner Bros. cartoon library and the MGM cartoons (the Tom and Jerry and Tex Avery cartoons) and then, perhaps inspired by Nickelodeon's success, went on to purchase the Hanna-Barbera library. Cartoon Network started in 1992 and, early on, mostly ran its library of existing cartoons. Scott Sassa, the head of Turner Broadcasting, sought to reinvigorate Hanna-Barbera Productions and brought in Fred Seibert, a marketing and branding expert from New York who had been involved with the branding of MTV and the rebranding of Nickelodeon. With limited funds and a desire to do original animation, Seibert worked with Cartoon Network to create a program of shorts. Hanna-Barbera put out the call for creators who could create seven-minute cartoons. The shorts would function as pilots; eventually a few went to series as half hours of three seven-minute cartoons.

Although there were many similarities between what Nickelodeon and Cartoon Network were doing, there were also some key differences. Where Nickelodeon emphasized character and humor in the form of half-hour series with two eleven-minute stories, Cartoon Network and Hanna-Barbera emphasized the completely gag-driven seven-minute short, inspired by the dominant form of animation from the Golden Age of Cartoons. The goal was simply to make funny shorts and to see what stuck with the audience. Both Nickelodeon and Cartoon Network were focused on finding innovative creators and on discovering unique and highly stylized designs. Also important were the quality of the animation and the varieties of humor. Nick's theme preference rested mainly with kid issues and what was funny for kids, whereas Cartoon Network in the early years tended to focus on whatever seemed funny. Many of the Hanna-Barbera shorts tried to recreate the feel of older cartoons, mostly through retro design. Many of the creators were also influenced by John Kricfalusi and created duos, similar both to Ren & Stimpy and the Hanna-Barbera canon (e.g., Pixie and Dixie, Snooper and Blabber, Sneezly and Breezly). Of interest was that both networks gained adult viewers early on, and not just parents.

In terms of style and overall influence, Nickelodeon was most influenced by the Looney Tunes, as well as the independent animation process, with designs that were easily identifiable as a certain creator's. At the same time, Cartoon Network seemed to favor not just Looney Tunes and older Hanna-Barbera styles but, in particular, Tex Avery. Avery's specialty was gags, not storytelling or character development, and consequently, the cartoons that borrowed the most from Avery were funny but generally did not make it to series for those reasons. The most character-driven of the shorts, *Dexter's Laboratory, Powerpuff Girls, Johnny Bravo, Cow and Chicken,* and *Courage the Cowardly Dog* were all shorts that made it to series in the 1990s.

Consequently, the most interesting animation of the 1990s was not only a reaction to the status quo but was most influenced by the cartoons of the 1940s. Besides underscoring the importance of animated shorts for a mass audience, both Nickelodeon and Cartoon Network put the power of series creation and development back in the hands of the creatives, and more specifically, the creators. Cable television executives were still ultimately accountable for the success of the series and the shorts but were knowledgeable enough of the history of funny cartoons to know that shows had the potential to be funnier if the creators and directors were hands-on through the entire production process.

One of the most successful and significant Cartoon Network directors from this period is Genndy Tartakovsky, the creator of *Dexter's Laboratory* and *Samurai Jack* and the producer of Craig McCracken's *Powerpuff Girls.* Tartakovsky helped define the new Hanna-Barbera and the Cartoon Network cartoon. Tartakovsky also drew on animation influences from the past. One of his major influences was UPA, specifically the director Bobe Cannon.

UNITED PRODUCTIONS OF AMERICA (UPA)

United Productions of America was a seminal animation studio formed in the latter half of the 1940s. The animators and designers combined the design elements of simple line-drawn characters and props, sparse backgrounds, color-card background styling that changed with moods, and stylized movement to create what can be considered the UPA style. This was in great contrast to the other studios of the day, which were still attempting to create the illusion of life or at least the illusion of comedic fluid animated movement against detailed design and backgrounds.

Also adding to the UPA style was the nature of the stories. More than any other studio, UPA tended to have adults in mind as viewers. The UPA shorts were notable in that they were often more literary than most of the animated shorts of the time. Rather than focusing on screwball gags or violence, the shorts were often animated versions of short stories, ranging from James Thurber to Edgar Allan Poe, and from Ludwig Bemelmans to Dr. Seuss. The shorts featured narration, sometimes in rhyme, as in *Gerald McBoing Boing.*

Also noteworthy for its color styling and contemporary design, UPA incorporated minimalist and abstract expressionist art tendencies into its backgrounds. The bright, flat backgrounds became reduced to representational colors and shapes and sometimes were only cut, textured, or patterned paper, quite unlike the detailed, realistic backgrounds of Disney films, for instance. UPA may also have been the first to use changing background color cards behind held characters to express moods and mood changes.

At the time, the work of the studio provided an alternative to the full animation and earnest storytelling of the Disney cartoons, as well as to the wisecracking cartoon anarchy of MGM and Warner Bros. The major studios were clearly influenced by the UPA style; this can be seen in several late-1950s Warner Bros. cartoons and some Disney animated films, most notably *Toot, Whistle, Plunk and Boom*.

ROBERT CANNON

Robert "Bobe" Cannon had been an animator at Leon Schlesinger's studio starting in 1934 through the early 1940s, where he animated cartoons for Chuck Jones and Bob Clampett. He also animated at Disney and MGM in that time before heading to UPA.[16] One of his most influential cartoons was *The Dover Boys at Pimento University*, a 1942 Looney Tunes cartoon directed by Chuck Jones and animated by Cannon. The characters in this cartoon move with a stiff, storybook-like stylization created by using fewer frames to create the movement. When the characters do move, they move quickly from pose to pose, with a frame of smear animation to create movement. This particular short turned out to be a seminal cartoon for many animators figuring out how to work with limited animation.

Bobe Cannon moved to UPA in the mid-1940s, as the studio was forming, and directed the film *Brotherhood of Man* (1945), a film that featured the flat stylized characters and design for which the studio would eventually be known. The UPA artist and executive Dave Hilberman noted to Leonard Maltin that "Bobe was the first animator who developed a style that organically grew out of the new kind of characters we were designing."[17]

In 1951 UPA released *Gerald McBoing Boing*, a film based on a radio play and short story by Theodore "Dr. Seuss" Geisel, about a boy who could not speak in words but in sound effects instead. The film featured flat, stylized settings and intentionally unrealistic movements. To this day *Gerald McBoing Boing* is the film to which people refer when describing UPA.

Cannon's work is known for the animator's ability to use design and color to communicate tone and emotions through the color-card backgrounds and the character's placement in the frame. Amid Amidi notes in his book *Cartoon Modern* that Cannon was a great designer, but "unlike most artists who designed characters or backgrounds, Cannon designed movement. Characters in his films move around in a wholly invented graphic manner that is as stylized as their designs. Cannon was unafraid to acknowledge the fact that the characters on screen were drawings made on a flat surface and that they could behave with designed mannerisms that would be impossible to replicate in real life."[18]

As I mentioned earlier, UPA's limited animation style would influence television animation twice, first in the late 1950s and 1960s, and later in the 1990s at Hanna-Barbera.

DEXTER'S LABORATORY AND GENNDY TARTAKOVSKY

In 1993 Hanna-Barbera and Cartoon Network, two companies connected through their parent company, Turner Broadcasting, announced a new program to encourage young filmmakers and emerging creators to develop their cartoon ideas and pitch them as shorts. The "World Premiere Toons" program ultimately brought in more than a thousand pitches; eventually, forty-eight were produced and aired on Cartoon Network. Several of these shorts were from a group of young animators who met at Cal Arts, shared similar interests in animation styles and influences, and ultimately ended up at Hanna-Barbera working on *Two Stupid Dogs*. The group included Genndy Tartakovsky, Craig McCracken, Paul Rudish, Rob Renzetti, Lou Romano, Miles Thompson, and Craig Kellman. Their collective style, which featured relatively flat, simply drawn characters with thick black outlines, was reminiscent of both early Hanna-Barbera and UPA. In the mid-1990s this style would be thought of as the "Cartoon Network style." This style eventually would go on to be a standard look for many animated series in the late 1990s and 2000s and would be seen on Nickelodeon, the Disney Channel, and even the Kids' WB.

The animator Genndy Tartakovsky created the cartoon *Dexter's Laboratory*, which aired on Cartoon Network and Boomerang. *Dexter's Laboratory* is a series that follows the life of Dexter, a boy genius who creates fantastic inventions in his huge laboratory, despite the interference of his annoying and playful older sister, Dee Dee. In his beloved lab, which seems to be located either in his attic or in a huge space off his bedroom, Dexter creates inventions and situations that seem to defy the universally accepted scientific laws of time and space. The show is not so much about Dexter's ability to invent, as much as it is about the havoc his inventions wreak. Despite his genius, he ultimately is unable to foil his pesky sister, who, despite her "limited mental capacity" (actually "normal" to the rest of us), is a formidable opponent to Dexter.

Much of the humor in *Dexter's Laboratory* comes from a combination of Dexter's obsession with his experiments, his blind ambition, and his arrogant and confident attitude, all of which are perfect counterpoints to his occasional encounters with humility and the demands of family life.

Dexter's Laboratory started out as a student film produced at Cal Arts in 1991–92. The first Dexter short, *Changes,* was produced as part of the World Premiere Toons project in 1995, and shortly thereafter, a second Dexter short, *The Big Sister,* was produced. The shorts were so successful on air and in viewer polls that *Dexter's Laboratory* became the first original series to be produced for Cartoon Network out of the forty-eight World Premiere Toons, premiering in April 1996.

Dexter's Laboratory took Cartoon Network in an interesting direction because of the way the shows were designed and directed. In terms of design the show made very little attempt to recreate reality. Dexter was designed to be more of an icon in some ways. His body was short and squat and his design was simple, with a black outline and relatively little detail. According to Tartakovsky, an assortment of influences and styles contributed to *Dexter's Laboratory*, including Hanna-Barbera, Japanese animation, Warner Bros. cartoons, and, of course, the UPA shorts.

Dexter was animated in a stylized limited way that Tartakovsky says was influenced by the cartoon *The Dover Boys at Pimento University*.[19] Unlike UPA's product, however, the Dexter cartoons were all staged cinematically, rather than flat and close to the screen, to leave space and depth for the action and gags in the lab, for instance. The show may be most notable for both this unique sense of design and space and for the sharp timing. The staging of the laboratory in Dexter's house created a sense of vastness, which is surprising given that from the outside establishing shots, the house is a standard suburban home.

Tartakovsky first saw UPA shorts as a sophomore at Columbia College in Chicago. At the time, his own taste in animation ran toward Don Bluth, but when he saw 16mm prints of *Gerald McBoing Boing, Rooty Toot Toot,* and *Robin Hoodlum,* he was able to appreciate their visual quality and the caricatures, as well as how well animated and unique they were.

Tartakovsky maintains that he learned to draw after seeing UPA cartoons and that before that, he had just copied other styles.[20] After seeing the UPA films, he thought more about simple shapes. As he learned to draw, he gravitated toward the cartoony aspects of UPA, pushing the style further to be funnier. As for the influence of UPA on Dexter, Tartakovsky noted that most people would associate *Dexter's* art direction with UPA, but to him, timing was most important, and the director Robert "Bobe" Cannon in his UPA period was most influential. Cannon, he noted, developed funny, interesting movement and timing for each character, so that every character moves in its own unique way. Tartakovsky noted that he tried to do the same with Dexter and Dee Dee and that each character moved with his or her own stylized animation. Dee Dee was developed as a girl who likes to dance; one can see she is the animated heir to Cannon's 1954 UPA short *Ballet-Oop,* with its dancers' long legs and similar dance style.

Since Tartakovsky knew he was developing Dexter for television, he purposely limited the design to some degree, designing the nose and mouth, for instance, in a Hanna-Barbera style to animate easily. Where UPA was as likely to have a simple line for a character's mouth, Hanna-Barbera mouths were also simple but designed to accommodate several different animators doing lip synch. He also was influenced by Hanna-Barbera's sillier voice characterizations, which he had always appreciated, and, in the spirit of UPA as well, worked to make sure the voice direction and storytelling shared the stage with the animation.[21]

Besides the clever use of staging to create the vastness of Dexter's laboratory, the series design was notable for its ability to play with size, proportion, and unusual angles for comedic effect. Dexter in some scenes would seem to shrink to the smallest possible size for effect. The directors made use of the comedic aspects of holding on funny frames, as well as repeating a gag several times as its own form of gag. (What comes to mind is an interstitial gag in an early episode where Dexter's hair is on fire. He circles Dee Dee many more times than necessary, each time yelling, "My hair is on fire!")

While combining several influences, Tartakovsky also attempted to push certain aspects of the show in a different direction, away from UPA and Hanna-Barbera influences. He found that UPA had a storybook quality that he was not looking for with Dexter. Dexter cartoons were more active, and much of the comedy was related to that action. Tartakovsky gave Dexter a different kind of energy, going for more character and real emotion. To Tartakovsky, UPA was slower paced, with different points of view and narration, and this kept the characters from seeming real. He attempted to create more energy through the cinematic shots, swish pans, and variable pacing. Whereas UPA was intent on proving that cartoons could be artistic and intelligent and still be successful, this was not a point that *Dexter's Laboratory* felt compelled to prove.

Tartakovsky's own influences for timing, besides Cannon, were Bob Clampett and Chuck Jones. His pacing, however, had more of an influence from live-action movies with more realistic movement and timing that accommodated the amount of time that it might take to walk from one point to another, for instance.

Tartakovsky's next project after Dexter was *Samurai Jack,* a cartoon that combined the clean design influence of UPA with action films and anime. This cartoon was a major shift in style and format for Cartoon Network, being the first noncomedic series that the network produced. He noted that "as UPA broke away from Disney, I'd like to break away from the norm as UPA did."[22]

What is notable about Tartakovsky's choice to make *Samurai Jack* is that he was given complete freedom by Cartoon Network to make the series he wanted. Based on his success with *Dexter's Laboratory* and his work producing *Powerpuff Girls,* the network believed that he had earned the opportunity to experiment. *Samurai Jack* was completely Tartakovsky's vision; there was little network interference beyond some broadcast standards questions. This made the series one of the best examples of a creator-driven series.

THE ANIMATION BOOM IN THE 1990S

Just as not every studio produced hilarious classic cartoons back in the 1940s and 1950s, not every studio producing cartoons in the 1990s was successful. Owing to the enormous success of both Nickelodeon and Cartoon Network, many studios jumped into animation. There was a sudden boom in feature animation and prime-time animation simultaneously, and by the mid-1990s, practically every studio was producing either for cable, for the networks, for Saturday morning, or for features. New studios were opening at a rapid pace, and it seemed that virtually anyone with a good idea and a sense of how to pitch a show could get something into development.

Many studios cherry-picked certain elements of the creator-driven process or did not bother at all to change their assembly-line process. Such decisions were usually at the discretion of the studio head rather than any larger corporate entity. Many seasoned producers were completely comfortable with established television production processes. They preferred the often cheaper and certainly easier and less time-consuming approach of hiring head writers to develop a story bible, oversee the writing of a series, and hand it off to a team of directors and storyboard artists. Often, their concession would be to pick up a show that had indeed been created by someone and then refer to it as "creator-driven" when, in actuality, its process had nothing to do with the creator-driven process or the auteur approach of the 1940s and 1950s. Animation divisions at established studios such as Sony, Warner Bros., and DreamWorks stuck to the more established writer-driven approach.

A director has a certain amount of power over the look of a show if that director is able to oversee the animation process. A major difference between the earlier era and the 1990s was that by the 1990s, almost no studios in the United States still did animation, and most did not do their own layouts. For hand-drawn animation it was much cheaper to storyboard and time out episodes domestically and then ship them overseas to Korea, India, or China for layout and animation. Most studios in the 1990s were not even able to find enough experienced layout artists! This would explain why so many studios and producers use Flash animation and other similar computer programs today. Despite the limitations of Flash, the animation is often completed onsite; even if it is done in another location, it is easier to keep the character designs consistent and easier to fix than cel animation.

This shift in philosophy in the 1990s completely changed animated shorts and brought a number of successes to television cartoons where there had been few. A new group of innovative and interesting television animation directors came out of this period. In addition to John Kricfalusi and Genndy Tartakovsky, other directors of note include David Silverman, Danny Antonucci, Craig McCracken, Stephen Hillenburg, Mike Judge, Rich Moore, Wes Archer, and Van Partible, to name a few.

It seems clear that cable television revived television animation by putting in place the right creative personnel, enacting appropriate budgets, and paying new attention to making animated series. In essence, this shift created a second studio system for cartoons, one that is run by cable networks. This second studio system has created a second group of star directors and a new stable of beloved characters. This newer studio system ushered in what some people have called the Second Golden Age of Cartoons.

Equally important, the success of these series showed that creator-driven shows work. And although trying to bring the process to television was not simple, the success showed that the creator-driven production process could be adapted to work within current television budgets and schedules.

In retrospect, it also seems evident that animators in the 1990s may have had an easier time bringing their vision to air. During the 1940s, directors such as Bob Clampett and Bobe Cannon were often only able to bring their sensibilities to existing characters. Yet in the 1990s, despite more attention from producers and network executives, John Kricfalusi and Genndy Tartakovsky were allowed to be auteurs, to create their own characters, and to envision their own universes and bring them to life.

As I write this in the early twenty-first century, cable television does not consistently offer as much of a creator-friendly culture for those who want to make funny cartoons. Most networks are not looking as aggressively for funny cartoons and characters. Also, creators are coming from other areas of the industry as writers, producers, and even researchers are creating successful and endearing characters. Surprisingly, much of the innovation in styles and techniques is happening in preschool animation, where programs for viewers ages two to five are as innovative as, and perhaps even more unusual than, anything made in the early 1990s, thanks to advances in technology and more opportunities to make animation for this age group.

The expectation is that in just a matter of a few years material will be produced for multiple platforms in multiple formats. Artists and executives alike are watching with great curiosity to see which platforms ultimately will be the most successful, as well as which ones will give the creative talent the most control.

NOTES

1. Tom Sito, telephone interview with author, Jan. 24, 2008.
2. Ibid.
3. Maltin, *Of Mice and Magic*, 337.
4. Barbera, *My Life in 'Toons*, 115.
5. Ibid.
6. For additional information on the history of Nickelodeon see my "The Early Days of Nicktoons."
7. Herb Scannell, telephone interview with author, July 3, 2002.
8. "Ottawa 06 Celebrates the Genius of Bob Clampett," 1.
9. Langer, "Bob Clampett at Warner Bros.," 36.
10. Ibid.

11. Kricfalusi, "The Importance of Having a Lot of Influences."

12. Quoted in McCracken, "My Intended Audience Was Everybody."

13. Kricfalusi, commentary on *The Great Piggy Bank Robbery,* *Looney Tunes Golden Collection,* vol. 2 (Burbank: Warner Bros., 2004), DVD, Disc Three, Track 13, commentary track.

14. Barrier, "An Exchange with John K."

15. Kricfalusi, "The Importance of Having a Lot of Influences."

16. Lenburg, *Who's Who in Animated Cartoons,* 42.

17. Maltin, *Of Mice and Magic,* 321.

18. Amidi, *Cartoon Modern,* 130.

19. Genndy Tartakovsky, telephone interview with author, Sept. 23, 1999.

20. Ibid.

21. Ibid.

22. Ibid.

BIBLIOGRAPHY

Aberdeen, J. J. *Hollywood Renegades: The Society of Independent Motion Picture Producers.* Los Angeles: Cobblestone Entertainment, 2000.

Adamson, Joe. *Tex Avery: King of Cartoons.* New York: Popular Library, 1975.

———. "'Where Can I Get a Good Corned Beef Sandwich?' An Oral History of Dave Fleischer (1969)." Courtesy of Center for Advanced Film Studies. American Film Institute Mayer Library, Los Angeles.

———. "With Disney on Olympus: An interview with Dick Huemer." *Funnyworld* 17 (1978): 37–45.

———. "Working for the Fleischers: An Interview with Dick Huemer." *Funnyworld* 16 (winter 1974–75): 23–25.

Adorno, Theodor W. "Chaplin in Malibu (1964)." In "Chaplin Times Two." Translated by John MacKay. *Yale Journal of Criticism* 9, no. 1 (1996): 58–61.

Allen, Jeanne Thomas. "Copyright and Early Theater, Vaudeville, and Film Competition." In Fell, *Film before Griffith,* 176–95.

Allen, Robert C. *Horrible Prettiness: Burlesque and American Culture.* Chapel Hill: University of North Carolina Press, 1991.

———. "Vaudeville and Film, 1895–1915: A Study in Media Interaction." PhD diss., University of Iowa, 1977.

Altman, Rick. *The American Film Musical.* Bloomington: Indiana University Press, 1989.

———. "The Sound of Sound: A Brief History of the Reproduction of Sound in Movie Theaters." *Cineaste* 21, nos. 1–2 (1995): 68–72.

Amidi, Amid. *Cartoon Modern: Style and Design in Fifties Animation.* San Francisco: Chronicle Books, 2006.

Appleton, Victor. *Tom Swift and His Airship.* New York: Grosset and Dunlap, 1910.

———. *Tom Swift and His Motor Cycle.* New York: Grosset and Dunlap, 1910.

Baker, Bob. "Max and Dave Fleischer." *Film Dope* (Feb. 1979): 27–29.

Bakhtin, M. M. *Rabelais and His World.* Bloomington: Indiana University Press, 1984.

Barbera, Joe. *My Life In 'Toons*. Atlanta: Turner Publishing, 1994.

Barrier, Michael. "An Exchange with John K." Michael Barrier.com. Aug. 21–Sept. 23, 2004. www.michaelbarrier.com/Feedback/feedback_johnk.htm.

———. *Hollywood Cartoons: American Animation in Its Golden Age*. New York: Oxford University Press, 1999.

———. "Interview with Frank Tashlin." In Garcia, *Frank Tashlin*, 155–60.

Barthes, Roland. "The Reality Effect." In *The Rustle of Language*, translated by Richard Howard, 141–48. Berkeley: University of California Press, 1989.

Bazelon, Irwin. *Knowing the Score: Notes on Film Music*. New York: Arco, 1975.

Bean, Annemarie, James Hatch, and Brooks McNamara, eds. *Inside the Minstrel Mask: Readings in Nineteenth-Century Blackface Minstrelsy*. Middletown, CT: Wesleyan University Press, 1996.

Belington, Monroe. "The New Deal Was a Joke: Political Humor during the Great Depression." *Journal of American Culture* 5, no. 33 (fall 1982): 15–21.

Benjamin, Walter. "The Work of Art in the Age of Its Technological Reproducibility." In *The Work of Art in the Age of Its Technological Reproducibility, and Other Writings on Media*, edited by Michael Jennings, Brigid Doherty, and Thomas Y. Levin, 19–55. Cambridge, MA: Harvard University Press, 2008.

Berger, Peter. *Redeeming Laughter: The Comic Dimension of Human Experience*. New York: Walter De Gruyter, 1997.

Bergson, Henri. *Laughter: An Essay on the Meaning of the Comic* (1904). Translated by Cloudesley Brereton and Fred Rothwell. New York: Macmillan, 1911. Repr. edited by Wylie Sypher. Garden City, NY: Doubleday Anchor, 1956.

Bisch, Louis E. "What Makes You Laugh?" *Photoplay*, June 1928, 34–35, 126.

Blackbeard, Bill, and Martin Williams. *The Smithsonian Collection of Newspaper Comics*. Washington: Smithsonian Institution Press, 1978.

Blum, Daniel. *A Pictorial History of the American Theatre, 1860–1970*. New York: Crown, 1971.

Borde, Raymond. "Le mystère bricolo." *Midi minuit fantastique* 17 (1967): 62–65.

Bordwell, David, and Kristin Thompson. *Film Art: An Introduction*. 7th edn. New York: McGraw-Hill, 2004.

Bower, Anthony. "Snow White and the 1,200 Dwarfs," *Nation*, May 10, 1941, 565.

The Bowers Mother Goose Movie Book. 1923. Repr. Putney, VT: Optical Toys, n.d. http://opticaltoys.com.

"Bowers Plans Comedy Series with Thomas." *Motion Picture Herald*, Feb. 24, 1934.

Bradley, Scott. "Music in Cartoons: Excerpts from a Talk Given at the Music Forum, October 28, 1944." *Film Music Notes* 4, no. 3 (Dec. 1944): unpaginated.

Braithwaite, Ronald L., and Kimberly R. J. Arriola. "Male Prisoners and HIV Prevention: A Call for Action Ignored." *American Journal of Public Health* 93 (May 2003): 759–63.

Bray, Glenn. *The Original Art of Basil Wolverton*. New York: Last Gasp, 2007.

Breton, André. "Note sur le cinéma à propos du film *It's a Bird*." In *Œuvres complètes*, vol. 2. Paris: Gallimard, 1992.

Brooks, Daphne. *Bodies in Dissent: Spectacular Performances of Race and Freedom, 1850–1910*. Durham, NC: Duke University Press, 2006.

Brophy, Philip. "The Animation of Sound." In *The Illusion of Life: Essays on Animation,* edited by Alan Cholodenko, 67–112. Sydney: Power Publications, 1991. www .philipbrophy.com/projects/sncnm/AnimationSound.html.

———. "The Body Horrible." *Intervention,* nos. 22/23 (1988). www.philipbrophy.com/ projects/bdyhrbl/BodyHorrible.html.

———. "I Scream in Silence: Cinema, Sex & the Sound of Women Dying." In *Cinesonic: The World of Sound in Film,* edited by Philip Brophy, 51–78. Sydney: AFTRS Publishing, 1999. www.philipbrophy.com/projects/cnsnc/1998_ScreamInSilence.html.

Brown, Jayna. *Babylon Girls: Black Women Performers and the Shaping of the Modern.* Durham, NC: Duke University Press, 2008.

Brown, Wendy. "Wounded Attachments." *Political Theory* 21, no. 3 (Aug. 1993): 390–410.

Bush, Stephen. "The Single Reel—II." *Moving Picture World,* July 4, 1914.

Caldwell, John T. "Welcome to the Viral Future of Cinema (Television)." *Cinema Journal* 45, no. 1 (fall 2005): 90–97.

Canemaker, John. "Art Babbitt: The Animator as Firebrand." *Millimeter* 3, no. 9 (Sept. 1975): 8–11, 42–45.

———. "The Birth of Animation." *Millimeter* 3, no. 4 (April 1975): 14–16.

———. *Felix: The Twisted Tale of the World's Most Famous Cat.* New York: Pantheon, 1991.

———. "A Final Interview with Otto Messmer." Dec. 31, 1984. Canemaker Collection, Fales Library, New York University.

———. "Otto Messmer Interview." March 5, 1975, Fort Lee, NJ. Canemaker Collection, Fales Library, New York University.

———. "Profile of an Animation Living Legend: J. R. Bray." *Filmmakers Newsletter* 8, no. 3 (Jan. 1975): n.p.

———. *Tex Avery: The MGM Years, 1942–1955.* Atlanta: Turner Publishing, 1996.

Carbaga, Leslie. *The Fleischer Story in the Golden Age of Animation.* New York: Nostalgia Press, 1976.

Carroll, Noël. "Notes on the Sight Gag." In *Comedy/Cinema/Theory,* edited by Andrew Horton, 25–42. Berkeley: University of California Press, 1991.

"Cartoon Making Kicked Around." *Variety,* May 28, 1947.

Cavalieri, Joey. "Jewish Mice, Bubblegum Cards, Comics Art, and Raw Possibilities." *Comics Journal* 65 (Aug. 1981): 98–125.

"Charles Bowers; Pioneer in Film Cartoons; Jersey Writer, Director and Producer's Career Began at 6 on Tightwire." *New York Herald Tribune,* Nov. 27, 1946. Charles Bowers clipping file. Billy Rose Theatre Collection, New York Public Library.

Chion, Michel. *Audio-Vision: Sound on Screen.* Edited and translated by Claudia Gorbman. New York: Columbia University Press, 1994.

Chude-Sokei, Louis. *The Last "Darky": Bert Williams, Black-on-Black Minstrelsy, and the African Diaspora.* Durham, NC: Duke University Press, 2006.

Churchill, Winston. "Everybody's Language" (1935). In Schickel, *The Essential Chaplin,* 205–14.

Clover, Carol. "Dancin' in the Rain." *Critical Inquiry* 21, no. 4 (summer 1995): 722–47.

Cockrell, Dale. *Demons of Disorder: Early Blackface Minstrels and Their World.* New York: Cambridge University Press, 1997.

Cohan, Steven, ed. *Hollywood Musicals, the Film Reader.* New York: Routledge, 2002.

Cohen, Karl F. *Forbidden Animation: Censored Cartoons and Blacklisted Animators in America.* Jefferson, NC: McFarland, 1997.

Coleman, Vera. Vera Coleman to William Welling. Sept. 15, 1934. Fleischer family collection.

Crafton, Donald. *Before Mickey: The Animated Film, 1898–1928.* Chicago: University of Chicago Press, 1993.

———. "The Last Night in the Nursery: Walt Disney's *Peter Pan.*" *Velvet Light Trap* 24 (fall 1989): 33–52.

———. "Pie and Chase: Gag, Spectacle and Narrative in Slapstick Comedy." In Karnick and Jenkins, *Classical Hollywood Comedy,* 106–19. Repr. in *The Cinema of Attractions Reloaded,* edited by Wanda Strauven, 335–64. Amsterdam: Amsterdam University Press, 2006.

———. "The View from Termite Terrace: Caricature and Parody in Warner Bros. Animation." In *Reading the Rabbit: Explorations in Warner Bros.,* edited by Kevin S. Sandler, 101–20. New Brunswick, NJ: Rutgers University Press, 1998.

Cripps, Thomas. Review of *Blackface, White Noise: Jewish Immigrants in the Hollywood Melting Pot,* by Michael Rogin. *Journal of American History* 83, no. 4 (March 1997): 1462–63.

———. *Slow Fade to Black: The Negro in American Films, 1900–1942.* New York: Oxford, 1995.

Critchley, Simon. *On Humor.* London: Routledge, 2002.

Crowther, Bosley. "Films for the Fair." *New York Times,* March 5, 1939.

Culhane, Shamus. Interview by Greg Ford, Jan. 3, 1979.

———. *Talking Animals and Other People.* New York: St. Martin's, 1986.

Curtis, James. *Between Flops: A Biography of Preston Sturges.* New York: Harcourt Brace Jovanovich, 1982.

"Cut Cartoon Output." *Variety,* June 11, 1947.

Deneroff, Harvey Raphael. *Popeye the Union Man: A Historical Study of the Fleischer Strike.* PhD diss., University of Southern California, 1985.

Derrida, Jacques. "History of the Lie." In *Futures of Jacques Derrida,* edited by Richard Rand, 65–98. Stanford: Stanford University Press, 2001.

de Seife, Ethan. *Cheerful Nihilism: The Films of Frank Tashlin.* Middletown, CT: Wesleyan University Press, forthcoming.

Dinerstein, Joel. *Swinging the Machine: Modernity, Technology, and African American Culture between the World Wars.* Amherst: University of Massachusetts Press, 2003.

Disney, Walt. "Growing Pains." *Journal of the Society of Motion Picture Engineers* 36 (1941): 30–40.

"Disney and RKO Discuss." *Motion Picture Herald,* July 2, 1938.

"Disney Feature." *Variety,* May 29, 1940.

"Disney Film Picketed." *New York Times,* July 25, 1941.

"Disney Preparing Eight New Features." *Motion Picture Herald,* June 1, 1946.

"Disney Rides a Baby Elephant Back into Hearts of His Fans." *Newsweek,* Oct. 27, 1941.

"Disney-RKO Deal." *Variety,* March 4, 1936.

"Disney's 800G Melon." *Variety,* June 29, 1938.

"Disney's 'Revolution.'" *Motion Picture Herald,* March 16, 1940.

"Disney's Self-Trailer." *Variety,* Oct. 2, 1940.

"Distribution for *Fantasia.*" *Variety,* Aug. 21, 1940.

Douglas, Susan J. *Inventing American Broadcasting, 1899–1922.* Baltimore: Johns Hopkins University Press, 1987.

"Draggin' Disney's *Dragon* into N.Y." *Variety,* July 23, 1941.

Dubin, Joe. "News Items . . . Comments." *Film Music Notes* 5, no. 5 (Jan. 1946): n.p.

Du Bois, W. E. B. *The Souls of Black Folk.* 1903. New York: Oxford University Press, 2007.

"*Dumbo.*" *Film Daily,* Oct. 1, 1941.

"*Dumbo.*" *Theatre Arts* (Dec. 1941): 907.

"*Dumbo.*" *Variety,* Oct. 1, 1941.

"*Dumbo* Gets Earlier Release." *Variety,* Dec. 11, 1940.

Du Pasquier, Sylvain. "Buster Keaton's Gags." *Journal of Modern Literature* 3, no. 2 (April 1973): 269–91.

Durgnat, Raymond. *The Crazy Mirror.* London: Faber and Faber, 1969.

Dyer, Richard. "Judy Garland and Camp." In Cohan, *Hollywood Musicals, the Film Reader,* 107–14.

Edsforth, Ronald. *The New Deal: America's Response to the Great Depression.* Malden, MA: Blackwell, 2000.

"Educational Acquires Vocafilm." *Motion Picture News,* Jan. 14, 1928.

Eisenstein, Sergei M. *On Disney.* Translated by Jay Leyda. London, Methuen, 1988.

Ely, Melvin P. *The Adventures of Amos 'n' Andy: A Social History of an American Phenomenon.* New York: Free Press, 1991.

Eugster, Al. Interview by Greg Ford, c. 1979.

———. Interview by Mark Langer, March 1975.

"Exhibitors Lining Up for Laugh Month." *Motion Picture News,* Dec. 18, 1926.

"Expansion of Short Subjects." *Film Daily,* May 30, 1926.

Fanon, Frantz. *Black Skin, White Masks.* New York: Grove, 1967.

"*Fantasia* Has Grossed." *Variety,* April 30, 1941.

"*Fantasia* under RKO Release." *Film Daily,* May 6, 1941.

Farnsworth, Marjorie. *The Ziegfeld Follies.* New York: Bonanza Books, 1956.

Faure, Elia. "The Art of Charlie Chaplin" (1923). In Schickel, *The Essential Chaplin,* 76–84.

F.B.O. [advertisement] *Motion Picture News,* May 22, 1926.

"F.B.O. Has 54 for 1926–27." *Motion Picture News,* May 22, 1926.

"F.B.O. Has New Comedy Series." *Motion Picture News,* May 8, 1926.

Fell, John L., ed. *Film before Griffith.* Berkeley: University of California Press, 1983.

———. "Motive, Mischief, and Melodrama: The State of Film Narrative in 1907." In Fell, *Film before Griffith,* 272–83.

Ferguson, Niall. "A Runaway Deficit May Soon Test Obama's Luck." *Financial Times,* Aug. 10, 2009.

Ferguson, Otis. "Two for the Show." *New Republic,* Oct. 27, 1941.

Ferriano, Frank. "Did He Write That? America's Great Unknown Song Writer, Harold Arlen." *Tracking* 3, no. 1 (Dec. 1990): 8–17.

Film Daily Yearbook, 1934. New York: Film Daily, 1934.

Finch, Christopher. *The Art of Walt Disney.* New York: Abrams, 1973.

Fleischer, Lou. Interview by Ray Pointer, 1972. Langer's private collection.

Ford, Greg. "'Cross-referred Media': Frank Tashlin's Cartoon Work." In Garcia, *Frank Tashlin,* 79–84.

Ford, Greg, and Richard Thompson. "Chuck Jones." *Film Comment* 11, no. 1 (Jan.-Feb. 1975): 21–38.

Franklin, Joe. *Joe Franklin's Encyclopedia of Comedians.* Secaucus, NJ: Citadel Press, 1979.

Freud, Sigmund. "Fetishism" (1927). In *Sexuality and the Psychology of Love.* Edited by Phillip Rieff. Translated by Joan Riviere, 204–9. New York: Touchstone Books, 1997.

———. "Humor" (1928). In *Character and Culture.* Edited by Phillip Rieff. Translated by Joan Riviere. New York: Collier Books, 1970.

———. "The Joke and the Varieties of the Comic" (1905). In *The Joke and Its Relation to the Unconscious.* Translated by Joyce Crick, 175–231. New York: Penguin, 2003.

———. "The Relation of Jokes to Dreams and to the Unconscious" (1905). In *Jokes and Their Relation to the Unconscious.* Edited and translated by James Strachey, 197–223. New York: Penguin, 1990.

———. "The Relation of the Joke to Dreams and to the Unconscious" (1905). In *The Joke and Its Relation to the Unconscious.* Translated by Joyce Crick, 154–74. New York: Penguin, 2003.

Gabbard, Krin. *Jammin' at the Margins: Jazz and the American Cinema.* Chicago: University of Chicago Press, 1996.

———, ed. *Representing Jazz.* Durham, NC: Duke University Press, 1995.

Gallup, George. Interview by Thomas Simonet, Princeton, NJ, Sept. 1977.

Garcia, Roger, ed. *Frank Tashlin.* London: British Film Institute, 1994.

Garity, W. E., and J. L. Ledeen. "The New Walt Disney Studio." *Journal of the Society of Motion Picture Engineers* 36 (1941): 7–8.

Geisel, Theodor, and Maurice Sendak. *The Secret Art of Dr. Seuss.* New York: Random House, 1995.

"General Distribution for Disney *Fantasia.*" *Motion Picture Herald,* May 3, 1941.

Gennari, John. *Blowin' Hot and Cool: Jazz and Its Critics.* Chicago: University of Chicago Press, 2006.

Giddens, Anthony. *The Consequences of Modernity.* Stanford: Stanford University Press, 1990.

Gilbert, Douglas. *American Vaudeville: Its Life and Times.* New York: Dover, 1963.

Goldmark, Daniel. *Tunes for 'Toons: Music and the Hollywood Cartoon.* Berkeley: University of California Press, 2005.

Goldstein, Donna M. *Laughter Out of Place: Race, Class, Violence, and Sexuality in a Rio Shantytown.* Berkeley: University of California Press, 2003.

Gomery, Douglas. *The Coming of Sound: A History.* New York: Routledge, 2005.

———. "Disney's Business History: A Reinterpretation." In *Disney Discourse: Producing the Magic Kingdom,* edited by Eric Smoodin, 71–86. New York: Routledge, 1994.

Gorbman, Claudia. *Unheard Melodies: Narrative Film Music.* Bloomington: Indiana University Press, 1987.

"Government Holds Off." *Variety,* July 16, 1941.

Green, Abel, and Joe Laurie Jr. *Showbiz from Vaude to Video.* New York: Henry Holt, 1951.

"Gross Rental from *Snow White*." *Variety,* July 19, 1939.

Groth, Gary, and Greg Sadowski. *Will Elder: The Mad Playboy of Art.* Seattle: Fantagraphics, 2003.

Gunning, Tom. "Attractions: How they Came into the World." In *The Cinema of Attractions Reloaded,* edited by Wanda Strauven, 31–39. Amsterdam: Amsterdam University Press, 2006.

———. "The Cinema of Attractions: Early Film, Its Spectator and the Avant-Garde." In *Early Cinema: Space, Frame, Narrative,* edited by Thomas Elsaesser, 56–62. London: British Film Institute, 1990.

———. "Crazy Machines in the Garden of Forking Paths: Mischief Gags and the Origins of American Film Comedy." In Karnick and Jenkins, *Classical Hollywood Comedy,* 87–105.

———. "Enigmas, Understanding, and Further Questions: Early Cinema Research in Its Second Decade since Brighton." *Persistence of Vision* 9 (1991): 4–9.

———. "An Unseen Energy Fills The Space." In Fell, *Film before Griffith,* 335–66.

Hall, Stuart. "Racist Ideologies and the Media." In *Media Studies: A Reader,* edited by Paul Marris and Sue Thornham, 271–82. New York: New York University Press, 2000.

Halttunen, Karen. *Confidence Men and Painted Women: A Study of Middle-Class Culture in America, 1830–1870.* New Haven, CT: Yale University Press, 1982.

Hamilton, Marie L. "Music and Theatrical Shorts." *Film Music Notes* 6, no. 2 (Nov. 1946): 19.

Hammond, Percy. "Cohan Is Too Busy to Resent Appellation." *New York Tribune,* March 12, 1922.

Hand, Dave. *Memoirs.* Cambria, CA: privately published, n.d.

Handzo, Stephen. "Appendix: A Narrative Glossary of Film Sound Technology." In *Film Sound: Theory and Practice,* edited by Elisabeth Weis and John Belton, 383–426. New York: Columbia University Press, 1985.

Hansen, Miriam Bratu. "The Mass Production of the Senses: Classical Cinema as Vernacular Modernism," *Modernism/Modernity* 6, no. 2 (1999): 59–77. Repr. in *Reinventing Film Studies,* edited by Christine Gledhill and Linda Williams, 332–50. London: Arnold, 2000.

———. "Of Mice and Ducks: Benjamin and Adorno on Disney." *South Atlantic Quarterly* 92, no. 1 (winter 1993): 27–61.

Hark, Ina Rae, ed. *American Cinema in the 1930s.* New Brunswick, NJ: Rutgers University Press, 2008.

Harris, Neil. *Humbug: The Art of P. T. Barnum.* Boston: Little, Brown, 1973.

Hartman, Saidiya. *Scenes of Subjection: Terror, Slavery, and Self-Making in Nineteenth-Century America.* New York: Oxford University Press, 1997.

Harvey, Doug. "The Closer You Look, the Prettier It Ain't: Basil Wolverton's Microscopic Grotesque." In *The Original Art of Basil Wolverton from the Collection of Glenn Bray,* 14–23. New York: Last Gasp, 2007.

Hefner, Hugh, ed. *Playboy's Little Annie Fannie.* New York: Dark Horse Comics, 2001.

Henderson, Brian. "Cartoon and Narrative in the Films of Frank Tashlin and Preston

Sturges," In *Comedy/Cinema/Narrative*, edited by Andrew Horton, 153–73. Berkeley: University of California Press, 1991.

Henderson, Schuyler. "Disregarding the Suffering of Others: Narrative, Comedy, and Torture." *Literature and Medicine* 24, no. 2 (fall 2005): 181–208.

Herrnstein, Richard J., and Charles Murray. *The Bell Curve: Intelligence and Class Structure in American Life*. New York: Free Press, 1994.

Hillier, Jim, ed. *Cahiers du cinéma, the 1950s: Neo-realism, Hollywood, New Wave*. Cambridge, MA: Harvard University Press, 1985.

Hoberman, J. "Vulgar Modernism." *Artforum* 20, no. 6 (Jan. 1982): 71–76. Repr. in Hoberman, *Vulgar Modernism*, 32–39.

———, ed. *Vulgar Modernism: Writing on Movies and Other Media*. Philadelphia: Temple University Press, 1991.

Holberg, Amelia. "Betty Boop: Jewish Film Star." *American Jewish History* 87, no. 4 (Dec. 1999): 291–312.

Hösle, Vittorio. *Woody Allen: An Essay on the Nature of the Comical*. Notre Dame: University of Notre Dame Press, 2007.

Howard, Hamp. *Max Fleischer Autobiography*. Miami: Fleischer Studios, 1938.

Howe, Irving. *World of Our Fathers*. New York: Bantam, 1980.

Huemer, Richard. "Humoresque." *Funnyworld* 19 (fall 1978): 35–36. In Charles Bowers clippings file. Billy Rose Theatre Collection, New York Public Library.

———. "Pioneer Portraits." *Cartoonist Profiles* 1, no. 3 (summer 1969): 14–18.

Huizinga, Johan. *Homo Ludens*. Boston: Beacon, 1955.

Ignatiev, Noel. *Race Traitor*. New York: Routledge, 1996.

Jacobs, Meg. *Pocketbook Politics: Economic Citizenship in Twentieth-Century America*. Princeton, NJ: Princeton University Press, 2005.

Jahn, Gary R. "The Aesthetic Theory of Leo Tolstoy's *What Is Art?*" *Journal of Aesthetics and Art Criticism* 34, no. 1 (autumn 1975): 59–65.

Jameson, Fredric. *Archaeologies of the Future: The Desire Called Utopia and Other Science Fictions*. London: Verso, 2005.

Jenkins, Henry. "'This Fellow Keaton Seems to Be the Whole Show': Buster Keaton, Interrupted Performance, and the Vaudeville Aesthetic." In *Buster Keaton's "Sherlock Jr.,"* edited by Andrew Horton, 29–66. Cambridge: Cambridge University Press, 1997.

———. *What Made Pistachio Nuts? Early Sound Comedy and the Vaudeville Aesthetic*. New York: Columbia University Press, 1992.

———. *The Wow Climax: Tracing Emotion through Popular Culture*. New York: New York University Press, 2006.

Jones, Chuck. "132 Takes/Th-Th-That's All Folks." *Film Comment* 25, no. 2 (March-April 1989): 2–3.

———. *Chuck Amuck*. London: Simon and Schuster, 1990.

———. *Chuck Reducks: Drawing from the Fun Side of Life*. New York: Warner Books, 1996.

———. "Music and the Animated Cartoon." *Hollywood Quarterly* 1, no. 4 (July 1946): 363–70. Repr. in *The Cartoon Music Book*, edited by Daniel Goldmark and Yuval Taylor, 93–102. Chicago: A Cappella Books, 2002.

Karlin, Fred, and Rayburn Wright. *On the Track: A Guide to Contemporary Film Scoring.* 2nd edn. New York: Routledge, 2004.

Karnick, Kristine Brunovska, and Henry Jenkins, eds. *Classical Hollywood Comedy.* New York: Routledge, 1995.

Kausler, Mark, John Cawley, and Jim Korkis. "Animated Oscars." *Cartoon Quarterly* 1 (1988): 15–18.

Kazin, Alfred. *A Walker in the City.* New York: Harcourt Brace, 1951.

Keaton, Buster, and Charles Samuels. *My Wonderful World of Slapstick.* New York: Da Capo, 1960.

Keezer, Dexter M. "The Consumer under the National Recovery Administration." *Annals of the American Academy of Political and Social Science* 172 (March 1934): 88–97.

Kerr, Walter. *The Silent Clowns.* New York: Knopf, 1975.

Keynes, John Maynard. *The Means to Prosperity.* New York: Harcourt, Brace, 1933.

Kiley, Dan. *The Peter Pan Syndrome: Men Who Have Never Grown Up.* New York: Dodd, Mead, 1983.

King, Geoff. *Film Comedy.* London: Wallflower, 2002.

King, Rob. "'Uproarious Inventions': The Keystone Film Company, Mass Culture, and the Art of the Motor." *Film History* 19, no. 3 (2007): 271–91.

Kinkle, Roger D., ed. *The Complete Encyclopedia of Popular Music and Jazz, 1900–1950.* 4 vols. New Rochelle, NY: Arlington House, 1974.

Kinney, Jack. *Walt Disney and Assorted Other Characters: An Unauthorized Account of the Early Years at Disney's.* New York: Harmony Books, 1988.

Klein, Norman M. *Seven Minutes: The Life and Death of the American Animated Cartoon.* New York: Verso, 1993.

Kline, Wendy. *Building a Better Race: Gender, Sexuality, and Eugenics from the Turn of the Century to the Baby Boom.* Berkeley: University of California Press, 2001.

Knight, Arthur. *Disintegrating the Musical: Black Performance and American Musical Film.* Durham, NC: Duke University Press, 2002.

Kozlenko, William. "The Animated Film and Walt Disney." *New Theatre* 3, no. 8 (Aug. 1936): 17–18.

Kracauer, Siegfried. "Cult of Distraction." Translated by Thomas Y. Levin. *New German Critique* 40 (winter 1987): 91–96.

———. "Preston Sturges or Laughter Betrayed." *Films in Review* 1, no. 1 (Feb. 1950): 11–13, 43–47.

Kricfalusi, John. "The Importance of Having a Lot of Influences." *John K. Stuff.* Sept. 27, 2006. http://johnkstuff.blogspot.com/2006/09/importance-of-having-lot-of-influences.html.

Krutnik, Frank. "The Clown-Prints of Comedy." *Screen* 24, no. 4/5 (July–Oct. 1984): 50–59.

"Labor Conciliator Steps In." *Variety,* July 9, 1941.

Lampe, J. Bodewalt. *Remick Folio of Moving Picture Music.* New York: J. H. Remick, 1914.

Landesman, Alter. *Brownsville: The Birth, Development and Passing of a Jewish Community in New York.* New York: Bloch, 1971.

———. "A Neighborhood Survey of Brownsville." Manuscript (1927). Jewish Division, New York Public Library.

Langer, Mark. "Bob Clampett at Warner Bros." Program guide, Sept. 2006. Ottawa 06 International Animation Festival. Ottawa, Ontario.

———. "The Disney-Fleischer Dilemma: Product Differentiation and Technological Innovation." *Screen* 33, no. 4 (winter 1992): 343–60.

———."The Fleischer Rotoscope Patent." *Animation Journal* 1, no. 2 (spring 1993): 66–73.

———. "Institutional Power and the Fleischer Studios: The *Standard Production Reference*," *Cinema Journal* 30, no. 2 (winter 1991): 3–22.

———. Interview with Richard Fleischer, Nov. 8, 1990.

———. "Max and Dave Fleischer." *Film Comment* 11, no. 1 (Jan.-Feb. 1975): 48–56.

———. "Polyphony and Heterogeneity in Early Fleischer Films: Comic Strips, Vaudeville, and New York Style." *Persistence of Vision* 13 (1997): 65–87.

Lanza, Joseph. "Rhapsody in Spew: Romantic Underscores in *The Ren & Stimpy Show*." In *The Cartoon Music Book,* edited by Daniel Goldmark and Yuval Taylor, 269–74. Chicago: A Cappella Books, 2002.

"'Laugh Recorder' Try Out in Los Angeles." *Motion Picture News,* March 31, 1928.

Laurie, Joe, Jr. *Vaudeville: From the Honky-Tonks to the Palace.* Port Washington, NY: Kennikat Press, 1972.

Lave, Jean, and Etienne Wenger. *Situated Learning: Legitimate Peripheral Participation.* Cambridge: Cambridge University Press, 1991.

Leach, William. *Land of Desire: Merchants, Power, and the Rise of a New American Culture.* New York: Pantheon, 1993.

Lears, T. J. Jackson. *Fables of Abundance: A Cultural History of Advertising in America.* New York: Basic Books, 1994.

———. *No Place of Grace: Antimodernism and the Transformation of American Culture, 1880–1920.* Chicago: University of Chicago Press, 1981.

Léger, Fernand. "A New Realism—the Object" (1926). In *Theories of Modern Art,* edited by Herschel B. Chipp, 279–80. Berkeley: University of California Press, 1968.

Lehman, Christopher P. *The Colored Cartoon: Black Representation in American Animated Short Films, 1907–1954.* Amherst: University of Massachusetts Press, 2007.

Lejeune, C. J. *Cinema.* London: Alexander Maclehose, 1931.

Lenburg, Jeff. *The Encyclopedia of Animated Cartoon Series.* New York: Da Capo, 1981.

———. *Who's Who in Animated Cartoons.* New York: Applause Theatre and Cinema Books, 2006.

Leslie, Esther. *Hollywood Flatlands: Animation, Critical Theory and the Avant-Garde.* London: Verso, 2002.

Levitt, Paul M. *Vaudeville Humor: The Collected Jokes, Routines, and Skits of Ed Lowry.* Carbondale: Southern Illinois University Press, 2002.

Lewis, Robert M., ed. *From Traveling Show To Vaudeville: Theatrical Spectacle In America, 1830 to 1910.* Baltimore: Johns Hopkins University Press, 2003.

Leyda, Jay, ed. *Eisenstein on Disney.* London: Methuen, 1988.

Lhamon, W. T. *Jump Jim Crow: Lost Plays, Lyrics, and Street Prose of the First Atlantic Popular Culture.* Cambridge, MA: Harvard University Press, 2003.

———. *Raising Cain: Blackface Performance from Jim Crow to Hip Hop.* Cambridge, MA: Harvard University Press, 1998.

Lindfors, Bernth, ed. *Africans on Stage: Studies in Ethnological Show Business.* Blooming-ton: Indiana University Press, 1999.

"Loss for Walt Disney." *Motion Picture Herald,* Dec. 28, 1940.

Lott, Eric. *Love and Theft: Blackface Minstrelsy and the American Working Class.* New York: Oxford University Press, 1993.

Lovett, Laura L. *Conceiving the Future: Pronatalism, Reproduction, and the Family in the United States, 1890–1938.* Chapel Hill: University of North Carolina Press, 2007.

"Lowell Thomas 'Tall Story' Comedies" [advertisement]. In *Film Daily Yearbook 1934,* 116. New York: Film Daily, 1934.

Luckett, Moya, "*Fantasia:* Cultural Constructions of Disney's 'Masterpiece.'" In *Disney Discourse,* edited by Eric Smoodin, 214–36. New York: Routledge, 1994.

Lutz, E. G. *Animated Cartoons: How They Are Made, Their Origin and Development.* New York: Charles Scribner's Sons, 1920. Facsimile repr. Bedford, MA: Applewood, 1998.

Mahar, William J. *Behind the Burnt Cork Mask: Early Blackface Minstrelsy and Ante-bellum American Popular Culture.* Urbana: University of Illinois Press, 1999.

Maltby, Richard. *Harmless Entertainment: Hollywood and the Ideology of Consensus.* Metuchen, NJ: Scarecrow Press, 1983.

Maltin, Leonard. *Of Mice and Magic.* New York: New American Library, 1980.

"Mammal-of-the-Year." *Time,* Dec. 29, 1941.

Marchand, Roland. *Advertising the American Dream: Making Way for Modernity, 1920–1940.* Berkeley: University of California Press, 1985.

Martin, André. *In Search of Raoul Barré.* Ottawa: Canadian Film Institute, 1976.

Martin, Waldo E. *"Brown v. Board of Education": A Brief History with Documents.* New York: St. Martins, 1998.

Marx, Karl. *Capital.* Vol. 1. Translated by Samuel Moore and Edward Aveling. Moscow: Foreign Languages Publishing House, 1961.

May, Lary. *Screening Out the Past.* Chicago: University of Chicago Press, 1980.

McCracken, Harry. "My Intended Audience Was Everybody." *Animato* 16 (spring 1988). www.harrymccracken.com/blog/my-intended-audience-was-everybody.

McGuire, Dewey. "Well, what do you know? The little light: It stays on!" *APATOONS* 121 (Aug. 2002): n.p.

McLaughlin, Robert. *Broadway and Hollywood: A History of Economic Interaction.* New York: Arno, 1974.

McLean, Albert F., Jr. *American Vaudeville as Ritual.* Lexington: University of Kentucky Press, 1965.

McNamara, Brooks. Introduction to *American Popular Entertainments: Jokes, Mono-logues, Bits, and Sketches,* edited by Brooks McNamara, 13–24. New York: Performing Arts Journal, 1983.

"Mediators Hope." *Variety,* June 18, 1941.

Merritt, Karen. "The Little Girl/Little Mother Transformation: The American Evolution of *Snow White and the Seven Dwarfs.*" In *Storytelling in Animation: The Art of the Animated Image,* vol. 2, edited by John Canemaker, 105–21. Los Angeles: American Film Institute, 1988.

Merritt, Russell, and J. B. Kaufman. *Walt Disney's Silly Symphonies.* Gemona, Italy: La Cineteca del Friuli, 2006.

"Mickey Mouse in Symphony." *Newsweek,* Nov. 25, 1940.

Miller, Ron, Rita Seiden Miller, and Stephen Karp. "The Fourth Largest City in America— A Sociological History of Brooklyn." In *Brooklyn USA: The Fourth Largest City in America,* edited by Rita Seiden Miller, 3–44. New York: Brooklyn College Press, 1979.

Moore, Deborah Dash. *At Home in America.* New York: Columbia University Press, 1981.

Moran, Kathleen, and Michael Rogin. "'What's the Matter with Capra?': *Sullivan's Travels* and the Popular Front." *Representations* 71 (summer 2000): 106–34.

Moritz, William. "Americans in Paris: Man Ray and Dudley Murphy." In *Lovers of Cinema: The First American Film Avant-Garde, 1919–1945,* edited by J. C. Horak, 120–30. Madison: University of Wisconsin Press, 1995.

———. "Some Observations on Non-Objective and Non-Linear Animation." In *Storytelling in Animation: The Art of the Animated Image,* vol. 2, edited by John Canemaker, 21–32. Los Angeles: American Film Institute, 1988.

Mounce, H. O. *Tolstoy on Aesthetics: What Is Art?* Aldershot, UK: Ashgate, 2001.

"Muller, Harold." *Motion Picture Studio Directory,* 1923/24.

Mumford, Lewis. *Technics and Civilization.* New York: Harcourt Brace, 1934.

Muscio, Giuliana. *Hollywood's New Deal.* Philadelphia: Temple University Press, 1996.

"Music and the Drama." *Chicago Record,* c. 1910. Robinson Locke Collection, New York Public Library.

Naremore, James. "Uptown Folks: Blackness and Entertainment in *Cabin in the Sky.*" In Gabbard, *Representing Jazz,* 169–92.

Nasaw, David. *Going Out: The Rise and Fall of Public Amusements.* New York: Basic Books, 1993.

Neupert, Richard. "Painting a Plausible World: Disney's Color Prototypes." In *Disney Discourse,* edited by Eric Smoodin, 106–17. New York: Routledge, 1994.

"The New Pictures." *Time,* Oct. 27, 1941.

"New Process." *Film Daily,* May 30, 1928.

Oberdeck, Kathryn. *The Evangelist and the Impresario: Religion, Entertainment, and Cultural Politics in America, 1884–1914.* Baltimore: Johns Hopkins University Press, 1999.

"Oil Industry Movie Presents New Hero." *New York Times,* May 23, 1939.

O'Meally, Robert. "Checking Our Balances: Ellison on Armstrong's Humor." *boundary 2* 30, no. 2 (2003): 115–36.

Omi, Michael, and Howard Winant. *Racial Formation in the United States from the 1960s to the 1990s.* New York: Routledge, 1994.

"Ottawa 06 Celebrates the Genius of Bob Clampett." Press release, Sept. 5, 2006. Ottawa 06 International Animation Festival. Ottawa, Ontario.

Page, Brett. *Writing for Vaudeville, with nine complete examples of various vaudeville forms by Richard Harding Davis, Aaron Hoffman, Edgar Allan Woolf, Taylor Granville, Louis Weslyn, Arthur Denvir, and James Madison.* Springfield, MA: Home Correspondence School, 1915.

Patterson, James T. *"Brown v. Board of Education": A Civil Rights Milestone and Its Troubled Legacy.* New York: Oxford University Press, 2002.

Peet, Bill. *An Autobiography.* Boston: Houghton Mifflin, 1989.

Place-Verghnes, Floriane. *Tex Avery: A Unique Legacy (1942–1955).* Eastleigh, UK: John Libbey Publishing, 2006.

Poe, Edgar Allan. "Diddling Considered as One of the Exact Sciences" (1850). http:// infomotions.com/etexts/literature/american/1800–1899/poe-diddling-433.htm.

Polan, Dana. "A Brechtian Cinema? Towards a Politics of Self-Reflexive Film." In *Movies and Methods,* vol. 2, edited by Bill Nichols, 661–71. Berkeley: University of California Press, 1985.

Prendergast, Roy M. *Film Music: A Neglected Art.* 2nd edn. New York: Norton, 1992.

"Prof. Semon at the Bijou." *Manitoba Free Press,* Nov. 5, 1895.

Prouty, Howard. "Filmography." In Garcia, *Frank Tashlin,* 197–240.

Pynchon, Thomas. "Mindful Mindlessness." Liner Notes for *Spiked! The Music of Spike Jones.* www.themodernword.com/pynchon/pynchon_music_jones.html.

Rabinovitz, Lauren. "The Coney Island Comedies: Bodies and Slapstick at the Amusement Park and the Movies." In *American Cinema's Transitional Era: Audiences, Institutions, Practices,* edited by Charlie Keil and Shelley Stamp, 171–90. Berkeley: University of California Press, 2004.

"'The Reluctant Dragon.'" *New York Times,* July 25, 1941.

Review of *Hop Off. Motion Picture News,* June 23, 1928.

Review of *Many a Slip. Motion Picture News,* Jan. 21, 1927.

Review of *Whoozit? Motion Picture News,* March 17, 1928.

RKO. ARI Correspondence File No. 2. In *RKO Papers.* Formerly at the RKO Studio, Culver City, California.

———. *Gallup Looks at the Movies: Audience Research Reports, 1940–1950.* Wilmington, DE: Scholarly Resources, 1979.

———. "President's Report of RKO Board Meeting, July 30, 1940." In Folder 681, Box 90, Record Group III 2C. Nelson Rockefeller Papers. Rockefeller Family Archives, Tarrytown, NY.

"RKO Radio Signs Pact." *Film Daily,* June 20, 1939.

"RKO Releasing *Fantasia.*" *Film Daily,* April 28, 1941.

"RKO's Budget." *Variety,* June 28, 1939.

Roberta. "Tintypes." *Fleischer's Animated News* 1, no. 10 (Sept. 1935).

Roberts, Richard M. "'Mixed Nuts' and Educational Pictures." *Classic Images,* Jan. 1992, 26–28.

Roberts, Sam. "A Nation of None and All of the Above." *New York Times,* Aug. 16, 2008.

Robinson, F. Miller. *The Man in the Bowler Hat.* Chapel Hill: University of North Carolina Press, 1993.

Roediger, David. *Towards the Abolition of Whiteness: Essays on Race, Politics, and Working Class History.* New York: Verso, 1994.

———. *The Wages of Whiteness: Race and the Making of the American Working Class.* New York: Verso, 1991.

Rogin, Michael. *Blackface, White Noise: Jewish Immigrants in the Hollywood Melting Pot.* Berkeley: University of California Press, 1996.

Rogoff, Barbara. *Everyday Cognition: Its Development in Social Context.* Cambridge, MA: Harvard University Press, 1984.

Roosevelt, Theodore. *American Ideals.* New York: G. P. Putnam's Sons, 1907.

———. *The New Nationalism.* New York: Outlook, 1911.

Rosenbaum, Jonathan. "Dream Masters II: Tex Avery." *Film Comment* 11, no. 1 (Jan.-Feb. 1975): 72–73.

Rourke, Constance. *American Humor: A Study of National Character.* New York: Harcourt Brace Jovanovich, 1931.

Rubin, Martin. "Movies and the New Deal in Entertainment." In Hark, *American Cinema of the 1930s: Themes and Variations,* 92–116.

Rydell, Robert W. *World of Fairs: The Century-of-Progress Expositions.* Chicago: University of Chicago Press, 1993.

Sampson, Henry T. *That's Enough, Folks: Black Images in Animated Cartoons, 1900–1960.* Lanham, MD: Scarecrow Press, 1998.

Samuel, Raphael. "Workshop of the World: Steam Power and Hand Technology in Mid-Victorian Britain." *History Workshop Journal* 3 (spring 1977): 6–72.

Sartin, Hank. "From Vaudeville to Hollywood, from Silence to Sound: Warner Bros. Cartoons of the Early Sound Era." In *Reading the Rabbit: Explorations in Warner Bros. Animation,* edited by Kevin Sandler, 67–85. New York: Routledge, 1998.

Saryian, Paul. "Out of the Inkwell with Betty Boop and Max Fleischer." Program for First Annual Nostalgia Convention, New York, 1975. Pacific Film Archives.

Schechner, Richard. *Performance Studies: An Introduction.* New York: Routledge, 2006.

Scheib, Ronnie. "Tex Arcana: The Cartoons of Tex Avery." In *The American Animated Cartoon: A Critical Anthology,* edited by Danny Peary and Gerald Peary, 110–27. New York: E. P. Dutton, 1980.

Schelly, William. *Harry Langdon.* Metuchen, NJ: Scarecrow Press, 1982.

Schickel, Richard. *The Disney Version: The Life, Times, Art, and Commerce of Walt Disney.* New York: Simon and Schuster, 1968; New York: Avon, 1969.

———, ed. *The Essential Chaplin.* Chicago: Ivan R. Dee, 2006.

———. "Introduction: The Tramp Transformed." In Schickel, *The Essential Chaplin,* 3–44.

Schneider, Steve. *That's All Folks! The Art of Warner Bros. Animation.* New York: Henry Holt, 1988.

Schroth, Raymond A. *"The Eagle" and Brooklyn.* Westport, CT: Greenwood Press, 1974.

Seidman, Steve. *Comedian Comedy: A Tradition in Hollywood Film.* Ann Arbor: UMI Research Press, 1981.

Seldes, Gilbert. "I Am Here Today" (1924/1957). In Schickel, *The Essential Chaplin,* 103–19.

Selznick, David O. Papers. Harry Ransom Humanities Research Center, University of Texas at Austin.

Sennett, Mack. Communication to Adolph Zukor, Dec. 13, 1917. Correspondence folder (1915–1919), General Files, Mack Sennett Collection. Margaret Herrick Library, Academy of Motion Picture Arts and Sciences.

Service, Robert W. *Songs of a Sourdough.* Toronto: William Briggs, 1907.

Seversky, Major Alexander P. de. *Victory through Air Power.* New York: Simon and Schuster, 1942.

Shale, Richard. *Donald Duck Joins Up: The Walt Disney Studio during World War II.* Ann Arbor: UMI Research Press, 1982.

Sharpsteen, Ben. Interview by Dave Smith, Feb. 6, 1974. Walt Disney Studio Archive.

"Short Subject Service Guide." *Motion Picture News,* April 15, 1927.

Simensky, Linda. "The Early Days of Nicktoons." In *Nickelodeon Nation,* edited by Heather Hendershot, 87–107. New York: New York University Press, 2004.

Singer, Ben. "Modernity, Hyperstimulus, and the Rise of Popular Sensationalism." In *Cinema and the Invention of Modern Life,* edited by Leo Charney and Vanessa Schwartz. Berkeley: University of California Press, 1995.

Sito, Tom. *Drawing the Line: The Untold Story of the Animation Unions from Bosko to Bart Simpson.* Lexington: University Press of Kentucky, 2006.

Sklar, Robert. "The Making of Cultural Myths—Walt Disney." In *The American Animated Cartoon: A Critical Anthology,* edited by Gerald Peary and Danny Peary, 58–65. New York: E. P. Dutton, 1980.

Slide, Anthony. *The Encyclopedia of Vaudeville.* Westport, CT: Greenwood Press, 1994.

Smith, Jeff. "Popular Songs and Comic Allusion in Contemporary Cinema." In *Soundtrack Available,* edited by Pamela Robertson Wojcik and Arthur Knight, 407–30. Durham, NC: Duke University Press, 2001.

Smith, Murray. *Engaging Characters: Fiction, Emotion, and the Cinema.* New York: Oxford University Press, 1995.

Smoodin, Eric. *Animating Culture: Hollywood Cartoons from the Sound Era.* New Brunswick, NJ: Rutgers University Press, 1993.

Smythe, Dallas. *Dependency Road: Communications, Capitalism, Consciousness and Canada.* Norwood, NJ: Ablex, 1981.

"*Snow White* Seen Headed for Record." *Motion Picture Herald,* Oct. 15, 1938.

Snyder, Robert W. *The Voice of the City: Vaudeville and Popular Culture in New York.* New York: Oxford University Press, 1989.

Sorin, Gerald. *The Nurturing Neighborhood.* New York: New York University Press, 1990.

Spiegelman, Art. *Breakdowns: Portrait of the Artist as a Young %@&*!* New York: Pantheon, 2008.

———. "Those Dirty Little Comics." In *Tijuana Bibles: Art and Wit in America's Forbidden Funnies,* edited by Bob Adelman. New York: Simon and Schuster, 1997.

Spiegelman, Art, and Chip Kidd. *Jack Cole and Plastic Man: Forms Stretched to Their Limits.* San Francisco: Chronicle Books, 2001.

Spitzer, Marian. *The Palace.* New York: Atheneum, 1969.

Standifer, James. "Musical Behaviors of Black People in American Society." *Black Music Research Journal* 1 (1980): 51–62.

"Start a Lecture Campaign in Your Theatre." *Triangle,* April 22, 1916.

Stein, Charles W. *American Vaudeville as Seen by Its Contemporaries.* New York: Alfred A. Knopf, 1984.

Sternfeld, Frederick W. "Kubik's McBoing Score with Excerpts of Score." *Film Music Notes* 10, no. 2 (Nov.-Dec. 1950): 8–16.

"Stoki-Disney *Fantasia* Roadshow Plan." *Variety,* March 20, 1940.

Stull, William. "*Fantasia* Sound." *Motion Picture,* Nov. 16, 1940. "Better Theaters" section.

———. "Fantasound." *American Cinematographer* (Feb. 1941): 58, 59, 80–81.

Sully, James. *An Essay on Laughter; Its Forms, Its Causes, Its Development and Its Value.* London: Longmans, Green, 1902.

Susman, Warren. "The People's Fair: Cultural Contradictions of a Consumer Society." In *Culture as History: The Transformation of American Society in the Twentieth Century.* New York: Pantheon, 1984.

Syrett, Harold Coffin. *The City of Brooklyn, 1865–1898.* New York: Columbia University Press, 1944.

Taussig, Michael. *Mimesis and Alterity: A Particular History of the Senses.* New York: Routledge, 1993.

Thomas, Frank, and Ollie Johnston. *Disney Animation: The Illusion of Life.* New York: Abbeville, 1981.

Thomas, Lowell. *Tall Stories: The Rise and Triumph of the Great American Whopper.* New York: Harcourt Brace Jovanovich, 1931.

Thompson, Kristin. "Implications of the Cel Animation Technique." In *The Cinematic Apparatus,* edited by Teresa de Lauretis and Stephen Heath, 106–20. New York: St. Martin's Press, 1980.

"Three-Minute Visit to Keystone Studio." *Triangle,* Nov. 27, 1915.

Tinkcom, Matthew. "'Working like a Homosexual': Camp Visual Cues and the Labor of Gay Subjects in the MGM Freed Unit." In Cohan, *Hollywood Musicals, the Film Reader,* 115–28.

Tolstoy, Leo. *What Is Art?* Translated by Richard Pevear and Larissa Volokhonsky. Harmondsworth, UK: Penguin, 1995.

U.S. Census Bureau. *The 1930 Federal Population Census Microfilm: District 163, Norwalk, Fairfield, Connecticut.* Washington: National Archives Trust Fund Board, 2002.

Villard, Oswald Garrison. "St. Clair McKelway." In *Proceedings of the Fifty-first Convention of the State of New York.* New York: n.p., 1915.

Vincendeau, Ginette. *Jean-Pierre Melville: An American in Paris.* London: British Film Institute, 2003.

"Vocafilm Busy Preparing New Acts." *Motion Picture News,* Jan. 21, 1928.

Walt Disney Studio. *Identification of Disney Characters.* Title Test Binder A–E, ARI Box 10, Walt Disney Studio Archives.

———. "The Walt Disney Studio Annual Report" for the fiscal year ending Sept. 27, 1947. Courtesy of Walt Disney Studio Investor Relations.

Wassenaar, Michael. "Strong to the Finich *[sic]*: Machines, Metaphor and Popeye the Sailor." *Velvet Light Trap* 24 (fall 1989): 20–32.

Weaver, William. "Studios Use Audience Research." *Motion Picture Herald,* July 20, 1946.

"The Week in Review." *Motion Picture News,* March 25, 1927.

Weinstein, David. "Interview with Otto Messmer, Creator of Felix the Cat." n.d. Canemaker Collection. Fales Library, New York University.

Wells, Paul. *The Animated Bestiary.* New Brunswick, NJ: Rutgers University Press, 2008.

———. "Building a Building: Animation as the Architecture of Modernity." In *Architecturanimation,* 126–53. Lleida: Actar, 2002.

———. *Understanding Animation.* London: Routledge, 1998.

White, Allon, and Peter Stallybrass. *The Politics and Poetics of Transgression.* New York: Cornell University Press, 1986.

Wilk, Christopher, ed. *Modernism: Designing a New World.* London: V and A Publications, 2006.

Williams, Raymond. *Marxism and Literature.* New York: Oxford University Press, 1977.

Williams, Rosalind. *Notes on the Underground: An Essay on Technology, Society, and the Imagination.* Cambridge, MA: MIT Press, 1990.

Winchell, Walter. "Walter Winchell on Broadway." *Nevada State Journal,* May 30, 1939.

Winokur, Mark. *American Laughter: Immigrants, Ethnicity, and 1930s Hollywood Film Comedy.* Basingstoke: Macmillan, 1995.

Wolverton, Basil. "Acoustics in the Comics." Originally published in 1948 for the *Daily Oregonian.* Repr. in ASIFA-Hollywood Animation Archive, Aug. 30, 2007. www.animation archive.org/2007/08/comics-basil-wolverton-on-cartoon.html.

Wright, Michelle M. *Becoming Black: Creating Identity in the African Diaspora.* Durham, NC: Duke University Press, 2004.

Young, Jordan R. *Spike Jones off the Record: The Man Who Murdered Music.* Boalsburg, PA: BearManor Media, 2005.

Young, Stark. "*The Circus.*" In Schickel, *The Essential Chaplin,* 183–87.

Žižek, Slavoj. *Enjoy Your Symptom! Jacques Lacan in Hollywood and Out.* London: Routledge, 1992.

———. *The Sublime Object of Ideology.* London: Verso, 1989.

Zupančič, Alenka. *The Odd One In: On Comedy.* Cambridge, MA: MIT Press, 2008.

CONTRIBUTORS

PHILIP BROPHY has directed experimental shorts such as *Salt, Saliva, Sperm and Sweat* and made his feature directorial debut with *Body Melt.* He composed the music and designed the sound for the feature *Mallboy,* as well as for numerous shorts. Many of his scores have been released on his own record label, Sound Punch. He is the founder and director of the CINESONIC International Conference on Film Scores and Sound Design and has edited three books from their proceedings. He has published articles on cinema in *The Wire, Film Comment,* and *Real Time.* His recent books include *100 Modern Soundtracks* and *100 Anime Films.*

DONALD CRAFTON is the Notre Dame Professor of Film and Culture in the Department of Film, Television, and Theatre, and the chairperson of the Department of Music. He was the founding director of the Yale Film Study Center and a director of the Wisconsin Center for Film and Theater Research. Among his books are *The Talkies: American Cinema's Transition to Sound, 1926–1931* and two books on early animation, including *Before Mickey: The Animated Film, 1898–1928.* The World Festival of Animation presented him with an award for his contributions to animation theory, and he is the recipient of the Jean Mitry prize in film history.

SCOTT CURTIS is associate professor in the Department of Radio/Television/Film at Northwestern University. He has published on a wide variety of topics, including early film theory, film sound, animation, Alfred Hitchcock, Douglas Fairbanks, the Motion Picture Patents Company, and scientific and industrial film. He also serves on the editorial board of *Animation Journal.* He is currently the president of Domitor, an international association dedicated to the study of early cinema.

ETHAN DE SEIFE is assistant professor in the Department of Radio, Television, and Film at Hofstra University. He has written a book on the film *This Is Spinal Tap,* and his book on the films of Frank Tashlin, from which his essay in this book is excerpted, will be published by Wesleyan University Press in 2012.

DANIEL GOLDMARK is associate professor in the Department of Music at Case Western Reserve University. He is series editor of the Oxford Music/Media Series and is the author and/or editor of several books on animation, film, and music, including *Tunes for 'Toons: Music and the Hollywood Cartoon.*

HENRY JENKINS is the Provost's Professor of Communication, Journalism, Cinematic Arts, and Education at the University of Southern California, having moved there recently after serving as codirector of the Comparative Media Studies Program at MIT. He is the author or editor of fourteen books, including *What Made Pistachio Nuts? Early Sound Comedy and the Vaudeville Aesthetic; Classical Hollywood Comedy; Convergence Culture: Where Old and New Media Collide;* and the forthcoming *Spreadable Media: Creating Value and Meaning in a Networked Culture.*

J. B. KAUFMAN is a film historian on the staff of the Walt Disney Family Foundation and has written extensively on Disney animation and American silent cinema. He is the author of *South of the Border with Disney;* and coauthor, with Russell Merritt, of *Walt in Wonderland: The Silent Films of Walt Disney* and *Walt Disney's Silly Symphonies: A Companion to the Classic Cartoon Series.*

CHARLIE KEIL is director of the Cinema Studies Institute and associate professor in the Department of History at the University of Toronto. He is the author of *Early American Cinema in Transition: Story, Style, and Filmmaking, 1907–1913;* coeditor, with Shelley Stamp, of *American Cinema's Transitional Era: Audiences, Institutions, Practices;* and coeditor, with Ben Singer, of *American Cinema of the 1910s: Themes and Variations.*

ROB KING is assistant professor of Cinema Studies and History at the University of Toronto. He is the author of *The Fun Factory: The Keystone Film Company and the Emergence of Mass Culture;* coeditor, with Tom Paulus, of *Slapstick Comedy;* and coeditor, with Richard Abel and Giorgio Bertellini, of *Early Cinema and the "National."*

MARK LANGER teaches in the Film Studies program at Carleton University and is president of the Ontario Confederation of University Faculty Associations. He has published on animation in many journals and has curated numerous film programs internationally.

RICHARD NEUPERT is Wheatley Professor of Film Studies and a Josiah Meigs Distinguished Teaching Professor in Film Studies at the University of Georgia. His books include *French Animation History; A History of the French New Wave Cinema;* and *The End.*

SUSAN OHMER is assistant provost, interim director of the Hesburgh Libraries, and the William T. and Helen Kuhn Carey Associate Professor of Modern Communication at the University of Notre Dame. She is the author of *George Gallup in Hollywood,* and her essays have appeared in the *Journal of Film and Video, Film History, Global Currents,* and the edited collection *Identifying Hollywood's Audiences.* She is working on a project assessing changing conceptions of animation at the Walt Disney Studio during the 1940s.

NICHOLAS SAMMOND is associate professor in Cinema Studies and English at the University of Toronto. His book *Babes in Tomorrowland: Walt Disney and the Making of the American Child, 1930–1960* received the 2006 Katherine Singer Kovács award from the Society for Cinema and Media Studies. He is also the editor of *Steel Chair to the Head: The Pleasure and Pain of Professional Wrestling* and has published articles in such journals as *Continuum, Television Quarterly,* and *Camera Obscura.* His current work involves examining blackface minstrelsy and the origins of American animation.

LINDA SIMENSKY is vice president of Children's Programming for PBS. She oversees the development and production of all children's series at PBS, including *Curious George, Dinosaur Train, The Cat in the Hat Knows a Lot about That,* and *WordGirl.* Simensky began her career with a nine-year tenure at Nickelodeon, where she helped build the animation department and launch such popular series as *Rugrats, Doug,* and *The Ren & Stimpy Show.* Most recently, she was senior vice president of Original Animation for Cartoon Network, where she oversaw the development and series production of *The Powerpuff Girls, Dexter's Laboratory, Samurai Jack, Courage the Cowardly Dog,* and other major projects. She holds a BA in communications with a minor in history from the University of Pennsylvania and an MA in media ecology from New York University.

PAUL WELLS is director of the Animation Academy at Loughborough University. He has published widely in the animation field, including *Understanding Animation; Animation and America; Fundamentals of Animation;* and *The Animated Bestiary.* He is also a successful scriptwriter and director in radio, television, and theater, and he tours worldwide to conduct workshops based on his book *Scriptwriting.*

INDEX

TEXT
10/12.5 Minion Pro

DISPLAY
Minion Pro (Open Type)

COMPOSITOR
BookMatters, Berkeley

PRINTER AND BINDER
Thomson-Shore, Inc.